Middle School 3-1

기말고사 완벽대비

적중100

영어 기출 문제집

중3

동아 | 이병민

Best Collection

구성과 특징

교과서의 주요 학습 내용을 중심으로 학습 영역별 특성에 맞춰 단계별로 다양한 학습 기회를 제공하여
단원별 학습능력 평가는 물론 중간 및 기말고사 시험 등에 완벽하게 대비할 수 있도록 내용을 구성

Words & Expressions

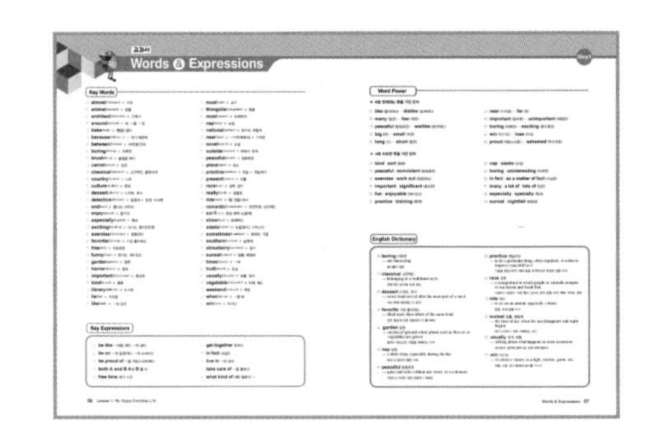

Step1 Key Words 단원별 핵심 단어 설명 및 풀이
Key Expression 단원별 핵심 숙어 및 관용어 설명
Word Power 반대 또는 비슷한 뜻 단어 배우기
English Dictionary 영어로 배우는 영어 단어

Step2 실력평가 단원별 수시평가 대비 주관식, 객관식 문제풀이

Step3 서술형 대비 학업성취도 및 수행능력평가 대비 서술형 문제풀이

Conversation

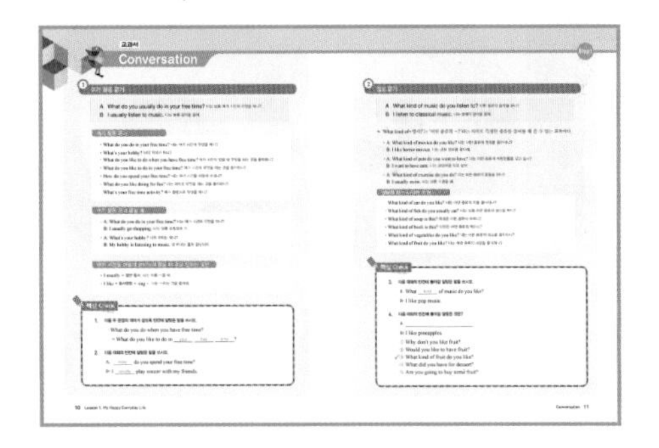

Step1 핵심 의사소통 소통에 필요한 주요 표현 방법 요약
핵심 Check 기본적인 표현 방법 및 활용능력 확인

Step2 대화문 익히기 교과서 대화문 심층 분석 및 확인

Step3 교과서 확인학습 빈칸 채우기를 통한 문장 완성 능력 확인

Step4 기본평가 시험대비 기초 학습 능력 평가

Step5 실력평가 단원별 수시평가 대비 주관식, 객관식 문제풀이

Step6 서술형 대비 학업성취도 및 수행능력평가 대비 서술형 문제풀이

Grammar

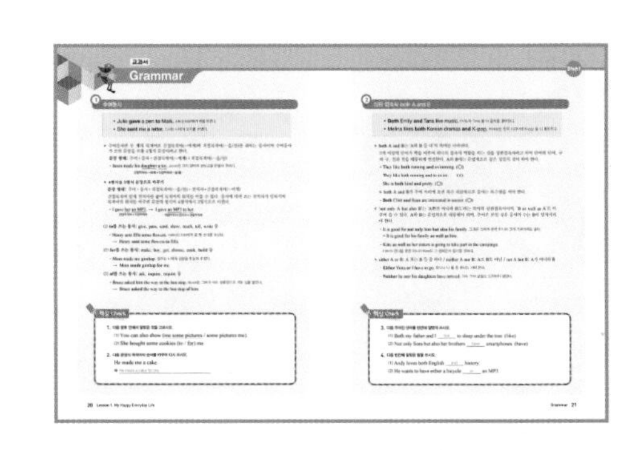

Step1 주요 문법 단원별 주요 문법 사항과 예문을 알기 쉽게 설명
핵심 Check 기본 문법사항에 대한 이해 여부 확인

Step2 기본평가 시험대비 기초 학습 능력 평가

Step3 실력평가 단원별 수시평가 대비 주관식, 객관식 문제풀이

Step4 서술형 대비 학업성취도 및 수행능력평가 대비 서술형 문제풀이

Reading

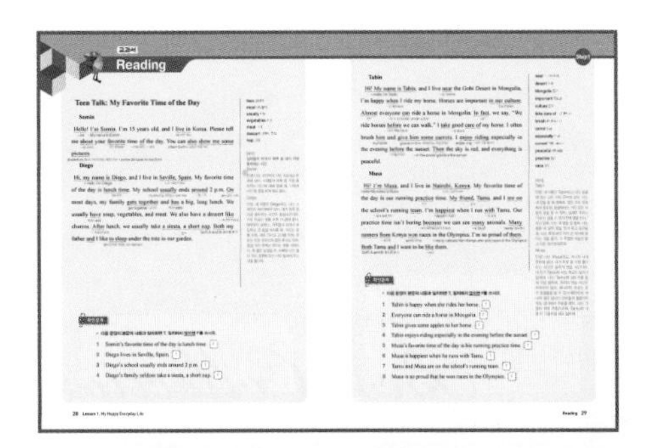

Step1 구문 분석 단원별로 제시된 문장에 대한 구문별 분석과 내용 설명
확인문제 문장에 대한 기본적인 이해와 인지능력 확인

Step2 확인학습A 빈칸 채우기를 통한 문장 완성 능력 확인

Step3 확인학습B 제시된 우리말을 영어로 완성하여 작문 능력 키우기

Step4 실력평가 단원별 수시평가 대비 주관식, 객관식 문제풀이

Step5 서술형 대비 학업성취도 및 수행능력평가 대비 서술형 문제풀이
교과서 구석구석 교과서에 나오는 기타 문장까지 완벽 학습

Composition

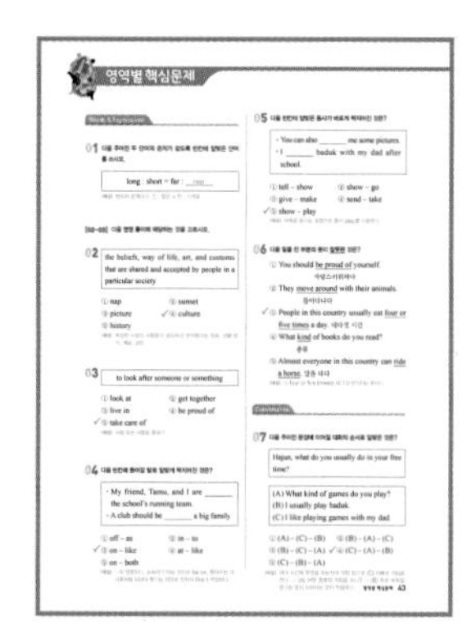

|영역별 핵심문제|

단어 및 어휘, 대화문, 문법, 독해 등 각 영역별 기출문제의 출제 유형을 분석하여 실전에 대비하고 연습할 수 있도록 문제를 배열

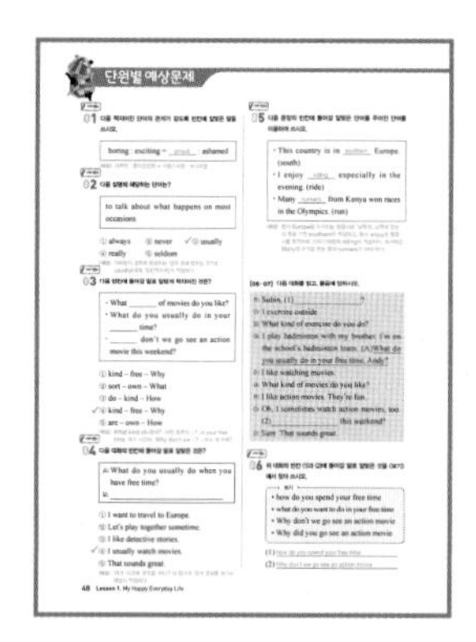

|단원별 예상문제|

기출문제를 분석한 후 새로운 시험 출제 경향을 더하여 새롭게 출제될 수 있는 문제를 포함하여 시험에 완벽하게 대비할 수 있도록 준비

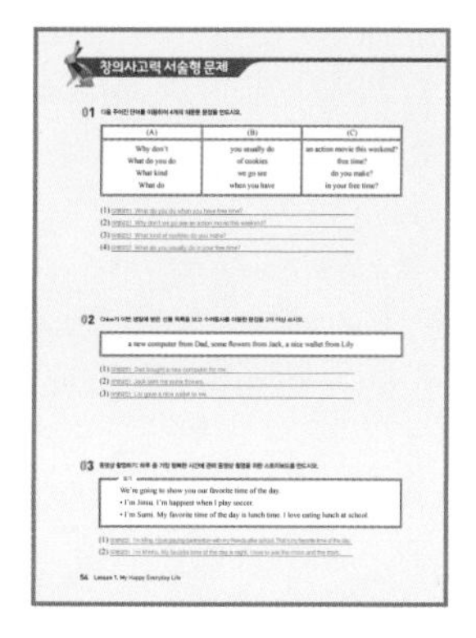

|서술형 실전 및 창의사고력 문제|

학교 시험에서 점차 늘어나는 서술형 시험에 집중 대비하고 고득점을 취득하는데 만전을 기하기 위한 학습 코너

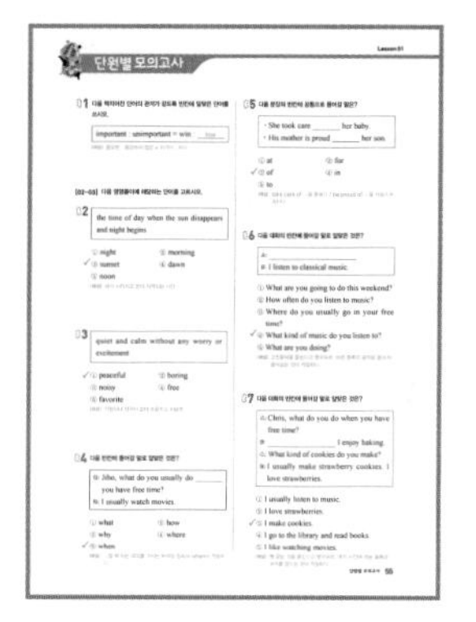

|단원별 모의고사|

영역별, 단계별 학습을 모두 마친 후 실전 연습을 위한 모의고사

교과서 파헤치기

- **단어Test1~3** 영어 단어 우리말 쓰기, 우리말을 영어 단어로 쓰기, 영영풀이에 해당하는 단어와 우리말 쓰기
- **대화문Test1~2** 대화문 빈칸 완성 및 전체 대화문 쓰기
- **본문Test1~5** 빈칸 완성, 우리말 쓰기, 문장 배열연습, 영어 작문하기 복습 등 단계별 반복 학습을 통해 교과서 지문에 대한 완벽한 습득
- **구석구석지문Test1~2** 지문 빈칸 완성 및 전문 영어로 쓰기

이책의 차례

Contents

Heal the World

의사소통 기능

- 원하는 행동 묻기
  A: What do you want me to do?
  B: Please put the clothes into the box.
- 당부하기
  A: Make sure you lock the doors.
  B: Okay, I will.

언어 형식

- 사역동사
  The project manager **had** us **meet** at 9 a.m.
- It ~ that 강조 구문
  It was a better tomorrow **that** we painted.

교과서

Words & Expressions

Key Words

- □ **amusement park** 놀이 공원
- □ **apply**[əplái] 동 지원하다
- □ **arrange**[əréindʒ] 동 배열하다
- □ **as** 접 ~할 때, ~하면서
- □ **background**[bǽkgraund] 명 배경
- □ **bake**[beik] 동 굽다
- □ **board**[bɔːrd] 명 칠판
- □ **clearly**[klíərli] 부 분명하게
- □ **decide**[disáid] 동 결심하다
- □ **deliver**[dilívər] 동 배달하다
- □ **divide**[diváid] 동 나누다
- □ **donation**[dounéiʃən] 명 기부, 기증
- □ **drawing**[drɔ́ːiŋ] 명 그림
- □ **elementary school** 초등학교
- □ **experience**[ikspíəriəns] 명 경험
- □ **friendly**[fréndli] 형 친절한
- □ **fur**[fəːr] 명 털
- □ **gym uniform** 체육복
- □ **land**[lænd] 동 내려앉다 명 땅, 육지
- □ **later**[léitər] 부 나중에, 후에
- □ **location**[loukéiʃən] 명 장소
- □ **manager**[mǽnidʒər] 명 운영자, 관리자
- □ **matter**[mǽtər] 동 문제되다, 중요하다
- □ **neat**[niːt] 형 깨끗한
- □ **neighborhood**[néidərhùd] 명 근처, 이웃
- □ **nursing home** 양로원
- □ **pack**[pæk] 동 짐을 꾸리다
- □ **paint**[peint] 명 물감 동 (그림물감으로) 그리다
- □ **plant**[plænt] 동 심다 명 식물
- □ **politely**[pəláitli] 부 예의 바르게
- □ **poster**[póustər] 명 벽보, 게시물
- □ **prepare**[pripέər] 동 준비하다
- □ **project**[prádʒekt] 명 과제
- □ **recycling bin** 재활용 쓰레기통
- □ **remove**[rimúːv] 동 없애다, 제거하다
- □ **reply**[riplái] 동 응답하다
- □ **rewarding**[riwɔ́ːrdiŋ] 형 보람 있는
- □ **select**[silékt] 동 선택하다, 선정하다
- □ **share**[ʃɛər] 동 나누다, 공유하다
- □ **shelf**[ʃelf] 명 책꽂이
- □ **site**[sait] 명 현장, 장소
- □ **soap**[soup] 명 비누
- □ **spot**[spɑt] 명 (특정한) 장소, 자리
- □ **suggest**[səgdʒést] 동 제안하다
- □ **the blind** 시각 장애인
- □ **the elderly** 나이 든 사람들
- □ **village**[vílidʒ] 명 마을
- □ **volunteer**[vɑ̀ləntíər] 명 자원봉사 동 자원봉사하다
- □ **vote**[vout] 동 투표하다
- □ **wall painting** 벽화
- □ **water**[wɔ́ːtər] 동 물을 주다
- □ **wing**[wiŋ] 명 날개

Key Expressions

- □ **a light goes on in the head** 머릿속에 좋은 생각이 떠오르다
- □ **Anything else**? 그 이외에 다른 것 있나요?
- □ **be on time** 제시간에 도착하다
- □ **be proud of** ~ ~을 자랑스러워하다
- □ **get along with** ~ ~와 사이좋게 지내다
- □ **get on** 타다
- □ **get together** 모이다
- □ **get up** 일어나다
- □ **give a bath** 목욕시키다
- □ **give** ~ **a hand** ~에게 도움을 주다
- □ **How about** ~? ~는 어떤가요?
- □ **in front of** ~ ~ 앞에서
- □ **It's time to** ~. ~해야 할 시간이다.
- □ **keep** ~ **in mind** ~을 명심하다
- □ **line up** 줄서다
- □ **make sure** ~ 꼭 ~하다
- □ **pick up** 치우다, 줍다
- □ **so** ~ **that** ... 너무 ~해서 …하다
- □ **take a break** 휴식을 취하다
- □ **take a picture** 사진을 찍다
- □ **That's it**. 다됐어., 그게 다예요.
- □ **turn off** 끄다
- □ **Why don't we** ~? ~하는 것이 어떨까?

Word Power

※ 서로 비슷한 뜻을 가진 어휘

- □ **arrange** 배열하다 - **array** 배열하다
- □ **decide** 결심하다 - **determine** 결정하다
- □ **manager** 관리자 - **director** 책임자
- □ **neat** 깨끗한 - **tidy** 깔끔한
- □ **clearly** 분명하게 - **obviously** 명백하게
- □ **divide** 나누다 - **split** 쪼개다
- □ **matter** 중요하다 - **count** 중요하다
- □ **remove** 제거하다 - **eliminate** 제거하다

※ 서로 반대의 뜻을 가진 어휘

- □ **background** 배경 ↔ **foreground** 전경
- □ **friendly** 친절한 ↔ **hostile** 적대적인
- □ **later** 나중에, 후에 ↔ **earlier** 이전에
- □ **pack** 짐을 꾸리다 ↔ **unpack** 짐을 풀다
- □ **divide** 나누다 ↔ **combine** 결합하다
- □ **land** 착륙하다 ↔ **take off** 이륙하다
- □ **neat** 깨끗한 ↔ **dirty** 지저분한
- □ **politely** 예의 바르게 ↔ **impolitely** 무례하게

※ 동사 – 명사

- □ **apply** 지원하다 - **application** 지원서, 적용
- □ **decide** 결심하다 - **decision** 결정
- □ **divide** 나누다 - **division** 분할
- □ **prepare** 준비하다 - **preparation** 준비
- □ **arrange** 배열하다 - **arrangement** 배열, 준비
- □ **deliver** 배달하다 - **delivery** 배달
- □ **manage** 관리하다 - **management** 관리
- □ **select** 선택하다 - **selection** 선택

※ 형용사 – 명사

- □ **blind** 눈이 먼 – **the blind** 시각 장애인
- □ **experienced** 경험 많은 - **the experienced** 경험 많은 사람들
- □ **elderly** 나이 든 – **the elderly** 나이 든 사람들

English Dictionary

□ **amusement park** 놀이 공원
→ a large park with many machines that you can ride on, such as roller coasters
롤러코스터 같은 탈 수 있는 많은 기계가 있는 큰 공원

□ **arrange** 정리하다
→ to put a group of things or people in a particular order or position
한 무리의 물건이나 사람을 특정한 순서나 위치에 두다

□ **background** 배경
→ the area that is behind the main thing that you are looking at
당신이 보고 있는 주된 것 뒤에 있는 영역

□ **bake** 굽다
→ to cook something using dry heat, in an oven
오븐에서 건열을 사용해서 요리하다

□ **deliver** 배달하다
→ to take something to a person or place
무언가를 어떤 사람이나 장소로 가져가다

□ **donation** 기부, 기증
→ something that you give to help a person or organization
사람이나 기관을 돕기 위해 주는 어떤 것

□ **drawing** 그림
→ a picture that you draw with a pencil, pen, etc.
펜, 연필 등으로 그리는 그림

□ **location** 장소
→ a particular place 특정한 장소

□ **manager** 관리자
→ someone whose job is to manage part or all of a company or other organization
회사나 다른 조직의 일부나 전체를 관리하는 일을 하는 사람

□ **matter** 중요하다
→ to be important 중요하다

□ **pack** 짐을 꾸리다
→ to put things into cases, bags, etc. ready for a trip
여행 준비로 상자나 가방에 짐을 넣다

□ **remove** 제거하다
→ to move or take something away from a place
어떤 것을 한 장소에서 옮기거나 치우다

□ **volunteer** 자원봉사자
→ a person who does a job without being paid
대가를 받지 않고 어떤 일을 하는 사람

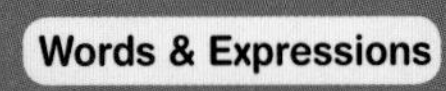

시험대비 실력평가

01 다음 밑줄 친 부분과 바꿔 쓸 수 있는 말을 고르시오.

> International travel can be a rich and rewarding adventure.

① expensive ② satisfying
③ informative ④ demanding
⑤ difficult

02 다음 빈칸에 들어갈 말을 고르시오.

> You're late again. It's important to be ______ time.

① at ② by ③ for ④ on ⑤ to

03 다음 <보기>에 있는 어휘를 이용하여 빈칸을 채울 수 없는 것을 고르시오. (형태 변화 가능)

> 보기
> do give have prepare

① Just make yourself at home while I ______ the baby a bath.
② You must ______ his advice in mind.
③ The most important thing is ______ our best.
④ Joe helped me ______ for the exam.
⑤ The children were ______ fun, chasing each other's shadows.

04 다음 밑줄 친 부분의 의미로 알맞지 않은 것은?

① You'd better pack your bags. We're leaving in an hour. (짐을 꾸리다)
② Soap and cold water will remove most food stains. (제거하다)
③ It doesn't matter what you wear, as long as you look neat and tidy. (문제, 어려움)
④ There was cat fur all over the chair. (털)
⑤ Even a small donation can make a big difference to one child's life. (기부)

05 다음 대화의 빈칸에 들어갈 말로 알맞은 것을 고르시오.

> A: I'm so tired.
> B: I ______ taking a rest.
> A: That's a good idea.

① suggest ② share ③ promise
④ explain ⑤ expect

06 다음 빈칸 (A)~(C)에 알맞은 말로 짝지어진 것을 고르시오.

> • He (A)______ together with some friends to plan a party for her.
> • Floor tiles can be difficult to clean. It is worth (B)______ in mind when you choose a new floor.
> • (C)______ sure to take this medicine after every meal.

	(A)		(B)		(C)
①	got	–	keeping	–	Take
②	got	–	keeping	–	Make
③	got	–	being	–	Take
④	had	–	being	–	Make
⑤	had	–	being	–	Take

Words & Expressions 서술형 시험대비

01 빈칸을 주어진 영영풀이에 해당하는 말을 이용하여 채우시오. (주어진 철자로 시작할 것.)

> to move or take something away from a place

> Illegally parked vehicles will be r________.

02 다음 빈칸에 알맞은 단어를 <보기>에서 골라 쓰시오. (단어는 한 번씩만 사용 가능)

보기: along on together up

(1) Get ________ early to be in time for the first train.
(2) They get ________ and study math on Wednesdays.
(3) We got ________ the train at Lime Street Station.
(4) I get ________ with my classmates.

03 두 문장의 의미가 같도록 문장을 완성할 때 빈칸에 들어갈 말을 쓰시오. (2 단어)

> It's time for self-introduction.
> ➡ It's time ____________ yourself.

[04~05] 다음 빈칸에 공통으로 들어갈 말을 쓰시오.

04

> • Why don't we pick ________ the trash?
> • Cars lined ________ waiting to board the ship.

05

> • Don't forget to water the ________ .
> • We will ________ tomatoes and carrots in the garden.

06 다음 우리말에 맞도록 빈칸에 알맞은 말을 쓰시오. (철자가 주어진 경우 주어진 철자로 시작할 것)

(1) 비행기는 안전하게 착륙했다.
➡ The plane l________ safely.

(2) 빗은 내가 머리를 단정하게 유지하는 것을 가능하게 한다.
➡ The comb enables me to keep my hair n________.

(3) Susan은 오후에 연세 드신 분들을 인터뷰할 것이다.
➡ Susan will interview ________ e________ people in the afternoon.

(4) Descartes는 그 파리가 똑같은 지점에 두 번 정말로 앉았는지 아닌지 궁금했다.
➡ Descartes wondered if the fly ever landed on the same s________ twice.

07 다음 우리말에 맞게 주어진 단어를 바르게 배열하시오.

(1) 그들은 스스로를 아주 자랑스러워해야 한다.
(must, themselves, they, so, of, proud, be)
➡ ________________________

(2) 이 상황이 아주 중요하다.
(situation, a, matters, this, lot)
➡ ________________________

(3) 내가 일찍 끝나면 도와줄게.
(I, I'll, finish, give, hand, early, a, if)
➡ ________________________

교과서

Conversation

1 원하는 행동 묻기

A: What do you want me to do? 내가 무엇을 하길 원하니?

B: Please put the clothes into the box. 옷을 상자 안에 넣어 줘.

- 'What do you want me to do?'는 상대방에게 도움을 주고자 할 때 그 사람이 구체적으로 필요로 하는 도움이 무엇인지 묻는 표현이다. 대답으로는 'I want you to ~.' 또는 Please로 시작하는 명령문을 사용해 말할 수 있다. 'What would you like to ~?'는 'What do you want to ~?'와 비슷한 표현이지만 더 부드럽게 말할 때 자주 쓰인다.
- 상대방이 원하는 행동을 물어볼 때 동사 'want, would like'는 '목적어+목적격보어(to부정사)'의 구조가 된다. 상대방이 누구에게 원하는지 그 대상을 목적어로 하고, 그가 해야 할 행동을 목적격보어로 써서 'What do you want 목적어+to부정사?', 'What would you like 목적어+to부정사?'의 구조가 되도록 한다.
- 상대방이 원하는 것을 물어보는 방법은 도움을 제안하는 표현으로도 나타낼 수 있다. 말하는 사람을 주어로 해서 상대에게 원하는 것을 물어볼 때는 'What can I do for you?', 'How may I help you?'가 될 수도 있다.

원하는 행동 묻기

- What would you like to ~?
- Do you want to ~?
- What do you want to ~?
- Would you like to ~?

도움을 제안하는 표현

- May/Can I help you? 도와 드릴까요?
- Would you like some help?
- Is there anything that I can help you?
- Do you need some help?
- What can I do for you?

핵심 Check

1. 다음 우리말과 일치하도록 빈칸에 알맞은 말을 쓰시오.

A: What are you doing?
B: I'm packing for my move tomorrow. Can you help me?
A: Sure. ______________________ (내가 무엇을 하길 원하니?)
B: Please put the clothes into the box.
A: No problem.

2 당부하기

A: Make sure you lock the door. 반드시 문을 닫아라.

B: Okay, I will. 알았어요.

- 'Make sure+주어+동사 ~.'는 상대방이 어떤 일을 잊지 않고 꼭 할 것을 당부할 때 사용할 수 있는 표현이다. 이에 대한 대답은 'Okay, I will.' 또는 'No problem.' 등으로 말할 수 있다. 'Make sure ~.'는 '~을 확실하게 하다.'의 뜻으로 명령문으로 나타내게 되면 '확실하게 해라, 반드시 ~해라.'의 의미로 상대에게 당부하는 표현이 된다. 'Be sure to ~.'도 마찬가지로 '반드시 ~해라.'의 의미가 된다.
- 상대방에게 '~할 것을 잊지 말아라., ~할 것을 기억해라.'라고 당부할 때는 'Don't forget to+동사원형 ~.'으로 말할 수 있고 'Remember to 동사원형 ~.'으로 나타내기도 한다.

당부하기

- Make sure (that) ~ . 반드시 ~해라.
- Be sure to ~ . 반드시 ~해라.
- Don't forget to ~. ~하는 것을 잊지 마라.
- Please remember to ~. ~할 것을 기억해 주세요.

핵심 Check

2. 다음 우리말과 일치하도록 주어진 말을 이용해 빈칸에 알맞은 말을 쓰시오.

A: It's time to go home.
B: Yes. 문을 잠그는 거 명심해. (make, lock)
A: Okay, I will. Anything else?
B: No, that's it. See you tomorrow.

 ____________________

3. 다음 주어진 문장을 적절하게 배열하시오.

A: Hi, I'm Minsu. I'm here for the volunteer work.
B: Thanks for coming, Minsu.
A: What do you want me to do today?
(A) Okay. Is there anything to keep in mind?
(B) Please give the dog a bath.
(C) Yes. Make sure you brush the fur first.
(D) Okay, I will.

 ____________________

Conversation 교과서 대화문 익히기

Listen and Speak 1 A

B: What are all these boxes ❶and books for?

G: I'm packing the books for the ❷donation center. ❸Can you give me a hand?

B: Sure. ❹What do you want me to do?

G: Please write ❺the address on the boxes.

B: No problem.

B: 이 박스와 책들은 다 무엇에 쓰려는 거니?

G: 기부 센터에 보내려고 책을 싸고 있어. 도와줄래?

B: 물론이야. 내가 무엇을 하길 원하니?

G: 박스에 주소를 좀 써 줘.

B: 그래.

❶ 접속사 and는 these boxes와 books를 연결하고 있다.

❷ donation: 기부, 기증

❸ 'give ~ a hand' 는 '~를 돕다'라는 관용적 표현으로, 이 표현을 이용해 'Can you give me a hand?'라고 하면, '나 좀 도와줄래?'의 의미로 상대방에게 도움을 요청할 때 사용하는 표현이다.

❹ 'What do you want me to do?'는 '너는 내가 무엇을 해 주기를 원하니?'라는 뜻으로 상대방이 원하는 행동이 무엇인지 물어보는 표현이다.

❺ address: 주소

Check(√) True or False

(1) The girl is packing the books. T ☐ F ☐

(2) The girl wants the boy to help her. T ☐ F ☐

Listen and Speak 2 A

B: Enjoy the concert, Mom.

W: Okay, ❶I will. Thanks. Your dinner is on the table.

B: All right. ❷Don't worry about me.

W: ❸Make sure you ❹feed the dog after you have dinner.

B: Okay. Mom, you should go now. Dad is waiting in the car.

B: 콘서트 재미있게 보세요, 엄마.

W: 그래. 고마워. 저녁은 식탁에 있어.

B: 알겠어요. 저는 걱정 마세요.

W: 저녁 먹은 후에 개 밥 주는 거 명심해라.

B: 알겠어요. 엄마, 이제 가셔야 해요. 아빠가 차에서 기다리고 계셔요.

❶ I will 다음에 enjoy the concert가 생략되어 있다.

❷ worry about: ~에 대해 걱정하다

❸ 'Make sure (that) 주어+동사 ~' 구문으로 상대방이 잊어버리지 않도록 중요한 일에 대해 강한 당부 또는 경고하는 의미를 나타낼 수 있다. '~을 확실히 하라, ~을 반드시 하라'의 뜻이다. 'Make sure (that) 주어+동사 ~' 대신에 'Make sure to+동사원형 ~', 'I think you should ~', 'Try to ~', 'Be sure to/that ~' 등을 통해서도 강한 당부, 충고, 경고의 의미를 나타낼 수 있다. '~을 반드시 하지 말 것'을 강하게 당부하거나 경고할 경우에는 'Make sure not to+동사원형' 또는 'Make sure (that) you don't ~'를 사용할 수 있다.

❹ feed: 먹이를 주다

Check(√) True or False

(3) Mom is going to go to the concert. T ☐ F ☐

(4) Mom is planning to eat dinner with the boy. T ☐ F ☐

Listen and Speak 1 B

B: What is this ❶mess?
G: I'm baking cookies.
B: Why are you baking so many cookies?
G: ❷They're for the people at the nursing home.
B: That's very nice of you.
G: ❸Can you give me a hand?
B: Sure. ❹What do you want me to do?
G: Please put the cookies in the gift boxes. Three cookies in each box.
B: Okay.

B: 이 엉망진창은 뭐니?
G: 쿠키를 굽고 있어.
B: 왜 이렇게 많은 쿠키를 굽고 있니?
G: 쿠키는 양로원에 계신 분들을 위한 거야.
B: 정말 착하구나.
G: 도와줄래?
B: 물론이야. 내가 무엇을 하길 원하니?
G: 선물 상자에 쿠키를 좀 넣어 줘. 상자 하나에 쿠키 3개씩.
B: 알겠어.

❶ mess: (지저분하고) 엉망인 상태
❷ 여기서 They는 many cookies를 받는 인칭대명사이다.
❸ 상대방에게 도움을 요청할 때 'Can you give me a hand?'로 말할 수 있다. 'Can you do me a favor?'로 바꿔 말할 수도 있다.
❹ 'What do you want to me to do?'는 '너는 내가 무엇을 하기를 원하니?'로 상대방이 원하는 것이 무엇인지 묻는 표현이다. 여기서 want는 5형식 동사로 'me'는 목적어 'to do'가 목적격보어로 사용되었다.

Check(√) True or False

(5) The boy will put three cookies in one box. T ☐ F ☐
(6) The girl is baking a few cookies. T ☐ F ☐

Real Life Talk Step 3

A: Hi, I'm Minsu. ❶I'm here for the volunteer work.
B: ❷Thanks for coming, Minsu.
A: ❸What do you want me to do today?
B: Please ❹give the dog a bath.
A: Okay. Is there anything ❺to keep in mind?
B: Yes. ❻Make sure you brush the fur first.
A: Okay, I will.

A: 안녕하세요. 저는 민수예요. 저는 봉사 활동을 하러 왔어요.
B: 와 주셔서 감사합니다.
A: 오늘 제가 무엇을 하길 원하세요?
B: 개를 목욕시켜 주세요.
A: 네. 명심해야 할 것이 있나요?
B: 네. 털을 먼저 빗길 것을 명심하세요.
A: 네. 그렇게 할게요.

❶ 'I'm here for 명사.'는 '~ 때문에 왔다, ~하러 왔다'라는 표현이며 'I'm here to 동사원형 ~.'으로 바꿔 쓸 수 있다. I'm here for the volunteer work. = I'm here to do volunteer work.
❷ thank (you) 뒤에 for를 쓰는 경우, for 뒤에 감사의 이유를 적는다.
❸ 상대방이 원하는 행동을 'What do you want me to do?(제가 무엇을 하기를 원하십니까?)'를 이용해서 물어볼 수 있다.
❹ give a bath: 목욕시키다
❺ to keep in mind가 앞의 anything을 수식하고 있다. keep in mind: 명심하다
❻ 상대방에게 당부의 말을 할 때는 '확실하게 하다'라는 의미의 make sure를 써서 'Make sure you+동사원형 ~'의 형태로 말한다. 비슷한 표현으로 'Don't forget to 동사원형 ~.'이 있다.

Check(√) True or False

(7) B wants Minsu to give the dog a bath. T ☐ F ☐
(8) Minsu should brush the fur after bathing the dog. T ☐ F ☐

Listen and Speak 1 C

A: What are you doing?

B: I'm ❶packing for my ❷move tomorrow. ❸Can you help me?

A: Sure. ❹What do you want me to do?

B: Please ❺move the chairs outside.

A: No problem.

❶ pack: 짐을 꾸리다

❷ move: 이사

❸ 상대방에게 도움을 요청할 때 'Can you help me?'로 말할 수 있다. 'Can you do me a favor?'나 'I was wondering if you could help me.'라고 바꿔 말할 수도 있다.

❹ 'What do you want me to do?'는 '너는 내가 무엇을 해 주기를 원하니?'라는 뜻으로 상대방이 원하는 행동이 무엇인지를 물어보는 표현이다.

❺ 여기서 move는 앞에 쓴 명사의 '이사'의 의미가 아니라 동사로 '옮기다'의 의미로 사용하였다. outside: 밖으로

Listen and Speak 2 B

B: Hello, class. Make groups of four people ❶and sit around the tables. Today ❷we're going to make bacon and egg sandwiches. ❸Keep in mind two rules for our class. First, ❹make sure you wash your hands before you start. Second, be careful ❺when you use a knife. All right, let's start.

❶ make와 sit은 접속사 and로 병렬로 연결되어 있다.

❷ 'be going to'는 '~할 것이다'의 의미로 가까운 미래의 계획을 말할 때 사용한다.

❸ keep in mind: 명심하다

❹ make sure ~: 꼭 ~해라, 확실하게 해라

❺ 여기서 when은 접속사로 '~할 때'의 의미로 사용되었다.

Listen and Speak 2 C

A: ❶It's time to go home.

B: Yes. ❷Make sure you lock the doors.

A: Okay, I will. Anything else?

B: No, that's it. See you tomorrow.

❶ It's time to 동사원형 ~: ~해야 할 시간이다

❷ 'Make sure (that) 주어 동사 ~'는 '꼭 ~해라, 확실하게 ~해라'라는 의미로 상대방에게 당부할 때 쓰는 표현이다. 'Be sure to 동사원형 ~.', 'Don't forget to 동사원형 ~.', 'Please remember to 동사원형 ~.' 등으로 바꿔 말할 수 있다.

Real Life Talk Watch a Video

Woman: Good morning. ❶What can I do for you?

Tony: Hi. ❷I'm here for the ❸volunteer work.

Woman: Oh, you ❹must be Tony.

Tony: That's right. ❺What do you want me to do today?

Woman: Please read this book for ❻the blind in the recording room.

Tony: No problem. Should I go in now?

Woman: Yes. Please go into Room 7.

Tony: Okay. Is there anything ❼to keep in mind?

Woman: Yes. ❽Make sure you read ❾slowly and clearly.

Tony: Okay. I'll ❿do my best.

❶ 'What can I do for you?'는 '무엇을 도와드릴까요?'의 의미로 상대방에게 도움을 제안할 때 사용하는 표현이다.

❷ 'I'm here for ~.'는 '나는 ~을 위해[~하러] 왔어요.'의 의미로 온 목적에 대해 말할 때 사용할 수 있다.

❸ volunteer: 자원봉사

❹ must는 '~임에 틀림없다'의 의미로 강한 추측을 나타낼 때 사용한다.

❺ 'What do you want me to do?'는 '제가 무엇을 하기 원하세요?'라는 뜻으로 상대방이 원하는 행동이 무엇인지를 물어보는 표현이다.

❻ 'the+형용사'는 복수 보통명사로 여기서 the blind는 blind people을 의미한다.

❼ to keep in mind는 앞의 명사 anything을 수식하고 있다. (to부정사의 형용사 용법) keep in mind: 명심하다

❽ make sure ~: 꼭 ~해라, 확실하게 ~해라

❾ slowly와 clearly는 앞의 동사인 read를 수식하고 있다.

❿ do one's best: 최선을 다하다

Real Life Talk Step 1

A: ❶What do you want to do?

B: I ❷want to ❸teach English to the children.

❶ 'What do you want to do?'는 '너는 무엇을 하기를 원하니?'로 상대방이 원하는 것이 무엇인지 묻는 표현이다.

❷ want는 to부정사를 목적어로 받는 동사이다.

❸ 'teach English to the children'을 4형식인 'teach the children English'로 바꿔 쓸 수 있다.

Conversation 교과서 확인학습

● 다음 우리말과 일치하도록 빈칸에 알맞은 말을 쓰시오.

Listen and Speak 1 A

B: ________ are all these boxes and books ________?

G: I'm ________ the books for the ________ center. Can you ________ ________ ________ hand?

B: Sure. What do you ________ me ________ do?

G: Please write the ________ ________ the boxes.

B: No problem.

Listen and Speak 1 B

B: What is ________ ________?

G: I'm ________ cookies.

B: ________ are you baking so ________ cookies?

G: ________ ________ the people at the nursing home.

B: That's very ________ ________ you.

G: ________ ________ ________ me a hand?

B: Sure. What ________ ________ ________ ________ to do?

G: Please ________ the cookies in the gift boxes. Three cookies in ________ box.

B: Okay.

Listen and Speak 1 C

1. A: What are you ________?

   B: I'm ________ ________ my move tomorrow. ________ ________ ________ me?

   A: Sure. ________ ________ ________ ________ me to do?

   B: Please ________ ________ ________ ________ the box.

   A: No problem.

2. A: What are you doing?

   B: I'm ________ ________ my ________ tomorrow. ________ ________ ________ ________?

   A: Sure. What do you want me to do?

   B: Please ________ the chairs ________.

   A: No problem.

B: 이 박스와 책들은 다 무엇에 쓰려는 거니?
G: 기부 센터에 보내려고 책을 싸고 있어. 도와줄래?
B: 물론이야. 내가 무엇을 하길 원하니?
G: 박스에 주소를 좀 써 줘.
B: 그래.

B: 이 엉망진창은 뭐니?
G: 쿠키를 굽고 있어.
B: 왜 이렇게 많은 쿠키를 굽고 있니?
G: 쿠키는 양로원에 계신 분들을 위한 거야.
B: 정말 착하구나.
G: 도와줄래?
B: 물론이야. 내가 무엇을 하길 원하니?
G: 선물 상자에 쿠키를 좀 넣어 줘. 상자 하나에 쿠키 3개씩.
B: 알겠어.

1. A: 너 뭐 하고 있니?
   B: 내일 이사를 위해 짐을 싸는 중이야. 도와줄래?
   A: 물론이지. 내가 무엇을 하길 원하니?
   B: 옷을 상자 안에 넣어 줘.
   A: 그래.

2. A: 너 뭐 하고 있니?
   B: 내일 이사를 위해 짐을 싸는 중이야. 도와줄래?
   A: 물론이지. 내가 무엇을 하길 원하니?
   B: 의자를 밖으로 옮겨 줘.
   A: 그래.

3. A: ________ ________ ________ ________?

   B: I'm ________ ________ my ________ tomorrow. ________ ________ ________ ________?

   A: Sure. ________ ________ ________ ________ ________ ________ ________?

   B: Please ________ ________ the trach.

   A: No problem.

해석

3. A: 너 뭐 하고 있니?
   B: 내일 이사를 위해 짐을 싸는 중이야. 도와줄래?
   A: 물론이지. 내가 무엇을 하길 원하니?
   B: 쓰레기를 밖에 갖다 버려 줘.
   A: 그래.

Listen and Speak 2 A

B: ________ the concert, Mom.

W: Okay, I ________. Thanks. Your dinner ________ ________ the table.

B: All right. Don't ________ ________ me.

W: ________ ________ ________ ________ the dog ________ you have dinner.

B: Okay. Mom, you ________ go now. Dad is waiting in the car.

B: 콘서트 재미있게 보세요, 엄마.
W: 그래, 고마워. 저녁은 식탁에 있어.
B: 알겠어요. 저는 걱정 마세요.
W: 저녁 먹은 후에 개 밥 주는 거 명심해라.
B: 알겠어요. 엄마, 이제 가셔야 해요. 아빠가 차에서 기다리고 계셔요.

Listen and Speak 2 B

B: Hello, class. ________ ________ ________ four people and ________ around the tables. Today we're going ________ ________ bacon and egg sandwiches. ________ ________ ________ two rules for our class. First, ________ ________ you wash your hands ________ ________ ________. ________, be careful ________ you use a knife. All right, ________ start.

B: 안녕하세요, 여러분. 4명씩 모둠을 만들어 탁자에 둘러앉으세요. 오늘 우리는 베이컨 달걀 샌드위치를 만들 거예요. 우리 수업의 두 가지 규칙에 유의하세요. 첫째, 시작하기 전에 손을 씻는 것을 명심하세요. 둘째, 칼을 사용할 때 조심하세요. 좋아요, 시작해 봐요.

Listen and Speak 2 C

1. A: It's time ________ ________ home.

   B: Yes. ________ ________ you lock the doors.

   A: Okay, I will. ________ else?

   B: No, ________ it. See you tomorrow.

2. A: It's ________ ________ go home.

   B: Yes. ________ ________ ________ ________ the board.

   A: Okay, I will. ________ ________?

   B: No, that's it. See you tomorrow.

3. A: ________ ________ ________ ________ home.

   B: Yes. ________ ________ you ________ ________ ________.

   A: Okay, I ________. Anything else?

   B: No, that's it. See you tomorrow.

1. A: 집에 갈 시간이야.
   B: 응. 문 잠그는 거 명심해.
   A: 알겠어, 그렇게 할게. 또 다른 건?
   B: 없어, 그게 전부야. 내일 보자.

2. A: 이제 집에 갈 시간이야.
   B: 응. 칠판 닦는 거 명심해.
   A: 알겠어, 그렇게 할게. 또 다른 건?
   B: 없어, 그게 전부야. 내일 보자.

3. A: 이제 집에 갈 시간이야.
   B: 응. 식물에 물 주는 거 명심해.
   A: 알겠어, 그렇게 할게. 또 다른 건?
   B: 없어, 그게 전부야. 내일 보자.

해석

Real Life Talk Watch a Video

Woman: Good morning. ________ ________ ________ ________ for you?

Tony: Hi. I'm ________ ________ the volunteer work.

Woman: Oh, you ________ ________ Tony.

Tony: That's right. ________ ________ ________ ________ ________ ________ ________ today?

Woman: Please ________ this book ________ ________ ________ in the recording room.

Tony: No problem. Should I go in now?

Woman: Yes. Please ________ ________ Room 7.

Tony: Okay. Is there ________ ________ ________ ________ mind?

Woman: Yes. ________ ________ ________ read ________ ________ ________.

Tony: Okay. I'll ________ ________ ________.

Woman: 안녕하세요. 무엇을 도와드릴까요?
Tony: 안녕하세요. 저는 봉사 활동을 하러 왔어요.
Woman: 오, Tony군요.
Tony: 맞아요. 오늘 제가 무엇을 하길 원하세요?
Woman: 녹음실에서 시각 장애인들을 위해 이 책을 읽어 주세요.
Tony: 알겠어요. 지금 들어가야 하나요?
Woman: 네. 7번 방으로 들어가 주세요.
Tony: 네. 명심해야 할 것이 있나요?
Woman: 네. 천천히 그리고 명확하게 읽어야 하는 것을 명심하세요.
Tony: 네. 최선을 다할게요.

Real Life Talk Step 3

1. **A:** Hi, I'm Minsu. ________ ________ ________ the volunteer work.
   B: Thanks ________ coming, Minsu.
   A: What ________ ________ ________ ________ ________ ________ today?
   B: Please ________ the dog ________ ________.
   A: Okay. ________ ________ ________ to keep in mind?
   B: Yes. ________ ________ you brush the fur first.
   A: Okay, I will
2. **A:** Hi, I'm Tony. ________ ________ ________ ________ ________.
   B: ________ ________ coming, Tony.
   A: ________ ________ ________ ________ ________ ________ ________ today?
   B: Please record a book ________ ________ ________.
   A: Okay. ________ ________ ________ ________ ________ ________ ________?
   B: Yes. Make ________ you read slowly and clearly.
   A: Okay, I will.

1. A: 안녕하세요. 저는 민수예요. 저는 봉사 활동을 하러 왔어요.
   B: 민수 군, 와 주셔서 감사합니다.
   A: 오늘 제가 무엇을 하길 원하세요?
   B: 개를 목욕시켜 주세요.
   A: 네. 명심해야 할 것이 있나요?
   B: 네. 털을 먼저 빗길 것을 명심하세요.
   A: 네. 그렇게 할게요.
2. A: 안녕하세요. 저는 Tony예요. 저는 봉사 활동을 하러 왔어요.
   B: Tony 군, 와 주셔서 감사합니다.
   A: 오늘 제가 무엇을 하길 원하세요?
   B: 시각 장애인들을 위해 책을 녹음해 주세요.
   A: 네. 유념해야 할 것이 있나요?
   B: 네. 천천히 그리고 명확하게 읽어야 하는 것을 명심하세요.
   A: 네. 그렇게 할게요.

[01~02] 다음 대화를 읽고 물음에 답하시오.

B: What are all these boxes and books for?
G: I'm packing the books for the donation center. Can you give me a hand?
B: Sure. What do you want (A)________?
G: (B)____
B: No problem.

01 빈칸 (A)에 알맞은 말을 고르시오.

① doing ② me doing ③ to do
④ me to do ⑤ me to have done

02 빈칸 (B)에 알맞은 말을 고르시오.

① Let's write the address on the boxes.
② I don't want to write the address on the boxes.
③ Did you write the address on the boxes?
④ Why don't we write the address on the boxes?
⑤ Please write the address on the boxes.

03 다음 대화의 빈칸에 들어갈 말을 <보기>에서 골라 순서대로 바르게 배열하시오.

B: What is this mess?
G: ________________________________
B: ________________________________
G: ________________________________
B: ________________________________
G: ________________________________
B: Sure. What do you want me to do?
G: Please put the cookies in the gift boxes. Three cookies in each box.
B: Okay.

보기

(A) They're for the people at the nursing home.
(B) That's very nice of you.
(C) I'm baking cookies.
(D) Can you give me a hand?
(E) Why are you baking so many cookies?

➡ ________________________

Conversation 시험대비 실력평가

Step5

01 중요 다음 대화의 빈칸에 들어갈 말로 알맞은 것을 고르시오.

> A: What are you doing?
> B: I'm packing for my move tomorrow. Can you help me?
> A: Sure. ________________
> B: Please move the chairs outside.
> A: No problem.

① What would you like me to do this year?
② What do you want me to do?
③ What do you want to do?
④ What did you move?
⑤ Why didn't you pack your books?

[02~04] 다음 대화를 읽고 물음에 답하시오.

> B: Enjoy the concert, Mom. (①)
> W: Okay, I will. Thanks. (②) Your dinner is on the table.
> B: All right. Don't worry about me. (③)
> W: Make (A)________ you feed the dog after you have dinner. (④)
> B: Okay. Mom, you should go now. (⑤)

02 위 대화의 ①~⑤ 중 주어진 문장이 들어갈 알맞은 곳은?

Dad is waiting in the car.

① ② ③ ④ ⑤

03 빈칸 (A)에 알맞은 말을 고르시오.

① such ② just ③ right
④ sure ⑤ true

04 중요 위 대화를 읽고 답할 수 없는 질문을 고르시오.

① What should the boy do after having dinner?
② What does the boy worry about?
③ Where is the boy's dinner?
④ Where is the boy's dad?
⑤ Where is the boy's mom going to go?

[05~07] 다음 대화를 읽고 물음에 답하시오.

> B: What are all these boxes and books for? (①)
> G: I'm (A)________ the books for the donation center. (②)
> B: Sure. (③) What do you want me to do?
> G: (④) Please write the address on the boxes. (⑤)
> B: No problem.

05 중요 위 대화의 ①~⑤ 중 주어진 문장이 들어갈 알맞은 곳은?

Can you give me a hand?

① ② ③ ④ ⑤

06 빈칸 (A)에 알맞은 말을 고르시오.

① packing ② picking
③ putting ④ spending
⑤ getting

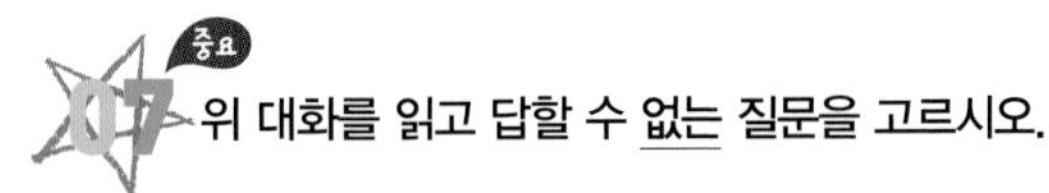

07 위 대화를 읽고 답할 수 없는 질문을 고르시오.

① Is the boy going to help the girl?
② What is the girl doing now?
③ How many books is the girl going to send to the donation center?
④ What are the books for?
⑤ What will the boy do after conversation?

08 다음 대화의 빈칸에 들어갈 말로 알맞은 것을 고르시오.

> A: Hi! I'm here for the volunteer work.
> B: Thanks for coming.
> A: What do you want me to do today?
> B: Please deliver meals to the elderly.
> A: Okay. Is there anything to keep in mind?
> B: Yes. ____________________
> A: Okay, I will.

① Make sure you greet them politely.
② Remember to make home-made meals.
③ Be sure to take two tablets with water before meals.
④ Don't forget not to eat between meals.
⑤ You'd better donate them to the elderly.

09 다음 중 짝지어진 대화가 어색한 것은?

① A: Your computer is always on. It uses a lot of electricity.
B: I'm sorry. I didn't know that.
A: Make sure you turn it off when you're not using it.

② A: You didn't water the plant. Make sure you water it regularly.
B: Okay. I will.

③ A: I forgot to close the window. It's all wet.
B: Be sure to close the window next time.

④ A: Did you say the movie starts at 7:00?
B: Yeah, make sure you go to the movie theater after 7:30.

⑤ A: It's really cold today.
B: Make sure you wear your warm coat.

[10~11] 다음 대화를 읽고 물음에 답하시오.

> B: (①) Hello, class. (②) Make groups of four people and sit around the tables. (③) Today we're going to make bacon and egg sandwiches. (④) First, make sure you wash your hands before you start. (⑤) Second, be careful when you use a knife. All right, let's start.

10 위 대화의 ①~⑤ 중 주어진 문장이 들어갈 알맞은 곳은?

> Keep in mind two rules for our class.

① ② ③ ④ ⑤

11 위 대화를 읽고 답할 수 없는 질문을 고르시오.

① What are they going to make?
② What class is it?
③ How many hours does it take to make bacon and egg sandwiches?
④ How many rules are there to keep in mind during the class?
⑤ How many people do make a group?

[01~03] 다음 대화를 읽고 물음에 답하시오.

Woman: Good morning. What can I do for you?
Tony: Hi. I'm here for the volunteer work.
Woman: Oh, you must be Tony.
Tony: That's right. 오늘 제가 무엇을 하길 원하세요?
Woman: (A)Please read this book for blind in the recording room.
Tony: No problem. Should I go in now?
Woman: Yes. Please go into Room 7.
Tony: Okay. Is there anything to keep ⓐ[at / in / for] mind?
Woman: Yes. Make sure you read slowly and clearly.
Tony: Okay. I'll ⓑ[do / keep / make] my best.

01 (중요) 위 대화의 괄호 ⓐ와 ⓑ에서 적절한 것을 골라 쓰시오.

➡ ⓐ ____________ ⓑ ____________

02 밑줄 친 우리말과 일치하도록 주어진 단어를 이용해 문장을 만드시오.

➡ ______________________________
(want, do)

03 밑줄 친 (A)에서 어색한 부분을 찾아 고쳐 쓰시오.

➡ ______________________________

04 다음 대화의 빈칸 (A)와 (B)에 알맞은 말을 쓰시오.

B: What is this mess?
G: I'm baking cookies.
B: Why are you baking so many cookies?
G: They're for the people at the nursing home.
B: That's very nice of you.
G: Can you (A)_____ me a hand?
B: Sure. What do you (B)_____ me to do?
G: Please put the cookies in the gift boxes. Three cookies in each box.
B: Okay.

➡ (A) ____________ (B) ____________

05 (중요) 다음 대화의 괄호 (A)와 (B)에서 적절한 것을 골라 쓰시오.

A: It's time (A)[to go / to going / going] home.
B: Yes. Make sure you (A)[lock / locking / to lock] the doors.
A: Okay, I will. Anything else?
B: No, that's it. See you tomorrow.

➡ (A) ____________ (B) ____________

06 다음 대화의 밑줄 친 문장과 같은 의미가 되도록 주어진 단어를 이용해 문장을 만드시오.

A: What are you doing?
B: I'm packing for my move tomorrow. Can you help me?
A: Sure. What do you want me to do?
B: Please take out the trash.
A: No problem.

➡ ______________________ (like)

교과서

Grammar

1 사역동사 have/make/let 5형식 문장

- The project manager **had** us **meet** at 9 a.m. 프로젝트 책임자는 우리를 오전 9시에 만나게 했다.
- We **had** the car **serviced.** 우리는 차를 점검 받았다.

■ 사역동사
- 의미: 목적어가 ~하게 하다[시키다]/두다
- 종류: make, have, let 등
- 형태: '주어+have/make/let+목적어+목적격보어(동사원형)'

■ 사역동사는 '사역동사+목적어+목적격보어'의 형태로 주어가 아니라 대상(목적어)이 행동을 하게 만들거나 하도록 허용한다는 의미를 가지는 동사를 말하며, have, make, let이 있다.

- Laughter can **make** us **feel** better. 웃음이 우리의 기분을 나아지게 할 수 있다.
- Don't **let** her **upset** you. 그녀 때문에 속 썩이지 마.

■ 목적격보어로 목적어와의 관계가 능동일 경우 동사원형이 오며 '~(목적어)가 …하게(목적격보어) 하다'의 뜻을 갖는다. 수동일 경우 '~(목적어)가 …(목적격보어)을 당하게[되게] 하다'의 뜻으로 make, have는 목적격보어로 과거분사를 쓰고, let은 'be p.p.' 형태를 쓴다.

- I **had** him **wash** my car. 〈능동〉 나는 그에게 내 차를 닦게 했다. (그가 차를 닦는 것으로 능동)
- I **had** my car **washed.** 〈수동〉 나는 내 차가 세차되도록 했다. (차가 세차되는 것으로 수동)

■ 'help'와 'get'의 쓰임

※ help는 목적격보어로 동사원형이나 to부정사가 오며 뜻의 차이는 없다.

- I **helped** Alisha **do** her science homework. 나는 Alisha가 과학 숙제를 하는 것을 도와주었다.
  = I **helped** Alisha **to do** her science homework.

※ get이 '~하게 하다'라는 사역동사의 뜻으로 쓰일 때 목적격보어로 to부정사를 쓴다.

- Mom **got** me **to eat** vegetables. 〈능동〉 엄마는 내가 야채를 먹도록 하셨다.
- I **got** my car **washed.** 〈수동〉 나는 내 차가 세차되도록 했다.

핵심 Check

1. 다음 괄호 안에서 알맞은 말을 고르시오.
   (1) Please let me (know / to know) your preferred date.
   (2) It makes me (feeling / feel) at home.

2 It is[was] ~ that 강조 구문

- **It was** a better tomorrow **that** we painted. 우리가 그린 것은 바로 더 나은 내일이었다.
- **It is** the book **that** everybody is talking about. 모든 사람이 말하고 있는 것은 바로 그 책이다.

■ It ~ that 강조 구문
- 의미: …한 것은 바로 ~이다[이었다]
- 형태: It is/was ~ that …

■ 'It ~ that 강조 구문'은 'It is/was ~ that …'의 형태로, 강조하고자 하는 부분을 It is/was와 that 사이에 넣고, 나머지 부분을 that 뒤에 써서 주어, 목적어, 부사(구/절) 등을 강조한다.

- I suggested this idea at the club meeting.
  → **It** was I **that** suggested this idea at the club meeting. (주어 강조)
  → **It** was this idea **that** I suggested at the club meeting. (목적어인 명사 강조)
  → **It** was at the club meeting **that** I suggested this idea. (부사구 강조)

■ 'It ~ that …' 강조 구문에서 강조하는 대상이 주어일 경우, that을 관계대명사 who(사람일 경우) 또는 which(사물이나 동물일 경우)로 바꿔 쓸 수 있다.

- I met her at the airport yesterday. 나는 그녀를 공항에서 어제 만났다.
  → **It was** I **that[who]** met her at the airport yesterday.
  → **It was** her **that[who/whom]** I met at the airport yesterday.

■ 'It ~ that …' 강조 구문에서 강조하는 대상이 부사(구/절)일 경우 that 다음에 완전한 절이 나오지만 그 외의 경우에는 불완전한 절이 나오는 것에 유의한다.

- **It is** a new computer **that[which]** I want to buy. 내가 사고 싶은 것은 바로 새 컴퓨터이다. (that 다음에 buy의 목적어가 없는 불완전한 절)
- **It was** at the party **that** I met Susan. 내가 Susan을 만난 것은 바로 그 파티에서였다. (that 다음에 완전한 절)

핵심 Check

2. 다음 괄호 안에서 알맞은 말을 고르시오.
(1) It is my watch (that / what) I am looking for.
(2) (It / That) was at the park that I met her by chance.
(3) It is her (whom / which) I love.

01 다음 빈칸에 들어갈 말로 알맞은 것은?

My mom had me ________ her food.

① taste ② tasted ③ to taste
④ tasting ⑤ to tasting

02 다음 각 문장의 빈칸에 공통으로 들어갈 말로 알맞은 것은?

• It was a big tree ________ he painted on the wall yesterday. • It was in 1969 ________ Apollo 11 landed on the moon.

① which ② when ③ who
④ that ⑤ what

03 다음 중 어법상 바르지 않은 것은?

① It was on the day that we had dinner together.
② It was Dan who broke the vase.
③ It is Lucy whom he loves.
④ It was in the park that we played basketball yesterday.
⑤ It was Jim which I met again.

04 다음 우리말에 맞게 주어진 어휘를 바르게 배열하시오.

(1) Brown 씨는 그의 아들이 파티에 가게 허락했다.
(Mr. Brown, the party, his son, go, let, to)
➡ ________________________________

(2) 프로젝트 책임자는 우리를 오전 9시에 만나게 했다.
(the project manager, us, had, meet, 9 a.m., at)
➡ ________________________________

(3) 그들은 내게 그 이야기 전체를 반복하게 만들었다.
(me, they, story, repeat, whole, made, the)
➡ ________________________________

(4) 그녀는 내가 이 숙제를 끝낼 수 있도록 도와주었다.
(this assignment, she, me, complete, helped, to)
➡ ________________________________

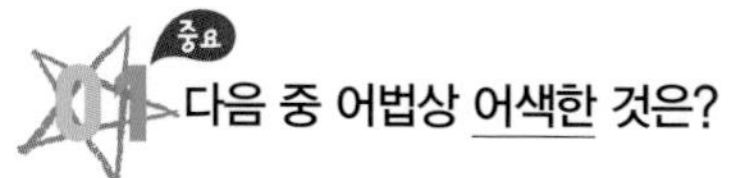

중요
01 다음 중 어법상 어색한 것은?

① He let me finishing playing the piano.
② Mom let me watch TV after I finished my homework.
③ The heavy traffic made me worry about being late.
④ She had her computer repaired.
⑤ Ms. White has us be on time for every class.

02 다음 중 어법상 옳은 것은?

① It was he which went to the station to see her off.
② It was the book which I bought last Saturday.
③ That was last Friday that I found the golden rings.
④ It was at the restaurant which I met Anna.
⑤ It was yesterday what I looked for the key.

서답형
03 다음 중 밑줄 친 부분의 쓰임이 <보기>와 같은 것을 모두 고르시오.

보기
Mom made me bake some bread.

ⓐ She made the waiter bring some water.
ⓑ He made me a model airplane.
ⓒ He made toward the door.
ⓓ The springshower makes the grass grow.
ⓔ It makes no difference.

➡ ____________________

[04~05] 다음 우리말을 알맞게 영작한 것을 고르시오. (04–1개, 05–2개)

04

선생님은 우리가 읽은 것에 관해 뭔가를 그리게 하셨다.

① The teacher had us drew something about what we had read.
② The teacher had us to draw something about that we had read.
③ The teacher had us drawing something about what we had read.
④ The teacher had us draw something about what we had read.
⑤ The teacher had us draw something about that we had read.

05

우리가 그린 것은 바로 더 나은 내일이었다.

① It was a better tomorrow what we painted.
② It was a better tomorrow which we painted.
③ It was a better tomorrow where we painted.
④ It was a better tomorrow when we painted.
⑤ It was a better tomorrow that we painted.

중요
06 다음 문장의 빈칸에 들어갈 말로 가장 적절한 것은?

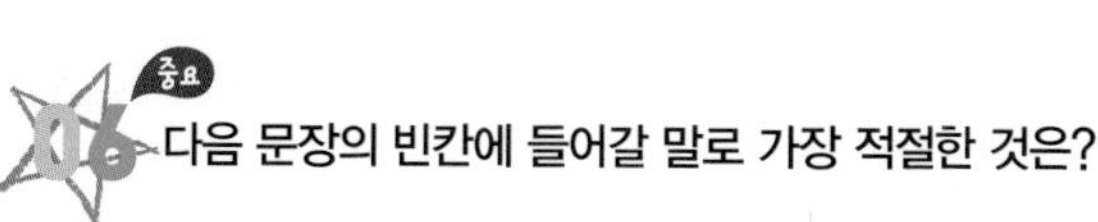
He made me ________ the work.

① finished ② finishing ③ finish
④ to finish ⑤ to finishing

07 다음 <보기>의 밑줄 친 that과 쓰임이 같은 것은?

보기

It was flowers that my club members planted in the garden on April 5th.

① He couldn't walk that fast.
② That's not the computer I bought last week.
③ It was the cookies that Amy made for me yesterday.
④ It is certain that he will come.
⑤ Give me that chair, not this one.

08 다음 문장의 빈칸 (A), (B), (C)에 들어갈 말로 가장 적절한 것은?

• Don't let him (A)______ your evening.
• I had the paper (B)________ for the meeting.
• They got their children (C)______ outside.

	(A)	(B)	(C)
①	spoiling	copied	to play
②	spoiling	copy	playing
③	spoil	to copy	play
④	spoil	copied	to play
⑤	spoil	copy	play

09 다음 중 It ~ that 쓰임이 나머지 넷과 다른 하나는?

① It was the vase that Jake broke at home yesterday.
② It is important that students develop an awareness of how the Internet can be used.
③ It was in the restaurant that I met Sam yesterday.
④ It was her wallet that she lost after playing badminton at the park.
⑤ It was yesterday that she made me bake some cake.

10 다음 문장의 빈칸 (A), (B)에 들어갈 말로 가장 적절한 것은?

Some teachers at school (A)_______ us advice. Ms. Green makes us (B)_______ quiet in class. Mr. Johns has us (C)______ up trash on the ground.

	(A)	(B)	(C)
①	give	be	pick
②	give	to be	picked
③	gives	be	picking
④	gives	to be	picked
⑤	giving	are	pick

[11~12] 다음 중 어법상 올바른 문장은?

11 ① Let her goes home right now.
② My mom had me cleaned my room.
③ The movie make me think about my own choices.
④ The teacher got us draw something strange.
⑤ The maid helped the princess to dress for the party.

12 ① It was on the last day of the festival which we finally enjoyed *samgyupsal*.
② It was last Saturday which the girl first saw the fireworks.
③ It was the hen that laid two eggs on the roof last week.
④ It was when Jake told me something which I realized my mistake.
⑤ It is in the city which my best friend met the girl.

서답형

13 다음 문장에서 어법상 어색한 부분을 바르게 고치시오.

(1) Carrie had her room paint white.

________ ➡ ________

(2) She let her daughter to play computer games.

________ ➡ ________

(3) Leslie helped him escaping from the pressures of living up to others' expectations.

________ ➡ ________

(4) It was last week which John borrowed a novel from the library.

________ ➡ ________

(5) It was his smartphone what Bob dropped in the toilet this morning.

________ ➡ ________

(6) It was in this school which I studied when I was young.

________ ➡ ________

서답형

14 다음 괄호 안에서 알맞은 것을 고르시오.

(1) His kindness made her (feel / to feel) good and (smile / to smile) at him.

(2) Clare got her computer (fix / fixed) at the store.

(3) I asked her (remain / to remain) seated.

(4) It was yesterday (which / that) they planted trees.

(5) It was Tom (who / which) broke it.

중요

15 다음 문장의 빈칸에 알맞지 않은 말은?

The woman _____ me clean the windows.

① made ② helped ③ let
④ had ⑤ got

16 주어진 문장을 'my favorite movie character'를 강조하는 문장으로 바르게 고친 것은?

I started to paint my favorite movie character.

① It was my favorite movie character where I started to paint.
② It was my favorite movie character what I started to paint.
③ It was my favorite movie character how I started to paint.
④ It is my favorite movie character what I started to paint.
⑤ It was my favorite movie character that I started to paint.

중요

17 다음 빈칸에 알맞은 말을 고르시오.

He always ______________ all of his appointments.

① gets her arrange
② gets her arranged
③ makes her arrange
④ makes her arranged
⑤ helps her arranged

18 다음 빈칸에 알맞은 말을 고르시오.

The team was ______________ increase the competition level.

① made ② making
③ to making ④ made to
⑤ to made

고난이도

01 다음 문장에서 어법상 어색한 것을 바르게 고쳐 다시 쓰시오.

(1) The project manager let us painted anything we wanted.

➡ ______________________

(2) She wasn't happy with our work and made us to start over.

➡ ______________________

(3) They immediately had the meeting cancel.

➡ ______________________

(4) When you cut them into pieces, let them marinated.

➡ ______________________

(5) You in this country helped us becoming free.

➡ ______________________

(6) It was Susan which I had a date with at the park last Saturday.

➡ ______________________

(7) It was the train which Kimberly lost her wallet.

➡ ______________________

(8) It was last Friday where Mina flew a drone at the school.

➡ ______________________

02 다음 두 문장을 주어진 〈조건〉에 맞춰 〈보기〉와 같이 한 문장으로 완성하시오.

보기
- My sister said her homework was difficult.
- So, my mom ordered me to help her.

→ My mom made me help my sister.

(1) 동사 let을 이용하여 8 단어로 쓸 것.

- I asked him to play the piano with me.
- So he allowed me to play the piano with him.

➡ ______________________

(2) 동사 have와 fix를 이용하여 5 단어로 쓸 것.

- Her computer was out of order.
- She called the repair shop and asked them to repair it.

➡ ______________________

중요

03 다음 그림을 보고 각 질문에 'It ~ that' 강조 구문을 사용하여 답하시오.

(1) Who found a deer behind a tree?

➡ ______________________

(2) What did Mina find behind a tree?

➡ ______________________

(3) Where did Mina find a deer?

➡ ______________________

고난이도

04 주어진 단어를 이용하여 〈보기〉와 같이 문장을 바꿔 쓰시오.

보기
Ms. Brown tells us to be quiet in class. (have)
→ Ms. Brown has us be quiet in class.

(1) I told my sister to bring my gym uniform. (have)
➡ ______________________

(2) Ashley asked me to fix dinner. (get)
➡ ______________________

(3) He ordered me to wash his car. (make)
➡ ______________________

(4) The doctor allowed her to return to work. (let)
➡ ______________________

05 다음 문장을 주어진 단어를 강조하는 문장으로 고쳐 쓰시오.

I bought this nice jacket at the store last Sunday.

(1) I
➡ ______________________

(2) bought
➡ ______________________

(3) this nice jacket
➡ ______________________

(4) at the store
➡ ______________________

(5) last Sunday
➡ ______________________

06 다음 그림을 보고 주어진 어휘를 이용하여 빈칸에 알맞은 말을 쓰시오.

My son feels ill. I'd better have him ________ to the hospital. (take)

중요

07 다음 우리말과 일치하도록 괄호 안에 주어진 어휘를 이용하여 영작하시오.

(1) Peter는 가끔 그의 개가 그의 침대에서 자게 내버려 둔다. (sometimes, let, on his bed)
➡ ______________________

(2) 우리 아빠는 내가 많은 책을 읽도록 시키신다. (my dad, make, lots of)
➡ ______________________

(3) 당신은 이 그림을 제가 어디다 걸기를 원하세요? (want, hang, this picture)
➡ ______________________

(4) John이 지난주에 한 도서관에서 빌린 것은 바로 그 소설이었다. (it, the novel, a library, borrow)
➡ ______________________

(5) 내가 그녀를 처음으로 만난 것은 바로 2014년이었다. (it, for the first time)
➡ ______________________

교과서

Reading

Paint a Better Tomorrow

Hi. My name is Homin. This is me in front of (~ 앞에) the wall painting. The wings are so pretty, aren't they (= the wings)? Many people like to take pictures in front of wall paintings. They (= Wall paintings) make old neighborhoods (목적어) bright and new (brightly and newly (×)).

Last month, I visited a village with (~이 있는) wall paintings in Yeosu. As I was taking a picture, a light went on in my head (머릿속에 좋은 생각이 떠올랐다). I thought, "I'm in the school art club. Why don't we do (= How[What] about doing ~?) wall paintings like (~와 같은(전치사)) these?" I suggested this idea at the next club meeting, and the members loved it (this idea(Homin's idea)).

We found a teen volunteer project on the Internet (인터넷에서). The project was to do (명사적 용법의 to부정사(보어)) a wall painting in our neighborhood. We applied for it (the project), and two weeks later, our club was selected (수동태)!

The day of the project finally (= at last = in the end: 마침내) came. The project manager had us meet (have+사람+원형부정사) at the painting site at 9 a.m. The wall was in very poor condition (be in poor[bad] condition: 상태가 나쁘다). There (유도부사) were (was(×)) strange writings and drawings (주어) on some parts. Other parts had old posters on them. We removed the posters first and painted over the writings and drawings with (~으로(도구)) white paint.

wing 날개
neighborhood 근처, 이웃
village 마을
teen 십 대의; 십 대
select 선택하다, 선정하다
manager 운영자, 관리자
site 현장, 장소
remove 없애다, 제거하다
spot (특정한) 장소, 자리
background (경치, 그림, 무대의) 배경

확인문제

● 다음 문장이 본문의 내용과 일치하면 T, 일치하지 않으면 F를 쓰시오.

1 Wall paintings make old neighborhoods bright and new. ☐
2 As Homin was painting a picture, a light went on in his head. ☐
3 Homin suggested his idea at the next club meeting, and the members loved it. ☐
4 Homin and the school art club members found a teen volunteer project on the Internet. ☐
5 Homin and the school art club members met at the painting site at 9 a.m. ☐
6 Homin and the school art club members removed the writings and drawings first and painted over the posters with white paint. ☐

The manager let us paint anything we wanted. We decided to paint something cute because the wall was near an elementary school. We divided into three groups and began painting. I was in the group with Minsu and Jiwon. I chose my spot and started to paint my favorite movie character. Minsu painted some flowers and Jiwon did some background drawings.

let+목적어+원형부정사 / = whatever / ~thing으로 끝나는 말은 형용사가 뒤에서 수식 / V1 / V2 / start+to부정사/동명사

Our club painted for about five hours. After we finished, we got together and shared the day's experiences. Minsu was very proud of his flower painting. He said, "My flower is so real that a bee landed on it." I said, "Drawing on a wall was much harder than drawing on paper."

for about: 약 ~ 동안 / ~한 후에 / be proud of = take pride in / so ~ that ...: 너무 ~해서 그 결과 …하다 / my flower / = even/still/far/ a lot :비교급 강조

We all agreed that our wall painting wasn't perfect. But it didn't matter. We made our neighborhood a little brighter and happier. We were proud of ourselves. We didn't just paint pictures on a wall that day. It was a better tomorrow that we painted.

= was imperfect / 중요하다(be important) / 비교급 강조 / us(X) / = only / It was ~ that 강조구문

decide to ~하기로 결정하다
cute 귀여운
elementary 초등의
character 등장인물, 캐릭터
background 배경
get together 모이다
land 내려앉다
matter 중요하다, 문제되다
perfect 완벽한
be proud of ~을 자랑스럽게 여기다

● 다음 문장이 본문의 내용과 일치하면 T, 일치하지 않으면 F를 쓰시오.

1 Homin and the school art club members decided to paint something cute because the wall was near an elementary school. ☐

2 They divided into four groups and began painting. ☐

3 Minsu painted some flowers and Jiwon did some background drawings. ☐

4 Drawing on paper was much harder than drawing on a wall. ☐

5 Homin and the school art club members all agreed that their wall painting wasn't perfect. ☐

6 Homin and the school art club members just painted pictures on a wall that day. ☐

• 우리말을 참고하여 빈칸에 알맞은 말을 쓰시오.

1 **Paint a** ________ ________

2 Hi. ________ ________ ________ Homin.

3 ________ ________ ________ in front of the wall painting.

4 The wings are so pretty, ________ ________?

5 Many people like to ________ ________ in front of wall paintings.

6 They make ________ ________ bright and new.

7 Last month, I visited a village ________ ________ ________ in Yeosu.

8 As I was taking a picture, ________ ________ ________ ________ ________ ________ ________.

9 I thought, "________ ________ the school art club.

10 ________ ________ ________ do wall paintings like these?"

11 I ________ ________ ________ at the next club meeting, and the members loved it.

12 We found a teen volunteer project ________ ________ ________.

13 The project was ________ ________ ________ ________ ________ in our neighborhood.

14 We ________ ________ it, and two weeks later, our club ________ ________!

15 The day of the project ________ ________.

16 The project manager ________ ________ ________ at the painting site at 9 a.m.

17 The wall ________ ________ ________ ________ ________.

1 더 나은 내일을 그려라

2 안녕. 내 이름은 호민이야.

3 벽화 앞에 있는 사람이 나야.

4 날개가 예뻐, 그렇지 않니?

5 많은 사람들이 벽화 앞에서 사진 찍는 것을 좋아해.

6 벽화는 오래된 마을을 밝고 새롭게 만들어.

7 지난달에 나는 여수에 있는 벽화 마을을 방문했어.

8 내가 사진을 찍을 때 머릿속에 좋은 생각이 떠올랐어.

9 나는 생각했어. "나는 학교 미술 동아리에 있잖아.

10 우리가 이것처럼 벽화를 그리면 어떨까?"

11 나는 이 아이디어를 다음 동아리 모임에서 제안했고, 동아리 부원들은 그것을 아주 좋아했어.

12 우리는 인터넷에서 청소년 봉사 프로젝트를 찾았어.

13 그 프로젝트는 우리 마을에 벽화를 그리는 것이었어.

14 우리는 거기에 지원했고, 2주 후에 우리 동아리가 선택되었어!

15 마침내 프로젝트 날이 되었어.

16 프로젝트 책임자는 우리를 오전 9시에 그림 그리는 곳에서 만나게 했어.

17 벽은 상태가 별로 좋지 않았어.

18 There were ________ ________ ________ ________ on some parts.

19 ________ ________ had old posters on them.

20 We removed the posters first and painted over the writings and drawings ________ ________ ________.

21 The manager ________ ________ ________ anything we wanted.

22 We decided to paint ________ ________ because the wall was near an elementary school.

23 We ________ ________ three groups and began painting.

24 I ________ ________ ________ ________ with Minsu and Jiwon.

25 I ________ ________ ________ and started to paint my favorite movie character.

26 Minsu painted some flowers and Jiwon ________ some ________ ________.

27 Our club painted ________ ________ five hours.

28 After we finished, we ________ ________ and ________ the day's experiences.

29 Minsu ________ ________ ________ ________ his flower painting.

30 He said, "My flower is ________ real ________ a bee landed on it."

31 I said, "Drawing on a wall was ________ ________ than drawing on paper."

32 We all agreed that our wall painting ________ ________.

33 But it didn't ________.

34 We made our neighborhood ________ ________ ________ ________ ________.

35 We were proud of ________.

36 We ________ ________ ________ pictures on a wall that day.

37 It was ________ ________ ________ that we painted.

18 몇 군데에는 이상한 낙서와 그림이 있었어.

19 다른 부분에는 오래된 포스터들이 붙어 있었어.

20 우리는 먼저 포스터들을 제거하고 낙서와 그림을 흰 페인트로 덧칠했어.

21 책임자는 우리가 원하는 어떤 것이든 그리게 했어.

22 우리는 그 벽이 초등학교 근처에 있어서 귀여운 뭔가를 그리기로 했어.

23 우리는 세 그룹으로 나뉘어 그리기 시작했어.

24 나는 민수와 지원이와 같은 그룹이었어.

25 나는 내 구역을 정해서 가장 좋아하는 영화 캐릭터를 그리기 시작했어.

26 민수는 몇 송이의 꽃을 그렸고 지원이는 배경 그림을 그렸어.

27 우리 동아리는 약 다섯 시간 동안 그림을 그렸어.

28 끝난 후에 우리는 모여서 그날의 경험을 함께 이야기했어.

29 민수는 자신이 그린 꽃 그림을 정말 자랑스러워했어.

30 그는 "내 꽃이 정말 진짜 같아서 벌이 꽃에 앉았어."라고 말했어.

31 나는 "벽에 그리는 것이 종이에 그리는 것보다 훨씬 힘들었어."라고 말했어.

32 우리 모두는 우리 벽화가 완벽하지는 않다는 것에 동의했어.

33 하지만 그것은 중요하지 않았어.

34 우리는 동네를 조금 더 밝고 행복하게 만들었어.

35 우리는 우리 자신이 자랑스러웠어.

36 우리는 그날 벽에 그림만 그린 게 아니었어.

37 우리가 그린 것은 바로 더 나은 내일이었어.

Reading 교과서 확인학습 B

- 우리말을 참고하여 본문을 영작하시오.

1 더 나은 내일을 그려라
➡ ____________________

2 안녕. 내 이름은 호민이야.
➡ ____________________

3 벽화 앞에 있는 사람이 나야.
➡ ____________________

4 날개가 예뻐, 그렇지 않니?
➡ ____________________

5 많은 사람들이 벽화 앞에서 사진 찍는 것을 좋아해.
➡ ____________________

6 벽화는 오래된 마을을 밝고 새롭게 만들어.
➡ ____________________

7 지난달에 나는 여수에 있는 벽화 마을을 방문했어.
➡ ____________________

8 내가 사진을 찍을 때 머릿속에 좋은 생각이 떠올랐어.
➡ ____________________

9 나는 생각했어. "나는 학교 미술 동아리에 있잖아.
➡ ____________________

10 우리가 이것처럼 벽화를 그리면 어떨까?"
➡ ____________________

11 나는 이 아이디어를 다음 동아리 모임에서 제안했고, 동아리 부원들은 그것을 아주 좋아했어.
➡ ____________________

12 우리는 인터넷에서 청소년 봉사 프로젝트를 찾았어.
➡ ____________________

13 그 프로젝트는 우리 마을에 벽화를 그리는 것이었어.
➡ ____________________

14 우리는 거기에 지원했고, 2주 후에 우리 동아리가 선택되었어!
➡ ____________________

15 마침내 프로젝트 날이 되었어.
➡ ____________________

16 프로젝트 책임자는 우리를 오전 9시에 그림 그리는 곳에서 만나게 했어.
➡ ____________________

17 벽은 상태가 별로 좋지 않았어.
➡ ____________________

18 몇 군데에는 이상한 낙서와 그림이 있었어.
➡ ______

19 다른 부분에는 오래된 포스터들이 붙어 있었어.
➡ ______

20 우리는 먼저 포스터들을 제거하고 낙서와 그림을 흰 페인트로 덧칠했어.
➡ ______

21 책임자는 우리가 원하는 어떤 것이든 그리게 했어.
➡ ______

22 우리는 그 벽이 초등학교 근처에 있어서 귀여운 뭔가를 그리기로 했어.
➡ ______

23 우리는 세 그룹으로 나뉘어 그리기 시작했어.
➡ ______

24 나는 민수와 지원이와 같은 그룹이었어.
➡ ______

25 나는 내 구역을 정해서 가장 좋아하는 영화 캐릭터를 그리기 시작했어.
➡ ______

26 민수는 몇 송이의 꽃을 그렸고 지원이는 배경 그림을 그렸어.
➡ ______

27 우리 동아리는 약 다섯 시간 동안 그림을 그렸어.
➡ ______

28 끝난 후에 우리는 모여서 그날의 경험을 함께 이야기했어.
➡ ______

29 민수는 자신이 그린 꽃 그림을 정말 자랑스러워했어.
➡ ______

30 그는 "내 꽃이 정말 진짜 같아서 벌이 꽃에 앉았어."라고 말했어.
➡ ______

31 나는 "벽에 그리는 것이 종이에 그리는 것보다 훨씬 힘들었어."라고 말했어.
➡ ______

32 우리 모두는 우리 벽화가 완벽하지는 않다는 것에 동의했어.
➡ ______

33 하지만 그것은 중요하지 않았어.
➡ ______

34 우리는 동네를 조금 더 밝고 행복하게 만들었어.
➡ ______

35 우리는 우리 자신이 자랑스러웠어.
➡ ______

36 우리는 그날 벽에 그림만 그린 게 아니었어.
➡ ______

37 우리가 그린 것은 바로 더 나은 내일이었어.
➡ ______

Reading 시험대비 실력평가

[01~04] 다음 글을 읽고 물음에 답하시오.

Hi. My name is Homin. This is me in front of the wall painting. ⓐThe wings are so pretty, isn't it? Many people like to take pictures in front of wall paintings. They make old neighborhoods bright and new.

(①) Last month, I visited a village with wall paintings in Yeosu. (②) I thought, "I'm in the school art club. (③) Why don't we do wall paintings like these?" (④) I suggested ⓑthis idea at the next club meeting, and the members loved it. (⑤)

We found a teen volunteer project on the Internet. The project was to do a wall painting in our neighborhood. We applied for it, and two weeks later, our club was selected!

서답형

01 위 글의 밑줄 친 ⓐ에서 어법상 틀린 부분을 찾아 고치시오.

➡ ______________________

02 위 글의 흐름으로 보아, 주어진 문장이 들어가기에 가장 적절한 곳은?

As I was taking a picture, a light went on in my head.

① ② ③ ④ ⑤

서답형

03 위 글의 밑줄 친 ⓑthis idea가 가리키는 것을 본문에서 찾아 쓰시오.

➡ ______________________

중요

04 According to the passage, which is NOT true?

① Wall paintings make old neighborhoods bright and new.
② Last month, Homin visited a village with wall paintings in Yeosu.
③ While Homin was taking a picture, a bright idea occurred to him.
④ The school art club members loved Homin's idea.
⑤ Homin's art club was selected for a teen volunteer project two weeks after he visited Yeosu.

[05~07] 다음 글을 읽고 물음에 답하시오.

The day of the project (A)finally came. The project manager had us meet at the painting site at 9 a.m. (B)벽은 상태가 별로 좋지 않았어. There were strange writings and drawings on some parts. Other parts had old posters on them. We ___ⓐ___ the posters first and painted over the writings and drawings with white paint.

05 위 글의 빈칸 ⓐ에 들어갈 알맞은 말을 고르시오.

① protected ② removed ③ prevented
④ maintained ⑤ destroyed

중요

06 위 글의 밑줄 친 (A)finally와 바꿔 쓸 수 있는 말을 모두 고르시오.

① above all ② at last ③ at least
④ most of all ⑤ in the end

서답형

07 위 글의 밑줄 친 (B)의 우리말에 맞게 주어진 어휘를 이용하여 7 단어로 영작하시오.

in, poor

➡ ________________________

[08~10] 다음 글을 읽고 물음에 답하시오.

Last month, I visited a village with wall paintings in Yeosu. As I was taking a picture, a light went on in my head. I thought, "I'm in the school art club. Why don't we do wall paintings like (A)these?" I suggested this idea at the next club meeting, and the members loved it.

We found a teen volunteer project ⓐ____ the Internet. The project was to do a wall painting in our neighborhood. We applied ⓑ____ it, and two weeks later, our club was selected!

08 위 글의 빈칸 ⓐ와 ⓑ에 들어갈 전치사가 바르게 짝지어진 것은?

	ⓐ ⓑ		ⓐ ⓑ
①	to – for	②	on – with
③	on – for	④	from – on
⑤	to – with		

서답형

09 본문의 내용과 일치하도록 다음 빈칸 (A)와 (B)에 알맞은 단어를 쓰시오.

Homin came up with an idea while he was (A)________ ________ ________ at a village with wall paintings in Yeosu, and suggested to the art club members that they should do (B)________ ________ like those.

서답형

10 위 글의 밑줄 친 (A)these가 가리키는 것을 10자에서 15자 사이의 우리말로 쓰시오.

➡ ________________________

[11~12] 다음 글을 읽고 물음에 답하시오.

Our club painted for about five hours. After we finished, we got together and shared the day's experiences. Minsu was very proud of his flower painting. He said, "My flower is so real that a bee landed on it." I said, "Drawing on a wall was much harder than drawing on paper."

We all agreed that our wall painting wasn't perfect. But it didn't ⓐmatter. We made our neighborhood a little brighter and happier. We were proud of ourselves. We didn't just paint pictures on a wall that day. It was a better tomorrow that we painted.

중요

11 위 글의 밑줄 친 ⓐmatter와 같은 의미로 쓰인 것을 고르시오.

① It's a private matter.
② Give me the printed matter.
③ Does it really matter who did it?
④ It's a matter of life and death.
⑤ All matter is solid, liquid, or gas.

중요

12 위 글의 제목으로 알맞은 것을 고르시오.

① Look! I Painted This Incredible Flower!
② Which Is Harder, Drawing on a Wall or Drawing on Paper?
③ Our Wall Painting Wasn't Perfect. So What?
④ We Painted Pictures on a Wall
⑤ What Did We Paint? A Better Tomorrow!

[13~14] 다음 글을 읽고 물음에 답하시오.

Our club painted ①during about five hours. After we finished, we got together and shared the day's experiences. Minsu was very proud of his flower painting. He said, "My flower is so real ②as to a bee landed on it." I said, "Drawing on a wall was much harder than drawing on paper."

We all agreed that our wall painting wasn't perfect. But ⓐit didn't matter. We made our neighborhood ③very brighter and happier. We were proud of ④us. We didn't just paint pictures on a wall that day. It was a better tomorrow ⑤what we painted.

13 위 글의 밑줄 친 ⓐ와 바꿔 쓸 수 없는 문장을 고르시오.

① it wasn't important
② it didn't count
③ it wasn't significant
④ it made a difference
⑤ it wasn't of importance

서답형

14 위 글의 밑줄 친 ①~⑤ 중 어법상 틀린 번호를 찾아 모두 고치시오.

➡ ______________________

____

[15~17] 다음 글을 읽고 물음에 답하시오.

The day of the project finally came. The project manager had us meet at the painting site at 9 a.m. The wall was in very ⓐpoor condition. There were strange writings and drawings on some parts. Other parts had old posters on them. We removed the posters first and painted over the writings and drawings with white paint.

The manager let us paint anything we wanted. ⓑWe decided to paint something cute so the wall was near an elementary school. We divided into three groups and began painting. I was in the group with Minsu and Jiwon. I chose my spot and started to paint my favorite movie character. Minsu painted some flowers and Jiwon did some background drawings.

<I: Homin>

서답형

15 위 글의 밑줄 친 ⓐpoor와 바꿔 쓸 수 있는 단어를 쓰시오.

➡ ______________________

서답형

16 위 글의 밑줄 친 ⓑ에서 흐름상 어색한 부분을 찾아 고치시오.

➡ ______________________

중요

17 Which question CANNOT be answered after reading the passage?

① When did they meet at the painting site?
② Was it possible for them to start doing a wall painting right away?
③ Were there any rules to follow about what to paint?
④ When they decided their subject matter, did they consider where the painting site was?
⑤ What was Homin's favorite movie character?

[18~20] 다음 글을 읽고 물음에 답하시오.

Last month, I visited a village with wall paintings in Yeosu. As I was taking a picture, a light went on in my head. I thought, "I'm in the school art club. Why don't we do wall paintings like these?" I suggested this idea at the next club meeting, and the members loved it.

We found a teen volunteer project on the Internet. The project was (A)to do a wall painting in our neighborhood. We applied for it, and two weeks later, our club ___ⓐ___!

<I: Homin>

서답형

18 위 글의 빈칸 ⓐ에 select를 알맞은 형태로 쓰시오.

➡ ______________________

19 위 글의 밑줄 친 (A)to do와 to부정사의 용법이 같은 것을 모두 고르시오.

① I think it valuable to do a wall painting.
② Are there any volunteers to do a wall painting?
③ What do we need to do a wall painting?
④ I chose my spot to do a wall painting.
⑤ My hobby is to do a wall painting.

중요

20 위 글의 제목으로 알맞은 것은?

① How about Doing Wall Paintings like These?
② The Hot Places with Wall Paintings
③ Taking Pictures before Wall Paintings
④ Why Don't We Volunteer Together?
⑤ Valuable Teen Volunteer Projects

[21~23] 다음 글을 읽고 물음에 답하시오.

The day of the project finally came. (A) The project manager had us to meet at the painting site at 9 a.m. The wall was in very poor condition. There were strange writings and drawings on ___ⓐ___ parts. ___ⓑ___ parts had old posters on them. We removed the posters first and painted over the writings and drawings with white paint.

(B)The manager let us to paint anything we wanted. We decided to paint something cute because the wall was near an elementary school. We divided into three groups and began painting. I was in the group with Minsu and Jiwon. I chose my spot and started to paint my favorite movie character. Minsu painted some flowers and Jiwon did some background drawings.

21 위 글의 빈칸 ⓐ와 ⓑ에 들어갈 알맞은 말을 고르시오.

① each – Another ② some – Others
③ a few – The other ④ each – Most
⑤ some – Other

서답형

22 위 글의 밑줄 친 (A)와 (B)에서 어법상 틀린 부분을 찾아 고치시오.

➡ (A) ______________________
(B) ______________________

중요

23 위 글의 주제로 알맞은 것을 고르시오.

① the explanation about the poor condition of the wall
② the strange writings and drawings on the wall
③ the process for doing a wall painting
④ the subject matter suitable for a wall painting
⑤ how to divide groups effectively

Reading 서술형 시험대비

[01~03] 다음 글을 읽고 물음에 답하시오.

> Hi. My name is Homin. (A)[It is / This is] me in front of the wall painting. The wings are (B)[so / such] pretty, ⓐ______ ______? Many people like to take pictures in front of wall paintings. ⓑThey make old neighborhoods (C)[bright and new / brightly and newly].

01 위 글의 빈칸 ⓐ에 들어갈 알맞은 부가의문문을 쓰시오.

➡ ______________________

중요

02 위 글의 괄호 (A)~(C)에서 어법상 알맞은 낱말을 골라 쓰시오.

➡ (A)________ (B)________ (C)________

03 위 글의 밑줄 친 ⓑThey가 가리키는 것을 본문에서 찾아 쓰시오.

➡ ______________________

[04~06] 다음 글을 읽고 물음에 답하시오.

> Last month, I visited a village with wall paintings in Yeosu. As I was taking a picture, ⓐ머릿속에 좋은 생각이 떠올랐어. I thought, "I'm in the school art club. Why don't we do wall paintings like these?" I suggested this idea at the next club meeting, and the members loved ⓑit.
>
> We found a teen volunteer project on the Internet. The project was to do a wall painting in our neighborhood. We applied for ⓒit, and two weeks later, our club was selected!
>
> <I: Homin>

고난이도

04 밑줄 친 ⓐ의 우리말에 맞게 주어진 어휘를 이용하여 7 단어로 영작하시오.

light, went

➡ ______________________

05 밑줄 친 ⓑit, ⓒit이 가리키는 것을 각각 본문에서 찾아 다음 빈칸에 쓰시오.

> ⓑit: this ___(A)___
> ⓒit: the ___(B)___ to do a wall painting in our neighborhood

➡ (A) ____________ (B) ____________

06 As a volunteer work, why did Homin suggest doing wall paintings of all things? Fill in the blanks with suitable words.

> He did so because he was in the ________ ________ ________.

[07~09] 다음 글을 읽고 물음에 답하시오.

> The day of the project finally came. The project manager had us meet at the painting site at 9 a.m. ⓐThe wall was in very poor condition. There were strange writings and drawings on some parts. Other parts had old posters on them. We removed the posters first and painted over the writings and drawings with white paint.
>
> The manager let us paint ⓑanything we wanted. We decided to paint something cute because the wall was near an elementary school. We divided into three groups and began painting. I was in the group with Minsu and Jiwon. I chose my spot and started to paint my favorite movie character. Minsu painted some flowers and Jiwon did some background drawings. <I: Homin>

07 위 글의 밑줄 친 ⓐ의 구체적인 내용을 우리말로 쓰시오.

➡ ______________________

____

중요

08 위 글의 밑줄 친 ⓑanything과 바꿔 쓸 수 있는 단어를 쓰시오.

➡ ______________

고난이도

09 위 글에서 호민이와 친구들이 벽화 작업을 한 과정을 우리말로 쓰시오.

➡ (1) ______________________
(2) ______________________
(3) ______________________
(4) ______________________
(5) ______________________

[10~11] 다음 글을 읽고 물음에 답하시오.

Our club painted for about five hours. After we finished, we got together and shared the day's experiences. Minsu was very proud of his flower painting. He said, "ⓐMy flower is so real that a bee landed on it." I said, "Drawing on a wall was much harder than drawing on paper."

We all agreed that our wall painting wasn't perfect. But it didn't matter. We made our neighborhood a little brighter and happier. We were proud of ourselves. We didn't just paint pictures on a wall that day. ⓑIt was a better tomorrow that we painted.

중요

10 (1) 위 글의 밑줄 친 ⓐ와 같은 뜻이 되도록 다음 빈칸에 알맞은 단어를 쓰시오. (2) 위 글의 밑줄 친 강조 구문 ⓑ를 강조되지 않은 보통의 문장으로 고치시오.

➡ (1) My flower is real ________ for a bee to land on.
(2) ______________________

11 본문의 내용과 일치하도록 다음 빈칸 (A)와 (B)에 알맞은 단어를 쓰시오.

Though all the club members agreed that their wall painting was (A)________, it didn't matter. They took (B)________ in themselves because they made their neighborhood a little brighter and happier.

[12~13] 다음 글을 읽고 물음에 답하시오.

Our club painted for about five hours. After we finished, we got together and ⓐ____ the day's experiences. Minsu was very proud of his flower painting. He said, "My flower is so real that a bee landed on it." I said, "ⓑDrawing on a wall was much harder than drawing on paper."

We all agreed that our wall painting wasn't perfect. But it didn't matter. We made our neighborhood a little brighter and happier. We were proud of ourselves. We didn't just paint pictures on a wall that day. It was a better tomorrow that we painted.

고난이도

12 다음과 같은 뜻이 되도록 위 글의 빈칸 ⓐ에 들어갈 알맞은 한 단어를 쓰시오.

had the day's experiences in common

➡ ______________________

13 밑줄 친 ⓑ를 다음과 같이 바꿔 쓸 때 빈칸에 들어갈 알맞은 단어를 쓰시오.

➡ (1) Drawing on paper was not ________ hard ________ drawing on a wall.
(2) Drawing on paper was much ________ hard than drawing on a wall.

교과서

구석구석

After You Read B

Project: Paint a Better Tomorrow
DATE: April 15
MEETING TIME: 9 a.m.
Do you like painting? Do you want to make your neighborhood brighter?
= to paint / 목적격보어로 쓰인 형용사(비교급)
Right now, the wall is in very poor condition.
상태
You need to remove the old posters and paint over the strange writings with white paint. You can paint anything you want!
= whatever
email: volunteer@1365.go.kr

구문해설
• neighborhood: 근처, 이웃 • right now: 지금은, 지금 당장 • remove: 없애다, 제거하다
• be in poor[bad] condition: 보존 상태가 나쁘다, 건강이 좋지 않다

해석

프로젝트: 더 나은 내일을 그려라
날짜: 4월 15일
만나는 시간: 오전 9시
당신은 그림 그리기를 좋아하십니까? 당신의 동네를 더 밝게 만들기를 원합니까? 지금, 벽은 상태가 별로 좋지 않습니다. 당신은 먼저 오래된 포스터들을 제거하고 이상한 낙서를 흰 페인트로 덧칠할 필요가 있습니다. 당신은 원하는 어떤 것이든 그릴 수 있습니다!
이메일: volunteer@1365.go.kr

Word Power

Sally got up early and prepared for school. She said goodbye to her mom. Her mom said, "Try to get along with your friends and have fun." Sally replied, "Okay, I will," and got on the school bus.

got up: (잠자리에서) 일어났다 / prepared for: ~을 준비했다 / try to 동사원형: ~하려고 노력하다 / get along with: ~와 잘 지내다 / have fun: 즐거운 시간을 보내다 / got on: (탈것에) 타다

Sally는 일찍 일어나서 학교에 갈 준비를 했다. 그녀는 엄마에게 작별인사를 했다. 엄마는 "친구들과 잘 지내고 즐거운 시간을 보내라."라고 말했다. Sally는 "그럴게요."라고 대답하고 스쿨 버스를 탔다.

Think and Write

Volunteer Work Diary
I volunteered at Dream Library. I read English books to children.
= I read children English books.
I tried to read like a voice actor. The volunteer manager had me arrange the books on the shelves. The books were so heavy that I had to take a break every 30 minutes. After I finished, the shelves looked very neat. I felt very proud. It was a fun and rewarding experience.

like: 전치사 / had: 사역동사 have+목적어+원형부정사 / arrange: 목적격보어(동사원형 / so ~ that: 너무 ~해서 …하다 / every 30 minutes: every+기수+복수 명사 / looked neat: look+형용사 보어 / felt proud: feel+형용사 보어

구문해설
• voice actor: 성우 • take a break: 쉬다 • rewarding: 득이 되는, 할 보람이 있는, (~할 만한) 가치가 있는

봉사 활동 일기
나는 Dream 도서관에서 자원봉사를 했다. 나는 아이들에게 영어책을 읽어 줬다. 나는 성우처럼 읽으려고 노력했다. 자원봉사 책임자는 내게 책을 책장에 정리하라고 했다. 책이 너무 무거워서 나는 30분마다 쉬어야 했다. 끝난 후에는 책장이 아주 깔끔해 보였다. 나는 매우 자랑스러움을 느꼈다. 재미있고 보람된 경험이었다.

영역별 핵심문제

Words & Expressions

01 다음 빈칸에 들어갈 알맞은 말을 고르시오.

> I was going to ______ breakfast so that my mom could rest in the morning.

① decide ② realize ③ ready
④ apply ⑤ prepare

02 다음 밑줄 친 부분의 의미가 다른 하나를 고르시오.

① He called me as I was writing a science report.
② As I got home, my little brother was crying.
③ You have to show your ticket as you go in.
④ As the elevator was broken, we had to walk up the stairs.
⑤ I saw Peter as I was getting off the bus.

03 밑줄 친 부분과 바꿔 쓸 수 있는 말을 주어진 철자로 시작하여 쓰시오.

> His clothes were always tidy and clean.

➡ n______________________

04 다음 빈칸에 공통으로 들어갈 말을 쓰시오.

> • Let's ________ a ten-minute break.
> • Do you want me to ________ a picture of you?

Conversation

[05~06] 다음 대화를 읽고 물음에 답하시오.

> B: What are all these boxes and books for? (①)
> G: I'm packing the books for the donation center. (②) (A)Can you give me a hand? (③)
> B: Sure. (④)
> G: (⑤) Please write the address on the boxes.
> B: No problem.

05 ①~⑤ 중 주어진 문장이 들어갈 곳은?

> What do you want me to do?

① ② ③ ④ ⑤

06 밑줄 친 (A)와 바꿔 쓸 수 있는 말을 고르시오.

① What can I do for you?
② Let me help you.
③ Can you do me a favor?
④ May I help you?
⑤ Can I give you a hand?

07 빈칸 ⓐ~ⓔ에 들어가지 않는 말을 고르시오. (대・소문자 무시)

> B: ⓐ________ the concert, Mom.
> W: Okay, I ⓑ__________. Thanks. Your dinner is on the table.
> B: All right. ⓒ________ about me.
> W: ⓓ__________ sure you feed the dog after you ⓔ________ dinner.
> B: Okay. Mom, you should go now. Dad is waiting in the car.

① make ② have ③ will
④ enjoy ⑤ worry

08 주어진 문장 이후에 올 대화의 순서를 바르게 배열한 것을 고르시오.

What are you doing?

(A) Please tape the boxes.
(B) I'm packing for my move tomorrow. Can you help me?
(C) Sure. What do you want me to do?
(D) No problem.

① (B) – (A) – (C) – (D)
② (B) – (C) – (A) – (D)
③ (C) – (A) – (B) – (D)
④ (C) – (B) – (A) – (D)
⑤ (C) – (D) – (B) – (A)

[09~12] 다음 대화를 읽고 물음에 답하시오.

Woman: Good morning. What can I do for you?
Tony: Hi. I'm here for the volunteer work. (①)
Woman: Oh, you (A)<u>must</u> be Tony. (②)
Tony: That's right. What do you want me to do today?
Woman: Please read this book for the blind in the recording room. (③)
Tony: No problem. (④)
Woman: Yes. Please go into Room 7.
Tony: Okay. (⑤) Is there anything to keep in mind?
Woman: Yes. Make sure you read slowly and clearly.
Tony: Okay. I'll do my best.

09 ①~⑤ 중 주어진 문장이 들어갈 곳은?

Should I go in now?

① ② ③ ④ ⑤

10 위 대화에서 다음 영영풀이에 해당하는 단어를 찾아 쓰시오.

someone who dose something without expecting any reward

➡ ____________________

11 밑줄 친 (A)<u>must</u>와 같은 의미로 쓰인 것을 고르시오.

① Sam <u>must</u> be nearly 90 years old now.
② You <u>must</u> not download the movie.
③ I <u>must</u> do my homework first.
④ You <u>must</u> not eat junk food.
⑤ You <u>must</u> study English every day.

12 위 대화를 읽고 답할 수 <u>없는</u> 질문을 고르시오.

① What will Tony keep in mind when he's reading the book?
② Has ever Tony volunteered?
③ Which room is Tony going to go into for recording?
④ For whom is Tony going to record the book?
⑤ What are Tony going to do for the blind?

Grammar

13 주어진 단어를 어법에 맞게 빈칸에 쓰시오.

(1) The police officer had him __________ the rule. (follow)
(2) Mr. Park makes us __________ many questions in class. (ask)
(3) The band let their photos __________ by the audience. (take)
(4) If you really hurry, you can have it __________ quite soon. (write)

14 다음 밑줄 친 부분과 바꿔 쓸 수 있는 것은?

> It was the amusement park <u>that</u> everyone voted for.

① what ② when ③ who
④ where ⑤ which

15 다음 문장을 각각의 주어진 단어를 강조하는 문장으로 고쳐 쓰시오.

> I played hide and seek with my friends in the park yesterday.

(1) I
➡ ______________________________

(2) played
➡ ______________________________

(3) hide and seek
➡ ______________________________

(4) with my friends
➡ ______________________________

(5) in the park
➡ ______________________________

(6) yesterday
➡ ______________________________

16 다음 중 어법상 바르지 <u>않은</u> 것은?

① I had my computer mend.
② Daniel made his brother turn off the TV.
③ Please don't let them be hurt.
④ It was no easy matter getting him to change his mind.
⑤ I let my dog sleep on my bed.

17 다음 중 어법상 올바른 문장을 고르시오.

① My sister always helps me cleans the garden.
② Ms. Parker made them watering the plants.
③ She had her daughter's name called through the speaker.
④ I remember hearing him came in.
⑤ He advised her not smoke.

18 밑줄 친 말을 강조할 때, 빈칸에 알맞은 말을 쓰시오.

> Suji found <u>her dog</u> in the park.
> ➡ ________ ________ her dog ________ Suji found in the park.

19 다음 괄호 안에서 어법상 알맞은 것을 고르시오.

(1) My grandpa made me (open / to open) the window.
(2) The teacher let us (read / reading) the book.
(3) It will make the request (take / be taken) seriously.

(4) It was in the park (which / that) Suji found her dog.
(5) It was potato pizza (which / what) we finally selected.
(6) It is every year (what / that) they plan to plant trees.

20 괄호 안에 주어진 어휘를 활용하여 글자 수에 맞게 다음 우리말을 영작하시오.

(1) Brown 선생님은 학생들이 체육관에서 줄을 서게 했다. (Mr. Brown, the gym, make, line up, the, 10 단어)
➡ ______________________

(2) 어제 창문을 깬 것은 바로 새였다. (the window, a bird, break, that, 9 단어)
➡ ______________________

Reading

[21~23] 다음 글을 읽고 물음에 답하시오.

Last month, I visited a village with wall paintings in Yeosu. As I was taking a picture, ⓐa light went on in my head. I thought, "I'm in the school art club. Why don't we do wall paintings like these?" I suggested this idea at the next club meeting, and the members loved it.

We found a teen volunteer project on the Internet. The project was to do a wall painting in our neighborhood. We applied for it, and two weeks later, our club was selected!

<I: Homin>

21 위 글의 밑줄 친 ⓐ와 바꿔 쓸 수 있는 말로 옳지 않은 것을 고르시오.

① a good idea occurred to me
② I hit upon a good idea
③ I was lost in a daydream
④ a good idea flashed on me
⑤ I came up with a good idea

22 위 글에서 알 수 있는 호민이의 성격으로 알맞은 것을 두 개 고르시오.

① active
② passive
③ selfish
④ considerate
⑤ arrogant

23 본문의 내용과 일치하도록 다음 빈칸에 알맞은 단어를 쓰시오.

> Homin and the school art club members decided to join a ________ ________ because they wanted to do wall paintings.

[24~26] 다음 글을 읽고 물음에 답하시오.

The day of the project finally came. (①) The project manager had us meet at the painting site at 9 a.m. (②) There were strange writings and drawings on some parts. (③) Other parts had old posters on them. (④) We removed the posters first and painted over the writings and drawings with white paint. (⑤)

The manager let us paint anything we wanted. We decided to paint something cute because the wall was near an elementary school. We divided into three groups and began painting. I was in the group with Minsu and Jiwon. I chose my spot and started to paint my favorite movie character. Minsu painted some flowers and Jiwon did some background drawings. <I: Homin>

24 위 글의 흐름으로 보아, 주어진 문장이 들어가기에 가장 적절한 곳은?

The wall was in very poor condition.

① ② ③ ④ ⑤

25 위 글의 제목으로 가장 알맞은 것을 고르시오.

① D-day for the Project Finally Has Come!
② The Poor Condition of the Wall
③ Let's Remove the Posters First
④ Wow! We Can Paint Anything We Want!
⑤ I'll Paint My Favorite Movie Character

26 According to the passage, which is NOT true?

① Homin and his friends met at the painting site at 9 a.m.
② Some parts of the wall had strange writings and drawings on them.
③ After painting over the writings and drawings with white paint, they removed the posters.
④ They decided to paint something cute because there was an elementary school near the painting site.
⑤ It was Minsu who painted some flowers.

[27~30] 다음 글을 읽고 물음에 답하시오.

Our club painted for about five hours. After we finished, we got together and shared the day's experiences. Minsu was very proud of his flower painting. He said, "My flower is so real that a bee landed on ⓐit." I said, "ⓑDrawing on a wall was much harder than drawing on paper."
We all agreed that our wall painting wasn't perfect. But ⓒit didn't matter. ⓓ우리는 동네를 조금 더 밝고 행복하게 만들었어. We were proud of ourselves. We didn't just paint pictures on a wall that day. It was a better tomorrow that we painted.

27 위 글의 밑줄 친 ⓐit, ⓒit이 가리키는 것을 각각 본문에서 찾아 쓰시오.

➡ ⓐ ______________, ⓒ ______________

28 아래 <보기>에서 위 글의 밑줄 친 ⓑDrawing과 문법적 쓰임이 같은 것의 개수를 고르시오.

보기
① Do you know the man drawing on a wall?
② It was no use drawing on a wall.
③ His hobby was drawing on a wall.
④ I saw them drawing on a wall.
⑤ He was drawing on a wall.

① 1개 ② 2개 ③ 3개 ④ 4개 ⑤ 5개

29 위 글의 밑줄 친 ⓓ의 우리말에 맞게 주어진 어휘를 이용하여 9 단어로 영작하시오.

little, bright, our neighborhood

➡ ______________________________

30 How long did it take for the club members to do the wall painting? Answer in English in a full sentence.

➡ ______________________________

단원별 예상문제

출제율 90%

01 빈칸에 들어갈 말이 나머지와 다른 하나를 고르시오.

① The boys ________ up and go to the bathroom.
② Please ________ off the light so that I can sleep.
③ Where can I ________ on the subway?
④ Many relatives can ________ together in the living room.
⑤ It is great that we ________ along with our friends.

출제율 95%

02 두 문장이 같은 의미가 되도록 빈칸을 채우시오.

The computer is too expensive for me to buy.
= The computer is ________ expensive ________ I can't buy it.

[03~04] 다음 빈칸에 들어갈 알맞은 말을 고르시오.

출제율 90%

03

I ________ to four universities and was accepted by all of them.

① divided ② replied ③ applied
④ suggested ⑤ mattered

출제율 95%

04

It was as if a light ________ on in their heads.

① had ② went ③ made
④ hit ⑤ stroke

[05~06] 다음 대화를 읽고 물음에 답하시오.

A: What are you doing?
B: (①) Can you help me?
A: Sure. (②) What do you want me to do? (③)
B: (④) (A)Please put the clothes into the box.
A: No problem. (⑤)

출제율 100%

05 ①~⑤ 중 주어진 문장이 들어갈 곳은?

I'm packing for my move tomorrow.

① ② ③ ④ ⑤

출제율 90%

06 밑줄 친 (A) 대신 쓸 수 있는 말을 모두 고르시오.

① I'm looking for putting the clothes into the box.
② I want to put the clothes into the box.
③ I'd like you to put the clothes into the box.
④ I hope to put the clothes into the box.
⑤ I want you to put the clothes into the box.

[07~08] 다음 글을 읽고 물음에 답하시오.

B: Hello, class. (A)_____ groups of four people and sit around the tables. Today we're going to (B)_______ bacon and egg sandwiches. 우리 수업의 두 가지 규칙에 유의하세요. First, (C)______ sure you wash your hands before you start. Second, be careful when you use a knife. All right, let's start.

출제율 90%

07 빈칸 (A)~(C)에 공통으로 들어갈 말을 쓰시오. (대・소문자 무시)

➡ ________________

출제율 95%

08 밑줄 친 우리말과 일치하도록 주어진 단어를 이용해 문장을 만드시오. (mind, for) (8 words)

➡ ________________________________

[09~12] 다음 대화를 읽고 물음에 답하시오.

A: Hi, I'm Minsu. (①)
B: Thanks (A)_______ coming, Minsu. (②)
A: What do you want me to do today?
B: Please (B)_______ the dog a bath. (③)
A: Okay. (④) Is there anything to keep in mind?
B: Yes. (⑤) Make sure you brush the fur first.
A: Okay, I will.

출제율 95%

09 ①~⑤ 중 주어진 문장이 들어갈 곳은?

I'm here for the volunteer work.

① ② ③ ④ ⑤

출제율 95%

10 빈칸 (A)에 알맞은 말을 고르시오

① for ② with ③ in ④ to ⑤ of

출제율 90%

11 빈칸 (B)에 알맞은 말을 쓰시오.

➡ ________________________

출제율 100%

12 A와 B 두 사람의 관계를 고르시오.

① teacher – student
② boss – employee
③ waiter – guest
④ volunteer – volunteer manager
⑤ client – staff

출제율 95%

13 다음 중 어법상 어색한 것은?

① She helped me to organize the party.
② The dentist made me open my mouth.
③ The manager let Minho use her phone.
④ The doctor had the pain reduce.
⑤ Ms. Kim has us get along with our friends.

출제율 100%

14 다음 중 어법상 올바른 문장을 모두 고르시오. (정답 2개)

① My friend let me riding his bike.
② Cloe had the trash on the ground pick up.
③ My father got me to bring him the newspaper.
④ Mom makes me to water the plants.
⑤ It was yesterday that Emily saw me at the mall.
⑥ It was the toilet that Bob dropped his smartphone this morning.
⑦ It was a drone who Mina flew at the park last Friday.

출제율 90%

15 밑줄 친 부분을 강조하는 문장으로 고쳐 쓰시오.

(1) What he said worried me.
➡ ________________________________

(2) I played soccer with my friends after school.
➡ ________________________________

(3) My club members planted flowers in the garden on April 5th.
➡ ________________________________
____

[16~18] 다음 글을 읽고 물음에 답하시오.

Last month, I visited a village with wall paintings in Yeosu. As I was taking a picture, a light went on in my head. I thought, "I'm in the school art club. Why don't we do wall paintings ⓐlike these?" I suggested this idea at the next club meeting, and the members loved it.

We found a teen volunteer project on the Internet. The project was to do a wall painting in our neighborhood. We applied for it, and two weeks later, our club was selected! <I: Homin>

출제율 95%

16 위 글의 밑줄 친 ⓐlike와 같은 의미로 쓰인 것을 고르시오.

① Which dress do you like best?
② They acted in like manner.
③ I have never seen the like before.
④ How did you like the book?
⑤ You have to do it like this.

출제율 100%

17 위 글의 주제로 알맞은 것을 고르시오.

① to introduce a village with wall paintings in Yeosu
② to do wall paintings as a volunteer work
③ how to take pictures in front of wall paintings well
④ the difficulty of having a good idea
⑤ the importance of the cooperative work

출제율 90%

18 본문의 내용과 일치하도록 다음 빈칸 (A)와 (B)에 알맞은 단어를 쓰시오.

> After the school art club members accepted Homin's (A)________, they did a search on the Internet and applied for a (B)________ ________ ________ to do a wall painting in their neighborhood. Two weeks later, their club was selected.

[19~21] 다음 글을 읽고 물음에 답하시오.

The day of the project finally came. The project manager had us meet at the painting site at 9 a.m. The wall was __ⓐ__ very poor condition. There were strange writings and drawings on some parts. Other parts had old posters on them. We removed the posters first and painted over the writings and drawings with white paint.

The manager let us paint anything we wanted. We decided to paint something cute because the wall was near an elementary school. We divided __ⓑ__ three groups and began painting. I was in the group with Minsu and Jiwon. I chose my spot and started to paint my favorite movie ⓒcharacter. Minsu painted some flowers and Jiwon did some background drawings.

<I: Homin>

출제율 95%

19 위 글의 빈칸 ⓐ와 ⓑ에 들어갈 전치사가 바르게 짝지어진 것은?

ⓐ ⓑ
① at – by
② in – by
③ in – into
④ at – for
⑤ on – into

출제율 90%

20 위 글의 밑줄 친 ⓒcharacter와 같은 의미로 쓰인 것을 고르시오.

① He is a man of good character.
② She has a face without any character.
③ What does this Chinese character mean?
④ She performed the leading character.
⑤ What is the character of the Americans?

출제율 95%

21 다음 중 위 글에 대한 이해가 옳지 않은 사람을 고르시오.

① 현경: At 9 a.m., Homin met his friends at the painting site where they would do the project.
② 정수: Yes. They removed the old posters first before they painted over the writings and drawings with white paint.
③ 단비: Besides, the manager had them paint something cute because the wall was near an elementary school.
④ 창훈: There were three groups and Homin was in the group with Minsu and Jiwon.
⑤ 명식: Exactly, and it was Jiwon who painted some background drawings.

[22~24] 다음 글을 읽고 물음에 답하시오.

Our club painted for about five hours. After we finished, we got together and shared the day's experiences. Minsu was very proud of his flower painting. He said, "My flower is so real that a bee landed on it." I said, "Drawing on a wall was much harder than drawing on paper."

We all agreed that our wall painting wasn't perfect. (①) We made our neighborhood a little brighter and happier. (②) We were proud of ourselves. (③) We didn't just paint pictures on a wall that day. (④) It was a better tomorrow that we painted. (⑤) <I: Homin>

출제율 90%

22 위 글의 흐름으로 보아, 주어진 문장이 들어가기에 가장 적절한 곳은?

But it didn't matter.

① ② ③ ④ ⑤

출제율 100%

23 마지막 부분에서 동아리 부원들이 느꼈을 심경으로 알맞은 것을 두 개 고르시오.

① disappointment ② satisfaction
③ depression ④ shame
⑤ self-esteem

출제율 95%

24 According to the passage, which is NOT true?

① After finishing the project, they got together and shared the day's experiences.
② To Homin, drawing on paper was much harder than drawing on a wall.
③ Homin's club members all agreed that their wall painting wasn't perfect.
④ Thanks to Homin's club members, their neighborhood became a little brighter and happier.
⑤ Homin's club members took pride in themselves.

[25~26] 다음 글을 읽고 물음에 답하시오.

Volunteer Work Diary

Name: Minsu Kim
Date: Friday, May 3rd

I volunteered at Dream Library. I read English books to children. I tried to read like a voice actor. The volunteer manager had me arrange the books on the shelves. The books were so heavy that I had to take a break every 30 (A)[minute / minutes]. After I finished, the shelves looked very (B)[neat / neatly]. I felt very proud. It was a fun and (C)[rewarding / rewarded] experience.

출제율 100%

25 위 글의 괄호 (A)~(C)에서 어법상 알맞은 낱말을 골라 쓰시오.

➡ (A)________ (B)________ (C)________

출제율 95%

26 위 글을 읽고 김민수의 봉사 활동에 대해 알 수 없는 것을 고르시오.

① When did he volunteer?
② Where did he volunteer?
③ What did he do?
④ How long did he volunteer?
⑤ How did he feel?

서술형 실전문제

01 대화의 흐름상 빈칸에 들어갈 말을 주어진 단어를 이용해 쓰시오. (2개)

> B: What are all these boxes and books for?
> G: I'm packing the books for the donation center. Can you give me a hand?
> B: Sure. ____________________
> G: Please write the address on the boxes.
> B: No problem.

➡ ____________________ (want, me)
➡ ____________________ (like, me)

[02~03] 다음 대화를 읽고 물음에 답하시오.

> Woman: Good morning. What can I do for you?
> Tony: Hi. I'm here for the volunteer work.
> Woman: Oh, you must be Tony.
> Tony: That's right. What do you want me to do today?
> Woman: Please read this book for the blind in the recording room.
> Tony: No problem. Should I go in now?
> Woman: Yes. Please go into Room 7.
> Tony: Okay. (A)Is there anything to keeping in mind?
> Woman: Yes. (B)Make sure you read slowly and clearly.
> Tony: Okay. I'll do my best.

02 밑줄 친 (A)에서 어법상 어색한 것을 찾아 바르게 고치시오.

➡ ____________________

03 밑줄 친 (B)와 바꿔 쓸 수 있는 문장을 주어진 조건에 맞춰 쓰시오.

➡ ____________________ (Be)
➡ ____________________ (forget)
➡ ____________________ (remember)

04 다음 우리말을 괄호 안에 주어진 어휘를 이용하여 영작하시오.

(1) 그는 우리가 그의 작품을 사진 찍도록 허용했다. (let, pictures, artwork)
➡ ____________________

(2) 내가 지금 그리고 있는 것은 흰색 곰이다. (that, a, draw)
➡ ____________________

(3) 카메라를 청소하려면 돈이 얼마나 들죠? (it, have, would, cost, clean, how)
➡ ____________________
____

05 어법상 어색한 것을 고쳐 문장을 다시 쓰시오.

(1) My mom made me to prepare dinner.
➡ ____________________

(2) My boss let the work done by tomorrow.
➡ ____________________

(3) Linda had her wallet steal on her way home.
➡ ____________________

(4) It was the restaurant that I saw Juliet calling her friend.
➡ ____________________
____

(5) It is because they have no jobs which they cannot afford to buy them.
➡ ____________________
____

[06~08] 다음 글을 읽고 물음에 답하시오.

Last month, I visited a village with wall paintings in Yeosu. As I was taking a picture, a light went on in my head. I thought, "I'm in the school art club. Why don't we do wall paintings like these?" I suggested this idea at the next club meeting, and the members loved it.

We found a teen volunteer project on the Internet. The project was to do a wall painting in our neighborhood. We ___ⓐ___ for it, and two weeks later, our club was selected! <I: Homin>

06 주어진 영영풀이를 참고하여 빈칸 ⓐ에 철자 a로 시작하는 단어를 시제에 맞게 쓰시오.

to write a letter or fill in a form in order to ask formally for something

➡ ________________

07 호민이가 자신의 아이디어를 동아리 모임에서 제안하는 내용을 (1) 동명사, (2) 부가의문문을 사용하여 쓰시오.

➡ (1) ________________ doing wall paintings like these?

(2) Let's do wall paintings like these, ________?

08 Where did Homin and the school art club members find a teen volunteer project? Answer in English in a full sentence. (6 words)

➡ ________________

[09~11] 다음 글을 읽고 물음에 답하시오.

The day of the project finally came. The project manager had us meet at the painting site at 9 a.m. The wall was in very (A)[good / poor] condition. There were strange writings and drawings on some parts. Other parts had old posters on ⓐthem. We removed the posters first and painted over the writings and drawings with white paint.

The manager let us paint anything we wanted. We decided (B)[to paint / painting] something cute because the wall was (C)[near / nearly] an elementary school. We divided into three groups and began painting. I was in the group with Minsu and Jiwon. I chose my spot and started to paint my favorite movie character. Minsu painted some flowers and Jiwon did some background drawings.

09 위 글의 괄호 (A)~(C)에서 문맥이나 어법상 알맞은 낱말을 골라 쓰시오.

➡ (A)________ (B)________ (C)________

10 위 글의 밑줄 친 ⓐthem이 가리키는 것을 본문에서 찾아 쓰시오.

➡ ________________

11 What did they have to do before they actually started to do a wall painting at the painting site? Answer in English in a full sentence.

➡ ________________

____

창의사고력 서술형 문제

01 다음 그림을 보고 당부하는 말을 주어진 단어를 이용하여 빈칸에 쓰시오.

A: It looks like it will rain in a minute.
B: Yeah. I think so, too.
A: I have to go to take class in half an hour.
B: ________________________________ with you. (take, sure, that)

02 다음 그림을 보고, 'It ~ that ...' 강조 구문을 활용하여 자유롭게 영작하시오.

(1) ________________________________
(2) ________________________________
(3) ________________________________
(4) ________________________________

03 다음 내용을 바탕으로 봉사 활동 일기를 쓰시오.

Date: Friday, May 3rd
Place: Dream Library
What I did:
- I read English books to children.
- I arranged the books on the shelves.

How I felt: I felt very proud.

Volunteer Work Diary

Name: Minsu Kim
Date: (A)____________

I volunteered at (B)____________ . I read (C)____________ to children. I tried to read like a voice actor. The volunteer manager had me (D)____________ on the shelves. The books were so heavy that I had to take a break every 30 minutes. After I finished, the shelves looked very neat. I felt (E)____________ . It was a fun and rewarding experience.

단원별 모의고사

01 다음 짝지어진 단어의 관계가 같도록 빈칸에 알맞은 말을 쓰시오.

neat : tidy = location : s________

02 빈칸 (A)와 (B)에 들어갈 말로 알맞은 것끼리 짝지어진 것을 고르시오.

- Please line (A)________ and take your turn.
- She must be very proud (B)______ herself.
- The bus came right (C)______ time.

(A) (B) (C)
① up – of – on
② up – in – on
③ on – of – at
④ for – in – at
⑤ for – of – on

03 〈보기〉에 있는 어휘를 이용하여 빈칸을 채울 수 <u>없는</u> 것을 고르시오. (형태 변화 가능) (한 단어는 한 번만 사용)

보기

plant reply select share

① We _______ four applicants for interview.
② They helped me _______ trees.
③ Her mother ________ that she should go and see the doctor.
④ 'Did you see Simon today?' 'Of course,' Nathalie _______ with a smile.
⑤ Will you _______ fries with me?

04 주어진 영영풀이에 해당하는 말을 이용하여 빈칸을 채우시오.

the area that is behind the main thing that you are looking at

It's important to understand other people, people from different __________s.

05 〈보기〉에서 빈칸 (A)와 (B)에 알맞은 말을 골라 쓰시오

보기

at for in out to with

A: What are you doing?
B: I'm packing for my move tomorrow. Can you help me?
A: Sure. What do you want me (A)________ do?
B: Please take (B)________ the trash.
A: No problem.

06 밑줄 친 부분에서 흐름상 또는 어법상 <u>어색한</u> 것을 바르게 고치시오.

B: Hello, class. <u>Make groups of four people and to sit around the tables.</u> Today we're going to make bacon and egg sandwiches. Keep in mind two rules for our class. <u>First, make sure you wash your hands after you start.</u> Second, be careful when you use a knife. All right, let's start.

➡ ______________________________

[07~09] 다음 대화를 읽고 물음에 답하시오.

B: What is this mess? (①)
G: I'm baking ⓐcookies. (②)
B: Why are you baking so ⓑmany?
G: ⓒThey're for the people at the nursing home. (③)
B: ⓓThat's very nice of you. (④)
G: Can you give me a hand?
B: Sure. (⑤)
G: Please put ⓔthem in the gift boxes. Three cookies in each box.
B: Okay.

07 ①~⑤ 중 주어진 문장이 들어갈 곳은?

What do you want me to do?

① ② ③ ④ ⑤

08 다음 ⓐ~ⓔ 중 가리키는 대상이 다른 하나를 고르시오.

① ⓐ ② ⓑ ③ ⓒ ④ ⓓ ⑤ ⓔ

09 위 대화를 읽고 답할 수 없는 질문을 고르시오.

① Is the boy going to help the girl?
② Why is the girl baking so many cookies?
③ How many cookies will the boy put in each box?
④ How many cookies has the girl baked?
⑤ What is the girl doing now?

10 밑줄 친 우리말과 일치하도록 주어진 어구를 이용하여 영작하시오.

A: It's time to go home.
B: Yes. 불을 끄는 거 명심해. (turn, make, the lights)
A: Okay, I will. Anything else?
B: No, that's it. See you tomorrow.

➡ ____________________

[11~13] 다음 대화를 읽고 물음에 답하시오.

Woman: Good morning. What can I do for you?
Tony: Hi. I'm here (A)______ the volunteer work.
Woman: Oh, you must be Tony.
Tony: That's right. What do you want me to do today?
Woman: Please read this book for the blind in the recording room.
Tony: No problem. Should I go in now?
Woman: Yes. Please go into Room 7.
Tony: Okay. (a)명심해야 할 것이 있나요?
Woman: Yes. Make sure you read (B)______.
Tony: Okay. I'll do my best.

11 빈칸 (A)에 알맞은 전치사를 쓰시오.

➡ ____________________

12 빈칸 (B)에 알맞은 말을 고르시오.

① slowly and clearly
② slow and steady
③ fast and early
④ hard and late
⑤ high and quick

13 밑줄 친 (a)의 우리말과 일치하도록 주어진 단어를 이용하여 영작하시오.

➡ ____________________
(anything, keep)

14 빈칸을 채워 주어진 문장과 같은 의미의 문장을 쓰시오.

Ms. Smith had us hand in the report on time.
= Ms. Smith had the report __________ __________ by us.

15 다음 문장의 밑줄 친 부분을 강조하는 문장을 쓰시오.

(1) We found a teen volunteer project on the Internet.

➡ ______________________

(2) We decided to paint something cute because the wall was near an elementary school.

➡ ______________________

(3) Our club was selected two weeks later.

➡ ______________________

(4) Mike built a tree house near the park.

➡ ______________________

16 다음 중 밑줄 친 부분의 쓰임이 다른 하나는?

① Climbing so high made me feel dizzy.
② They made him bulid a windmill at the top of the mountain.
③ Sandra made her daughter a nice dress.
④ The teacher made Minsu paint some flowers on the wall.
⑤ My mom made me get up at 7 every morning.

17 다음 중 어법상 어색한 것을 모두 고르시오.

① Suji made him find her dog.
② Mr. White had his bags check when he passed the gate.
③ She had me help the old lady getting on the bus.
④ It was on the roof that the hen laid two eggs last week.
⑤ It was in 2010 that Tom met Sarah in New York.
⑥ It was saw that Emily me at the mall yesterday.
⑦ It was carefully that he rescued the injured.

[18~20] 다음 글을 읽고 물음에 답하시오.

Last month, I visited a village with wall paintings in Yeosu. ⓐAs I was taking a picture, a light went on in my head. I thought, "I'm in the school art club. Why don't we do wall paintings like these?" I suggested this idea at the next club meeting, and the members loved it.

ⓑWe founded a teen volunteer project on the Internet. The project was to do a wall painting in our neighborhood. We applied for it, and two weeks later, our club was selected!

<I: Homin>

18 위 글의 밑줄 친 ⓐAs와 문법적 쓰임이 같은 것을 고르시오.

① This is twice as large as that.
② Do in Rome as the Romans do.
③ As he is honest, he is trusted by everyone.
④ He came up as I was speaking.
⑤ He regarded me as a fool.

19 위 글의 밑줄 친 ⓑ에서 흐름상 어색한 부분을 찾아 고치시오.

➡ ______________________

20 위 글을 읽고 답할 수 없는 질문을 고르시오.

① Where did Homin visit last month?
② How many pictures did Homin take there?
③ What school club is Homin in?
④ Did Homin's club members accept his suggestion?
⑤ What project did Homin and his club members apply for?

[21~23] 다음 글을 읽고 물음에 답하시오.

Our club painted for about five hours. After we finished, we got together and shared the day's experiences. Minsu was very proud of his flower painting. He said, "My flower is so real that a bee landed on it." I said, "ⓐ벽에 그리는 것이 종이에 그리는 것보다 훨씬 힘들었어."

We all agreed that our wall painting wasn't perfect. But it didn't matter. We made our neighborhood a little brighter and happier. We were proud of ourselves. ⓑWe didn't just paint pictures on a wall that day. It was a better tomorrow that we painted.

21 위 글의 밑줄 친 ⓐ의 우리말에 맞게 한 단어를 보충하여, 주어진 어휘를 알맞게 배열하시오.

harder / on paper / drawing / on a wall / than / was / drawing

➡ ______________________________
____

22 위 글의 밑줄 친 ⓑ를 다음과 같이 바꿔 쓸 때 빈칸에 들어갈 알맞은 말을 세 단어로 쓰시오.

➡ What we painted on a wall that day was rather ________ ________ ________, not just pictures.

23 위 글의 주제로 알맞은 것을 고르시오.

① sharing the experience of laborious wall painting
② the difficulty of drawing on a wall
③ self-esteem gained by rewarding volunteer work
④ carrying out a mission imperfectly
⑤ trying to make our neighborhood more convenient

[24~25] 다음 글을 읽고 물음에 답하시오.

Project: Paint a Better Tomorrow
DATE: April 15
MEETING TIME: 9 a.m.
Do you like painting? Do you want to make your neighborhood brighter? Right now, the wall is in very poor condition. You need to remove the old posters and paint over the strange writings with white paint. You can paint anything you want!
email: volunteer@1365.go.kr

24 위 글의 종류로 알맞은 것을 고르시오.

① article ② essay
③ summary ④ review
⑤ advertisement

25 다음 문장에서 위 글의 내용과 다른 부분을 찾아서 고치시오.

If you are interested in this project, you can apply for it by sending a text message.

➡ ______________________________

Lesson 4

Open a Book, Open Your Mind

의사소통 기능

- 의견 묻기
  A: How do you feel about single food diet?
  B: I think it's easy but unhealthy.
- 동의하기
  A: I think reading books on a smartphone is good. We can read anytime.
  B: I'm with you on that.

언어 형식

- the+비교급 ~, the+비교급 …
  The more Stanley dug, **the stronger** he became.
- 접속사 since
  It couldn't be real gold **since** it was too light.

교과서

Words & Expressions

Key Words

- □ **acting**[ǽktiŋ] 명 (연극, 영화에서의) 연기
- □ **actually**[ǽktʃuəli] 부 실제로
- □ **adventure**[ədvéntʃər] 명 모험
- □ **assign**[əsáin] 동 (사람을) 배치하다
- □ **awake**[əwéik] 형 잠들지 않은, 깨어 있는
- □ **beat**[biːt] 동 (심장이) 고동치다, 때리다
- □ **bone**[boun] 명 뼈
- □ **bottom**[bátəm] 명 맨 아래, 바닥
- □ **brain**[brein] 명 머리, 지능
- □ **brush**[brʌʃ] 동 털다
- □ **caffeine**[kæfíːn] 명 카페인
- □ **carefully**[kɛ́ərfəli] 부 조심스럽게
- □ **character**[kǽriktər] 명 품성, 인격
- □ **convenience**[kənvíːnjəns] 명 편리, 편의
- □ **convenient**[kənvíːnjənt] 형 편리한
- □ **cruel**[krúːəl] 형 잔혹한, 잔인한
- □ **detective**[ditéktiv] 명 형사, 탐정
- □ **dig**[dig] 동 (구멍 등을) 파다
- □ **dirt**[dəːrt] 명 흙
- □ **driverless**[dráivərlis] 형 운전사가 없는
- □ **helpful**[hélpfəl] 형 유용한, 도움이 되는
- □ **hole**[houl] 명 구덩이, 구멍
- □ **letter**[létər] 명 문자, 편지
- □ **light**[lait] 형 가벼운
- □ **marry**[mǽri] 동 결혼하다
- □ **muscle**[mʌ́sl] 명 근육
- □ **object**[ábdʒikt] 명 물건
- □ **popular**[pápjulər] 형 인기 있는
- □ **raise**[reiz] 동 키우다, 기르다
- □ **return**[ritə́ːrn] 동 돌려주다, 반품하다
- □ **scary**[skɛ́əri] 형 무서운
- □ **scene**[siːn] 명 장면
- □ **shiny**[ʃáini] 형 빛나는, 반짝거리는
- □ **skip**[skip] 동 (일을) 거르다, 빼먹다
- □ **sleepy**[slíːpi] 형 졸리는
- □ **sneakers**[sníːkərz] 명 운동화
- □ **spend**[spend] 동 쓰다
- □ **steal**[stiːl] 동 훔치다
- □ **suddenly**[sʌ́dnli] 부 갑자기
- □ **summary**[sʌ́məri] 명 요약, 개요
- □ **tube**[tjuːb] 명 통, 관
- □ **unfortunately**[ənfɔ́rtʃənətli] 부 불행히도
- □ **wide**[waid] 형 폭넓은, 폭이 ~인
- □ **yell**[jel] 동 고함치다

Key Expressions

- □ **a pair of** 한 쌍의
- □ **at the bottom of** ~의 바닥에서
- □ **be full of** ~로 가득 차다
- □ **belong to** ~의 것이다, ~ 소유이다
- □ **brush off** 털다
- □ **build character** 덕성을 기르다, 인성을 키우다
- □ **day off** 휴일, 쉬는 날
- □ **end up** 결국 ~이 되다
- □ **fall in love with** ~와 사랑에 빠지다
- □ **I'm with you on that.** 그 점에 대해서는 동의해.
- □ **in fact** 사실
- □ **look like** ~처럼 보이다
- □ **look up** 찾아보다
- □ **not ~ at all** 전혀 ~가 아닌
- □ **pick up** ~을 집다
- □ **put down** 내려놓다
- □ **stand for** ~을 의미하다
- □ **stay awake** 깨어 있다
- □ **That is why ~** 그것이 ~한 이유이다
- □ **try one's best** 최선을 다하다

Word Power

※ 서로 비슷한 뜻을 가진 어휘

- □ **actually** 실제로 - **really** 사실은
- □ **carefully** 조심스럽게 - **thoughtfully** 신중하게
- □ **dangerous** 위험한 - **risky** 위험한
- □ **assign** 배치하다 - **allocate** 배치하다
- □ **cruel** 잔혹한 - **brutal** 잔혹한
- □ **focus** 집중하다 - **concentrate** 집중하다

※ 서로 반대의 뜻을 가진 어휘

- □ **awake** 잠들지 않은 ↔ **asleep** 잠든
- □ **carefully** 조심스럽게 ↔ **carelessly** 부주의하게
- □ **leave** 떠나다 ↔ **arrive** 도착하다
- □ **marry** 결혼하다 ↔ **divorce** 이혼하다
- □ **useful** 유용한 ↔ **useless** 쓸모없는
- □ **bottom** 맨 아래 ↔ **top** 꼭대기
- □ **convenient** 편리한 ↔ **inconvenient** 불편한
- □ **light** 가벼운 ↔ **heavy** 무거운
- □ **unfortunately** 불행히도 ↔ **fortunately** 다행히도

※ 동사 – 명사

- □ **assign** (사람을) 배치하다 - **assignment** 배치
- □ **inform** 알려주다 - **information** 정보
- □ **detect** 탐지하다 - **detective** 형사
- □ **marry** 결혼하다 - **marriage** 결혼

※ 명사 – 형용사

- □ **adventure** 모험 - **adventurous** 모험적인
- □ **convenience** 편리, 편의 - **convenient** 편리한
- □ **information** 정보 - **informative** 유익한, 정보를 주는
- □ **thirst** 갈증 - **thirsty** 목마른
- □ **character** 품성, 인격 - **characteristic** 특유의
- □ **danger** 위험 - **dangerous** 위험한
- □ **reason** 이유 - **reasonable** 합리적인

English Dictionary

□ **assign** (사람을) 배치하다
→ to send someone to a particular group or place as part of a job
누군가를 일의 일부로 특정 집단이나 장소로 보내다

□ **awake** 잠들지 않은, 깨어 있는
→ not sleeping
잠자고 있지 않은

□ **bottom** 맨 아래, 바닥
→ the lowest part of something
무언가의 가장 낮은 부분

□ **brush** 털다
→ to remove something with a brush or with your hand
손이나 솔로 무언가를 제거하다

□ **day off** 휴일, 쉬는 날
→ a day when you do not go to work, school, etc.
출근 또는 출석하지 않는 날

□ **dig** (구멍 등을) 파다
→ to move soil, sand, snow, etc., in order to create a hole
구덩이를 만들기 위하여 흙, 모래, 눈 등을 이동시키다

□ **hole** 구덩이, 구멍
→ an empty space in something solid
무언가 단단한 것에 비어 있는 공간

□ **muscle** 근육
→ a body tissue that can contract and produce movement
동작을 만들어 내고 수축할 수 있는 신체 조직

□ **object** 물건
→ a thing that you can see and touch but is not alive
볼 수 있고 만질 수 있지만 살아 있지 않은 것

□ **shiny** 빛나는, 반짝거리는
→ smooth and bright 매끄럽고 반짝이는

□ **skip** (일을) 거르다, 빼먹다
→ to pass over or not do something
지나치거나 어떤 일을 하지 않다

□ **tube** 통, 관
→ a long and empty object that is usually round, like a pipe
파이프처럼 보통 둥근, 길고 속이 비어 있는 물건

□ **wide** 폭이 ~인
→ measured from side to side
옆에서 옆으로 측정된

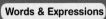

중요 **01** 다음 빈칸에 들어갈 말로 적절한 것을 고르시오.

> The new teacher was ________ to the science laboratory.

① promoted ② appeared
③ made ④ encouraged
⑤ assigned

중요 **02** 다음 밑줄 친 부분의 의미로 알맞지 않은 것은?

① In fact, Kobe was too busy to spend time looking out the window. (사실은, 실제로는)
② The money belongs to him. (~의 소유이다)
③ Many people have to look up the meaning of this word in the dictionary. (위를 보다)
④ I could not put the book down, so I read it in one sitting. (내려놓다)
⑤ The mud at the bottom of rivers and lakes also provides food and shelter. (~의 바닥에서)

03 다음 영영풀이가 나타내는 말을 고르시오.

> an empty space in something solid

① pole ② bone ③ hole
④ wound ⑤ hall

[04~05] 다음 밑줄 친 부분과 의미가 가장 가까운 것을 고르시오.

04

> When you hit the drum, you feel good.

① fall ② catch ③ keep
④ beat ⑤ reach

05

> A: What do the letters "U.S.A" mean?
> B: It means United States of America.

① calls for ② gets on ③ takes in
④ stands for ⑤ runs into

06 다음 빈칸에 들어갈 말이 나머지와 다른 하나를 고르시오. (대·소문자 구분 안 함)

① He bought ________ sneakers.
② All he needed was ________ glasses.
③ There was ________ scissors on the table.
④ ________ clothes were piled high on the chair.
⑤ ________ gloves is a nice present.

중요 **07** 다음 빈칸 (A)~(C)에 알맞은 말로 짝지어진 것을 고르시오.

> • I (A)________ in love with him because of his kind nature.
> • Reading good books helps to (B)________ good character.
> • I am so tired that it is difficult for me to (C)________ awake.

	(A)	(B)	(C)
①	fell	build	try
②	fell	build	stay
③	fell	catch	stay
④	began	catch	try
⑤	began	catch	stay

중요
[01~02] 다음 빈칸에 공통으로 들어갈 말을 쓰시오.

01

- She bent down to pick ________ her glove.
- Can you look ________ the opening times on the website?
- Online shopping is the reason I end ________ spending all my money.

02

- I've known Joanna ________ she was born.
- ________ nobody cared, they didn't know about his hobby.

고난이도
03 다음 괄호 안의 단어를 문맥에 맞게 고쳐 쓰시오.

____________(fortunate), I won't be able to attend the meeting.

04 다음 우리말에 맞게 주어진 단어를 바르게 배열하시오.

그들에게 우주 정착지를 설계하라는 과제가 맡겨졌다. (assigned, a, were, to, they, settlement, design, Space)

➡ ________________________________

중요
05 다음 빈칸에 알맞은 단어를 <보기>에서 골라 쓰시오.

보기
convenient detective driverless wide

(1) It should be ________ enough to allow plenty of space for food preparation.
(2) Google says the ________ cars are safer than those with human drivers.
(3) The family thought it was more ________ to eat in the kitchen.
(4) She hired a private ________ in an attempt to find her daughter.

고난이도
06 다음 우리말에 맞도록 빈칸에 알맞은 말을 쓰시오. (철자가 주어진 경우, 주어진 철자로 시작할 것)

(1) 장발장은 결국 감옥에 들어가게 되었다.
➡ Jean Valjean e________ ________ in prison.
(2) 그는 나의 어깨를 때렸다.
➡ He h________ ________ ________ the shoulder.
(3) 이 소스는 준비하고 요리하는 데 25분이 걸린다.
➡ This sauce ________ 25 minutes ________ prepare and cook.
(4) 우리가 높이 올라갈수록 점점 더 추워진다.
➡ ________ ________ we go up, ________ ________ it becomes.
(5) 그게 바로 내가 배가 심하게 아팠던 이유였어.
➡ That ________ ________ I had such a bad pain in my belly.

교과서

Conversation

1 의견 묻기

A: How do you feel about single food diet?
너는 한 가지 음식만 먹는 다이어트에 대하여 어떻게 생각하니?
B: I think it's easy but unhealthy. 그것은 쉽지만 건강에 좋지 않다고 생각해.

- 주어진 주제에 관하여 상대방의 의견을 물어볼 때는 'How do you feel about ~?(~에 관해 어떻게 생각하니?)', 'What do you think about ~?(~에 대하여 어떻게 생각하니?)', 'What's your opinion on[about] ~?(~에 대한 의견이 무엇이니?)'와 같은 표현을 사용하여 의견을 물어볼 수 있으며, 'I think ~.'의 표현을 사용해 자신의 의견을 말할 수 있다. 'How do you like ~?'는 '~가 마음에 드니?'의 의미로 상대방이 만족하는지 등의 의견을 물어보는 표현이다.
- 경험한 일을 바탕으로 하여 상대방의 의견이나 감정을 물을 때는 'Do you find it ~?(너는 ~가 …하다고 생각하니?)'를 사용할 수 있다. 주로 가목적어 it을 사용하여 'find it+형용사+to부정사'의 형태가 되고 목적격보어로 쓰이는 다양한 형용사 다음에 진목적어인 to부정사가 따라온다.
- 상대방의 의견을 물어보는 표현으로 'Do you think it is easy/hard to ~?(너는 ~하는 것이 쉽다고/어렵다고 생각하니?)'를 사용할 수 있고, 'Would you find it easy/hard to ~ if you had the chance to ~?(만약 네가 ~할 기회가 있다면 너는 ~하는 것이 쉽다고/어렵다고 생각하니?)'와 같이 물어볼 수 있다.

상대방의 의견 묻기

- How do you feel about ~? (~에 대하여 어떻게 생각하니?)
- What do you think about ~? (~에 대하여 어떻게 생각하니?)
- What's your opinion on[about] ~? (~에 대한 의견이 무엇이니?)
- How do you like ~? (~가 마음에 드니?)
- Can you give me your thoughts on ~? (~에 대한 네 생각을 알려줄래?)
- Do you have any opinions on[about] ~? (~에 대한 의견이 있니?)

핵심 Check

1. 다음 대화의 빈칸에 주어진 의미에 해당하는 적절한 말을 쓰시오. (주어진 단어를 이용할 것)

B: Hi, Amy. Welcome to Korea.
G: Long time no see, Minho. How have you been?
B: Great. How did you come here from the airport?
G: I came here by subway.
B: ______________________________? (feel)
(한국 지하철에 대해서 어떻게 생각하니?)
G: I think it's very clean.

2 동의하기

A: I think reading books on a smartphone is good. We can read anytime.
나는 스마트폰으로 책을 읽는 것이 좋다고 생각해. 우리는 언제든지 읽을 수 있어.

B: I'm with you on that. 나는 그 점에 대해 너에게 동의해.

- 상대방의 말이나 의견에 동의할 때는 'I agree (with you).(나는 동의한다.)', 'I'm with you on that.(나는 그 점에 대해서 너에게 동의한다.)', 'You can say that again.(맞아.)' 등으로 말한다. 또한 상대방의 의견에 동의하지 않을 때는 'I don't agree.' 또는 'I don't think so.' 등으로 표현할 수 있고, 반대하는 의견을 제기할 때는 'I am against+명사.(나는 ~에 반대한다.)'로 표현할 수 있다.
- 상대방의 말이나 의견에 전적으로 동의할 때, 다음과 같은 표현을 쓸 수 있다.
  - You're telling me. / That's precisely my point. 내 말이 바로 그 말이야.
  - You can say that again. / I'm in favor of that. 너의 의견에 동의해.
- 상대방의 말에 동의할 때는 '나도 그래.'의 의미로 'Me, too.' 또는 'So + 동사 + 주어.'의 형태를 쓸 수 있다. 이때 사용하는 동사는 be동사, do, does, did를 포함하는 조동사이다. 부정문에 이어지는 경우에는 so 대신 neither를 사용하여 'Neither+동사+주어.'라고 하거나 'Me neither.'라고 할 수 있다.

동의하기

- I couldn't agree with you more. (전적으로 동감이다.)
- No doubt about it. (그렇고말고.)
- You have a point there. (그것은 일리가 있어요.)
- That's exactly how I feel. (내 생각도 바로 그거야.)
- You are absolutely right. (당신이 전적으로 옳습니다.)
- You read my mind. (텔레파시가 통했나 보구나.)

반대하기

- I don't agree with you. (나는 동의하지 않아.)
- I am against+명사. (나는 ~에 반대한다.)
- I don't think so. (나는 그렇게 생각하지 않아.)

핵심 Check

2. 다음 밑줄 친 말을 대신해서 쓰기에 적절하지 않은 것은?

B: Did you enjoy the movie?
G: Yes, I liked it a lot.
B: What did you like most about it?
G: The acting was so great.
B: I'm with you on that.

① I agree with you. ② You can say that again. ③ You're telling me.
④ You read my mind. ⑤ I'm against that.

Listen and Speak 1 A

B: Hi, Amy. Welcome to Korea.
G: ❶Long time no see, Minho. ❷How have you been?
B: ❸Great. How did you come here from the airport?
G: I came here ❹by subway.
B: ❺How do you feel about the subway in Korea?
G: ❻I think it's very clean.

B: 안녕, Amy. 한국에 온 걸 환영해.
G: 오랜만이야, 민호야. 어떻게 지냈니?
B: 잘 지냈어. 공항에서 여기에 어떻게 왔니?
G: 여기까지 지하철을 타고 왔어.
B: 한국 지하철에 관해 어떻게 생각하니?
G: 매우 깨끗하다고 생각해.

❶ Long time no see.: 오랜만이야.
❷ 안부를 묻는 표현에는 'How are you?' 이외에도 'How have you been?', 'What's up?' 'What's going on?'과 같은 다양한 표현들이 있다.
❸ 'How have you been?'에 대한 응답을 할 때 'I've been'은 생략되기도 한다.
❹ by+교통수단: 교통수단을 이용해, 교통수단으로
❺ 'How do you feel about ~?'은 '~에 관해 어떻게 생각하니?'라는 뜻으로 상대방의 의견을 묻는 표현이다. about이 전치사이므로 뒤에 동사가 오려면 '-ing' 형태의 동명사를 써야 한다. 비슷한 표현으로 'What do you think of[about] ~?', 'What's your opinion about ~?', 'What do you say to ~?' 등이 있다. (= What do you think of[about] the subway in Korea? = What's your opinion about the subway in Korea? = What do you say to the subway in Korea?)
❻ think와 it's 사이에는 접속사 that이 생략되어 있다. 여기서 it은 앞 문장의 the subway in Korea(한국 지하철)를 받는 인칭대명사이다.

Check(√) True or False

(1) The boy and the girl are at the airport. T☐ F☐
(2) The girl thinks that the subway in Korea is dirty. T☐ F☐

Listen and Speak 2 A

B: Did you enjoy the movie?
G: Yes, I ❶liked it ❷a lot.
B: ❸What did you like most about it?
G: The acting was so great.
B: ❹I'm with you on that.

B: 영화 재미있었니?
G: 응, 아주 좋았어.
B: 무엇이 가장 좋았니?
G: 연기가 아주 멋졌어.
B: 나도 그 점에 동의해.

❶ 'Did you ~?'로 질문했으므로, 과거시제인 liked로 대답하고 있다.
❷ a lot: 많이
❸ 'What did you like most about it?'은 의문사 what(무엇)을 사용해 무엇이 가장 좋았는지를 묻고 있다.
❹ 'I'm with you on that.'은 '나는 그 점에 동의해.'라는 뜻으로 상대방의 의견에 동의할 때 사용할 수 있는 표현이다.

Check(√) True or False

(3) The girl enjoyed the movie. T☐ F☐
(4) The boy and the girl liked the acting most about the movie. T☐ F☐

Listen and Speak 1 B

G: Brian, did you hear the news?
B: ❶What news?
G: We can use smartphones ❷during classes from next week.
B: Yes, I heard that.
G: ❸How do you feel about it?
B: ❹I think it will be very useful. I can ❺look up words ❻I don't know.
G: Yeah. We can also find information on the Internet.
B: Right. It will be very ❼helpful.

G: Brian, 너 그 소식 들었니?
B: 어떤 소식?
G: 우리는 다음 주부터 수업 중에 스마트폰을 사용할 수 있어.
B: 응, 그 소식을 들었어.
G: 넌 그것에 관해 어떻게 생각하니?
B: 매우 유용할 거라고 생각해. 모르는 단어들을 찾아볼 수 있잖아.
G: 그래. 우리는 또한 인터넷으로 정보를 찾을 수도 있어.
B: 맞아. 매우 도움이 될 거야.

❶ What은 의문형용사로 뒤에 명사가 오며, '어떤 ~' 또는 '무슨 ~'으로 해석한다.
❷ during은 '~ 동안에'의 의미로, 전치사이기 때문에 뒤에 명사가 온다.
❸ 'How do you feel about ~?'은 '~에 관해 어떻게 생각하세요?'라는 뜻으로 상대방의 의견을 물을 때 사용하는 표현이다. about 뒤에는 명사(구)나 동명사(구)를 넣어 말한다.
❹ 의견을 묻는 질문에 'I think ~.'의 표현을 사용해 자신의 의견을 말할 수 있다.
❺ look up: (사전 · 참고 자료 · 컴퓨터 등에서 정보를) 찾아보다
❻ words와 I don't know 사이에 목적격 관계대명사 which나 that이 생략되어 있다.
❼ helpful: 도움이 되는

Check(√) True or False

(5) The girl and the boy can look up words by using smartphones during classes. T ☐ F ☐
(6) The girl doesn't agree with the boy's idea that using smarphones during classes is very useful. T ☐ F ☐

Listen and Speak 2 C

A: ❶How do you feel about reading books on a smartphone?
B: I think it's good. We can read anytime.
A: ❷I'm with you on that. / I don't agree. It's not good for our eyes.

A: 스마트폰으로 책 읽는 것에 대해 어떻게 생각하니?
B: 좋다고 생각해. 언제든지 읽을 수 있잖아.
A: 동의해. / 동의하지 않아. 그것은 우리의 눈에 나빠.

❶ 'How do you feel about ~?'은 '~에 관해 어떻게 생각하니?'라는 뜻으로 상대방의 의견을 물을 때 사용하는 표현이다. about 뒤에는 명사(구)나 동명사(구)를 넣어 말한다. 비슷한 표현으로 'What do you think about ~?', 'What's your opinion on ~?', 'Can you give me your thoughts on ~?', 'Do you have any opinions on[about] ~?' 등이 있다.
❷ 'I'm with you on that.'은 '나는 그 말에 동의해.'라는 뜻으로 상대방의 의견에 동의할 때 사용할 수 있는 표현이다. 동의하지 않을 때는 'I don't agree.' 또는 'I don't think so.' 등으로 표현할 수 있다.

Check(√) True or False

(7) B thinks that reading books on a smartphone is good for our eyes. T ☐ F ☐
(8) By using smartphones, people can read books anytime. T ☐ F ☐

Listen and Speak 1 C

A: ❶Can I ask you a difficult question?

B: Sure. ❷I'll try my best.

A: ❸How do you feel about the ❹driverless car?

B: ❺I think it's ❻convenient but dangerous.

❶ 어떤 내용을 요청할 때에는 'Can I ~?(내가 ~해도 되나요?)'를 사용할 수 있다. 여기서 ask는 4형식 구조로 간접목적어(you)와 직접목적어(a difficult question)를 취하고 있다.
❷ try one's best: 최선을 다하다
❸ '~에 대해 어떻게 생각하니?'라고 상대방의 의견을 묻는 표현으로는 'How do you feel about ~?', 'What do you think about ~?', 'What's your opinion on ~?', 'Can you give me your thoughts on ~?', 'Do you have any opinions on[about] ~?' 등이 있다.
❹ driverless: 운전사가 없는
❺ 'I think that ~.'은 의견을 말할 때 사용하는 표현으로 'In my opinion, ~'과 같은 의미이다.
❻ convenient: 편리한

Listen and Speak 2 B

B: Hey, Jessica. Why ❶are you always drinking energy drinks?

G: Because ❷they ❸help me ❹stay awake.

B: ❺I'm with you on that, but they have too much caffeine.

G: Well, they help me ❻focus on my studies.

B: ❼Did you know that too much caffeine can hurt your bones?

G: Oh, I didn't know that.

B: ❽I think you should drink energy drinks less often.

G: Maybe you're right. Thanks, Tom.

❶ 부사(구) always, all the time 등과 현재진행형(be+동사ing)을 사용해 습관적인 행동을 표현할 수 있다.
❷ they는 앞 문장의 energy drinks를 의미한다.
❸ 동사 help는 뒤에 목적어와 목적격보어가 나와서 '(목적어)가 ~하는 것을 돕다'의 의미를 나타낸다. 이때 목적격보어로는 동사원형과 to부정사 모두 올 수 있다.
❹ stay는 자동사로 뒤에 형용사가 오며 '~인 채로 있다'의 의미를 가진다. awake: 잠들지 않은, 깨어 있는
❺ 상대방의 말이나 의견에 동의할 때, 'I'm with you on that.(나는 그 말에 동의해.)'을 사용할 수 있다.
❻ focus on: ~에 집중하다
❼ 'Did[Do] you know that ~?'는 '너는 ~을 알고 있었니?'의 의미로 상대방에게 무언가에 대해 알고 있는지 물어보는 표현이다. 'Have you heard about ~?'으로도 물어볼 수 있다.
❽ 'I think you should+동사원형 ~.'은 '내 생각에 너는 ~해야 해.'의 의미로 상대방에게 충고할 때 쓰는 표현이다. 그 외에 'You'd better ~.', 'Why don't you ~?', 'What[How] about ~?', 'I advise you to ~.' 등을 쓸 수 있다.

Real Life Talk Watch a Video

Tony: What are all these boxes, Suji?

Suji: ❶They're items I ordered online.

Tony: You like shopping on the Internet, don't you?

Suji: Yes, I do. ❷How do you feel about online shopping, Tony?

Tony: ❸I don't like it at all.

Suji: Why?

Tony: ❹It's very difficult to know what an item actually looks like.

Suji: ❺I'm with you on that.

Tony: It's also difficult ❻to return an item if you don't like it.

Suji: ❼You're right, but I think ❽it's very convenient.

Tony: Well, ❾convenience ❿isn't everything.

❶ items와 I ordered online 사이에 목적격 관계대명사 which나 that이 생략되어 있다.
❷ 'How do you feel about ~?'은 '~에 관해 어떻게 생각하세요?'라는 뜻으로 상대방의 의견을 물을 때 사용하는 표현이다. about 뒤에는 명사(구)나 동명사(구)를 넣어 말한다.
❸ not ~ at all: 전혀 ~가 아닌
❹ 문장 맨앞의 It은 가주어이며, 'to know what an item actually looks like'는 진주어이다. know의 목적어로 '의문사+주어+동사'의 간접의문문이 사용되었다.
❺ 'I'm with you on that.'은 '나는 그 말에 동의해.'라는 뜻으로 상대방의 의견에 동의할 때 사용할 수 있는 표현이다. 동의하지 않을 때는 'I don't agree.' 또는 'I don't think so.' 등으로 표현할 수 있다.
❻ to return은 진주어로 to부정사의 명사적 용법으로 사용되었다. return: 돌려주다, 반품하다. if는 '만약 ~라면'의 의미로 조건의 부사절을 이끄는 접속사이다.
❼ 'You're right.'은 상대방의 의견에 동의할 때 사용하는 표현이다.
❽ think와 it's very convenient 사이에 접속사 that이 생략되어 있다. 인칭대명사 it은 online shopping 또는 shopping on the Internet을 받는다. convenient: 편리한
❾ convenience: 편리, 편의
❿ not과 전체를 나타내는 말(always, all, every 등)이 함께 쓰이면 '항상[모두] ~인 것은 아니다'란 의미로 일부를 부정한다.

Conversation 교과서 확인학습

• 다음 우리말과 일치하도록 빈칸에 알맞은 말을 쓰시오.

Listen and Speak 1 A

B: Hi, Amy. Welcome ________ Korea.

G: ________ time ________ see, Minho. ________ have you ________?

B: Great. ________ did you come ________ ________ the airport?

G: I came here ________ subway.

B: ________ do you feel ________ the subway in Korea?

G: I think it's very ________.

B: 안녕, Amy. 한국에 온 걸 환영해.
G: 오랜만이야, 민호야. 어떻게 지냈니?
B: 잘 지냈어. 공항에서 여기에 어떻게 왔니?
G: 여기까지 지하철을 타고 왔어.
B: 한국 지하철에 관해 어떻게 생각하니?
G: 매우 깨끗하다고 생각해.

Listen and Speak 1 B

G: Brian, ________did you ________ the news?

B: ________ news?

G: We ________ use smartphones ________ classes ________ next week.

B: Yes, I ________ that.

G: ________ do you feel about it?

B: I think it will be very ________. I can ________ ________ ________ ________ ________ ________.

G: Yeah. We can also ________ information on the Internet.

B: Right. It will be very ________.

G: Brian, 너 그 소식 들었니?
B: 어떤 소식?
G: 우리는 다음 주부터 수업 중에 스마트폰을 사용할 수 있어.
B: 응, 그 소식을 들었어.
G: 넌 그것에 관해 어떻게 생각하니?
B: 매우 유용할 거라고 생각해. 모르는 단어들을 찾아볼 수 있잖아.
G: 그래. 우리는 또한 인터넷으로 정보를 찾을 수도 있어.
B: 맞아. 매우 도움이 될 거야.

Listen and Speak 1 C

1. A: ________ ________ ________ you a difficult question?

   B: Sure. I'll try my ________.

   A: ________ do you ________ about the ________ food diet?

   B: I think it's easy but ________.

2. A: Can I ________ you a ________ question?

   B: Sure. I'll ________ my best.

   A: ________ ________ ________ ________ about the AI robot?

   B: I think it's ________ ________ scary.

3. A: ________ ________ ________ ________ a difficult question?

   B: Sure. I'll ________ ________ ________.

   A: ________ ________ ________ ________ ________ animal testing?

   B: I think it's ________ ________ ________.

1. A: 어려운 질문을 해도 될까?
   B: 물론이지. 최선을 다할게.
   A: 싱글 푸드 다이어트에 대해 어떻게 생각하니?
   B: 쉽지만 건강에 해롭다고 생각해.

2. A: 어려운 질문을 해도 될까?
   B: 물론이지. 최선을 다할게.
   A: AI 로봇에 대해 어떻게 생각하니?
   B: 도움이 되지만 무섭다고 생각해.

3. A: 어려운 질문을 해도 될까?
   B: 물론이지. 최선을 다할게.
   A: 동물 실험에 대해 어떻게 생각하니?
   B: 도움이 되지만 잔인하다고 생각해.

Listen and Speak 2 A

B: ________ ________ ________ the movie?
G: Yes, I liked it ________ lot.
B: ________ ________ ________ ________ most about it?
G: The acting ________ so great.
B: I'm ________ ________ ________ that.

해석

B: 그 영화 재미있었니?
G: 응, 아주 좋았어.
B: 무엇이 가장 좋았니?
G: 연기가 아주 멋졌어.
B: 나도 그 점에 동의해.

Listen and Speak 2 B

B: Hey, Jessica. ________ are you ________ ________ energy drinks?
G: Because they ________ ________ ________ awake.
B: ________ ________ ________ ________ that, but they have ________ much caffeine.
G: Well, they ________ ________ ________ ________ my studies.
B: Did you ________ ________ ________ ________ ________ can hurt your bones?
G: Oh, I didn't know that.
B: I think you ________ ________ energy drinks ________ often.
G: Maybe you're right. Thanks, Tom.

B: 얘, Jessica. 너는 왜 늘 에너지 음료를 마시니?
G: 에너지 음료가 깨어 있는 데 도움이 되기 때문이야.
B: 그 점에는 동의하지만, 에너지 음료에는 카페인이 너무 많아.
G: 음, 공부에 집중하는 데 도움이 돼.
B: 너무 많은 카페인은 뼈를 다치게 할 수 있다는 것을 알고 있었니?
G: 아, 그건 몰랐어.
B: 내 생각에 넌 에너지 음료를 덜 자주 마셔야 해.
G: 네 말이 맞는 거 같아. 고마워, Tom.

Listen and Speak 2 C

1. A: ________ ________ ________ ________ ________ ________ books on a smartphone?
   B: I think it's good. We can read ________.
   A: I'm ________ ________ ________ ________. / I don't agree. It's ________ ________ ________ our eyes.
2. A: ________ ________ ________ ________ ________ skipping breakfast?
   B: I think it's good. We can sleep ________.
   A: ________ ________ ________ ________ ________. / I don't agree. Our brain may not work well.
3. A: ________ ________ ________ ________ ________ eating fast food?
   B: I think it's bad. Fast food has a lot of fat.
   A: ________ ________ ________ ________ ________. / ________ ________ ________. We can save time.

1. A: 스마트폰으로 책 읽는 것에 대해 어떻게 생각하니?
   B: 좋다고 생각해. 언제든지 읽을 수 있잖아.
   A: 동의해. / 동의하지 않아. 그것은 우리의 눈에 나빠.
2. A: 아침을 건너뛰는 것을 어떻게 생각하니?
   B: 좋다고 생각해. 우리는 잠을 더 잘 수 있어.
   A: 동의해. / 나는 동의하지 않아. 우리의 뇌가 잘 작동하지 않을 수 있어.
3. A: 패스트 푸드를 먹는 것에 대해 어떻게 생각하니?
   B: 나쁘다고 생각해. 패스트 푸드는 많은 지방을 가지고 있어.
   A: 동의해. / 나는 동의하지 않아. 우리는 시간을 절약할 수 있어.

Real Life Talk Watch a Video

Tony: ________ are all these boxes, Suji?

Suji: ________ ________ ________ ________ online.

Tony: You like shopping on the Internet, don't you?

Suji: Yes, I do. ________ ________ ________ ________ ________ online shopping, Tony?

Tony: I don't like it ________ ________.

Suji: Why?

Tony: It's very ________ ________ ________ ________ an item actually looks ________.

Suji: I'm with you on that.

Tony: It's also ________ ________ ________ an item if you don't like it.

Suji: You're right, but I think it's very ________.

Tony: Well, ________ isn't everything.

해석

Tony: 이 상자들은 전부 뭐니, 수지야?
수지: 내가 온라인으로 주문한 물건들이야.
Tony: 너 인터넷으로 쇼핑하는 걸 좋아하는구나, 그렇지 않니?
수지: 응, 그래. 넌 온라인 쇼핑에 관해 어떻게 생각하니, Tony?
Tony: 난 전혀 좋아하지 않아.
수지: 왜?
Tony: 물건이 실제로 어떻게 생겼는지 알기가 매우 어렵거든.
수지: 그 점에는 동의해.
Tony: 만약 물건이 마음에 들지 않으면 물건을 돌려보내는 것도 어려워.
수지: 네 말이 맞지만, 온라인 쇼핑은 매우 편리하다고 생각해.
Tony: 음, 편리함이 전부는 아니야.

Real Life Talk Step 2

1. **A:** How do you ________ ________ ________ on the Internet?
   B: I like it a lot.
   A: ________ ________ ________ ________ the reason?
   B: I can ________ ________ I want.
   A: ________ ________ ________ on that.
2. **A:** ________ ________ ________ ________ ________ ________ pets?
   B: I don't like it.
   A: Can you tell me the reason?
   B: It's a lot of ________ ________ ________ ________ ________ them.
   A: I ________ ________. They're so cute and ________ ________ ________.

1. A: 인터넷에서 쇼핑하는 것을 어떻게 생각해?
   B: 나는 아주 좋아해.
   A: 이유를 말해 줄 수 있니?
   B: 내가 원할 때마다 쇼핑할 수 있어.
   A: 나도 동의해.
2. A: 애완동물을 기르는 것을 어떻게 생각해?
   B: 나는 좋아하지 않아.
   A: 이유를 말해 줄 수 있니?
   B: 애완동물을 돌보기 위해 할 일이 많아.
   A: 나는 동의하지 않아. 그들은 아주 귀엽고, 우리를 기쁘게 해줘.

Check up Dialogue Champion

A: ________ ________ ________ ________ ________ ________ smartphones in class?

B: I think smartphones are ________ in class. We can ________ ________ information on them.

A: I'm ________ ________ ________ ________.

A: 수업 시간에 스마트폰을 사용하는 것에 대해 어떻게 생각해?
B: 수업 시간에 스마트폰은 유용하다고 생각해. 우리는 스마트폰으로 정보를 찾을 수 있어.
A: 나는 그 점에 동의해.

01 다음 대화의 밑줄 친 부분과 바꿔 쓸 수 없는 것은?

> A: How do you feel about shopping on the Internet?
> B: I like it a lot.
> A: Can you tell me the reason?
> B: I can shop whenever I want.
> A: I'm with you on that.

① I couldn't agree with you more.
② That's exactly how I feel.
③ I don't think so.
④ You are absolutely right.
⑤ No doubt about it.

02 다음 빈칸에 알맞은 말을 고르시오.

> G: Brian, did you hear the news?
> B: What news?
> G: We can use smartphones during classes from next week.
> B: Yes, I heard that.
> G: ______________________________
> B: I think it will be very useful. I can look up words I don't know.

① Have you heard about it? ② How do you feel about it?
③ Why do you think so? ④ What do you mean?
⑤ What do you know about it?

03 대화가 자연스럽게 연결되도록 (A)~(D)를 순서대로 가장 적절하게 배열한 것은?

> (A) I think it's helpful but cruel.
> (B) How do you feel about animal testing?
> (C) Can I ask you a difficult question?
> (D) Sure. I'll try my best.

① (B)-(A)-(C)-(D) ② (B)-(C)-(A)-(D)
③ (C)-(A)-(B)-(D) ④ (C)-(B)-(A)-(D)
⑤ (C)-(D)-(B)-(A)

[01~02] 다음 대화를 읽고 물음에 답하시오.

B: Hi, Amy. Welcome to Korea. (①)
G: Long time no see, Minho. (②)
B: Great. (③) How did you come here from the airport?
G: I came here by subway. (④)
B: How do you feel about the subway in Korea? (⑤)
G: I think it's very clean.

01 위 대화의 ①~⑤ 중 주어진 문장이 들어갈 알맞은 곳은?

How have you been?

① ② ③ ④ ⑤

02 중요 위 대화의 내용과 일치하지 않거나 알 수 없는 것은?

① Amy thinks that the subway in Korea is very clean.
② Amy came here from the airport by subway.
③ Minho and Amy haven't seen each other for a long time.
④ Amy has never been to Korea before.
⑤ Minho has been great.

[03~04] 다음 대화를 읽고 물음에 답하시오.

B: Hey, Jessica. Why are you always drinking energy drinks?
G: ______________________
B: I'm with you on that, but they have too much caffeine.
G: Well, they help me focus on my studies.
B: Did you know that too much caffeine can hurt your bones?
G: Oh, I didn't know that.
B: I think you should drink energy drinks less often.
G: Maybe you're right. Thanks, Tom.

03 위 대화의 빈칸에 들어갈 말로 알맞은 것을 고르시오.

① Because I like to drink herb tea.
② Because I haven't slept well lately.
③ I don't like to drink energy drinks.
④ I'm always drinking water these days.
⑤ Because they help me stay awake.

04 위 대화의 내용과 일치하지 않는 것은?

① Tom은 너무 많은 카페인이 뼈를 다치게 한다는 것을 알고 있다.
② Tom은 카페인이 집중하는 데 도움이 된다는 것에 동의하고 있다.
③ Jessica는 에너지 음료를 늘 마신다.
④ Jessica는 대화 후에 에너지 음료를 덜 마실지도 모른다.
⑤ Tom은 Jessica에게 에너지 음료를 덜 자주 마시라고 충고하고 있다.

[05~06] 다음 대화를 읽고 물음에 답하시오.

G: Brian, did you hear the news?
B: What news?
G: ______________________
B: ______________________
G: ______________________
B: ______________________
G: Yeah. We can also find information on the Internet.
B: ⓐ____________ It will be very helpful.

중요
05 위 대화의 빈칸에 들어갈 말을 <보기>에서 골라 순서대로 바르게 배열한 것은?

보기
(A) How do you feel about it?
(B) We can use smartphones during classes from next week.
(C) Yes, I heard that.
(D) I think it will be very useful. I can look up words I don't know.

① (B) – (A) – (C) – (D)
② (B) – (C) – (A) – (D)
③ (C) – (A) – (B) – (D)
④ (C) – (B) – (A) – (D)
⑤ (C) – (D) – (B) – (A)

06 빈칸 ⓐ에 알맞은 말이 <보기>에서 모두 몇 개인지 고르시오.

보기
• I'm with you on that.
• You have a point there.
• I couldn't agree with you more.
• That's exactly how I feel.
• No doubt about it.
• You are absolutely right.

① 2개 ② 3개 ③ 4개 ④ 5개 ⑤ 6개

[07~08] 다음 대화를 읽고 물음에 답하시오.

A: (A)__________ do you feel about using smarphones in class?
B: I don't like it.
A: Can you tell me the reason?
B: Many students will play games on the smartphones.
A: (B)______________ It can be very helpful to search for information on the smartphones.

07 위 대화의 빈칸 (A)에 알맞은 말을 고르시오.

① How ② Why ③ What
④ Which ⑤ How about

중요
08 위 대화의 빈칸 (B)에 알맞은 말을 모두 고르시오.

① I couldn't agree with you more.
② I don't think so.
③ I totally disagree.
④ No doubt about it.
⑤ I'm not sure about that.

중요
09 다음 중 짝지어진 대화가 어색한 것을 모두 고르시오.

① A: The movie is interesting. Don't you think so?
B: I don't think so. In my opinion, the story is good.
② A: I think that the new teacher is very kind.
B: I think so, too. She also teaches very well.
③ A: I think science is an interesting subject. How do you feel about science?
B: I think so, too.
④ A: How do you feel about online shopping?
B: In my opinion, it saves time.
⑤ A: How do you feel about the school lunch?
B: I don't think so. I think the food is delicious.

[01~02] 다음 대화를 읽고 물음에 답하시오.

G: Brian, did you hear the news?
B: What news?
G: We can use smartphones during classes from next week.
B: Yes, I heard that.
G: (A)넌 그것에 관해 어떻게 생각하니?
B: I think it will be very useful. I can look (B)_______ words I don't know.
G: Yeah. We can also find information on the Internet.
B: Right. It will be very helpful.

고난이도

01 밑줄 친 (A)를 주어진 단어를 이용하여 영작하시오.

➡ ____________________________ (how)

중요

02 빈칸 (B)에 알맞은 말을 쓰시오.

➡ ____________________

[03~05] 다음 대화를 읽고 물음에 답하시오.

Tony: What are all these boxes, Suji?
Suji: (A)____________________ (ordered, items, they, online, I, are)
Tony: You like shopping on the Internet, don't you?
Suji: Yes, I do. How do you feel about online shopping, Tony?
Tony: I don't like it at all.
Suji: Why?
Tony: It's very difficult to know what an item actually looks like.
Suji: I'm ⓐ______ you ⓑ______ that.
Tony: It's also difficult to return an item if you don't like it.
Suji: You're right, but I think it's very (B)__________.
Tony: Well, convenience isn't everything.

중요

03 빈칸 (A)를 괄호 안에 주어진 단어를 알맞게 배열하여 채우시오.

➡ ______________________________

04 상대방의 의견에 동의하는 말을 할 때 빈칸 ⓐ와 ⓑ에 알맞은 말을 쓰시오.

➡ ⓐ ____________ ⓑ ____________

고난이도

05 빈칸 (B)에 들어갈 말을 대화에 나오는 단어를 이용하여 알맞은 형태로 바꿔 쓰시오.

➡ ____________________

[06~07] 다음 대화를 읽고 물음에 답하시오.

A: (A)패스트 푸드를 먹는 것에 대해 어떻게 생각하니?
B: I think it's bad. Fast food has a lot of fat.
A: (B)____________ We can save time.

06 밑줄 친 (A)를 주어진 단어를 이용하여 영작하시오.

➡ ____________________________
(feel, eat)

중요

07 대화의 흐름상 빈칸 (B)에 들어갈 말을 주어진 단어를 이용해서 쓰시오.

➡ ____________________________ (agree)

교과서

Grammar

1 'the 비교급 ~ the 비교급…'

- **The more** Stanley dug, **the stronger** he became.
  Stanley는 많이 파면 팔수록, 더 힘이 세졌다.
- **The more** I want to get something done, **the less** I call it work.
  나는 뭔가가 이루어지기를 원하면 원할수록 그것을 더 일이라고 생각하지 않는다.

■ the 비교급(+주어+동사) ~, the 비교급+주어+동사 …
- 형태: The+비교급(+주어+동사) ~, the+비교급(+주어+동사) …
- 의미: ~하면 할수록 더 …하다

■ 'the 비교급(+주어+동사) ~, the 비교급(+주어+동사) …' 구문은 정도가 점점 더해지거나 덜해지는 것을 표현할 때 사용한다.
- **The sooner**, **the better**. 빠르면 빠를수록 더 좋다.

■ 최상급이 아닌 비교급임에도 the를 쓰는 것에 주의해야 하며, be동사나 반복되는 어구는 종종 생략된다. 'the 비교급(+주어+동사) ~, the 비교급+주어+동사 …'에서 앞에 나오는 'the'는 관계부사이며, 뒤에 나오는 'the'는 지시부사이다.
- **The higher** we climb, **the colder** it will become. 우리가 높이 오르면 오를수록, 더 추워질 것이다.
- Paradoxically, **the less** she ate, **the fatter** she got. 역설적이게도 그녀는 적게 먹을수록 더 살이 쪘다.

■ 'the 비교급+주어+동사 ~, the 비교급+주어+동사 …' 구문은 'As+주어+동사+비교급 ~, 주어+동사+비교급 …'으로 바꿔 쓸 수 있다.
- **The more** you chase money, **the harder** it is to catch it.
  = As you chase money more, it is harder to catch it. 돈은 더 좇을수록 손에 쥐기 힘들어진다.

cf. '비교급 and 비교급'은 '점점 더 ~하다'의 뜻이다.
- It's getting **harder and harder** to find parking close to the office.
  사무실 근처에 주차할 데 찾기가 갈수록 힘들어요.

핵심 Check

1. 다음 괄호 안에서 알맞은 말을 고르시오.
   (1) The (long / longer) he stayed there, the less he liked the people.
   (2) The more you have, the (more / most) you want.

2 접속사 since

- It couldn't be real gold **since** it was too light. 그것은 너무 가벼웠기 때문에 진짜 금일 리가 없었다.
- It's years **since** we last met. 우리가 마지막으로 만난 후로 오래 되었다.

■ since는 이유를 나타내는 접속사로 쓰여, '~이기 때문에'의 뜻으로 이유를 나타내는 부사절을 이끌며 because, as로 바꿔 쓸 수 있다.

- **Since** we live in the computer era, you should get used to personal computers.
  = **Because**[**As**] we live in the computer era, you should get used to personal computers.
  우리는 컴퓨터 시대에 살고 있으니까 PC를 익혀야 한다.

■ since의 그 밖의 쓰임

(1) 시간의 접속사: '~한 이후로'의 뜻으로, 시간의 부사절을 이끄는 since와 함께 쓰는 주절은 현재완료나 과거완료 시제로 쓴다.

- It's been three years to the day **since** we met. 우리가 만난 지 정확히 3년이다.
- He has been collecting stamps **since** he was eight. 그는 8살 때부터 우표를 모아 오고 있다.

(2) 전치사: '~ 이후(from then till now)'의 뜻으로, 'since+명사(구)'나 'ever since+명사(구)'의 형태로 쓰인다.

- You've grown **since** the last time I saw you! 지난번 봤을 때보다 많이 컸구나!
- The rain has been continuous **since** this morning. 비가 오늘 아침부터 계속 내리고 있다.

(3) 부사: '그 이후로'의 뜻이며, 주로 완료형 동사나 'ever since'의 형태로 쓰인다.

- He left home two weeks ago and we haven't heard from him **since**.
  그는 2주 전에 집을 떠났는데 그 이후로 우리는 그에게서 소식을 못 들었다.
- I have not seen him **since**. 그 후로 나는 그를 만나지 못했다..

핵심 Check

2. 다음 괄호 안에서 알맞은 말을 고르시오.

(1) We canceled the picnic (since / though) it rained a lot.
(2) He has changed a lot (unless / since) the accident.
(3) (Because / Before) he was so happy, he was smiling broadly.

Grammar 시험대비 기본평가

01 다음 빈칸에 들어갈 말로 알맞은 것은?

The ___________ you give, the more you get back.

① few ② many ③ little
④ more ⑤ most

02 다음 문장의 빈칸에 공통으로 들어갈 말로 알맞은 것은? (대·소문자 무시)

• _________ she was tired, she took some rest. • Many diets fail _________ they are boring.

① Unless ② If ③ Since
④ That ⑤ Though

03 다음 중 어법상 바르지 않은 것은?

① The older we grow, the weaker we become.
② The long the nails get, the more strange they become.
③ The more you practice, the better you do.
④ She hasn't seen Laura since her schooldays.
⑤ We thought that, since we were in the area, we'd stop by and see them.

04 다음 우리말에 맞게 주어진 어휘를 바르게 배열하시오.

(1) Stanley는 많이 파면 팔수록, 더 힘이 세졌다.
(Stanley, he, became, dug, stronger, more, the, the)
➡ ______________________________

(2) 나는 그에 대해 더 많이 들을수록, 그에 대한 동정심이 더 많아졌다.
(I, I, felt, heard, him, him, sympathetic, more, more, the, the, for, about)
➡ ______________________________

(3) 그는 아팠기 때문에 학교에 갈 수 없었다. (부사절로 시작할 것)
(he, he, school, go, was, couldn't, sick, since, to)
➡ ______________________________

Grammar 시험대비 실력평가

Step3

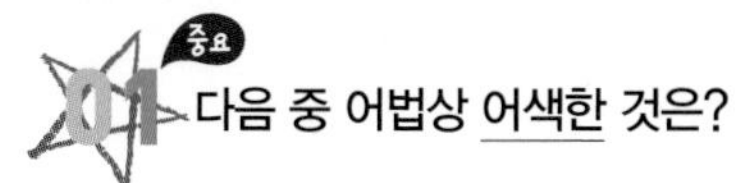

01 다음 중 어법상 어색한 것은?

① The more you exercise, the healthier you become.
② The much sugar in the orange juice, the short the shelf life.
③ The longer, the better.
④ The more you study, the more you get to know all the scientific stuff.
⑤ The warmer it gets, the less clothes you need.

02 다음 중 어법상 옳은 것은?

① Jane was bored since she waited so long.
② He didn't go to school though it was a holiday.
③ Such changes have not been seen because the invention of the printing press.
④ Unless Tom was tired, he stopped working.
⑤ I was bitten by a dog once and I've been afraid of them ever before.

03 다음 문장과 같은 뜻의 문장은?

As he gets older, he becomes wiser.

① Because he gets old, he becomes wise.
② He got the old, so he became the wise.
③ The old he gets, the wise he becomes.
④ The older he gets, the wiser he becomes.
⑤ The oldest he gets, the wisest he becomes.

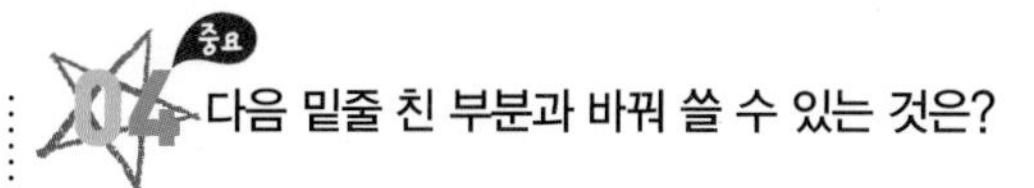

04 다음 밑줄 친 부분과 바꿔 쓸 수 있는 것은?

It couldn't be real gold <u>since</u> it was too light.

① whether ② that ③ if
④ unless ⑤ because

[05~06] 다음 우리말을 알맞게 영작한 것을 모두 고르시오.

05

너는 공부를 열심히 하면 할수록, 더 영리해질 것이다.

① Harder you study, smarter you will become.
② The hardest you study, the smartest you will become.
③ The harder you study, the smarter you will become.
④ Because you study harder, you will become the smarter.
⑤ As you study harder, you will become smarter.

06

피곤했기 때문에 나는 일찍 집에 갔다.

① Unless I felt very tired, I went home early.
② If I felt very tired, I went home early.
③ Since I felt very tired, I went home early.
④ When I felt very tired, I went home early.
⑤ Because I felt very tired, I went home early.

07 다음 우리말과 일치하는 문장을 쓸 때, 빈칸에 알맞은 말은?

음식이 매울수록 그녀는 더 좋아한다. = _______ the food is, the more she likes it.

① Spice ② Spicer ③ Spicest
④ The spicier ⑤ The spiciest

중요
08 다음 〈보기〉의 밑줄 친 since와 쓰임이 같은 것은?

보기
Since I was busy, I couldn't help my friend.

① We've lived here since 1994.
② I have permission to get married since I am old enough.
③ She has moved house six times since she came here.
④ It's a long time since her death.
⑤ I have not seen him since.

중요
09 다음 문장의 빈칸 (A), (B)에 들어갈 말로 가장 적절한 것은?

(A)_________ the race, (B)_________ the warm-up.

	(A)	(B)
①	The shorter	the longer
②	The shorter	longer
③	The short	the long
④	Shorter	the longer
⑤	Shorter	longer

10 다음 문장의 빈칸에 알맞은 말을 모두 고르시오.

I couldn't sleep _________ the bed was so uncomfortable.

① since ② that ③ what
④ because ⑤ where

중요
11 다음 문장과 비슷한 뜻이 되도록 비교급을 사용하여 바꿔 쓰시오.

(1) As it is colder, the hole becomes larger and deeper.
➡ ______________________________

(2) If you have stronger will, you will learn more.
➡ ______________________________

12 다음 중 since의 쓰임이 나머지와 다른 하나는?

① Many improvements have been made since this century began.
② I can get away from the office since we're not very busy just now.
③ We have both changed since we parted.
④ He has worked since he left school.
⑤ He has learned a lot since he came here.

서답형
13 다음 문장을 어법에 맞게 고쳐 쓰시오.

(1) This book is better of the two.
➡ ______________________________

(2) Harder he tried to get out, deeper he went.
➡ ______________________________

(3) Little people spend, slow the economy growth becomes.
➡ ______________________________
____

[14~15] 다음 중 어법상 올바른 문장은?

14
① The older she got, the pretty she got.
② The less I tell you, the more safe you'll be.
③ The lower a country's GNP is, the happier the country's people are.
④ Smaller portion of the two will be paid to him.
⑤ It was getting dark and dark, and we hurried to the shore.

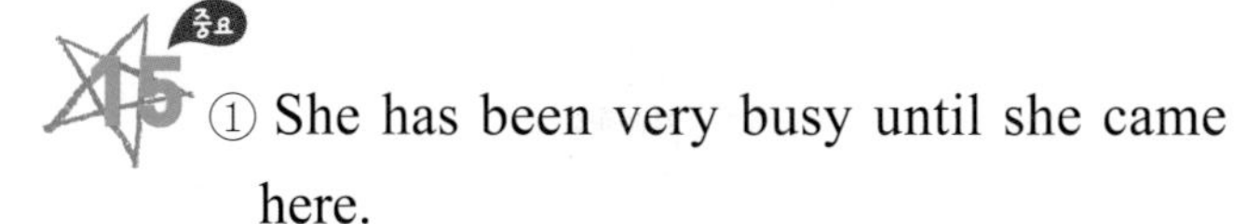

중요
15
① She has been very busy until she came here.
② We lost because of we played badly.
③ I was forced to take a taxi while the last bus had left.
④ The train was delayed though a tree had fallen across the line.
⑤ Life was harder then because neither of us had a job.

서답형
16 다음 문장에서 어법상 어색한 부분을 바르게 고치시오.

(1) Though I had no time to text you yesterday, I could not reply.
_____________ ➡ _____________

(2) She didn't come to the meeting if she was busy last weekend.
_____________ ➡ _____________

(3) He took his jacket off because the heat.
_____________ ➡ _____________

서답형
17 다음 괄호 안에서 알맞은 것을 고르시오.

(1) (The more / The much) stress I get, (the more / the much) nervous I become.
(2) (The closer / Close) I got to her, (the happier / happy) I became.
(3) (Bigger / The bigger) the eyes, (better / the better) the eyesight.
(4) (Although / Because) I was so tired, I couldn't concentrate.
(5) He resigned (since / because of) bad health.

18 다음 빈칸에 들어갈 수 없는 것은?

The harder I practice, _____________ I become.

① the more merry ② the better
③ the more interested ④ the happier
⑤ the more excited

중요
19 다음 주어진 문장과 의미가 같은 것을 모두 고르시오.

He gave up his job in advertising because he couldn't stand the pace.

① He gave up his job in advertising if he couldn't stand the pace.
② He gave up his job in advertising since he couldn't stand the pace.
③ He gave up his job in advertising although he couldn't stand the pace.
④ He gave up his job in advertising whether he couldn't stand the pace.
⑤ He gave up his job in advertising as he couldn't stand the pace.

Grammar 서술형 시험대비

01 다음 두 문장을 〈보기〉와 같이 한 문장으로 완성하시오.

보기
- You laugh much.
- You become happy.

→ The more you laugh, the happier you become.

(1) • You are young.
• It is easy to learn.
➡ ______________________

(2) • The picture is large.
• It will take long for people to download.
➡ ______________________
____

고 난이도

02 다음 문장에서 어법상 어색한 것을 바르게 고쳐 다시 쓰시오.

(1) The old he grew, the poor his memory became.
➡ ______________________
____

(2) I think the hard I work, the much I move up in the world.
➡ ______________________
____

(3) Ann is taller and more beautiful of the two sisters.
➡ ______________________
____

(4) This dictionary is a lot better of the two.
➡ ______________________

(5) The plan failed because lack of money.
➡ ______________________

(6) The accident happened because of nobody paid attention to the warning signs.
➡ ______________________
____

(7) They've been best friends before they were children.
➡ ______________________

(8) She had only spoken to him once though the party.
➡ ______________________

중요

03 다음 그림을 보고 주어진 어휘를 이용하여 빈칸에 알맞은 말을 쓰시오.

(1) __________ it gets, __________________ she becomes. (hot, exhausted)

(2) __________ she wants to drink something cold, __________________ she feels. (much, thirsty)

04 다음 두 문장을 since를 이용해 한 문장으로 쓰시오.

(1) • I was hungry.
• I had a whole pizza.
(since로 시작하는 부사절이 주절의 앞에 위치할 것)
➡ ________________________________

(2) • I didn't enjoy the book.
• I couldn't identify with any of the main characters.
(since로 시작하는 부사절이 주절의 뒤에 위치할 것)
➡ ________________________________
____

고난이도

05 다음 문장과 비슷한 뜻이 되도록 비교급을 사용하여 바꿔 쓰시오.

(1) If you read many books, you will know many things.
➡ ________________________________
____

(2) If you start early, you arrive there soon.
➡ ________________________________
____

(3) As you win more arguments, you'll have fewer friends.
➡ ________________________________
____

(4) As one's mind is healthier, one's body will be healthier.
➡ ________________________________
____

06 괄호 안에 주어진 어휘를 이용하여 빈칸에 알맞은 말을 쓰시오.

(1) The more you practice, ____________. (you, do, good)

(2) The hotter you feel, ________________ ____________. (you, drink, much, water)

(3) The fewer hours they work, __________ ____________________. (they, have, little, holiday time)

중요

07 다음 우리말과 일치하도록 괄호 안에 주어진 어휘를 이용하여 영작하시오.

(1) 우리는 나이가 들면 들수록, 더 현명해진다. (grow, become, old, wise)
➡ ________________________________

(2) 너는 높이 올라가면 올라갈수록, 더 멀리 본다. (climb, see, high, far)
➡ ________________________________

(3) 너는 덜 쓰면 덜 쓸수록, 더 많이 절약한다. (save, spend, much, little)
➡ ________________________________

(4) 나는 돈이 없어서 먹을 것을 하나도 살 수 없었다. (buy, anything, since, no money)
➡ ________________________________
____

(5) 그녀는 대학을 떠난 이후로 많은 책을 써 왔다. (has written, since, left college)
➡ ________________________________
____

교과서

Reading

HOLES

"Dig harder, Stanley! The harder you dig, the faster you'll finish!"
The+비교급(+주어+동사) ~, the+비교급(+주어+동사): ~할수록, (점점) 더 …하다
yelled Mr. Sir. Stanley Yelnats couldn't dig any harder since every
any: 부정문에서 '전혀, 조금도'의 뜻으로 형용사나 부사의 의미를 강조 since: 이유나 원인을 나타내는 절을 이끄는 접속사 every: 모든, 단수 명사와 함께 쓰임.
single muscle hurt. He was thirsty and hungry. He wanted to go home. Unfortunately, Stanley's home for the next 18 months would be right
과거 시제에서 will의 과거형으로 would를 쓴다.
here, at Camp Green Lake.
here와 at Camp Green Lake는 동격으로 콤마(,)로 연결

Camp Green Lake was a terrible name. It wasn't green and there was no lake. Camp Green Lake was hot and full of sand. In fact, it wasn't
실제로는, 사실은
even a camp. It was a place for bad boys. Then what was a good boy
예상 밖의 놀라운 일을 나타내는 말, ~조차도
like Stanley doing here? He was sent to the camp for stealing a pair of
쌍을 이루는 물건의 수량을 표현할 때 사용
sneakers.

Stanley didn't really steal a pair of sneakers. He was just in the wrong place at the wrong time. One day, he was walking home from school.
One day: 미래의 어느 시기나 과거의 특정한 날을 가리킨다. 과거진행형: ~하는 중이었다
Suddenly, a pair of old sneakers fell from the sky. The sneakers hit him
'갑자기'라는 뜻의 부사로 문장 전체를 수식 fall from the sky: 하늘에서 떨어지다
on the head.
hit+사람+on+the+신체 부위: ~의 …을 때리다

He started running with the sneakers to tell his father what happened.
to부정사의 부사적 용법(목적) 간접의문문(의문사 주어+동사)
A few minutes later, the police stopped Stanley and asked him why
시간+later: ~ 시간이 지난 후에 ~를 멈추게 했다
he was running. Unfortunately for Stanley, the sneakers belonged to
asked의 직접목적어로 쓰인 간접의문문
a famous baseball player, Clyde Livingstone. That was why Stanley
그것이 ~한 이유였다.
ended up at Camp Green Lake.
end up+특정 장소나 상황: 결국 (어떤 처지)에 처하게 되다

hole 구덩이, 구멍
dig (구멍 등을) 파다
muscle 근육
unfortunately 불행히도
belong to ~의 소유이다[것이다]
end up 결국 ~이 되다

• 다음 문장이 본문의 내용과 일치하면 T, 일치하지 않으면 F를 쓰시오.

1 Because every single muscle hurt, Stanley Yelnats couldn't dig any harder. ☐
2 Stanley's home for the next two years would be at Camp Green Lake. ☐
3 Camp Green Lake wasn't green and there was no lake. ☐
4 Stanley started to run with the sneakers to tell his father what happened. ☐
5 The sneakers belonged to a famous basketball player, Clyde Livingstone. ☐

Step1

Stanley was assigned to Group D in the camp. There were six other boys in Stanley's group. They all had cool names like X-Ray, Zigzag and Zero. Each boy had to dig one hole every day. It had to be about 150cm deep and 150cm wide. Mr. Sir said, "You are digging to build character."

be assigned to: ~에 배치되다. 능동태: assign+목적어+to. ~(목적어)를 …에 배치하다
Stanley를 포함하면 총 7명의 소년이 있었다.
~해야 했다(의무)
각 소년이 매일 파야 하는 구멍이
깊이와 너비가 150센티미터 정도가 되어야 함을 의미
to부정사의 부사적 용법(목적)

The more Stanley dug, the stronger he became. It took less time to finish his hole each day. In his second week, as Stanley was finishing his hole, he saw something shiny in the dirt. Stanley's heart beat faster. He heard that anyone who found something interesting would be given the day off. He carefully picked up the shiny object and brushed off the dirt. It was a small gold tube. But it couldn't be real gold since it was too light. There were two letters, *KB*, at the bottom of the tube. What did KB stand for? Stanley's heart beat even faster.

It+takes+시간+to부정사구: ~하는 데 (…의) 시간이 걸리다
~하는 동안에(접속사)
-thing으로 끝나는 부정대명사를 수식하는 형용사는 뒤에 위치
heard의 목적어를 이끄는 접속사
주격 관계대명사
-thing으로 끝나는 부정대명사를 수식하는 형용사는 뒤에 위치
the small gold tube.
couldn't: ~일 리가 없었다(강한 부정적인 추측)
since: 원인이나 이유를 나타내는 절을 이끄는 접속사
= represent = symbolize: ~을 상징하다
'훨씬, 더욱'(비교급을 강조)

assign (사람을) 배치하다
wide 폭이 ~인
character 품성, 인격
shiny 빛나는, 반짝거리는
dirt 흙
beat (심장이) 고동치다, 때리다
day off 휴일, 쉬는 날
object 물건
brush off 털다, 털어 내다
tube 통, 관
bottom 맨 아래, 바닥
stand for ~을 의미하다

확인문제

- 다음 문장이 본문의 내용과 일치하면 T, 일치하지 않으면 F를 쓰시오.

1 There were seven boys in Stanley's group including Stanley. ☐
2 The hole each boy had to dig every day had to be about 150cm deep and 150cm wide. ☐
3 It took more time for Stanley to finish his hole each day. ☐
4 In his second week, Stanley saw something shiny in the dirt. ☐
5 The shiny object was a small tube which was made of real gold. ☐

Reading 교과서 확인학습 A

- 우리말을 참고하여 빈칸에 알맞은 말을 쓰시오.

HOLES

1 "Dig _______, Stanley!

2 The _______ you dig, _______ _______ you'll finish!" yelled Mr. Sir.

3 Stanley Yelnats couldn't dig _______ _______ since every single muscle hurt.

4 He was _______ and _______.

5 He wanted to _______ _______.

6 Unfortunately, Stanley's home for the next 18 months _______ _______ right here, at Camp Green Lake.

7 Camp Green Lake was a _______ name.

8 It wasn't green and there was _______ _______.

9 Camp Green Lake was hot and _______ _______ _______.

10 _______ _______, it wasn't _______ a camp.

11 It was _______ _______ _______ _______ _______.

12 Then what was a good boy _______ Stanley doing here?

13 He was sent to the camp _______ _______ a pair of sneakers.

14 Stanley _______ _______ _______ a pair of sneakers.

15 He was just _______ _______ _______ _______ at the wrong time.

16 One day, he was walking home _______ _______.

17 Suddenly, a pair of old sneakers _______ _______ the sky.

18 The sneakers _______ _______ _______ _______ _______.

구덩이

1 "더 열심히 파, Stanley!

2 네가 열심히 파면 팔수록, 너는 더 빨리 끝낼 거야!" Sir 씨가 소리를 질렀다.

3 Stanley Yelnats는 모든 근육 하나하나가 아팠기 때문에 더 열심히 팔 수가 없었다.

4 그는 목이 마르고 배가 고팠다.

5 그는 집에 가고 싶었다.

6 불행히도, 앞으로 18개월 동안 Stanley의 집은 바로 여기 Green Lake 캠프가 될 것이었다.

7 Green Lake 캠프는 형편없는 이름이었다.

8 그곳은 초록색도 아니었고 호수도 없었다.

9 Green Lake 캠프는 뜨거웠고 온통 모래였다.

10 사실 그곳은 캠프조차 아니었다.

11 그곳은 나쁜 소년들을 위한 곳이었다.

12 그렇다면 Stanley 같이 착한 소년이 여기서 무엇을 하고 있었을까?

13 그는 운동화 한 켤레를 훔쳤다는 이유로 캠프에 보내졌다.

14 Stanley가 정말로 운동화 한 켤레를 훔친 것은 아니었다.

15 그는 그저 잘못된 시간에 잘못된 장소에 있었다.

16 어느 날, 그는 학교에서 집으로 걸어가고 있었다.

17 갑자기, 낡은 운동화 한 켤레가 하늘에서 떨어졌다.

18 그 운동화는 그의 머리에 맞았다.

19 He started running with the sneakers to tell his father _______ _______.

20 A few minutes later, the police _______ Stanley and asked him _______ _______ _______ _______.

21 Unfortunately _______ Stanley, the sneakers _______ _______ a famous baseball player, Clyde Livingstone.

22 _______ _______ _______ Stanley ended up at Camp Green Lake.

23 Stanley _______ _______ _______ Group D in the camp.

24 There were _______ _______ _______ in Stanley's group.

25 They all had _______ names _______ X-Ray, Zigzag and Zero.

26 Each boy had to dig _______ _______ _______ _______.

27 It had to be _______ 150cm _______ and 150cm _______.

28 Mr. Sir said, "You are digging _______ _______ _______."

29 _______ _______ Stanley dug, _______ _______ he became.

30 _______ _______ less time _______ _______ his hole each day.

31 In his second week, as Stanley was finishing his hole, he saw _______ _______ in the dirt.

32 Stanley's heart _______ _______.

33 He heard that _______ _______ found something interesting would _______ _______ _______ _______ _______.

34 He carefully picked up the shiny object and _______ _______ the dirt.

35 It was a _______ _______ _______.

36 But it _______ _______ real gold _______ it was too light.

37 There were two letters, *KB*, _______ _______ _______ _______ the tube.

38 What did KB _______ _______?

39 Stanley's heart beat _______ faster.

19 그는 그의 아버지에게 무슨 일이 일어났는지 말하기 위해 운동화를 가지고 달리기 시작했다.

20 몇 분 후에, 경찰이 Stanley를 멈춰 세웠고 그가 왜 달리고 있었는지를 그에게 물었다.

21 Stanley에게는 불행히도, 그 운동화는 유명한 야구 선수인 Clyde Livingstone의 것이었다.

22 그것이 Stanley가 Green Lake 캠프에 오게 된 이유였다.

23 Stanley는 캠프에서 D 그룹에 배치되었다.

24 Stanley의 그룹에는 6명의 다른 소년들이 있었다.

25 그들은 모두 X-Ray, Zigzag, Zero와 같은 멋진 이름을 가지고 있었다.

26 각 소년은 매일 구덩이 하나를 파야 했다.

27 그것은 150cm 정도 깊이와 150cm 정도 너비여야 했다.

28 Sir 씨는 "너희들은 인격을 수양하기 위해 구덩이를 파고 있는 것이야."라고 말했다.

29 Stanley는 많이 파면 팔수록, 더 힘이 세졌다.

30 하루하루 구덩이를 끝내는 데 시간이 덜 걸렸다.

31 그가 온 지 두 번째 주, Stanley가 자기 구덩이를 끝내 가고 있었을 때, 그는 흙 속에서 빛나는 뭔가를 봤다.

32 Stanley의 심장은 더 빨리 뛰었다.

33 그는 흥미로운 뭔가를 발견한 사람은 그 날을 쉬게 된다고 들었다.

34 그는 조심스럽게 그 빛나는 물체를 집어 흙을 털어 냈다.

35 그것은 작은 금색 통이었다.

36 그러나 그것은 너무 가벼웠기 때문에 진짜 금일 리가 없었다.

37 그 통의 바닥에는 KB라는 두 글자가 있었다.

38 KB는 무엇을 의미할까?

39 Stanley의 심장은 훨씬 더 빨리 뛰었다.

Reading 교과서 확인학습 B

- 우리말을 참고하여 본문을 영작하시오.

HOLES

1. "더 열심히 파, Stanley!
➡ ______________________

2. 네가 열심히 파면 팔수록, 너는 더 빨리 끝낼 거야!" Sir 씨가 소리를 질렀다.
➡ ______________________

3. Stanley Yelnats는 모든 근육 하나하나가 아팠기 때문에 더 열심히 팔 수가 없었다.
➡ ______________________

4. 그는 목이 마르고 배가 고팠다.
➡ ______________________

5. 그는 집에 가고 싶었다.
➡ ______________________

6. 불행히도, 앞으로 18개월 동안 Stanley의 집은 바로 여기 Green Lake 캠프가 될 것이었다.
➡ ______________________

7. Green Lake 캠프는 형편없는 이름이었다.
➡ ______________________

8. 그곳은 초록색도 아니었고 호수도 없었다.
➡ ______________________

9. Green Lake 캠프는 뜨거웠고 온통 모래였다.
➡ ______________________

10. 사실 그곳은 캠프조차 아니었다.
➡ ______________________

11. 그곳은 나쁜 소년들을 위한 곳이었다.
➡ ______________________

12. 그렇다면 Stanley 같이 착한 소년이 여기서 무엇을 하고 있었을까?
➡ ______________________

13. 그는 운동화 한 켤레를 훔쳤다는 이유로 캠프에 보내졌다.
➡ ______________________

14. Stanley가 정말로 운동화 한 켤레를 훔친 것은 아니었다.
➡ ______________________

15. 그는 그저 잘못된 시간에 잘못된 장소에 있었다.
➡ ______________________

16. 어느 날, 그는 학교에서 집으로 걸어가고 있었다.
➡ ______________________

17. 갑자기, 낡은 운동화 한 켤레가 하늘에서 떨어졌다.
➡ ______________________

18. 그 운동화는 그의 머리에 맞았다.
➡ ______________________

19 그는 그의 아버지에게 무슨 일이 일어났는지 말하기 위해 운동화를 가지고 달리기 시작했다.
➡ ______

20 몇 분 후에, 경찰이 Stanley를 멈춰 세웠고 그가 왜 달리고 있었는지를 그에게 물었다.
➡ ______

21 Stanley에게는 불행히도, 그 운동화는 유명한 야구 선수인 Clyde Livingstone의 것이었다.
➡ ______

22 그것이 Stanley가 Green Lake 캠프에 오게 된 이유였다.
➡ ______

23 Stanley는 캠프에서 D 그룹에 배치되었다.
➡ ______

24 Stanley의 그룹에는 6명의 다른 소년들이 있었다.
➡ ______

25 그들은 모두 X-Ray, Zigzag, Zero와 같은 멋진 이름을 가지고 있었다.
➡ ______

26 각 소년은 매일 구덩이 하나를 파야 했다.
➡ ______

27 그것은 150cm 정도 깊이와 150cm 정도 너비여야 했다.
➡ ______

28 Sir 씨는 "너희들은 인격을 수양하기 위해 구덩이를 파고 있는 것이야."라고 말했다.
➡ ______

29 Stanley는 많이 파면 팔수록, 더 힘이 세졌다.
➡ ______

30 하루하루 구덩이를 끝내는 데 시간이 덜 걸렸다.
➡ ______

31 그가 온 지 두 번째 주, Stanley가 자기 구덩이를 끝내 가고 있었을 때, 그는 흙 속에서 빛나는 뭔가를 봤다.
➡ ______

32 Stanley의 심장은 더 빨리 뛰었다.
➡ ______

33 그는 흥미로운 뭔가를 발견한 사람은 그 날을 쉬게 된다고 들었다.
➡ ______

34 그는 조심스럽게 그 빛나는 물체를 집어 흙을 털어 냈다.
➡ ______

35 그것은 작은 금색 통이었다.
➡ ______

36 그러나 그것은 너무 가벼웠기 때문에 진짜 금일 리가 없었다.
➡ ______

37 그 통의 바닥에는 KB라는 두 글자가 있었다.
➡ ______

38 KB는 무엇을 의미할까?
➡ ______

39 Stanley의 심장은 훨씬 더 빨리 뛰었다.
➡ ______

Reading 시험대비 실력평가

[01~03] 다음 글을 읽고 물음에 답하시오.

"Dig harder, Stanley! The harder you dig, the faster you'll finish!" yelled Mr. Sir. Stanley Yelnats couldn't dig any harder (A) since every single muscle hurt. He was thirsty and hungry. He wanted to go home. Unfortunately, Stanley's home for the next 18 months would be right here, at Camp Green Lake.

Camp Green Lake was a terrible name. It wasn't green and there was no lake. Camp Green Lake was hot and full of sand. In fact, it wasn't even a camp. It was a place ⓐ________ bad boys. Then what was a good boy like Stanley doing here? He was sent to the camp ⓑ______ stealing a pair of sneakers.

서답형

01 위 글의 빈칸 ⓐ와 ⓑ에 공통으로 들어갈 알맞은 전치사를 쓰시오.

➡ ____________________

02 위 글의 밑줄 친 (A)since와 문법적 쓰임이 같은 것을 고르시오.

① It is two years since I left school.
② She's been off work since Tuesday.
③ He hasn't phoned since he went to Berlin.
④ Since we live in the computer era, you should get used to personal computers.
⑤ He left home two weeks ago and we haven't heard from him since.

중요

03 According to the passage, which is NOT true?

① Mr. Sir yelled at Stanley.
② Stanley was unable to dig any harder.
③ Camp Green Lake was named after its color.
④ Camp Green Lake was filled with sand.
⑤ Camp Green Lake wasn't even a camp.

[04~06] 다음 글을 읽고 물음에 답하시오.

ⓐStanley는 많이 파면 팔수록, 더 힘이 세져 갔다. ⓑIt took less time finishing his hole each day. In his second week, as Stanley was finishing his hole, he saw something shiny in the dirt. Stanley's heart beat faster. He heard that anyone who found something interesting would be given the day off. He carefully picked up the shiny object and brushed off the dirt. It was a small gold tube. But it couldn't be real gold since it was too light. There were two letters, *KB*, at the bottom of the tube. What did KB stand for? Stanley's heart beat ⓒeven faster.

서답형

04 위 글의 밑줄 친 ⓐ의 우리말에 맞게 주어진 어휘를 이용하여 8 단어로 영작하시오.

the, became

➡ ____________________

서답형

05 위 글의 밑줄 친 ⓑ에서 어법상 틀린 부분을 찾아 고치시오.

➡ ____________________

중요

06 위 글의 밑줄 친 ⓒeven과 바꿔 쓸 수 없는 말을 고르시오.

① much ② still ③ far
④ very ⑤ a lot

[07~09] 다음 글을 읽고 물음에 답하시오.

Stanley didn't really steal a pair of sneakers. He was just in the wrong place at the wrong time. One day, he was walking home from school. ⓐSuddenly, a pair of old sneakers fell from the sky. The sneakers hit him on the head.

He started running with the sneakers to tell his father what happened. A few minutes later, the police stopped Stanley and asked him why he was running. Unfortunately for Stanley, the sneakers belonged to a famous baseball player, Clyde Livingstone. That was why Stanley ended up at Camp Green Lake.

07 위 글에서 Stanley가 느꼈을 심경으로 가장 알맞은 것을 고르시오.

① ashamed ② unfair ③ excited
④ pleased ⑤ bored

08 위 글의 밑줄 친 ⓐSuddenly와 바꿔 쓸 수 없는 말을 고르시오.

① All at once ② Abruptly
③ All of a sudden ④ Urgently
⑤ Unexpectedly

09 중요 위 글을 읽고 알 수 없는 것을 고르시오.

① Did Stanley really steal a pair of sneakers?
② What was Stanley doing when a pair of sneakers fell from the sky?
③ What did the sneakers hit when they fell from the sky?
④ Why did a pair of sneakers fall from the sky?
⑤ When did the police stop Stanley?

[10~12] 다음 글을 읽고 물음에 답하시오.

ⓐThe more Stanley dug, the stronger he became. It took less time to finish his hole each day. In his second week, as Stanley was finishing his hole, he saw ①something shiny in the dirt. Stanley's heart beat faster. He heard that anyone who found something interesting would be given the day off. He carefully picked up ②the shiny object and brushed off the dirt. It was a small gold tube. But ③it couldn't be real gold since ④it was too light. There were two letters, *KB*, at the bottom of the tube. What did ⑤KB stand for? Stanley's heart beat even faster.

10 밑줄 친 ①~⑤ 중에서 가리키는 대상이 나머지 넷과 다른 것은?

① ② ③ ④ ⑤

서답형
11 위 글의 밑줄 친 ⓐ를 As를 사용하여 아래와 같이 바꿨을 때, 문법적으로 어색한 부분을 찾아 고치시오.

As Stanley dug the more, he became the stronger.

➡ ______________________________

서답형
12 Why did Stanley's heart beat faster? Answer in English beginning with "Because".

➡ ______________________________

____

[13~15] 다음 글을 읽고 물음에 답하시오.

Stanley was assigned to Group D in the camp. There were six other boys in Stanley's group. They all had cool names like X-Ray, Zigzag and Zero. Each boy had to dig one hole every day. It had to be about 150cm deep and 150cm wide. Mr. Sir said, "You are digging ⓐto build character."

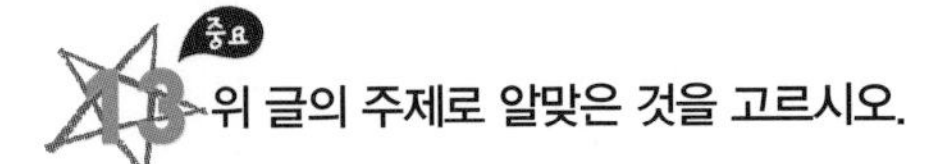

13 위 글의 주제로 알맞은 것을 고르시오.

① the number of the members of Group D to which Stanley was assigned
② the cool names of the boys in Group D to which Stanley was assigned
③ the size of the hole that each boy had to dig every day
④ the duty the members of Group D had to do every day
⑤ the reason Mr. Sir said that the boys were digging the hole to build character

14 아래 〈보기〉에서 위 글의 밑줄 친 ⓐto build와 to부정사의 용법이 다른 것의 개수를 고르시오.

보기
① I expect him to build it.
② How many people do you need to build it?
③ Who was the first man to build it?
④ Is it easy to build it?
⑤ I have no money to build it.

① 1개 ② 2개 ③ 3개 ④ 4개 ⑤ 5개

서답형
15 What was the size of the hole the boys had to dig every day? Fill in the blanks (A) and (B) with suitable words.

The (A)________ of the hole was about 150 centimeters and its (B)________ was also about 150 centimeters.

[16~18] 다음 글을 읽고 물음에 답하시오.

Stanley didn't really steal a pair of sneakers. He was just in the wrong place at the wrong time. One day, he was walking home from school. Suddenly, a pair of old sneakers fell from the sky. The sneakers hit him on the head.
He started running with the sneakers ⓐto tell his father what happened. A few minutes later, the police stopped Stanley and asked him why he was running. Unfortunately for Stanley, the sneakers belonged to a famous baseball player, Clyde Livingstone. That was why Stanley ended up at Camp Green Lake.

중요
16 위 글의 제목으로 알맞은 것을 고르시오.

① Sneakers from the Sky? Unbelievable!
② Unjustly Accused Stanley
③ Wow, I Got the Free Sneakers!
④ Why Was Stanley in the Wrong Place?
⑤ Clyde Livingstone Lost His Sneakers

17 위 글의 밑줄 친 ⓐto tell과 to부정사의 용법이 같은 것을 모두 고르시오.

① He was happy to tell his father the news.
② It's time to tell his father the news.
③ It was too late to tell his father the news.
④ He tried to tell his father the news.
⑤ He had no courage to tell his father the news.

서답형
18 Whose were the sneakers which fell from the sky? Answer in English in a full sentence. (4 words)

➡ ______________________________

[19~22] 다음 글을 읽고 물음에 답하시오.

"Dig harder, Stanley! (A)네가 열심히 파면 팔수록, 너는 더 빨리 끝낼 거야!" yelled Mr. Sir. Stanley Yelnats couldn't dig any harder since every single muscle hurt. He was thirsty and hungry. He wanted to go home. Unfortunately, Stanley's home for the next 18 months would be right here, at Camp Green Lake.

Camp Green Lake was a terrible name. It wasn't green and there was no lake. Camp Green Lake was hot and full of sand. ⓐ_____, it wasn't even a camp. It was a place for bad boys. Then what was a good boy like Stanley doing here? He ___ⓑ___ to the camp for stealing a pair of sneakers.

19 위 글의 빈칸 ⓐ에 들어갈 알맞은 말을 고르시오.

① Therefore
② In fact
③ By contrast
④ However
⑤ Similarly

서답형

20 위 글의 빈칸 ⓑ에 send를 알맞은 형태로 쓰시오.

➡ ______________________

서답형

21 위 글의 밑줄 친 (A)의 우리말에 맞게 주어진 어휘를 알맞게 배열하시오.

you'll / harder / finish / the / dig / faster / you / the / ,

➡ ______________________

서답형

22 Why couldn't Stanley dig any harder? Answer in English in a full sentence using "since".

➡ ______________________

[23~25] 다음 글을 읽고 물음에 답하시오.

Stanley was ___ⓐ___ to Group D in the camp. There were six other boys in Stanley's group. They all had cool names like X-Ray, Zigzag and Zero. Each boy had to dig one hole every day. It had to be about ⓑ150cm deep and 150cm wide. Mr. Sir said, "You are digging to build ⓒcharacter."

서답형

23 주어진 영영풀이를 참고하여 빈칸 ⓐ에 철자 a로 시작하는 단어를 알맞은 형태로 쓰시오.

to send someone to a particular place, group, or person, usually in order to work at that place or for that person

➡ ______________________

서답형

24 위 글의 밑줄 친 ⓑ를 영어로 읽는 법을 쓰시오.

➡ ______________________

중요

25 위 글의 밑줄 친 ⓒcharacter와 같은 의미로 쓰인 것을 고르시오.

① He was a man of character.
② Who is the major character in the book?
③ I like the character of the country.
④ Your password can only start with an alphabetic character or number.
⑤ This area has the character of desert areas.

[01~02] 다음 글을 읽고 물음에 답하시오.

The more Stanley dug, the stronger he became. It took (A)[less / more] time to finish his hole each day. In his second week, as Stanley was finishing his hole, he saw something shiny in the dirt. Stanley's heart beat faster. He heard that anyone who found something interesting would ___ⓐ___ the day off. He carefully picked up the shiny object and brushed off the dirt. It was a small gold tube. But it couldn't be real gold (B)[if / since] it was too light. There were two letters, *KB*, at the bottom of the tube. What did KB stand (C)[by / for]? Stanley's heart beat even faster.

01 위 글의 빈칸 ⓐ에 give를 알맞은 형태로 쓰시오.

➡ ________________

중요

02 위 글의 괄호 (A)~(C)에서 문맥이나 어법상 알맞은 낱말을 골라 쓰시오.

➡ (A)________ (B)________ (C)________

[03~05] 다음 글을 읽고 물음에 답하시오.

Stanley didn't really steal a pair of sneakers. ⓐHe was just in the right place at the right time. One day, he was walking home from school. Suddenly, a pair of old sneakers fell from the sky. The sneakers hit him on the head.

He started running with the sneakers to tell his father what happened. A few minutes later, the police stopped Stanley and asked him why he was running. Unfortunately for Stanley, the sneakers belonged to a famous baseball player, Clyde Livingstone. ⓑ그것이 Stanley가 Green Lake 캠프에 오게 된 이유였다.

03 위 글의 밑줄 친 ⓐ에서 흐름상 어색한 부분을 찾아 고치시오. (두 군데)

➡ ________________

고난이도

04 위 글의 밑줄 친 ⓑ의 우리말에 맞게 주어진 어휘를 이용하여 10 단어로 영작하시오.

why, ended up

➡ ________________

____

05 Why did Stanley start running with the sneakers? Fill in the blanks with suitable words.

He started running with them in order that he ________ ________ his father what happened.

[06~07] 다음 글을 읽고 물음에 답하시오.

Stanley was assigned to Group D in the camp. There were six other boys in Stanley's group. They all had cool names like X-Ray, Zigzag and Zero. Each boy had to dig one hole every day. ⓐ그것은 150cm 정도 깊이와 150cm 정도 너비여야 했다. Mr. Sir said, "You are digging to build character."

06 다음 문장에서 위 글의 내용과 다른 부분을 찾아서 고치시오.

There were six boys including Stanley in Group D.

➡ ____________________

중요
07 위 글의 밑줄 친 ⓐ의 우리말에 맞게 주어진 어휘를 알맞게 배열하시오.

deep / about / it / 150cm / to / 150cm / and / had / be / wide

➡ ______________________________

[08~09] 다음 글을 읽고 물음에 답하시오.

The more Stanley dug, the stronger he became. ⓐIt took less time to finish his hole each day. In his second week, as Stanley was finishing his hole, he saw something shiny in the dirt. Stanley's heart beat faster. He heard that anyone who found something interesting would be given the day off. He carefully picked up the shiny object and brushed off the dirt. It was a small gold tube. But it couldn't be real gold since it was too light. There were two letters, *KB*, at the bottom of the tube. What did KB ⓑstand for? Stanley's heart beat even faster.

08 밑줄 친 ⓐ를 다음과 같이 바꿔 쓸 때 빈칸에 들어갈 알맞은 단어를 쓰시오.

➡ Stanley spent less time ________ his hole each day.

09 위 글의 밑줄 친 ⓑstand for와 바꿔 쓸 수 있는 단어를 쓰시오.

➡ ______________________________

[10~12] 다음 글을 읽고 물음에 답하시오.

"Dig harder, Stanley! ⓐThe harder you dig, the faster you'll finish!" yelled Mr. Sir. Stanley Yelnats couldn't dig any harder since every single muscle hurt. He was thirsty and hungry. He wanted to go home. Unfortunately, Stanley's home for the next 18 months would be right here, at Camp Green Lake.

Camp Green Lake was a terrible name. It wasn't green and there was no lake. Camp Green Lake was hot and full of sand. In fact, it wasn't even a camp. It was a place for bad boys. Then what was a good boy ⓑlike Stanley doing here? He was sent to the camp for stealing a pair of sneakers.

10 위 글의 밑줄 친 ⓐ를 As로 시작하여 고치시오.

➡ ______________________________

중요
11 위 글의 밑줄 친 ⓑ와 바꿔 쓸 수 있는 말을 쓰시오.

➡ ____________________

고난이도
12 다음 빈칸 (A)~(C)에 알맞은 단어를 넣어 Camp Green Lake에 대한 소개를 완성하시오.

Camp Green Lake was not (A)________ ________ but a place for bad boys. Unlike its name, it wasn't (B)________ and there was no lake. In fact, it was hot and filled with (C)________.

교과서

구석구석

After You Read B

Monday, August 5th
Unfortunately, the camp isn't green and there is no lake. I'm in Group D. My group members have cool names like X-Ray, Zigzag and Zero. We have to dig one hole about 150cm deep and 150cm wide. The good news is this: anyone who finds something interesting can get the day off. I hope I can be the one.

- Unfortunately ↔ Fortunately
- like = such as
- have to = must
- deep 명사: depth
- wide 명사: width
- this 뒤에 나오는 내용을 가리킨다.
- anyone who = whoever
- something interesting -thing으로 끝나는 대명사를 수식하는 형용사는 대명사 뒤에 위치
- the one 뒤에 'who can get the day off'가 생략됨.

구문해설 • unfortunately: 불행히도 • dig: (구멍 등을) 파다 • hole: 구덩이, 구멍 • wide: 폭이 ~인

해석
8월 5일, 월요일
불행히도, 캠프는 초록색도 아니고 호수도 없다. 나는 D 그룹에 있다. 나의 그룹 멤버들은 X-Ray, Zigzag, Zero와 같은 멋진 이름들을 가지고 있다. 우리는 150cm 정도 깊이와 150cm 정도 너비의 구덩이 하나를 파야 한다. 좋은 소식은 다음과 같다. 흥미로운 뭔가를 발견한 사람은 그 날을 쉴 수 있다. 내가 그 사람이기를 바란다.

Word Power

- She bought a pair of shoes for 15 dollars.
  a pair of shoes: 쌍으로 이루어진 것, 2개의 비슷한 것이 하나의 물건을 이룰 때 'a pair of+복수명사'의 형태로 쓴다.
- I found a pair of glasses under the chair.
  a pair of glasses: 안경 한 개(2개의 비슷한 것이 하나의 물건을 이루는 것)
- He packed three pairs of jeans in his bag.
  three pairs of jeans: three가 있으므로 pair에 명사의 복수형 어미 s가 들어간다.

구문해설 • pack: (짐을) 싸다

- 그녀는 구두 한 켤레를 15 달러에 샀다.
- 나는 의자 아래에서 안경 한 개를 찾았다.
- 그는 가방에 청바지 세 벌을 쌌다.

Think and Write

Kate Barlow was a teacher in Green Lake. She was very popular.

Many rich men in the town wanted to marry her. But Kate fell in love with Sam, a poor man. The rich men tried to hurt Sam.

Later, Sam was found dead. Kate became sad and left the town.

- in the town: 형용사구
- to marry: 명사적 용법의 to부정사
- Sam, a poor man: 동격
- to hurt: 명사적 용법의 to부정사
- dead: 보어로 쓰인 형용사

구문해설 • fall in love with: ~와 사랑에 빠지다

Kate Barlow는 그린 레이크 마을의 교사였다. 그녀는 매우 인기가 있었다. 마을의 많은 부유한 남자들이 그녀와 결혼하고 싶어했다. 그러나 Kate는 가난한 남자인 Sam과 사랑에 빠졌다. 부유한 남자들은 Sam을 다치게 하려고 했다. 나중에 Sam은 죽은 채로 발견되었다. Kate는 슬퍼서 마을을 떠났다.

영역별 핵심문제

Words & Expressions

01 다음 짝지어진 단어의 관계가 같도록 빈칸에 알맞은 말을 쓰시오.

asleep : awake = ________ : top

[02~03] 다음 빈칸에 알맞은 단어를 고르시오.

02

The ____________ of a man is known from his conversations.

① education ② community ③ taste
④ character ⑤ production

03

You can __________ the next chapter if you have covered the topic in class.

① count ② skip ③ publish
④ include ⑤ figure

04 다음 우리말에 맞도록 빈칸에 알맞은 말을 쓰시오.

(1) 그것이 자외선 차단제를 사용하는 것이 중요한 이유이다.
➡ That is ________ it is important to use sunscreen.

(2) 그 케이크는 자동차처럼 보이게 장식되어 있었다.
➡ The cake was decorated to ________ ________ a car.

(3) 나는 이 단어를 사전에서 찾아보았는데 실려 있지 않았다.
➡ I've tried to ________ ________ this word in the dictionary, but haven't been able to find it.

Conversation

[05~06] 다음 대화를 읽고 물음에 답하시오.

B: Hi, Amy. Welcome (A)______ Korea.
G: Long time no see, Minho. ⓐ________ have you been?
B: Great. How did you come here (B)______ the airport?
G: I came here (C)______ subway.
B: ⓑ______ do you feel (D)______ the subway in Korea?
G: I think it's very clean.

05 빈칸 (A)~(D)에 들어가지 않는 말을 고르시오.

① from ② for ③ to
④ about ⑤ by

06 빈칸 ⓐ와 ⓑ에 공통으로 들어갈 말을 쓰시오.

➡ ____________________

[07~08] 다음 대화를 읽고 물음에 답하시오.

G: Brian, did you hear the news?
B: What news?
G: We can use smartphones (A)[during / while / after / when] classes from next week.
B: Yes, I heard that.
G: How do you feel about it?
B: I think it will be very (B)[different / useless / useful / careful]. (C)____________(look, don't, I, know, words, I, up, can)
G: Yeah. We can also find information on the Internet.
B: Right. It will be very helpful.

07 위 대화의 괄호 (A)와 (B)에서 적절한 것을 골라 쓰시오.

➡ (A) ____________ (B) ____________

08 빈칸 (C)를 괄호 안에 주어진 단어를 알맞게 배열하여 채우시오.

➡ ______________________________

[09~12] 다음 대화를 읽고 물음에 답하시오.

Tony: What are all these boxes, Suji?
Suji: They're items I ordered online. (①)
Tony: You like shopping on the Internet, don't you? (②)
Suji: Yes, I do. (③)
Tony: I don't like it at all.
Suji: Why?
Tony: It's very difficult to know what an item actually looks like. (④)
Suji: 그 점에는 동의해.
Tony: It's also difficult to (A)_______ an item if you don't like it. (⑤)
Suji: You're right, but I think it's very convenient.
Tony: Well, convenience isn't everything.

09 ①~⑤ 중 주어진 문장이 들어갈 곳은?

How do you feel about online shopping, Tony?

① ② ③ ④ ⑤

10 빈칸 (A)에 알맞은 말을 고르시오.

① borrow ② result ③ save
④ lend ⑤ return

11 밑줄 친 우리말과 일치하도록 주어진 단어를 사용해 영작하시오. (on)

➡ ______________________________

12 위 대화의 내용과 일치하지 않는 것을 모두 고르시오.

① Tony doesn't like shopping on the Internet.
② Suji doesn't agree with the idea that Tony has about online shopping.
③ Suji ordered items online.
④ Tony thinks that online shopping has many benefits.
⑤ Suji likes online shopping.

Grammar

13 다음 중 어법상 알맞은 것은?

① The more angrier Judy got, the more loudly she yelled.
② The high the expectation, the great the disappointment.
③ The more I got to know her, the more I liked her.
④ More technology develops, more people seem to miss traditional forms of communication.
⑤ The more you exercise, the healthier get.

14 주어진 단어의 형태가 바르게 짝지어진 것은?

> _______ you are to someone, _______ you need to be. (close, respectful)

① Close – respectful
② Closer – more respectful
③ The close – more respectful
④ The closer – the much respectful
⑤ The closer – the more respectful

15 다음 밑줄 친 부분과 바꿔 쓸 수 있는 것을 <u>모두</u> 고르면?

> <u>Because</u> I got up late, I had to run to school.

① Since ② That ③ What
④ As ⑤ While

16 다음 그림을 보고 주어진 어휘를 이용하여 빈칸에 알맞은 말을 쓰시오.

(1) __________ he works, ________________ he becomes. (much, tired)
(2) __________ he tries to be awake, ________________ he feels. (much, sleepy)

17 다음 중 빈칸에 들어갈 가장 적절한 말은?

> Tim fell asleep during English class since ________________________________.

① he stayed up the night before
② he felt awakening
③ it made him awake
④ it was very interesting
⑤ it was too bright to sleep

18 우리말과 일치하도록 괄호 안에 주어진 어휘를 이용하여 빈칸에 알맞게 쓰시오.

(1) 과일이 신선하면 할수록, 그것은 더 맛이 좋다.
➡ ____________________, the better it tastes. (the fruit, fresh)

(2) 햇빛이 매우 강했기 때문에 그녀는 모자를 써야 했다.
➡ ________________________________, she had to wear her hat. (the sunlight, strong)

19 다음 괄호 안에서 어법상 알맞은 것을 고르시오.

(1) (The nearer / nearer) the inn, (the longer / longer) the road.
(2) The Earth keeps getting (the warmer and the warmer / warmer and warmer) every year.
(3) My throat is sore (because / because of) a very bad cold.
(4) I couldn't call my friend (since / while) I didn't have my phone.
(5) (As / Before) it was raining, we couldn't go out.

Reading

[20~22] 다음 글을 읽고 물음에 답하시오.

"Dig harder, Stanley! The harder you dig, the faster you'll finish!" yelled Mr. Sir. Stanley Yelnats couldn't dig any harder since every single muscle hurt. He was thirsty and hungry. He wanted to go home. Unfortunately, Stanley's home for the next 18 months would be right here, at Camp Green Lake.

①Camp Green Lake was a terrible name. ②It wasn't green and there was no lake. Camp Green Lake was hot and full of sand. ⓐIn fact, ③it wasn't even ④a camp. It was a place for bad boys. ⓑ그렇다면 Stanley 같이 착한 소년이 여기서 무엇을 하고 있었을까? He was sent to ⑤the camp for stealing a pair of sneakers.

20 밑줄 친 ①~⑤ 중에서 가리키는 대상이 나머지 넷과 다른 것은?

① ② ③ ④ ⑤

21 위 글의 밑줄 친 ⓐIn fact와 바꿔 쓸 수 없는 말을 고르시오. (2개)

① Actually
② Thus
③ Reasonably
④ To tell the truth
⑤ As a matter of fact

22 위 글의 밑줄 친 ⓑ의 우리말에 맞게 주어진 어휘를 이용하여 10 단어로 영작하시오.

good, like

➡ ______________________

[23~25] 다음 글을 읽고 물음에 답하시오.

Stanley didn't really steal a pair of sneakers. (①) He was just in the wrong place at the wrong time. (②) One day, he was walking home from school. (③) Suddenly, a pair of old sneakers fell from the sky. (④)

He started running with the sneakers to tell his father __ⓐ__ happened. (⑤) A few minutes later, the police stopped Stanley and asked him why he was running. ⓑUnfortunately for Stanley, the sneakers were belonged to a famous baseball player, Clyde Livingstone. That was why Stanley ended up at Camp Green Lake.

23 위 글의 빈칸 ⓐ에 들어갈 알맞은 말을 고르시오.

① which
② when
③ that
④ where
⑤ what

24 위 글의 흐름으로 보아, ①~⑤ 중 다음 주어진 문장이 들어가기에 가장 적절한 곳은?

The sneakers hit him on the head.

① ② ③ ④ ⑤

25 위 글의 밑줄 친 ⓑ에서 어법상 틀린 부분을 찾아 고치시오.

➡ ______________________

[26~27] 다음 글을 읽고 물음에 답하시오.

Stanley was assigned to Group D in the camp. There were six other boys in Stanley's group. They all had ⓐcool names like X-Ray, Zigzag and Zero. Each boy had to dig one hole every day. It had to be about 150cm deep and 150cm wide. Mr. Sir said, "You are digging to build character."

26 위 글의 밑줄 친 ⓐcool과 같은 의미로 쓰인 것을 고르시오.

① She tried to remain cool and calm.
② It's a cool movie.
③ Let's sit in the shade and keep cool.
④ The rain will cool the air.
⑤ He felt sorry to receive a cool response from the public.

27 According to the passage, which is NOT true?

① Stanley belonged to Group D in the camp.
② There were seven boys in Stanley's group including Stanley.
③ The names of the other boys in Stanley's group were cool.
④ The boys cooperated to dig a hole every day.
⑤ The depth of the hole was the same as its width.

[28~30] 다음 글을 읽고 물음에 답하시오.

Stanley didn't really steal a pair of sneakers. He was just in the wrong place at the wrong time.

One day, he was walking (A)[home / to home] from school. Suddenly, a pair of old sneakers fell from the sky. The sneakers hit him on (B)[his / the] head.

He started running with the sneakers to tell his father what happened. A few minutes later, the police stopped Stanley and asked him why he was running. Unfortunately ⓐ_____ Stanley, the sneakers belonged ⓑ_____ a famous baseball player, Clyde Livingstone. That was (C)[because / why] Stanley ended up at Camp Green Lake.

28 위 글의 빈칸 ⓐ와 ⓑ에 들어갈 전치사가 바르게 짝지어진 것은?

	ⓐ ⓑ		ⓐ ⓑ
①	for – to	②	on – at
③	to – on	④	for – at
⑤	on – to		

29 위 글의 괄호 (A)~(C)에서 문맥이나 어법상 알맞은 낱말을 골라 쓰시오.

➡ (A)_______ (B)_______ (C)_______

30 According to the passage, which is NOT true?

① Stanley wasn't a thief who stole a pair of sneakers.
② A pair of awesome sneakers fell from the sky.
③ Stanley started to run with the sneakers so as to tell his father what happened.
④ The police stopped Stanley and asked him the reason for which he was running.
⑤ Clyde Livingstone was a famous baseball player.

단원별 예상문제

출제율 95%

01 빈칸 (A)와 (B)에 들어갈 말로 알맞은 것끼리 짝지어진 것을 고르시오.

• It wasn't her fault, but she was (A) ________ her best to help.
• It's good to (B)________ on developing something that'll be more profitable.

	(A)	(B)
①	trying	share
②	making	share
③	trying	focus
④	making	focus
⑤	trying	attend

출제율 100%

02 다음 빈칸에 들어갈 말을 <보기>에서 찾아 쓰시오. (단어는 한 번씩만 사용, 형태 변화 가능.)

보기
brush dig order raise

(1) Remember to specify your size when ________ clothes.
(2) She said that the world is too dangerous to ________ children.
(3) Mud ________ off easily when it is dry.
(4) The worker uses a machine to ________ the hole.

[03~04] 빈칸에 공통으로 들어갈 말을 쓰시오. (주어진 철자로 시작할 것.)

출제율 90%

03

• He couldn't e________ open the door.
• The female blue whale is e________ bigger than the male.

출제율 90%

04

• I've earned my own living s________ I was seven.
• Washing without soap would be best, s________ all soaps can pollute lakes and streams.

출제율 95%

05 다음 빈칸 (A)와 (B)에 들어갈 말로 알맞게 짝지어진 것은?

A: How do you feel about shopping on the Internet?
B: (A)________________
A: Can you tell me the (B)____________?
B: I can shop whenever I want.
A: I'm with you on that.

	(A)	(B)
①	I like it a lot.	– reason
②	I like it a lot.	– purpose
③	I like it a lot.	– way
④	I don't like it.	– opinion
⑤	I don't like it.	– reason

출제율 95%

06 다음 대화의 괄호 (A)~(C)에서 적절한 것을 골라 쓰시오.

A: How do you feel about (A)[eating / to eat] fast food?
B: I think it's (B)[bad / good]. Fast food has a lot of fat.
A: I don't agree. We can (C)[save / spend] time.

[07~09] 다음 대화를 읽고 물음에 답하시오.

B: Hey, Jessica. Why are you always ⓐto drink energy drinks?
G: Because they help me ⓑstaying awake.
B: (A)________________, but they have too ⓒ many caffeine.
G: Well, they help me focus ⓓin my studies.
B: Did you know that too ⓒmany caffeine ⓔ can hurt your bones?
G: Oh, I didn't know that.
B: I think you should drink energy drinks less often.
G: Maybe you're right. Thanks, Tom.

출제율 95%

07 빈칸 (A)에 알맞은 말이 〈보기〉에서 모두 몇 개인지 고르시오.

보기
• I couldn't agree with you more.
• Absolutely not.
• You're absolutely right.
• I'm not sure about that.
• No doubt about it.

① 1개 ② 2개 ③ 3개 ④ 4개 ⑤ 5개

출제율 95%

08 ⓐ~ⓔ 중 흐름상 또는 어법상 옳은 것을 고르시오.

① ⓐ ② ⓑ ③ ⓒ ④ ⓓ ⑤ ⓔ

출제율 90%

09 위 대화에서 다음 영영풀이에 해당하는 단어를 찾아 쓰시오.

not sleeping

➡ ________________

[10~12] 다음 대화를 읽고 물음에 답하시오.

Tony: What are all these boxes, Suji?
Suji: They're items I ordered online. (①)
Tony: You like shopping on the Internet, don't you?
Suji: Yes, I do. (②) 넌 온라인 쇼핑에 관해 어떻게 생각하니, Tony?
Tony: I don't like ⓐit at all.
Suji: Why? (③)
Tony: ⓑIt's very difficult to know what an item actually looks like.
Suji: I'm with you on that. (④)
Tony: ⓒIt's also difficult to return an item if you don't like ⓓit.
Suji: You're right, but I think ⓔit's very convenient.
Tony: Well. (⑤)

출제율 100%

10 ①~⑤ 중 주어진 문장이 들어갈 곳은?

Convenience isn't everything.

① ② ③ ④ ⑤

출제율 90%

11 밑줄 친 우리말과 일치하도록 주어진 단어를 이용해 영작하시오.

➡ ________________
(feel, about, online)

출제율 95%

12 밑줄 친 ⓐ~ⓔ 중 가리키는 것이 같은 것끼리 모은 것을 고르시오.

① ⓐ, ⓑ ② ⓐ, ⓒ
③ ⓐ, ⓓ ④ ⓐ, ⓔ
⑤ ⓐ, ⓓ, ⓔ

출제율 95%

13 다음 중 어법상 올바른 것은?

① The more you chew bread, the sweet it tastes.
② I think the more he has, the more he wants.
③ Since the mother began to clean it, the lamp was very dirty.
④ He bought two pair of sneakers and a cap at the store.
⑤ Though he had a headache, Jack went to see the doctor.

출제율 100%

14 다음 중 어법상 올바른 문장을 모두 고르시오. (정답 2개)

① The hard you study, the good you will do.
② This is because hotter it is, more energy it has.
③ The more we recycle, the less garbage ends up in landfills.
④ While he was sleepy, Mr. Smith went to bed early.
⑤ The game will be canceled since the weather is bad.
⑥ Because of he was sick, he couldn't go to school.
⑦ Ann drank two glass of waters since she was thirsty.

출제율 85%

15 괄호 안에 주어진 어휘를 활용하여 글자 수에 맞게 다음 우리말을 영작하시오.

(1) 그 의자가 좋으면 좋을수록, 너는 더 편하게 느낀다. (good, comfortable, the chair, feel, 10 단어)

➡ ______________________

(2) Tom은 피곤했기 때문에 일하는 것을 멈췄다. (since, tired, stop, work, 7 단어)

➡ ______________________

[16~18] 다음 글을 읽고 물음에 답하시오.

> Stanley ___ⓐ___ to Group D in the camp. There were six other boys in Stanley's group. They all had cool names like X-Ray, Zigzag and Zero. ⓑ각 소년은 매일 구덩이 하나를 파야 했다. It had to be ⓒabout 150cm deep and 150cm wide. Mr. Sir said, "You are digging to build character."

출제율 90%

16 위 글의 빈칸 ⓐ에 assign을 알맞은 형태로 쓰시오.

➡ ______________________

출제율 95%

17 위 글의 밑줄 친 ⓑ의 우리말에 맞게 주어진 어휘를 이용하여 9 단어로 영작하시오.

each, one, every

➡ ______________________

출제율 90%

18 위 글의 밑줄 친 ⓒabout과 바꿔 쓸 수 있는 말을 모두 고르시오.

① accurately ② roughly
③ around ④ exactly
⑤ approximately

[19~20] 다음 글을 읽고 물음에 답하시오.

> Kate Barlow was a teacher in Green Lake. She was very popular. ⓐMany rich men in the town wanted to marry with her. But Kate fell in love with Sam, a poor man. The rich men tried to hurt Sam. Later, Sam was found dead. Kate became sad and left the town.
>
> After 20 years, Kate returned to Green Lake with a lot of treasure. But Green Lake became a desert. She hid all her treasure somewhere in Green Lake. Many people wanted to find the treasure.

출제율 90%

19 위 글의 밑줄 친 ⓐ에서 어법상 틀린 부분을 찾아 고치시오.

➡ ______________________

출제율 100%

20 위 글을 읽고 알 수 없는 것을 고르시오.

① Where did Kate Barlow teach?
② Why was Kate Barlow very popular?
③ With whom did Kate fall in love?
④ What did the rich men try to do?
⑤ Where did Kate hide all her treasure?

[21~23] 다음 글을 읽고 물음에 답하시오.

"Dig harder, Stanley! The harder you dig, the faster you'll finish!" yelled Mr. Sir. Stanley Yelnats couldn't dig any harder since every single muscle hurt. He was thirsty and hungry. He wanted to go home. Unfortunately, Stanley's home for the next 18 months would be (A)right here, at Camp Green Lake.

Camp Green Lake was a terrible name. (①) It wasn't green and there was no lake. (②) Camp Green Lake was hot and full of sand. (③) In fact, it wasn't even a camp. (④) Then what was a good boy like Stanley doing here? (⑤) He was sent to the camp for stealing ⓐ_____ _____ sneakers.

출제율 90%

21 위 글의 빈칸 ⓐ에 들어갈 알맞은 말을 쓰시오.

➡ ______________________

출제율 100%

22 위 글의 밑줄 친 (A)right와 같은 의미로 쓰인 것을 고르시오.

① Turn right at the end of the street.
② I don't feel quite right today.
③ What gives you the right to do that?
④ Take the first street on the right.
⑤ Lee was standing right behind her.

출제율 95%

23 위 글의 흐름으로 보아, 주어진 문장이 들어가기에 가장 적절한 곳은?

It was a place for bad boys.

① ② ③ ④ ⑤

[24~25] 다음 글을 읽고 물음에 답하시오.

Monday, August 5th
Unfortunately, the camp isn't green and there is no lake. I'm in Group D. My group members have cool names like X-Ray, Zigzag and Zero. We have to dig one hole about 150cm deep and 150cm wide. The good news is this: anyone who finds something interesting can get the ⓐ_____ _____. I hope I can be the one.

출제율 95%

24 주어진 영영풀이를 참고하여 빈칸 ⓐ에 철자 d로 시작하는 단어를 쓰시오.

a day when you do not go to work, even though it is usually a working day

➡ ______________________

출제율 100%

25 위 글의 종류로 알맞은 것을 고르시오.

① e-mail ② essay
③ diary ④ review
⑤ article

서술형 실전문제

01 다음 대화에서 흐름상 어색한 것을 찾아 바르게 고치시오.

> B: Hey, Jessica. ①Why are you always drinking energy drinks?
> G: ②Because they help me stay awake.
> B: I'm with you on that, but they have too much caffeine.
> G: Well, they help me focus on my studies.
> B: Did you know that too much caffeine can hurt your bones?
> G: Oh, ③I didn't know that.
> B: ④I think you should drink energy drinks more often.
> G: ⑤Maybe you're right. Thanks, Tom.

➡ ____________________

02 다음 대화의 밑줄 친 부분 중 흐름상 어색한 것을 찾아 바르게 고치시오.

> A: How do you feel about reading books on a smartphone?
> B: I think it's good. We can read anytime.
> A: I'm with you on that. It's not good for our eyes.

➡ ____________________

03 밑줄 친 문장과 바꿔 쓸 수 있는 문장을 주어진 단어를 써서 바꿔 쓰시오.

> B: Hey, Jessica. Why are you always drinking energy drinks?
> G: Because they help me stay awake.
> B: I'm with you on that, but they have too much caffeine.
> G: Well, they help me focus on my studies.

➡ ____________________
(couldn't, more)

04 어법상 어색한 것을 찾아 바르게 고쳐 문장을 다시 쓰시오.

(1) I think older she grows, smarter she becomes.
➡ ____________________

(2) Ann drank a lot of water though she was thirsty.
➡ ____________________

(3) He closed the window because of the wind was blowing outside.
➡ ____________________

(4) Venus is hot though it is near the sun.
➡ ____________________

05 다음 문장을 접속사가 없는 문장으로 바꿔 쓰시오.

(1) As you dig harder, you'll finish faster.
➡ ____________________

(2) As we go up higher, it becomes colder.
➡ ____________________

[06~08] 다음 글을 읽고 물음에 답하시오.

"Dig harder, Stanley! The harder you dig, the faster you'll finish!" yelled Mr. Sir. ⓐStanley Yelnats couldn't dig any harder though every single muscle hurt. He was thirsty and hungry. He wanted to go home. Unfortunately, Stanley's home for the next ⓑ18 months would be right here, at Camp Green Lake.

Camp Green Lake was a terrible name. It wasn't green and there was no lake. Camp Green Lake was hot and full of sand. In fact, it wasn't even a camp. It was a place for bad boys. Then what was a good boy like Stanley doing here? He was sent to the camp for stealing a pair of sneakers.

06 위 글의 밑줄 친 ⓐ에서 흐름상 어색한 부분을 찾아 고치시오.

➡ ________________

07 위 글의 밑줄 친 ⓑ를 다음과 같이 바꿔 쓸 때 빈칸에 들어갈 알맞은 말을 두 단어로 쓰시오.

➡ one and ________ ________ years 또는 one year and ________ ________

08 Why was Stanley Yelnats sent to Camp Green Lake? Fill in the blank with a suitable word.

He was sent there on the grounds that he ________ a pair of sneakers.
*on the grounds that: …라는 이유로

[09~11] 다음 글을 읽고 물음에 답하시오.

Stanley didn't really steal a pair of sneakers. He was just in the wrong place at the wrong time. One day, he was walking home from school. Suddenly, a pair of old sneakers fell from the sky. The sneakers hit him on the head.

He started running with the sneakers to tell his father what happened. ⓐA few minutes later, the police stopped Stanley and asked him why was he running. Unfortunately for Stanley, the sneakers belonged to a famous baseball player, Clyde Livingstone. ⓑThat was why Stanley ended up at Camp Green Lake.

09 위 글의 밑줄 친 ⓐ에서 어법상 틀린 부분을 찾아 고치시오.

➡ ________________

10 위 글의 밑줄 친 ⓑ를 다음과 같이 바꿔 쓸 때 빈칸에 들어갈 알맞은 단어를 쓰시오.

➡ For that ________, Stanley ended up at Camp Green Lake.

11 위 글의 내용을 다음과 같이 정리하고자 한다. 빈칸 (A)와 (B)에 들어갈 알맞은 단어를 본문에서 찾아 쓰시오.

One day, a pair of old sneakers fell from the sky and hit Stanley (A)________ ________ ________. He ran with the sneakers just to tell his father what happened, but he (B)________ ________ at Camp Green Lake because of the sneakers.

창의사고력 서술형 문제

01 친구와 한국 음식 중 가장 맛있는 음식에 대한 의견을 말하고 있다. 다음 주어진 표현과 〈조건〉을 보고 대화를 완성하시오.

조건
- 동의하기나 반대 의견 말하기에 관한 표현을 반드시 사용할 것.
- 완벽한 문장으로 답할 것.

A: I think Kimchi is the best Korean food. How ____________________ (about, feel)
B: ____________________ (on, with)
A: Can you tell me why?
B: ________________________________ (delicious, healthy)

02 다음 그림을 보고, since를 활용하여 자유롭게 영작하시오.

(1) ________________________________
(2) ________________________________

03 다음 내용을 바탕으로 Stanley의 관점에서 경험한 내용을 쓴 글을 완성하시오.

1. A pair of sneakers fell from the sky. Stanley picked them up and started running home.
2. The police stopped Stanley. He was sent to Camp Green Lake.
3. Stanley met six other boys in Group D. Each boy had to dig one hole every day.
4. Stanley found a shiny gold tube in the dirt. He saw two letters at the bottom of it.

On my way home, I was hit by (A)______________. I picked them up and started (B)______________. The police stopped me and I was sent to (C)______________.
At the camp, I met six other boys in Group D. I had to dig (D)______________. One day, I found a shiny gold tube with two letters (E)______________ of it.

단원별 모의고사

01 빈칸을 주어진 영영풀이에 해당하는 말을 이용하여 채우시오.

to send someone to a particular group or place as part of a job

If an individual is ________ to a position out of his or her abilities, success will be harder to expect.

02 두 단어의 관계가 나머지와 다른 하나를 고르시오.

① dangerous – risky
② useful – useless
③ cruel – brutal
④ focus – concentrate
⑤ assign – allocate

03 빈칸 (A)와 (B)에 들어갈 말로 알맞은 것끼리 짝지어진 것을 고르시오.

• My suitcase was full (A)______ books. • The crown stands (B)_______ royal dignity.

(A) (B)
① of – for
② of – on
③ with – for
④ with – on
⑤ with – in

04 다음 우리말에 맞도록 빈칸에 알맞은 말을 쓰시오.

(1) 한 시간 후에, 혈당 수치를 측정하기 위해서 피검사를 할 것이다.
➡ One ________ ________, you'll have a blood test to measure your blood sugar level.

(2) 커피는 그가 자지 않고 깨어 있도록 도와줄 것이다.
➡ The coffee will help him ________ ________.

(3) 저 사진은 전혀 그녀처럼 보이지 않는다.
➡ That photograph doesn't look ________ her ________ ________.

05 주어진 문장 다음에 이어질 대화의 순서를 바르게 배열한 것을 고르시오.

How do you feel about shopping on the Internet?

(A) I can shop whenever I want. (B) Can you tell me the reason? (C) I like it a lot. (D) I'm with you on that.

① (B) – (A) – (C) – (D)
② (B) – (C) – (A) – (D)
③ (C) – (A) – (B) – (D)
④ (C) – (B) – (A) – (D)
⑤ (C) – (D) – (B) – (A)

[06~07] 다음 대화를 읽고 물음에 답하시오.

A: 수업 시간에 스마트폰을 사용하는 것에 대해 어떻게 생각해?
B: I think smartphones are useful in class. (A) ____________________(can, them, on, for, we, search, information)
A: I'm with you on that.

06 빈칸 (A)를 괄호 안에 주어진 단어를 알맞게 배열하여 채우시오.

➡ ______________________________

07 밑줄 친 우리말과 일치하도록 주어진 단어를 이용해 문장을 만드시오.

➡ ______________________________
____

(feel, use, in, about)

[08~10] 다음 대화를 읽고 물음에 답하시오.

B: Hey, Jessica. (A)[What / Why / How] are you always drinking energy drinks?
G: Because they help me stay awake.
B: ⓐ _______________ (caffeine, with, they, you, much, on, I'm, have, too, that, but)
G: Well, ⓑ공부에 집중하는 데 도움이 돼.
B: Did you know (B)[what / that] too much caffeine can hurt your bones?
G: Oh, I didn't know that.
B: I think you should drink energy drinks less often.
G: Maybe you're right. Thanks, Tom.

08 빈칸 ⓐ를 괄호 안에 주어진 단어를 알맞게 배열하여 채우시오.

➡ ______________________________
____

09 위 대화의 괄호 (A), (B)에서 적절한 것을 고르시오.

➡ (A) ___________ (B) ___________

10 밑줄 친 ⓑ의 우리말과 일치하도록 주어진 단어를 이용해 영작하시오.

➡ ______________________________ (they, focus, 7 단어)

[11~12] 다음 대화를 읽고 물음에 답하시오.

B: Hi, Amy. Welcome to Korea. (①)
G: Long time no see, Minho. (②) How have you been? (③)
B: Great. (④)
G: I came here by subway. (⑤)
B: (A)How do you feel about the subway in Korea?
G: I think it's very clean.

11 ①~⑤ 중 주어진 문장이 들어갈 곳은?

How did you come here from the airport?

① ② ③ ④ ⑤

12 밑줄 친 문장 (A)와 바꿔 쓸 수 있는 문장을 주어진 단어를 이용해 쓰시오.

➡ ______________________________
(about, what)

➡ ______________________________
(opinion)

13 빈칸을 채워 주어진 문장과 같은 의미의 문장을 쓰시오.

(1) As you fear something more, it will appear to be bigger.
= The more ______________________________
______________________.

(2) As the top of a tower is higher, it commands a finer view.
= The higher ______________________________
______________________.

14 다음 우리말을 주어진 어휘를 이용하여 영작하시오.

(1) 화가 날수록 카멜레온의 색깔은 더 밝아진다. (the chameleon, its color, become, angry, bright)
➡ ______________________

(2) 더 열심히 공부할수록 너는 더 좋은 성적을 얻을 수 있을 거야. (grades, study, get, good, hard)
➡ ______________________

(3) 그 운동화 때문에 그는 Camp Green Lake로 보내졌다. (because, sneakers, send)
➡ ______________________

(4) 지난여름 이후 모든 것이 매우 많이 달라졌다. (everything, have, change, since, so)
➡ ______________________

15 다음 문장의 빈칸에 들어갈 수 없는 말을 고르시오.

The ________, the better.

① shorter ② longer ③ richer
④ less ⑤ sweater

16 다음 중 어법상 어색한 것을 모두 고르시오.

① The drier the air is, the more water you need.
② The early they start, the soon they will arrive.
③ The more you study, the more you learn.
④ We didn't go on a picnic because of it rained a lot.
⑤ Stanley Yelnats couldn't dig any harder since every single muscle hurt.
⑥ Mina went home early though she felt very tired.
⑦ Since everything can be done by robots, life is more convenient.

[17~18] 다음 글을 읽고 물음에 답하시오.

"Dig harder, Stanley! The harder you dig, the faster you'll finish!" yelled Mr. Sir. Stanley Yelnats couldn't dig any harder since every single muscle hurt. He was thirsty and hungry. He wanted to go home. Unfortunately, Stanley's home for the next 18 months would be right here, at Camp Green Lake.

Camp Green Lake was a ___ⓐ___ name. It wasn't green and there was no lake. Camp Green Lake was hot and full of sand. In fact, it wasn't even a camp. It was a place for bad boys. Then what was a good boy ⓑlike Stanley doing here? He was sent to the camp for stealing a pair of sneakers.

17 위 글의 빈칸 ⓐ에 들어갈 알맞은 말을 고르시오.

① cool ② terrific
③ reasonable ④ awesome
⑤ terrible

18 위 글의 밑줄 친 ⓑlike와 같은 의미로 쓰인 것을 고르시오.

① She's wearing a dress like mine.
② Which bag do you like best?
③ Wild flowers like primroses are becoming rare.
④ He ran like the wind.
⑤ She acts like she owns the place.

[19~20] 다음 글을 읽고 물음에 답하시오.

Stanley didn't really steal a pair of sneakers. He was just in the wrong place at the wrong time. One day, he was walking home from school. Suddenly, a pair of old sneakers fell from the sky. ⓐ그 운동화는 그의 머리에 맞았다.
ⓑHe started running with the sneakers to tell his father what was happened. A few minutes later, the police stopped Stanley and asked him why he was running. Unfortunately for Stanley, the sneakers belonged to a famous baseball player, Clyde Livingstone. That was why Stanley ended up at Camp Green Lake.

19 위 글의 밑줄 친 ⓐ의 우리말에 맞게 주어진 어휘를 이용하여 7 단어로 영작하시오.

hit, on

➡ ____________________

20 위 글의 밑줄 친 ⓑ에서 어법상 틀린 부분을 찾아 고치시오.

➡ ____________________

[21~22] 다음 글을 읽고 물음에 답하시오.

The more Stanley dug, the stronger he became. (①) It took less time to finish his hole each day. (②) Stanley's heart beat faster. (③) He heard that anyone who found something interesting would be given the day off. (④) He carefully picked up the shiny object and brushed off the dirt. (⑤) It was a small gold tube. But it couldn't be real gold since it was too light. There were two letters, *KB*, at the bottom of the tube. What did KB stand for? Stanley's heart beat even faster.

21 위 글의 흐름으로 보아, 주어진 문장이 들어가기에 가장 적절한 곳은?

In his second week, as Stanley was finishing his hole, he saw something shiny in the dirt.

① ② ③ ④ ⑤

22 According to the passage, which is NOT true?

① As Stanley dug more, he became stronger.
② Stanley spent less time finishing his hole each day.
③ Anyone who found something interesting would be given the day off.
④ What Stanley found was a small gold tube.
⑤ There were two letters, *KB*, at the top of the tube.

[23~24] 다음 글을 읽고 물음에 답하시오.

Stanley was assigned to Group D in the camp. There were six other boys in Stanley's group. They all had cool names like X-Ray, Zigzag and Zero. Each boy had to dig one hole every day. ⓐIt had to be about 150cm deep and 150cm wide. Mr. Sir said, "ⓑYou are digging to build character."

23 위 글의 밑줄 친 ⓐIt이 가리키는 것을 본문에서 찾아 쓰시오.

➡ ____________________

24 위 글의 밑줄 친 ⓑ를 다음과 같이 바꿔 쓸 때 빈칸에 들어갈 알맞은 말을 쓰시오.

➡ (1) You are digging __________ build character. (2) You are digging __________ you _______ build character.

Believe in Yourself

의사소통 기능

- 기대 표현하기
  A: Are you going to travel to Jeju-do next week?
  B: Yes, I'm really looking forward to riding a horse.
- 거절하기
  A: Do you want to join me?
  B: I'd love to, but I can't. I have to do my homework.

언어 형식

- 가정법과거
  If I **were** a bird, I **would fly**.
- 의문사+to부정사
  We didn't know **how to read** music.

교과서

Words & Expressions

Key Words

- □ **afford** [əfɔ́:rd] 동 ~할 형편이 되다
- □ **appear** [əpíər] 동 나타나다
- □ **award** [əwɔ́:rd] 명 상
- □ **battle** [bǽtl] 명 전쟁, 전투
- □ **bored** [bɔ:rd] 형 지루해하는
- □ **cheek** [ʧi:k] 명 볼, 뺨
- □ **cheer** [ʧiər] 동 응원하다
- □ **drone** [droun] 명 무인 항공기
- □ **educator** [édʒukèitər] 명 교육자
- □ **environmental** [invàiərənméntl] 형 환경의
- □ **excited** [iksáitid] 형 신이 난, 흥분한
- □ **giant** [dʒáiənt] 형 거대한
- □ **gym** [dʒim] 명 운동, 체육관
- □ **gym class** 체육 수업
- □ **journey** [dʒɔ́:rni] 명 여행
- □ **landfill** [lǽndfil] 명 쓰레기 매립지
- □ **mostly** [móustli] 부 대부분, 일반적으로
- □ **musical instrument** 악기
- □ **none** [nʌn] 대 아무도 ~ 않다
- □ **ocean** [óuʃən] 명 바다
- □ **orchestra** [ɔ́:rkəstrə] 명 오케스트라, 관현악단
- □ **parade** [pəréid] 명 퍼레이드, 가두 행진
- □ **patience** [péiʃəns] 명 인내심
- □ **performance** [pərfɔ́:rməns] 명 공연
- □ **respect** [rispékt] 동 존경하다
- □ **roll** [roul] 동 구르다, 굴러가다
- □ **scared** [skɛərd] 형 무서워하는, 겁먹은
- □ **singing contest** 노래 경연 대회
- □ **speech** [spi:ʧ] 명 연설
- □ **stick** [stik] 동 붙이다
- □ **still** [stil] 부 아직도, 여전히
- □ **surprised** [sərpráizd] 형 놀란, 놀라는
- □ **talented** [tǽləntid] 형 재능 있는
- □ **thrilled** [θrild] 형 황홀해하는, 아주 신이 난
- □ **title** [táitl] 명 제목
- □ **trash** [træʃ] 명 쓰레기
- □ **tune** [tju:n] 명 곡, 곡조, 선율
- □ **violinist** [vàiəlínist] 명 바이올린 연주자
- □ **worried** [wɔ́:rid] 형 걱정하는

Key Expressions

- □ **a few+셀 수 있는 명사** 약간의, 몇 개의
- □ **be able to 동사원형** ~할 수 있다
- □ **be known as** ~로 알려지다
- □ **be made into** ~로 만들어지다
- □ **be made of** ~로 만들어지다
- □ **can't afford to 동사원형** ~할 형편이 못되다
- □ **cheer for** 응원하다
- □ **from then on** 그때부터 계속
- □ **give a big hand** 큰 박수를 보내다
- □ **give up** 포기하다
- □ **help with** ~를 돕다
- □ **how to 동사원형** ~하는 방법, 어떻게 ~할지
- □ **look forward to (동)명사** ~를 기대하다, 고대하다
- □ **one another** 서로
- □ **out of tune** 음이 맞지 않는
- □ **put ~ into practice** ~을 실행에 옮기다
- □ **step by step** 점차로, 차근차근, 하나씩
- □ **take care of** ~를 돌보다
- □ **take part in** ~에 참가하다
- □ **That's why ~.** 그것이 ~한 이유이다.
- □ **turn A into B** A를 B로 바꾸다

Word Power

※ 서로 비슷한 뜻을 가진 어휘

□ **award** (상) - **prize** (상)
□ **mostly** (대부분, 일반적으로) - **mainly** (주로, 대개는)
□ **take part in** (~에 참가하다) - **participate in** (~에 참가하다)
□ **journey** (여행) - **travel** (여행)
□ **take care of** (~를 돌보다) - **look after** (~를 돌보다)

※ 감정을 나타내는 동사의 형용사 쓰임

주어가 감정을 느끼는 주체일 경우에는 감정을 나타내는 형용사로 과거분사 형태를 쓰고, 주어가 감정을 느끼게 하는 경우에는 현재분사(동사원형-ing) 형태를 쓴다.

(1) 주어가 감정을 느끼는 주체인 경우

□ **thrilled** (아주 신이 난)
□ **excited** (신이 난, 흥분한)
□ **surprised** (놀란, 놀라는)
□ **worried** (걱정하는)
□ **scared** (무서워하는, 겁먹은)
□ **bored** (지루해하는)

(2) 주어가 감정을 느끼게 하는 경우

□ **thrilling** (아주 신나는)
□ **exciting** (신나는, 흥분하게 하는)
□ **surprising** (놀라운, 놀랄)
□ **worrying** (걱정할 만한)
□ **scaring** (겁주는, 위협적인)
□ **boring** (재미없는, 지루한)

English Dictionary

□ **afford** ~할 형편이 되다
→ to be able to pay for something
어떤 것의 비용을 지불할 수 있는

□ **award** 상
→ a prize or certificate that a person is given for doing something well
어떤 것을 잘해서 누군가에게 주어지는 상이나 증명서

□ **bored** 지루해하는
→ to feel tired and impatient because you have lost interest in something or because you have nothing to do
어떤 것에 흥미를 잃었거나 할 것이 없어져서 피곤함이나 짜증을 느끼는

□ **cheek** 볼, 뺨
→ either side of the face below the eyes
얼굴의 눈 아래 양쪽

□ **landfill** 쓰레기 매립지
→ an area where waste is buried under the ground
쓰레기가 땅 밑에 묻히는 지역

□ **look forward to (동)명사** ~를 기대하다, 고대하다
→ to want it to happen because you think you will enjoy it
당신이 그것을 즐길 것이라 생각해서 그것이 일어나기를 바라다

□ **patience** 인내심
→ the ability to stay calm and accept a delay or suffering without complaining
침착하고 불평 없이 지연이나 고통을 받아들이는 능력

□ **practice** 실행, 실천
→ action rather than ideas
생각보다는 행동

□ **scared** 무서워하는, 겁먹은
→ frightened of someone or something
어떤 사람이나 어떤 것에 대해 겁을 내는

□ **step by step** 점차로, 차근차근, 하나씩
→ in a gradual manner
점진적인 방식으로

□ **talented** 재능 있는
→ able or skillful
능력 있고 기술이 좋은

□ **thrilled** 황홀해하는, 아주 신이 난
→ very excited and happy
매우 신이 나고 행복한

□ **tune** 곡, 곡조, 선율
→ a series of musical notes that make a pleasing sound when played together
함께 연주되었을 때 유쾌한 소리를 내는 일련의 음표

01 빈칸에 'ing'나 'ed' 둘 중 하나가 들어갈 때 들어갈 말이 나머지와 다른 하나를 고르시오.

① They were frighten_____ of snakes.
② She was shock_____ to hear the news.
③ His stories are always interest_____.
④ I am thrill_____ to see him in person.
⑤ He was disappoint_____ at the test result.

중요
02 밑줄 친 부분의 단어가 의미상 어색한 것을 고르시오.

① I was surprised that he won the game.
② She is bored not only with music but also with arts.
③ Everybody was scared at the news that they won the gold medal.
④ I'm worried about the English test tomorrow.
⑤ The children were excited about their presents.

03 주어진 문장에서 밑줄 친 still의 뜻으로 사용되지 않은 것을 고르시오.

I still haven't done my English homework.

① Your friend is still waiting for you there.
② They still live in that house.
③ The house was still being built.
④ The rain became still heavier.
⑤ I'm still looking for work.

중요
04 주어진 두 문장이 같은 의미가 되도록 빈칸에 알맞은 말을 고르시오.

Who's going to look after the children while you're away? = Who's going to _______ the children while you're away?

① look forward to
② put off
③ look down on
④ take after
⑤ take care of

05 다음 영영풀이에 해당하는 단어로 알맞은 것은?

very excited and happy

① bored
② thrilled
③ worried
④ talented
⑤ scared

06 빈칸 (A)와 (B)에 알맞은 말로 짝지어진 것을 고르시오.

• He soon turned his dreams (A)_______ reality. • They went to Busan to take part (B)_______ the Busan International Film Festival.

(A) (B)
① into – in
② into – from
③ in – from
④ in – in
⑤ into – to

중요

01 다음 문장들에서 쓰임이 자연스럽지 않은 것을 찾아 고치시오.

ⓐ Can you show me how to do it?
ⓑ We can't afford to going abroad this summer.
ⓒ I'm really looking forward to work with you.

➡ ______________________

중요

02 다음 괄호 안의 단어를 문맥에 맞게 고쳐 빈칸에 쓰시오.

(1) The show was very _______. (bore)
(2) The news was _______ to everyone. (shock)
(3) His new book is really _______! (amaze)
(4) Mike was too _______ to do bungee jumping. (scare)

03 다음 빈칸에 공통으로 들어갈 말을 쓰시오.

- The novel, *Beauty and the Beast*, has been made _______ a movie.
- Gwanghwamun Plaza in central Seoul has been turned _______ a skating rink.
- She's determined to put her new ideas _______ practice.

고난이도

04 다음 우리말에 맞도록 빈칸에 알맞은 말을 쓰시오. (철자가 주어진 경우 주어진 철자로 시작할 것.)

(1) 나는 일을 서두르지 않고 차근차근 하는 중이다.
➡ I am not rushing things and I'm taking it _______ _______ _______.

(2) 그곳은 그 도시에서 가장 위험한 지역으로 알려져 있다.
➡ It's _______ _______ the most dangerous part of the city.

(3) 기타의 음이 맞지 않는다.
➡ The guitar is _______ of t_______.

(4) 그 이후 계속 그는 치아 관리를 잘 하게 됐어요.
➡ F_______ _______ _______, he started to _______ good care of his teeth.

(5) 야생동물 사진은 많은 인내심을 필요로 한다.
➡ Wildlife photography requires a lot of _______.

(6) 그 여행이 얼마나 걸릴 것인지 추정하기가 어렵다.
➡ It's difficult to judge how long the j_______ will take.

05 빈칸을 주어진 영영풀이에 해당하는 말을 이용하여 채우시오.

to be able to pay for something

➡ I'm not sure how they are able to _______ such expensive holidays.

교과서

Conversation

1 기대 표현하기

A Are you going to travel to Jeju-do next week? 다음 주에 제주도 여행을 갈 거니?
B Yes, I'm really looking forward to riding a horse. 응, 나는 말 타기를 정말 고대하고 있어.

- 'I'm looking forward to (동)명사 ~.'는 '나는 ~하기를 기대한다.'라는 뜻으로, 기대를 나타낼 때 사용하는 표현이다. to는 전치사로 뒤에 명사 또는 동명사(-ing)를 쓴다. 간절히 고대하는 것은 'I'm really looking forward to (동)명사 ~.'로 표현한다.
- 'I'm looking forward to (동)명사 ~.' 대신 쓸 수 있는 표현으로, 'I can't wait to ~'가 있는데 'can't wait to' 다음에는 동사원형을 써야 한다.

기대 표현하기

- I'm looking forward to (동)명사 ~. (나는 ~하기를 기대한다.)
- I'm excited about (동)명사 ~. (나는 ~하는 것이 신이 나.)
- I can't wait to 동사원형 ~. (나는 ~하는 것이 기다려져.)

핵심 Check

1. 다음 우리말과 일치하도록 빈칸에 알맞은 말을 쓰시오.

A: Are you going to Joohun's birthday party this Sunday?
B: Yes, I am. I'm ________ ________ ________ it. (나는 그것을 기대하고 있어.)

2. 다음 대화의 괄호 안에서 알맞은 말을 고르시오.

A: Are you going to go to the school festival next week?
B: Yes. I'm really looking forward to (go / going) there.

3. 다음 주어진 문장 이후에 올 대화의 순서를 바르게 배열하시오.

I'm looking forward to my school festival.
(A) It's this Friday. Anyone can come and join the festival.
(B) School festival? When is it?
(C) Sounds interesting! I'll go there.
➡ ______________________

2 거절하기

A Do you want to join me? 너는 나랑 함께 하고 싶니?
B I'd love to, but I can't. I have to do my homework. 그러고 싶지만, 그럴 수 없어. 숙제해야 해.

- 'I'd love to, but I can't.'는 '그러고 싶지만, 할 수 없어.'라는 뜻으로 상대방의 제안을 거절할 때 사용할 수 있는 표현이다. but 뒤에 거절할 수밖에 없는 이유를 부연하여 상대방의 이해를 구할 수 있다.
- 'I'd love to, but I can't.' 대신에 'I'm sorry, but I can't.', 'I'm afraid I can't.' 등을 사용할 수 있다.

거절하기

- I'd love to, but I can't. (그러고 싶지만, 그럴 수 없어.)
- I'm sorry, but I can't. (미안하지만, 안 되겠어.)
- I'm afraid I can't. (안 될 것 같아.)
- I'll take a rain check. (다음에 할게.)
- I wish I could, but I have to ~. (할 수 있으면 좋겠는데, 하지만 나는 ~해야 해.)
- Your suggestion sounds great, but ~. (너의 제안은 좋아보여, 하지만 ~.)

핵심 Check

4. 다음 우리말과 일치하도록 주어진 단어를 알맞게 배열하여 문장을 만드시오.

A: Do you want to watch a movie after school?
B: <u>그러고 싶지만, 나는 숙제를 해야 해.</u> (love, do, homework, I'd, to, my, have, but, I, to)
➡ ______________________________

5. 다음 대화의 빈칸에 알맞은 말을 쓰시오.

A: I'm planning to go on a picnic. Do you want to join me?
B: I'd ________ ________, ________ ________ ________. I have to visit my grandparents.

6. 다음 대화의 순서를 바르게 배열하시오.

(A) I'd love to, but I can't. I have to go to the Spanish class on Sunday.
(B) Yes, I like them.
(C) Great! Let's go to the K-pop concert this Sunday.
(D) Tony, are you interested in Korean pop songs?
➡ ____________________

Conversation 교과서 대화문 익히기

Listen and Speak 1 A

B: Hey, Bora. Welcome to our rock band.

G: Thanks. ❶I'm looking forward to playing in a concert with you.

B: We're ❷excited ❸to have a new guitar player.

G: Yeah. See you on Friday.

B: 얘, 보라야. 우리 록 밴드에 온 걸 환영해.
G: 고마워. 공연에서 너희들과 함께 연주할 게 기대돼.
B: 우리는 새로운 기타 연주자를 갖게 되어서 신나.
G: 잘됐다. 금요일에 봐.

❶ 'I'm looking forward to (동)명사 ~.'는 '~을 기대하다, 고대하다'라는 뜻으로, 어떤 일을 즐거운 마음으로 기대하는 상황에서 사용하는 표현이다.
❷ excited: 신난. 감정을 나타내는 동사의 형용사형으로 주어가 감정을 느끼는 주체일 경우에는 과거분사 형태를 쓰고, 주어가 감정의 대상인 경우에는 현재분사(동사원형-ing) 형태를 쓴다.
❸ to부정사의 부사적 용법 중 감정의 원인으로 '~하니까, ~해서'로 해석한다.

Check(√) True or False

(1) Bora is going to play in a concert. T ☐ F ☐

(2) They have practiced a lot for the concert. T ☐ F ☐

Listen and Speak 2 A

G: Minho, did you finish the math homework?

B: Not yet. Math is difficult.

G: Yes, but ❶it's interesting, too.

B: Then can you ❷help me with my math homework?

G: ❸I'd love to, but I can't. I ❹have to take care of my brother.

G: 민호야, 너 수학 숙제 끝냈니?
B: 아직. 수학은 어려워.
G: 맞아, 그렇지만 재미있기도 해.
B: 그럼 내 수학 숙제 좀 도와줄래?
G: 그러고 싶지만, 안 돼. 내 남동생을 돌봐야 해.

❶ it은 앞에서 언급된 math를 지칭한다. interesting: 흥미로운, 재미있는
❷ help A with B: A가 B하는 것을 돕다
❸ 'I'd love to, but I can't.'는 '그러고 싶지만, 할 수 없어.'라는 뜻으로 상대방의 제안을 거절할 때 사용할 수 있는 표현이다. but 뒤에 거절할 수밖에 없는 이유를 부연하여 상대방의 이해를 구할 수 있다.
❹ have to 동사원형: ~해야 한다 take care of: ~를 돌보다

Check(√) True or False

(3) Minho finished the math homework. T ☐ F ☐

(4) The girl will help Minho with his homework. T ☐ F ☐

Listen and Speak 1 B

G: Jiho, what are you reading?
B: I'm reading a book about baseball player ❶named Jim Abbott.
G: Oh, the man ❷who was born without a right hand?
B: That's right. He tried really hard and even ❸won the MVP award.
G: Yeah. His story ❹was made into a movie. ❺I'm going to watch it this Saturday.
B: Really? What's the title?
G: *Our Hero*. ❻I'm really looking forward to watching it.
B: Can I join you?
G: Sure. See you on Saturday.

G: 지호야, 뭘 읽고 있니?
B: Jim Abbott이라는 이름의 야구 선수에 관한 책을 읽고 있어.
G: 오, 오른손이 없이 태어난 그 사람?
B: 맞아. 그는 정말 열심히 노력해서 최우수 선수상까지 받았어.
G: 그래. 그의 이야기가 영화로 만들어졌어. 난 이번 주 토요일에 그 영화를 볼 거야.
B: 정말? 제목이 뭐니?
G: 'Our Hero'야. 그 영화를 볼 게 정말 기대돼.
B: 나도 너와 함께해도 될까?
G: 물론이지. 토요일에 봐.

❶ named는 동사 name(이름 짓다)의 과거분사형으로 '이름이 ~인'의 의미를 가지며, 앞의 명사 baseball player를 수식하고 있다.
❷ who는 주격 관계대명사로, 'who was born without a right hand'가 'the man'을 수식하고 있다. who 대신에 that을 사용할 수 있다. without: ~ 없이
❸ tried와 won은 접속사 and로 연결되어 있다.
❹ be made into ~: ~로 만들어지다
❺ 계획을 말할 때는 'be going to+동사원형'으로 말할 수 있다.
❻ 'I'm looking forward to ~.'는 앞으로 일어날 일에 대한 기대를 표현할 때 사용하는 표현으로, '나는 ~하기를 기대한다'의 의미이며 to 뒤에는 명사나 동명사가 온다. 비슷한 표현으로 'I'm excited about (동)명사 ~. (나는 ~하는 것이 신이 나.)', 'I can't wait to 동사원형 ~. (나는 ~하는 것이 기다려져.)' 등이 있다.

Check(√) True or False

(5) The movie, *Our Hero*, is about the man who was born without a left hand. T ☐ F ☐

(6) They are going to see the movie this Saturday. T ☐ F ☐

Listen and Speak 2 C

A: ❶What are you going to do this afternoon?
B: I'm going to ride my bike. Do you want to join me?
A: ❷I'd love to, but I can't. I have to ❸do my homework.
B: Okay, then next time.

A: 오늘 오후에 뭐 할 거니?
B: 나는 자전거를 탈 거야. 같이 탈래?
A: 그러고 싶지만, 안 돼. 나는 숙제를 해야 해.
B: 알겠어. 다음에 하자.

❶ 상대방에게 무엇을 할 계획인지(또는 어떤 계획이 있는지) 물어볼 때 'What are you planning[going] to+동사원형~?'을 사용할 수 있다.
❷ 'I'd love to, but I can't.'는 '그러고 싶지만, 할 수 없어.'라는 뜻으로 상대방의 제안을 거절할 때 사용할 수 있는 표현이다. but 뒤에 거절할 수밖에 없는 이유를 부연하여 상대방의 이해를 구할 수 있다.
❸ do one's homework: 숙제를 하다

Check(√) True or False

(7) A is going to ride a bike with B. T ☐ F ☐

(8) A should do his or her homework this afternoon. T ☐ F ☐

Listen and Speak 1 C

A: You ❶look happy today. ❷What's going on?
B: I'm so excited. I'm going to travel to Jeju-do.
A: That sounds great!
B: Yes, ❸I'm really looking forward to riding a horse.

❶ look+형용사: ~하게 보이다
❷ 'What's going on?'은 '무슨 일이야?'의 의미로, 여기에서는 상대방에게 행복해 보이는 이유를 물어보고 있다.
❸ 'I'm looking forward to (동)명사 ~.'는 '나는 ~하기를 기대한다.'라는 뜻으로, 기대를 나타낼 때 사용하는 표현이다. to는 전치사로 뒤에 명사 또는 동명사(-ing)를 쓴다. 간절히 고대하는 것은 'I'm really looking forward to (동)명사 ~.'로 표현한다.

Listen and Speak 2 B

G: Alex, ❶I'm going to take part in a singing contest next Monday.
B: That's great, Sumin!
G: You know ❷how to play the guitar, right?
B: Yes, ❸I've played the guitar for 3 years.
G: Great. Can you play the guitar ❹while I sing in the contest?
B: ❺I'd love to, but I can't. I hurt my hand in gym class yesterday.
G: Oh! ❻I'm sorry to hear that.
B: Thanks. But I'll be there to ❼cheer for you.

❶ be going to 동사원형: ~할 예정이다 take part in: ~에 참가하다
❷ '의문사+to부정사'는 주어, 목적어, 보어로 쓰인다. 여기서 'how to 동사원형(~하는 방법)'은 know의 목적어로 사용되었다.
❸ 'have p.p.'는 과거의 특정 시점에서 시작된 일이 현재까지 계속되고 있음을 나타내는 현재완료의 형태로, 여기서는 계속적 용법으로 사용되고 있다.
❹ while: ~하는 동안
❺ 'I'd love to, but I can't.', 'I'm sorry, but I can't.', 'I'm afraid I can't.' 등의 표현들은 상대방의 제안을 거절할 때 사용할 수 있다.
❻ 어떤 상황에 대하여 유감이나 동정을 표현할 때 'I'm sorry to hear that.'이라고 말할 수 있다
❼ cheer for: ~을 응원하다

Real Life Talk Watch a Video

Linda: Hi, Tony! ❶What are you going to do this weekend?
Tony: I'm going to watch the musical, *Billy Elliot*.
Linda: *Billy Elliot*? What is it about?
Tony: It's about a boy ❷who became a famous dancer. ❸I'm looking forward to watching it.
Linda: ❹Sounds interesting. Who is the main actor?
Tony: Jason Kim. He's a great dancer.
Linda: He's my favorite actor. I watched his musical last year.
Tony: Oh, really? Do you ❺want to join me?
Linda: ❻I'd love to, but I can't. I have volunteer work this weekend.
Tony: Okay. Maybe next time!

❶ 상대방에게 무엇을 할 계획인지(또는 어떤 계획이 있는지) 물어볼 때 'What are you planning[going] to+동사원형 ~?'을 사용할 수 있다.
❷ 선행사 'a boy'를 관계대명사절인 'who became a famous dancer'가 수식하고 있다.
❸ 'I'm looking forward to ~.'는 앞으로 일어날 일에 대한 기대를 표현할 때 사용하는 표현으로, '나는 ~하기를 기대한다.'의 의미이며 to 다음에는 명사나 동명사가 온다.
❹ sound+형용사: ~하게 들리다
❺ want는 to부정사를 목적어로 취하는 동사이다.
❻ 'I'd love to, but I can't.'는 '그러고 싶지만, 할 수 없어.'라는 뜻으로 상대방의 제안을 거절할 때 사용할 수 있는 표현이다. but 뒤에 거절할 수밖에 없는 이유를 부연하여 상대방의 이해를 구할 수 있다.

Real Life Talk Step 2

A: What are you going to do first?
B: I'm going to watch a parade at 10:30. ❶I'm really looking forward to watching it.
A: Sounds fun.
B: Do you want to join me?
A: ❷Yes, I'd love to. / I'd love to, but I can't. I'm going to get my face painted at that time.

❶ 'I'm looking forward to (동)명사 ~.'는 '나는 ~하기를 기대한다.'라는 뜻으로, 기대를 나타낼 때 사용하는 표현이다. to는 전치사로 뒤에 명사 또는 동명사(−ing)를 쓴다. 간절히 고대하는 것은 'I'm really looking forward to (동)명사 ~.'로 표현한다.
❷ 상대방의 제안에 응할 때는 'Yes, I'd love to.', 그렇지 않을 때는 'I'd love to, but I can't.'를 사용해서 대답할 수 있다. 거절할 때는 뒤에 거절할 수밖에 없는 이유를 부연하여 상대방의 이해를 구할 수 있다.

교과서 확인학습

Step3

• 다음 우리말과 일치하도록 빈칸에 알맞은 말을 쓰시오.

Listen and Speak 1 A

B: Hey, Bora. Welcome ________ our rock band.
G: Thanks. I'm ________ ________ to playing in a concert with you.
B: We're ________ ________ have a new guitar player.
G: Yeah. ________ ________ ________ Friday.

B: 얘, 보라야. 우리 록 밴드에 온 걸 환영해.
G: 고마워. 공연에서 너희들과 함께 연주할 게 기대돼.
B: 우리는 새로운 기타 연주자를 갖게 되어서 신나.
G: 잘됐다. 금요일에 봐.

Listen and Speak 1 B

G: Jiho, ________ ________ you reading?
B: I'm ________ a book ________ baseball player ________ Jim Abbott.
G: Oh, the man ________ ________ ________ ________ a right hand?
B: That's right. He tried really hard and ________ ________ the MVP award.
G: Yeah. His story ________ ________ ________ a movie. I'm ________ ________ watch it this Saturday.
B: Really? What's the title?
G: *Our Hero*. ________ ________ ________ ________ ________ watching it.
B: Can I join you?
G: Sure. See you ________ Saturday.

G: 지호야, 뭘 읽고 있니?
B: Jim Abbott이라는 이름의 야구 선수에 관한 책을 읽고 있어.
G: 오, 오른손이 없이 태어난 사람?
B: 맞아. 그는 정말 열심히 노력해서 최우수 선수상까지 받았어.
G: 그래. 그의 이야기가 영화로 만들어졌어. 난 이번 주 토요일에 그 영화를 볼 거야.
B: 정말? 제목이 뭐니?
G: 'Our Hero'야. 그 영화를 볼 게 정말 기대돼.
B: 나도 너와 함께해도 될까?
G: 물론이지. 토요일에 봐.

Listen and Speak 1 C

1. A: You look happy today. ________ going on?
   B: I'm so ________. ________ ________ ________ ________ to Jeju-do.
   A: That sounds great!
   B: Yes. I'm ________ ________ ________ ________ riding a horse.

2. A: You ________ ________ today. What's going on?
   B: I'm so excited. I'm going to ________ ________ ________ a drone.
   A: That sounds great!
   B: Yes. ________ ________ ________ forward ________ ________ a drone in the park.

3. A: You look happy today. What's ________ ________?
   B: I'm ________ ________. ________ ________ to see Jackson's concert.
   A: That sounds great!
   B: Yes. I'm really ________ ________ ________ ________ Jackson's performance.

1. A: 너 오늘 행복해 보인다. 무슨 일이야?
   B: 나는 아주 신나. 제주도로 여행을 갈 거야.
   A: 좋겠다!
   B: 응, 나는 말 타기를 정말 고대하고 있어.

2. A: 너 오늘 행복해 보인다. 무슨 일이야?
   B: 나는 아주 신나. 드론을 날리는 것을 배울 거야.
   A: 좋겠다!
   B: 응. 공원에서 드론을 날리는 것이 정말 기대돼.

3. A: 너 오늘 행복해 보인다. 무슨 일이야?
   B: 나는 아주 신나. Jackson의 콘서트를 볼 거야.
   A: 좋겠다!
   B: 응. Jackson의 공연을 보는 것이 정말 기대돼.

Listen and Speak 2 A

G: Minho, did you ________ the math homework?
B: Not yet. Math is ________.
G: Yes, but it's ________, ________.
B: Then can you ________ ________ ________ my math homework?
G: ________ ________ ________, but I can't. I ________ ________ ________ ________ ________ my brother.

해석
G: 민호야, 너 수학 숙제 끝냈니?
B: 아직. 수학은 어려워.
G: 맞아, 그렇지만 재미있기도 해.
B: 그럼 내 수학 숙제 좀 도와줄래?
G: 그러고 싶지만, 안 돼. 내 남동생을 돌봐야 해.

Listen and Speak 2 B

G: Alex, I'm going to ________ ________ ________ a singing contest next Monday.
B: That's great, Sumin!
G: You know ________ ________ ________ the guitar, right?
B: Yes, ________ ________ the guitar for 3 years.
G: Great. ________ ________ ________ the guitar while I sing in the contest?
B: I'd love to, ________ ________ ________. I hurt my hand in gym class yesterday.
G: Oh! I'm ________ ________ ________ that.
B: Thanks. But I'll be there to ________ ________ you.

G: Alex, 나 다음 월요일에 노래 대회에 참가할 거야.
B: 대단하다, 수민아!
G: 너 기타 칠 줄 알지, 그렇지?
B: 응, 3년 동안 기타를 쳤어.
G: 잘됐다. 내가 대회에서 노래하는 동안 기타를 쳐 줄 수 있니?
B: 그러고 싶지만, 안 돼. 어제 체육 수업 중에 손을 다쳤어.
G: 오! 유감이다.
B: 고마워. 하지만 너를 응원하러 거기에 갈게.

Listen and Speak 2 C

1. A: What are you ________ ________ ________ this afternoon?
   B: I'm going to ride my bike. Do you ________ ________ join me?
   A: I'd love to, ________ ________ ________. I ________ ________ do my homework.
   B: Okay, then ________ ________.

2. A: What ________ ________ ________ ________ do this afternoon?
   B: I'm going to play soccer. Do you want to ________ ________?
   A: ________ ________ ________, but I can't. I have ________ ________ my grandparents.
   B: Okay, then ________ ________.

1. A: 오후에 뭐 할 거니?
   B: 나는 자전거를 탈 거야. 같이 할래?
   A: 그러고 싶지만, 안 돼. 나는 숙제를 해야 해.
   B: 알겠어, 다음에 하자.

2. A: 오후에 뭐 할 거니?
   B: 나는 축구를 할 거야. 같이 할래?
   A: 그러고 싶지만, 안 돼. 나는 조부모님 댁을 방문해야 해.
   B: 알겠어, 다음에 하자.

Real Life Talk Watch a Video

Linda: Hi, Tony! ________ ________ ________ ________ to do this weekend?

Tony: I'm going to ________ the musical, *Billy Elliot*.

Linda: *Billy Elliot*? What is ________ ________?

Tony: It's ________ ________ ________ ________ ________ a famous dancer. I'm ________ ________ ________ ________ it.

Linda: Sounds ________. Who is the main actor?

Tony: Jason Kim. He's a great dancer.

Linda: He's my favorite actor. I ________ his musical last year.

Tony: Oh, really? Do you ________ ________ ________ me?

Linda: I'd love to, ________ ________ ________. I have ________ work this weekend.

Tony: Okay. Maybe ________ time!

해석

Linda: 안녕, Tony! 이번 주말에 뭐 할 거니?
Tony: 나는 뮤지컬 'Billy Elliot'를 볼 거야.
Linda: 'Billy Elliot'? 무슨 내용이니?
Tony: 유명한 무용수가 된 한 소년에 관한 내용이야. 그 뮤지컬을 볼 게 기대돼.
Linda: 재미있겠다. 주연 배우가 누구니?
Tony: Jason Kim이야. 그는 훌륭한 무용수야.
Linda: 그는 내가 가장 좋아하는 배우야. 작년에 그의 뮤지컬을 봤어.
Tony: 오, 정말? 나와 함께 가고 싶니?
Linda: 그러고 싶지만, 안 돼. 이번 주말에 자원봉사 활동이 있어.
Tony: 알겠어. 다음에 같이 가자!

Real Life Talk Step 2

1. **A:** What are you going to do first?
   B: ________ ________ ________ ________ a parade at 10:30. I'm really looking forward ________ ________ it.
   A: Sounds ________.
   B: Do you want to join me?
   A: Yes, I'd ________ ________. / I'd love to, ________ ________ ________. I'm going to get ________ ________ ________ at that time.

2. **A:** What are you ________ ________ ________ ________?
   B: I'm going to play a water balloon game ________ 12:30. ________ ________ ________ forward to ________ ________.
   A: ________ fun.
   B: Do you want to join me?
   A: Yes, I'd love to. / ________ ________ ________, ________ I can't. I'm going to have the longest hot dog at that time.

1. **A:** 처음에 무엇을 할 거니?
   B: 10시 30분에 퍼레이드를 볼 거야. 퍼레이드 보는 것이 정말 기대돼.
   A: 재미있겠다.
   B: 너도 같이 할래?
   A: 응, 그래. / 그러고 싶지만, 안 돼. 나는 그 때 얼굴에 페이스 페인팅을 할 거야.

2. **A:** 다음에 무엇을 할 거니?
   B: 물풍선 게임을 12시 30분에 할 거야. 나는 그것을 하는 것이 정말 기대돼.
   A: 재미있겠다.
   B: 너도 같이 할래?
   A: 응, 그래. / 그러고 싶지만, 안 돼. 나는 그 때 가장 긴 핫도그를 먹을 거야.

[01~02] 다음 대화의 빈칸에 알맞은 것을 고르시오.

01

G: Minho, did you finish the math homework?
B: Not yet. Math is difficult.
G: Yes, but it's interesting, too.
B: Then can you help me with my math homework?
G: ____________________ I have to take care of my brother.

① I'd love to, but I can't.
② Sure, I can.
③ I don't know what you meant.
④ Yes, I'd love to.
⑤ No, I am not.

02

A: You look happy today. What's going on?
B: I'm so excited. I'm going to learn to fly a drone.
A: That sounds great!
B: Yes, ______________________________.

① I'm not interested in flying a drone in the park
② I'm really looking forward to flying a drone in the park
③ I don't want to fly a drone in the park
④ I didn't wait to fly a drone in the park
⑤ I'm not good at flying a drone in the park

03 다음 대화의 밑줄 친 부분과 바꿔 쓸 수 없는 것은? (2개)

B: Hey, Bora. Welcome to our rock band.
G: Thanks. <u>I'm looking forward to playing in a concert with you.</u>
B: We're excited to have a new guitar player.
G: Yeah. See you on Friday.

① I can't wait to play in a concert with you.
② I'm not interested in playing in a concert with you.
③ I really want to play in a concert with you.
④ I want to be good at playing in a concert with you.
⑤ I'm excited about playing in a concert with you.

[01~03] 다음 대화를 읽고 물음에 답하시오.

G: Jiho, what are you reading?
B: I'm reading a book about baseball player named Jim Abbott. (①)
G: Oh, the man who was born without a right hand?
B: That's right. (②) He tried really hard and even won the MVP award. (③)
G: Yeah. (④) I'm going to watch it this Saturday.
B: Really? What's the title?
G: *Our Hero*. (⑤) ________ (A) ________
B: Can I join you?
G: Sure. See you on Saturday.

중요

01 위 대화의 ①~⑤ 중 주어진 문장이 들어갈 알맞은 곳은?

His story was made into a movie.

① ② ③ ④ ⑤

02 빈칸 (A)에 알맞은 말을 모두 고르시오.

① I'm really looking forward to watch it.
② I really want to watching it.
③ I can't wait to watching it.
④ I'm really looking forward to watching it.
⑤ I can't wait to watch it.

03 위 대화의 내용과 일치하는 것을 모두 고르시오.

① 지호와 소녀는 토요일에 만나서 영화를 같이 볼 것이다.
② 소녀는 Jim Abbott과 관련된 영화의 제목을 모르고 있다.
③ Jim Abbott은 오른손이 없는 야구 선수이다.
④ 지호는 토요일에 Jim Abbott에 관한 책을 읽을 것이다.
⑤ 소녀는 Jim Abbott이 누구인지 몰랐다.

[04~06] 다음 대화를 읽고 물음에 답하시오.

G: Minho, did you finish the math homework?
B: Not yet. Math is difficult.
G: Yes, ___ⓐ___ it's interesting, too.
B: Then can you help me ___(A)___ my math homework?
G: I'd love to, ___ⓑ___ I can't. I have to take care of my brother.

04 빈칸 (A)에 알맞은 말을 고르시오.

① in ② on ③ with
④ off ⑤ to

05 빈칸 ⓐ와 ⓑ에 공통으로 들어갈 말을 고르시오.

① and ② so ③ but
④ nor ⑤ for

06 위 대화의 내용과 일치하는 것을 고르시오.

① Minho has a brother.
② The girl can't help Minho to do his homework.
③ Minho thinks that math is easy.
④ The girl thinks that math is not interesting but difficult.
⑤ Minho has finished his math homework.

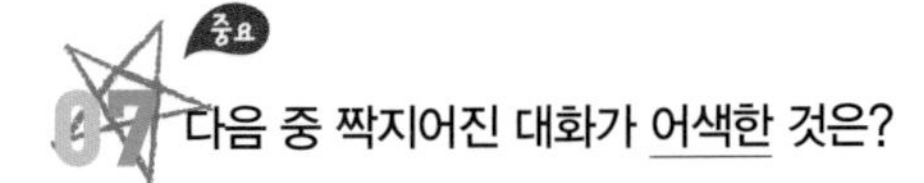

07 다음 중 짝지어진 대화가 어색한 것은?

① A: I'm excited that we're going to high school next March.
B: Yeah. I can't wait to start high school.

② A: What are you looking forward to doing in high school?
B: I'm looking forward to making a lot of new friends.

③ A: I want to go skiing this winter. How about you?
B: I'm looking forward to taking a trip.

④ A: Could I ask you to give me a ride?
B: I'd love to, but I'm very busy now.

⑤ A: I'm going to visit Insa-dong this Sunday. Will you join me?
B: Sure. I'd love to, but I can't.

[08~10] 다음 대화를 읽고 물음에 답하시오.

Linda: Hi, Tony! What are you going to do this weekend?
Tony: I'm going to watch the musical, *Billy Elliot*.
Linda: *Billy Elliot*? What is it about?
Tony: It's about a boy who became a famous dancer. (a)I'm looking forward to watch it.
Linda: Sounds interesting. Who is the main actor?
Tony: Jason Kim. He's a great dancer.
Linda: He's my favorite actor. I watched his musical last year.
Tony: Oh, really? Do you want to join me?
Linda: ________(A)________ I have volunteer work this weekend.
Tony: Okay. Maybe next time!

08 <보기>에서 위 대화의 빈칸 (A)에 알맞은 말이 모두 몇 개인지 고르시오.

보기
ⓐ I'm afraid I can't.
ⓑ I wish I could, but
ⓒ Your suggestion sounds great. I would
ⓓ Of course.
ⓔ I'm sorry, but I can't.
ⓕ I'd love to, but I can't.
ⓖ Yes, I do.

① 2개 ② 3개 ③ 4개 ④ 5개 ⑤ 6개

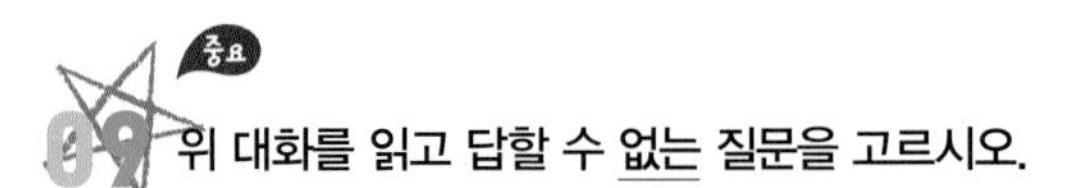

09 위 대화를 읽고 답할 수 없는 질문을 고르시오.

① What is the musical, *Billy Elliot*, about?
② How long has Linda had volunteer work?
③ When did Linda watch the musical in which Jason Kim acted?
④ What is Tony going to do this weekend?
⑤ Who is the main actor in *Billy Elliot*?

서답형

10 밑줄 친 (a)에서 어법상 어색한 것을 바르게 고치시오.

__________ ➡ __________

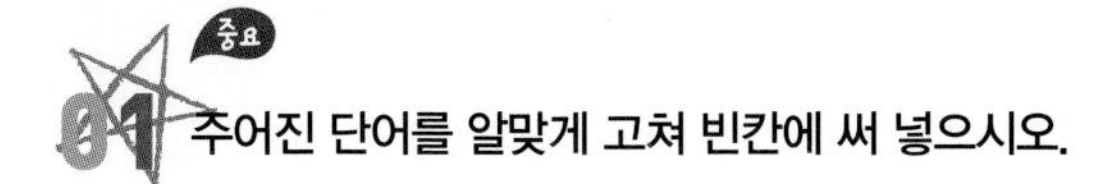

중요

01 주어진 단어를 알맞게 고쳐 빈칸에 써 넣으시오.

> G: Jiho, what are you reading?
> B: I'm reading a book about baseball player ___(A)___ (name) Jim Abbott.
> G: Oh, the man who was born without a right hand?
> B: That's right. He tried really hard and even won the MVP award.
> G: Yeah. His story was made into a movie. I'm going to watch it this Saturday.
> B: Really? What's the title?
> G: *Our Hero*. I'm really looking forward ___(B)___ (watch) it.
> B: Can I join you?
> G: Sure. See you on Saturday.

(A) ______________
(B) ______________(2 단어)

[02~03] 다음 대화를 읽고 물음에 답하시오.

> G: Minho, did you finish the math homework?
> B: Not yet. Math is difficult.
> G: Yes, but it's interesting, too.
> B: Then can you help me with my math homework?
> G: I'd love to, ___(A)___. I have to take care ___(B)___ my brother.

02 대화의 흐름상 빈칸 (A)에 들어갈 알맞은 말을 주어진 단어를 이용하여 쓰시오. (3 words)

(can)

➡ ______________

03 빈칸 (B)에 알맞은 전치사를 쓰시오.

➡ ______________

[04~05] 다음 대화를 읽고 물음에 답하시오.

> Linda: Hi, Tony! (A)What are you going to do this weekend?
> Tony: I'm going to watch the musical, *Billy Elliot*.
> Linda: *Billy Elliot*? What is it about?
> Tony: (B)It's about a boy who became a famous dancer. (a)그 뮤지컬을 볼 게 기대돼.
> Linda: Sounds interesting. Who is the main actor?
> Tony: Jason Kim. He's a great dancer.
> Linda: He's my favorite actor. (C)I watched his musical last year.
> Tony: Oh, really? (D)Do you want to join me?
> Linda: (E)Of course. I have volunteer work this weekend.
> Tony: Okay. Maybe next time!

04 밑줄 친 (A)~(E) 중 흐름상 어색한 것을 고르고 바르게 고치시오.

➡ ______________

05 밑줄 친 (a)의 우리말을 주어진 단어를 이용하여 영작하시오.

look, watch, it

➡ ______________

교과서

Grammar

1 가정법과거

• **If** I **were** a bird, I **would fly.** 내가 새라면, 날아갈 텐데.

■ '만약 ~라면 …할 텐데'라는 뜻으로, 현재 사실을 반대로 가정하거나 실현 가능성이 없는 일에 대해서 가정할 때 쓰며, 'If+주어+were/동사의 과거형 ~, 주어+조동사의 과거형(would/should/could/might)+동사원형 …'의 형태로 나타낸다. 가정법이 사용된 문장이라는 표시로 if절에 과거 동사를 사용할 뿐이며, 의미상 과거를 나타내지 않는다.

■ 가정법과거 문장은 현재시제의 직설법으로 바꿔 쓸 수 있다.

• If she **knew** how, she **would apply** to the university. 그녀가 방법을 알면 대학에 지원할 텐데.
(가정법과거, 현재 사실의 반대 가정)
= As she doesn't know how, she won't apply to the university.
그녀는 방법을 모르기 때문에, 대학에 지원하지 않을 것이다.
cf. If she knows how, she will apply to the university. 그녀가 방법을 안다면, 대학에 지원할 것이다.
(조건문, 사실)

■ 'be'동사는 주어의 인칭 및 수와 무관하게 'were'를 쓰지만, 구어체에서는 주어가 'I' 또는 3인칭 단수인 경우 'was'를 쓰기도 한다.

• If I **were[was]** rich enough, I **would buy** it. 내가 돈이 넉넉하면 그것을 살 텐데.

■ 가정법의 다양한 표현

• As she is poor, she cannot buy that house. 그녀는 가난하기 때문에, 그 집을 살 수 없다. (직설법)
= If she were not poor, she could buy that house. 그녀가 가난하지 않다면, 그 집을 살 수 있을 텐데. (가정법)
= Were she not poor, she could buy that house. (가정법)

• If it were not for the sun, we could not live at all. 만일 태양이 없다면, 우리는 전혀 살 수 없을 텐데.
= Were it not for the sun, we could not live at all. (If 생략 후 도치)
= Without the sun, we could not live at all. (without = if it were not for)

※ if절의 동사가 'were' 또는 'had'일 때 if를 생략하여 쓸 수 있으며, 이때 주어와 동사가 도치된다.

핵심 Check

1. 다음 우리말에 맞게 괄호 안의 단어를 바르게 배열하시오.
내가 너라면, 좀 더 오래 기다릴 텐데. (you, I, I, if, wait, would, were, longer, a little)
➡ ______________________________

2 의문사+to부정사

- We didn't know **how to read** music. 우리는 악보를 읽는 방법을 알지 못했다.
- Don't tell me **what to do**! 나한테 이래라저래라 하지 말아요!

■ '의문사+to부정사'는 'what/when/where/how/which/who(m)+to부정사'의 형태로 쓰이며, 문장 속에서 주어, 목적어, 보어 역할을 하는 명사구로 사용되며, '~할지'라는 뜻을 나타낸다. 주로 동사의 목적어로 사용된다. 'why+to부정사'는 쓰이지 않는다.

- **How to save** money is very important. (주어) 돈을 저축하는 방법은 매우 중요하다.
- I don't know **how to save** money. (know의 목적어) 나는 돈을 저축하는 방법을 모르겠어.

의문사	to부정사	의미
what	to do	무엇을 해야 할지
when	to begin	언제 시작해야 할지
where	to go	어디로 가야 할지
how	to make	어떻게 만드는지(만드는 방법)
which	to select	어떤 것을 선택해야 할지
who(m)	to call	누구에게 전화를 해야 할지

■ 의문사가 의문형용사로 쓰여 '의문형용사+명사+to부정사'나 '의문부사+형용사+to부정사' 형태로도 사용된다.

- I hesitated over **which one to choose**. 난 어떤 것을 고를지 몰라 우물쭈물했다.
- I didn't know **how much to bring**. 나는 얼마나 많이 가져와야 할지 몰랐다.

■ '의문사+to부정사'는 '의문사+주어+should[can]+동사원형'으로 바꿔 쓸 수 있다.

- I can't decide **what to wear**. 무엇을 입을 것인지 결정할 수가 없어.
  = I can't decide **what I should wear**.
- She knows **how to persuade** her dad. 그녀는 자기 아빠를 설득시키는 법을 안다.
  = She knows **how she can persuade** her dad.

핵심 Check

2. 다음 우리말에 맞게 빈칸에 알맞은 말을 쓰시오.

(1) 이 팩스 사용할 줄 아세요?

➡ Do you know ________ ________ ________ this fax machine?

(2) 어디에 제 차를 주차해야 할지 제게 말해주시겠어요?

➡ Can you tell me ________ ________ ________ my car?

01 다음 가정법 문장에서 어법상 어색한 단어를 한 개씩 찾아 고치시오.

(1) If I have a lot of money, I would travel around the world.

__________ ➡ __________

(2) If I were a teacher, I will not make my students do much homework.

__________ ➡ __________

(3) If I know your address, I would send you a letter.

__________ ➡ __________

(4) I will start looking for another job if I were you.

__________ ➡ __________

02 다음 중 어법상 바르지 않은 것은?

① We didn't know how to make a kite.
② You will be instructed where to go as soon as the plane is ready.
③ I can't find why to stay here.
④ The problem lies in deciding when to start.
⑤ Nobody knew what to say.

03 다음 빈칸에 들어갈 말로 알맞은 것은?

If I ________ a famous movie star, I would hold many fan meetings.

① had ② am ③ have been
④ were ⑤ be

04 다음 문장을 should를 이용하여 다시 쓰시오.

I did not know whom to thank for the gift.

➡ ______________________________

Grammar 시험대비 실력평가

Step3

01 다음 중 어법상 어색한 문장은?

① If I had wings, I could get out of this maze.
② If it were not for the expense, I would go.
③ If it were raining, I would put on the rain coat.
④ What will you do if another war occurred?
⑤ If the weather were nice, we would go outside.

02 다음 빈칸에 알맞은 것은?

I don't know ________ to cook the eggs.

① how ② what ③ that
④ why ⑤ whom

03 다음 문장의 밑줄 친 단어들 중 어법상 어색한 단어는?

①If I ②have a time machine, I ③would ④go back to ⑤ancient Korea.

① ② ③ ④ ⑤

04 다음 중 어법상 바르지 않은 것은?

① Do you know how to make spaghetti?
② Let me know whom to ask about the problem.
③ Have you decided where to go?
④ I will contact you later to advise you when to come.
⑤ I don't know what to do it next.

05 다음 중 같은 뜻을 가진 문장끼리 짝지어진 것은?

① It is snowy, so she wants to make a snowman.
= If it is snowy, she would want to make a snowman.
② Jim didn't have a car, so he couldn't drive.
= If Jim had a car, he couldn't drive.
③ I don't have a computer, so I can't get better grades.
= If I had a computer, I'd get better grades.
④ Mina doesn't have a smartphone, so she wants to have one.
= Mina wants a smartphone if she had a smartphone.
⑤ I can't send an e-mail to her, so I don't know her address.
= I could send an e-mail to her if I knew her address.

06 주어진 문장의 밑줄 친 부분과 용법이 다른 것은?

Miranda doesn't know how to use the copy machine.

① People are pleased to use the copy machine.
② He told me when to use the copy machine.
③ We started to use the copy machine last month.
④ Can you teach me how to use the copy machine?
⑤ We plan to use the copy machine at our office.

[07~08] 다음 우리말을 바르게 영작한 것을 고르시오.

07

내가 타임머신이 있다면, 세종대왕을 만나러 갈 수 있을 텐데.

① If I have a time machine, I can go to meet King Sejong.
② If I have a time machine, I could go to meet King Sejong.
③ If I had a time machine, I could go to meet King Sejong.
④ If I had a time machine, I can go to meet King Sejong.
⑤ If I had had a time machine, I could have gone to meet King Sejong.

08

Alex는 그 책을 어디에서 사야 할지 알아냈다.

① Alex found out when to buy the book.
② Alex found out where to buy the book.
③ Alex found out to buy the book where.
④ Alex found out the book to buy where.
⑤ Alex found out to buy where the book.

서답형

09 다음 괄호 안에서 어법상 바른 것을 고르시오.

(1) If you (are / were) a doctor, what would you do?
(2) If I (have / had) a magic lamp, I would make three wishes.
(3) He knows (what / how) to ride a bicycle.
(4) I didn't know when (to go / going) to the station.

중요

10 다음 문장의 빈칸 (A)~(C)에 들어갈 말로 가장 적절한 것은?

• If there ___(A)___ more workers, the company could take better care of them.
• Were it not for water and air, what ___(B)___ become of us?
• If I ___(C)___ a lot of money, I would travel around the world.

	(A)	(B)	(C)
①	was	will	have
②	was	could	have
③	will be	could	had had
④	were	would	had
⑤	were	will	had

서답형

11 두 문장의 의미가 같도록 빈칸에 알맞은 말을 쓰시오.

(1) I sometimes teach them how to write Hangul.
= I sometimes teach them ________ ________ ________ ________ Hangul.

(2) I don't know when to bring the birthday cake in.
= I don't know ________ ________ ________ ________ the birthday cake in.

(3) Please tell me what to do.
= Please tell me ________ ________ ________ ________.

12 다음 문장과 같은 의미의 문장을 고르시오.

If there were no air, we couldn't live.

① We can live so there is air.
② There is no air, so we can't live.
③ Though there is air, we can live.
④ As there is no air, we can't live.
⑤ As there is air, we can live.

13 다음 빈칸에 적절한 것을 모두 고르시오.

They talked about ________ to meet again and said goodbye.

① what ② where ③ which
④ when ⑤ why

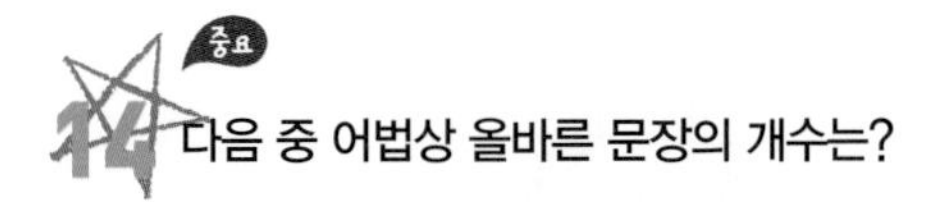

14 다음 중 어법상 올바른 문장의 개수는?

ⓐ If I have a million dollars, I would buy a driverless car.
ⓑ If he were a policeman, he will help people.
ⓒ I want to learn how to fly a drone.
ⓓ Have you decided where going for your vacation?
ⓔ David wanted to know where to send those goods.
ⓕ My family is exciting about the trip to America.
ⓖ The child was so scare at the big dog.

① 1개 ② 2개 ③ 3개 ④ 4개 ⑤ 5개

15 다음 우리말을 영작할 때, 바르지 않은 문장을 고르시오.

만일 컴퓨터가 없다면 우리 생활은 매우 불편할 텐데.

① But for no computers, our lives would be very inconvenient.
② If it were not for computers, our lives would be very inconvenient.
③ If there are no computers, our lives would be very inconvenient.
④ Were it not for computers, our lives would be very inconvenient.
⑤ Without computers, our lives would be very inconvenient.

서답형

16 다음 문장에서 틀린 것을 고쳐 다시 쓰시오.

(1) If it snows all night, I would not leave tomorrow morning.
➡ ________________________________
____

(2) My mom taught me to bake cookies how.
➡ ________________________________

서답형

17 다음 문장에서 어법상 어색한 부분을 찾아서 한 단어만 고치시오.

(1) If I had the choice, I will stop working tomorrow.
____________ ➡ ____________

(2) The man showed the girl what to play chess.
____________ ➡ ____________

Grammar 서술형 시험대비

[01~02] 다음 우리말과 일치하도록 괄호 안에 주어진 단어들을 바르게 배열하시오.

01

그가 내 주소를 안다면, 내게 편지를 보낼 텐데.
(he, he, me, a letter, my address, knew, send, would, if)

➡ ________________________________

02

나는 언제 개에게 먹이를 줄지 그에게 말했다.
(I, him, the dog, feed, told, when, to)

➡ ________________________________

고난이도

03 다음 문장과 같은 뜻이 되도록 괄호 안에 주어진 어휘를 활용하여 빈칸을 채우시오.

Without injustice, men would not know justice.

(1) ______ ______ ______ ______ ______ injustice, men would not know justice. (it, be)

(2) ______ ______ ______ ______ injustice, men would not know justice. (it, be)

(3) ______ ______ ______ ______ injustice, men would not know justice. (there, no)

(4) ______ ______ injustice, men would not know justice. (but)

(5) ______ ______ ______ injustice, men will know justice.
(as, 직설법으로 쓸 것.)

04 다음 그림을 보고, 주어진 어휘를 이용하여 대화의 빈칸을 알맞게 채우시오.

A: Did you decide ________________?
(which, buy, 4 단어)
B: Yeah. I'll buy the purple one.

➡ ________________

05 다음 그림을 보고, 괄호 안에 주어진 단어를 빈칸에 알맞게 채우시오.

If Linda ______(sing) well, I would listen to her singing attentively.

➡ ________________

중요

06 우리말에 맞게 빈칸에 알맞은 말을 쓰시오.

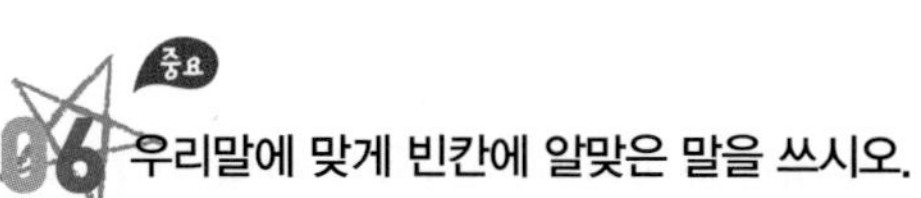

그녀는 어디로 가야 할지를 몰랐다.
➡ She didn't know ______ ______ ______.

07 다음 주어진 문장과 뜻이 같도록 빈칸을 알맞게 채우시오.

I don't speak 4 languages, so I can't be a good interpreter.
→ If I _______ 4 languages, I _______ _______ a good interpreter.

중요

08 다음 우리말을 괄호 안에 주어진 단어들을 활용하여 영작하시오.

(1) 만약 내가 슈퍼맨이라면, 나는 위험에 처한 사람들을 구할 텐데.
(Superman, save, people in danger)
➡ _______________

(2) 그가 감기에 걸리지 않았다면, 나와 함께 쇼핑을 갈 수 있을 텐데. (have a cold)
➡ _______________

(3) 아무도 악기를 연주할 줄 몰랐다.
(no one, musical instruments)
➡ _______________

(4) 어느 기차를 타야 할지 말해 줄 수 있니?
(can, which, take)
➡ _______________

09 다음 글에서 어법상 잘못 쓰인 것을 찾아 알맞게 고치시오. (3곳)

It was amazed that you received a Nobel Peace Prize at the age of 17. If I am the president of your country, I will let girls go to school.

_______ ➡ _______
_______ ➡ _______
_______ ➡ _______

고난이도

10 다음 직설법 문장을 가정법 문장으로 고쳐 쓰시오.

(1) As I am not a bird, I don't fly.
➡ _______________

(2) It doesn't rain, so I won't put on the boots.
➡ _______________

(3) Since she doesn't have enough eggs, she can't bake bread for her family.
➡ _______________

(4) Because I don't have a magic carpet, I won't travel all around the world.
➡ _______________

11 다음 문장을 바꿔 쓸 때, 빈칸에 알맞은 말을 쓰시오.

(1) Let me know where to put the eggs.
➡ Let me know _______________.

(2) I don't know how to use this camera.
➡ I don't know _______________.

(3) They have to decide when to take action.
➡ They have to decide _______________.

중요

12 다음 문장에서 어법상 어색한 부분을 찾아 고치시오.

(1) If he has enough time, he would visit us.
_______ ➡ _______

(2) He asked me when taking out the eggs.
_______ ➡ _______

교과서

Reading

From Trash to Music

Tears of joy are rolling down my cheeks. I'm so happy and thrilled. If I were a bird, I would fly. I look around. The other members in my orchestra are hugging one another. Our concert has just finished and everyone is standing and giving us a big hand. None of us ever expected that this day would come. It has been a long journey.

주어가 감정을 느끼는 주체일 경우 과거분사 사용
가정법과거: 현재 사실에 반대되는 내용을 가정, '만약 ~라면, …할 텐데'
주어가 The other members이므로 동사는 are
현재완료 완료 용법
everyone은 3인칭 단수로 취급하므로 is를 사용
우리에게 큰 박수를 보내다
부정의 의미로 '아무도 ~ 않다'
우리의 콘서트가 끝나고 모든 사람이 큰 박수를 보내는 날

My name is Andrea and I'm a violinist in the Recycled Orchestra. Why is it called the Recycled Orchestra? It's because our musical instruments are made of objects from a landfill. That's why it's also known as the Landfill Harmonic Orchestra.

오케스트라가 Recycled Orchestra로 불리는 이유를 묻는 수동태 문장
be made of는 '~로 만들어지다', 물건들을 그대로 활용하여 악기를 만든 것을 의미.
그것이 ~한 이유이다
~로 알려지다
it과 the Landfill Harmonic Orchestra는 동일한 대상

Most of us in the orchestra are from Cateura, a small town in Paraguay. There is a huge landfill in our town. Some people even say that Cateura itself is a giant landfill. Many of us are poor. There weren't many hopes and dreams in our town. Everything began to change, however, when we met Favio Chávez.

콤마(,)로 연결된 Cateura와 a small town in Paraguay는 동격 관계
'심지어'라는 뜻의 부사로 say를 수식
재귀대명사로 주어 Cateura를 지칭

trash 쓰레기
tear 눈물
joy 기쁨
roll 구르다, 굴러가다
cheek 볼, 뺨
thrilled 황홀해하는, 아주 신이 난
one another 서로
journey 여행
orchestra 오케스트라, 관현악단
musical instrument 악기
landfill 쓰레기 매립지

확인문제

● 다음 문장이 본문의 내용과 일치하면 T, 일치하지 않으면 F를 쓰시오.

1 The other members in the orchestra are hugging one another. ☐
2 Everyone expected that this day would come. ☐
3 Andrea is a violinist in the Recycled Orchestra. ☐
4 Their musical instruments are bought from a landfill. ☐
5 Cateura is a small town in Paraguay. ☐
6 There were many hopes and dreams in Cateura. ☐

Favio was an environmental educator and a musician. He wanted to teach us music, but there was a big problem. There were only a few ('약간의, 몇 개의'라는 뜻의 수량형용사, 셀 수 있는 명사 앞에 위치) musical instruments in the whole town. We couldn't afford to ('~할 형편이 못되었다') buy new ones (= musical instruments). But Favio didn't give up. He said that we could make musical instruments with objects from the landfill. A talented man named (주어인 A talented man을 수식) Nicholas was able to ('~할 수 있었다') put this idea into practice (이 생각을 실행에 옮기다). He made violins from oil drums. He turned water pipes into flutes. (A를 B로 바꾸었다)

We had another problem. No one knew how to play (how to+동사원형: ~하는 방법, 어떻게 ~할지) musical instruments. We didn't even know how to read music. Favio taught us with great patience (= very patiently). Step by step, we began to make some sounds on our instruments. I still (아직도, 여전히(부사)) remember the first piece of music that (목적격 관계대명사) we played. It (= The first piece of music that we played) was very short and mostly out of tune (음이 맞지 않는). But it was the most beautiful music to us. We felt a new hope in our hearts. From then on (그때부터), we gathered to practice (목적을 나타내는 부사적 용법의 to부정사) every day. One day, Favio told us some great news. We were going to have a concert, a real concert!

And here we are now in front of hundreds of (수백 명의) people. They (= Hundreds of people) love our music. The world sends us trash, but we send back music!

environmental 환경의
educator 교육자
afford ~할 형편이 되다
talented 재능 있는
be able to ~할 수 있다
put ~ into practice ~을 실행에 옮기다
patience 인내심
step by step 점차로, 차근차근, 하나씩
mostly 대부분, 일반적으로
out of tune 음이 맞지 않는

확인문제

- 다음 문장이 본문의 내용과 일치하면 T, 일치하지 않으면 F를 쓰시오.

1 Favio was an environmental educator and a musician. ☐

2 There were not a few musical instruments in the whole town. ☐

3 Nicholas made violins from oil drums. ☐

4 They began to make some sounds on their instruments quickly. ☐

5 The first piece of music that they played was very short and mostly out of tune. ☐

6 They gathered to practice every Sunday. ☐

Reading 교과서 확인학습 A

• 우리말을 참고하여 빈칸에 알맞은 말을 쓰시오.

1 From ________ to ________

2 ________ ________ ________ are rolling down my cheeks.

3 I'm so happy and ________.

4 If I ________ a bird, I ________ ________.

5 I ________ ________.

6 ________ ________ ________ in my orchestra are hugging one another.

7 Our concert ________ ________ ________ and everyone is standing and ________ ________ ________ ________ ________.

8 None of us ________ ________ that this day would come.

9 ________ ________ ________ a long journey.

10 My name is Andrea and ________ ________ ________ in the Recycled Orchestra.

11 ________ ________ ________ ________ the Recycled Orchestra?

12 It's because our musical instruments ________ ________ ________ objects ________ a landfill.

13 ________ ________ it's also known as the Landfill Harmonic Orchestra.

14 Most of us in the orchestra ________ ________ Cateura, a small town in Paraguay.

15 There is ________ ________ ________ in our town.

16 Some people even say that Cateura ________ is a giant landfill.

17 ________ ________ ________ are poor.

18 There weren't ________ ________ ________ ________ in our town.

19 Everything ________ ________ ________, however, when we met Favio Chávez.

20 Favio was ________ ________ ________ and a musician.

21 He wanted to ________ ________ ________, but there was a big problem.

1 쓰레기를 음악으로
2 기쁨의 눈물이 내 볼에 흘러내리고 있다.
3 나는 정말 기쁘고 황홀하다.
4 내가 새라면, 날아오를 텐데.
5 나는 주변을 본다.
6 우리 오케스트라의 다른 단원들은 서로 껴안고 있다.
7 우리의 공연은 이제 막 끝났고 모든 사람들이 서서 우리에게 큰 박수를 보내고 있다.
8 우리 중 아무도 이 날이 올 거라고 예상하지 못했다.
9 긴 여정이었다.
10 내 이름은 Andrea이고 나는 Recycled Orchestra의 바이올리니스트이다.
11 오케스트라가 왜 Recycled Orchestra라고 불리냐고?
12 그것은 우리의 악기들이 쓰레기 매립지에서 나온 물건들로 만들어지기 때문이다.
13 그것이 오케스트라가 Landfill Harmonic Orchestra로도 알려진 이유이다.
14 오케스트라의 우리들 대부분은 파라과이의 작은 마을인 카테우라 출신이다.
15 우리 마을에는 거대한 쓰레기 매립지가 있다.
16 몇몇 사람들은 심지어 카테우라 자체가 거대한 쓰레기 매립지라고 말한다.
17 우리들 중 많은 이들이 가난하다.
18 우리 마을에는 꿈과 희망이 많지 않았다.
19 그러나 우리가 Favio Chávez 선생님을 만났을 때 모든 것이 바뀌기 시작했다.
20 Favio 선생님은 환경 교육가이자 음악가였다.
21 그는 우리에게 음악을 가르치고 싶어 했지만, 큰 문제가 있었다.

22 There were ________ ________ ________ musical instruments in the whole town.

23 We ________ ________ ________ buy new ones.

24 But Favio didn't ________ ________.

25 He said that we could make musical instruments ________ ________ ________ ________ ________.

26 A talented man ________ Nicholas was able to ________ this idea ________ ________.

27 He ________ violins ________ oil drums.

28 He ________ water pipes ________ flutes.

29 We had ________ ________.

30 No one knew ________ ________ ________ musical instruments.

31 We didn't even know ________ ________ ________ music.

32 Favio taught us ________ ________ ________.

33 ________ ________ ________, we began to make some sounds on our instruments.

34 I still remember ________ ________ ________ ________ ________ that we played.

35 It was very short and mostly ________ ________ ________.

36 But it was ________ ________ ________ ________ to us.

37 We ________ ________ ________ ________ in our hearts.

38 ________ ________ ________, we gathered to practice every day.

39 One day, Favio told us ________ ________ ________.

40 We ________ ________ ________ ________ a concert, a real concert!

41 And here we are now in front of ________ ________ ________.

42 They love ________ ________.

43 The world ________ ________ ________, but we ________ ________ ________!

22 온 마을에 악기가 단지 몇 개뿐이었다.
23 우리는 새 악기를 살 형편도 아니었다.
24 그러나 Favio 선생님은 포기하지 않았다.
25 그는 우리가 쓰레기 매립지의 물건들로 악기를 만들 수 있다고 말했다.
26 재능이 많은 Nicholas 아저씨가 이 생각을 실행에 옮길 수 있었다.
27 그는 기름통으로 바이올린을 만들었다.
28 그는 수도관을 플루트로 바꾸었다.
29 우리에게 또 다른 문제가 있었다.
30 아무도 악기를 연주할 줄 몰랐다.
31 우리는 심지어 악보를 읽는 방법도 알지 못했다.
32 Favio 선생님은 엄청난 인내심으로 우리를 가르쳤다.
33 점차로, 우리는 악기로 어떤 소리를 만들어 내기 시작했다.
34 나는 아직도 우리가 연주했던 첫 곡을 기억한다.
35 그 곡은 매우 짧고 대부분은 음이 맞지 않았다.
36 그러나 그것은 우리에게 가장 아름다운 곡이었다.
37 우리는 마음속에 새로운 희망을 느꼈다.
38 그때부터, 우리는 매일 연습을 하기 위해 모였다.
39 어느 날, Favio 선생님은 우리에게 엄청난 소식을 말해 줬다.
40 우리는 공연을, 진짜 공연을 하게 될 것이었다!
41 그리고 여기 우리는 지금 수백 명의 사람들 앞에 있다.
42 그들은 우리의 음악을 사랑한다.
43 세상은 우리에게 쓰레기를 보내지만, 우리는 음악을 돌려보낸다!

Reading 교과서 확인학습 B

● 우리말을 참고하여 본문을 영작하시오.

1 쓰레기를 음악으로
➡ ______________________________

2 기쁨의 눈물이 내 볼에 흘러내리고 있다.
➡ ______________________________

3 나는 정말 기쁘고 황홀하다.
➡ ______________________________

4 내가 새라면, 날아오를 텐데.
➡ ______________________________

5 나는 주변을 본다.
➡ ______________________________

6 우리 오케스트라의 다른 단원들은 서로 껴안고 있다.
➡ ______________________________

7 우리의 공연은 이제 막 끝났고 모든 사람들이 서서 우리에게 큰 박수를 보내고 있다.
➡ ______________________________

8 우리 중 아무도 이 날이 올 거라고 예상하지 못했다.
➡ ______________________________

9 긴 여정이었다.
➡ ______________________________

10 내 이름은 Andrea이고 나는 Recycled Orchestra의 바이올리니스트이다.
➡ ______________________________

11 오케스트라가 왜 Recycled Orchestra라고 불리냐고?
➡ ______________________________

12 그것은 우리의 악기들이 쓰레기 매립지에서 나온 물건들로 만들어지기 때문이다.
➡ ______________________________

13 그것이 오케스트라가 Landfill Harmonic Orchestra로도 알려진 이유이다.
➡ ______________________________

14 오케스트라의 우리들 대부분은 파라과이의 작은 마을인 카테우라 출신이다.
➡ ______________________________

15 우리 마을에는 거대한 쓰레기 매립지가 있다.
➡ ______________________________

16 몇몇 사람들은 심지어 카테우라 자체가 거대한 쓰레기 매립지라고 말한다.
➡ ______________________________

17 우리들 중 많은 이들이 가난하다.
➡ ______________________________

18 우리 마을에는 꿈과 희망이 많지 않았다.
➡ ______________________________

19 그러나 우리가 Favio Chávez 선생님을 만났을 때 모든 것이 바뀌기 시작했다.
➡ ______________________________

20 Favio 선생님은 환경 교육가이자 음악가였다.
➡ ______________________________

21 그는 우리에게 음악을 가르치고 싶어 했지만, 큰 문제가 있었다.
➡ ______________________________

22 온 마을에 악기가 단지 몇 개뿐이었다.
➡ ______________________________

23 우리는 새 악기를 살 형편도 아니었다.
➡ ______________________________

24 그러나 Favio 선생님은 포기하지 않았다.
➡ ______________________________

25 그는 우리가 쓰레기 매립지의 물건들로 악기를 만들 수 있다고 말했다.
➡ ______________________________

26 재능이 많은 Nicholas 아저씨가 이 생각을 실행에 옮길 수 있었다.
➡ ______________________________

27 그는 기름통으로 바이올린을 만들었다.
➡ ______________________________

28 그는 수도관을 플루트로 바꾸었다.
➡ ______________________________

29 우리에게 또 다른 문제가 있었다.
➡ ______________________________

30 아무도 악기를 연주할 줄 몰랐다.
➡ ______________________________

31 우리는 심지어 악보를 읽는 방법도 알지 못했다.
➡ ______________________________

32 Favio 선생님은 엄청난 인내심으로 우리를 가르쳤다.
➡ ______________________________

33 점차로, 우리는 악기로 어떤 소리를 만들어 내기 시작했다.
➡ ______________________________

34 나는 아직도 우리가 연주했던 첫 곡을 기억한다.
➡ ______________________________

35 그 곡은 매우 짧고 대부분은 음이 맞지 않았다.
➡ ______________________________

36 그러나 그것은 우리에게 가장 아름다운 곡이었다.
➡ ______________________________

37 우리는 마음속에 새로운 희망을 느꼈다.
➡ ______________________________

38 그때부터, 우리는 매일 연습을 하기 위해 모였다.
➡ ______________________________

39 어느 날, Favio 선생님은 우리에게 엄청난 소식을 말해 줬다.
➡ ______________________________

40 우리는 공연을, 진짜 공연을 하게 될 것이었다!
➡ ______________________________

41 그리고 여기 우리는 지금 수백 명의 사람들 앞에 있다.
➡ ______________________________

42 그들은 우리의 음악을 사랑한다.
➡ ______________________________

43 세상은 우리에게 쓰레기를 보내지만, 우리는 음악을 돌려보낸다!
➡ ______________________________

Reading 시험대비 실력평가

[01~04] 다음 글을 읽고 물음에 답하시오.

Tears of joy are rolling down my cheeks. I'm so happy and (A)[thrilling / thrilled]. ⓐ 내가 새라면, 날아오를 텐데. I look around. The other members in my orchestra (B)[is / are] hugging one another. Our concert ⓑhas just finished and everyone is standing and (C) [gave / giving] us a big hand. None of us ever expected that this day would come. It has been a long journey.

서답형

01 위 글의 괄호 (A)~(C)에서 어법상 알맞은 낱말을 골라 쓰시오.

(A) ________ (B) ________ (C) ________

서답형

02 위 글의 밑줄 친 ⓐ의 우리말에 맞게 8 단어로 영작하시오.

➡ ______________________________

03 위 글의 밑줄 친 ⓑ와 현재완료의 용법이 같은 것을 모두 고르시오.

① She has been sick since yesterday.
② Have you seen it already?
③ How many times have you read it?
④ I have lived here for 10 years.
⑤ She has not washed the dishes yet.

중요

04 According to the passage, which is NOT true?

① The writer is weeping for joy.
② The concert has just ended.
③ The writer saw the other members in the orchestra hugging one another.
④ Everyone is applauding.
⑤ The writer expected that this day would come.

[05~07] 다음 글을 읽고 물음에 답하시오.

My name is Andrea and I'm a violinist in the Recycled Orchestra. Why is it called the Recycled Orchestra? It's because our musical instruments are made of objects from a landfill. (A)That's why it's also known by the Landfill Harmonic Orchestra.

Most of us in the orchestra are from Cateura, a small town in Paraguay. There is a huge landfill in our town. Some people even say that Cateura itself is a giant landfill. Many of us are poor. There weren't many hopes and dreams in our town. Everything began to change, ___ⓐ___, when we met Favio Chávez.

05 위 글의 빈칸 ⓐ에 들어갈 알맞은 말을 고르시오.

① instead
② therefore
③ that is
④ however
⑤ in addition

서답형

06 위 글의 밑줄 친 (A)에서 어법상 틀린 부분을 찾아 고치시오.

__________ ➡ __________

중요

07 위 글의 주제로 알맞은 것을 고르시오.

① the description of the violinist of the Recycled Orchestra
② how to make musical instruments with objects from a landfill
③ the reason why the orchestra is called the Recycled Orchestra
④ the poor living condition of the people in Cateura
⑤ the way Favio Chávez changed everything

[08~11] 다음 글을 읽고 물음에 답하시오.

Favio was an environmental educator and a musician. He wanted to teach us music, but there was a big problem. There were only a few musical instruments in the whole town. We couldn't afford to buy new ___ⓐ___. But Favio didn't give up. He said that ⓑ우리가 쓰레기 매립지의 물건들로 악기를 만들 수 있다. A talented man named Nicholas was able to put this idea into practice. He made violins from oil drums. He turned water pipes into flutes.

서답형

08 위 글의 빈칸 ⓐ에 들어갈 알맞은 대명사를 쓰시오.

➡ ________________

서답형

09 위 글의 밑줄 친 ⓑ의 우리말에 맞게 주어진 어휘를 알맞게 배열하시오.

objects / musical instruments / from / we / the landfill / with / could make

➡ ________________________________

____

중요

10 위 글의 제목으로 알맞은 것을 고르시오.

① Favio, an Environmental Educator and a Musician
② How to Teach Music
③ Oops! A Few Musical Instruments in the Whole Town?
④ From Trash to Musical Instruments
⑤ A Talented Man Named Nicholas

11 위 글을 읽고 알 수 없는 것을 고르시오.

① Who was Favio?
② What did Favio want to teach?
③ What musical instruments were there in the town?
④ With what objects could they make musical instruments?
⑤ Who was able to put Favio's idea into practice?

[12~14] 다음 글을 읽고 물음에 답하시오.

We had another problem. No one knew how to play musical instruments. We didn't even know how to read music. Favio taught us ___ⓐ___ great patience. Step by step, we began to make some sounds ___ⓑ___ our instruments. I still remember the first piece of music that we played. It was very short and mostly out of tune. But it was the most beautiful music to us. We felt a new hope in our hearts. From then on, we gathered to practice every day. One day, Favio told us some great news. We were going to have a concert, a real concert!

And here we are now in front of hundreds of people. They love our music. The world sends us trash, but we send back music!

*We: the children of Cateura

12 위 글의 빈칸 ⓐ와 ⓑ에 들어갈 전치사가 바르게 짝지어진 것은?

	ⓐ	ⓑ		ⓐ	ⓑ
①	for	at	②	with	on
③	to	on	④	for	to
⑤	with	at			

13 위 글의 앞에 올 내용으로 가장 알맞은 것을 고르시오.

① the problem of burying waste in landfill
② the challenge of having a concert in front of hundreds of people
③ the process of organizing the orchestra
④ the difficulty of reading music while they were practicing musical instruments
⑤ the difficulty of getting musical instruments

중요
14 Which question CANNOT be answered after reading the passage?

① Was there any one that knew how to play musical instruments?
② Was there any one that knew how to read music?
③ Who taught music to the children of Cateura?
④ What was the first piece of music that the children of Cateura played?
⑤ What did the children of Cateura think about their first piece of music that they played?

[15~17] 다음 글을 읽고 물음에 답하시오.

> My name is Andrea and I'm a violinist in the Recycled Orchestra. (①) Why is it called the Recycled Orchestra? (②) That's why it's also known as the Landfill Harmonic Orchestra. (③)
> Most of us in the orchestra are from Cateura, a small town in Paraguay. (④) There is a huge landfill in our town. (⑤) Some people even say that Cateura ⓐitself is a giant landfill. Many of us are poor. There weren't many hopes and dreams in our town. Everything began to change, however, when we met Favio Chávez.

중요
15 위 글의 흐름으로 보아, 주어진 문장이 들어가기에 가장 적절한 곳은?

> It's because our musical instruments are made of objects from a landfill.

① ② ③ ④ ⑤

서답형
16 주어진 영영풀이에 해당하는 단어를 본문에서 찾아 쓰시오.

> a large deep hole in which very large amounts of trash are buried

➡ ____________________

중요
17 위 글의 밑줄 친 ⓐitself와 문법적 쓰임이 같은 것을 모두 고르시오.

① History repeats itself.
② We enjoyed ourselves very much.
③ I did it myself.
④ Please help yourself to the cake.
⑤ I saw Mr. Smith himself.

[18~20] 다음 글을 읽고 물음에 답하시오.

> Favio was an environmental educator and a musician. He wanted to teach us music, but there was (A)a big problem. There were only a few musical instruments in the whole town. (B)We couldn't afford buying new ones. But Favio didn't give up. He said that we could make musical instruments with objects from the landfill. A talented man named Nicholas was able to put this idea ___ⓐ___ practice. He made violins from oil drums. He turned water pipes ___ⓑ___ flutes.

18 위 글의 빈칸 ⓐ와 ⓑ에 공통으로 들어갈 알맞은 전치사를 고르시오.

① by ② on ③ into
④ for ⑤ at

서답형

19 위 글의 밑줄 친 (A)a big problem이 가리키는 것을 우리말로 쓰시오.

➡ ______________________
____

서답형

20 위 글의 밑줄 친 (B)에서 어법상 틀린 부분을 찾아 고치시오.

__________ ➡ __________

[21~24] 다음 글을 읽고 물음에 답하시오.

We had another problem. No one knew how to play musical instruments. We didn't even know how to read music. Favio taught us with great patience. ⓐStep by step, we began to make some sounds on our instruments. I still remember the first piece of music that we played. ⓑIt was very short and mostly in tune. But it was the most beautiful music to us. We felt a new hope in our hearts. From then on, we gathered ⓒto practice every day. One day, Favio told us some great news. We were going to have a concert, a real concert!

And here we are now in front of hundreds of people. They love our music. The world sends us trash, but we send back music!

*We: the children of Cateura

중요

21 위 글의 밑줄 친 ⓐStep by step과 바꿔 쓸 수 있는 말을 모두 고르시오.

① Gradually ② Side by side
③ Time after time ④ By degrees
⑤ Little by little

서답형

22 위 글의 밑줄 친 ⓑ에서 흐름상 어색한 부분을 찾아 고치시오.

__________ ➡ __________

23 아래 <보기>에서 위 글의 밑줄 친 ⓒto practice와 to부정사의 용법이 다른 것의 개수를 고르시오.

보기
① This water is not good to drink.
② How to live is an important question in life.
③ She was very happy to get the birthday present.
④ He awoke to find himself famous.
⑤ My plan is to master English in a year.

① 1개 ② 2개 ③ 3개 ④ 4개 ⑤ 5개

중요

24 위 글의 주제로 알맞은 것을 고르시오.

① many problems the children of Cateura experienced
② the patient lesson of Favio
③ the difficult process up to the performance of a concert
④ the first piece of music that the children of Cateura played
⑤ the deeply moved audience of a concert

Reading 서술형 시험대비

[01~03] 다음 글을 읽고 물음에 답하시오.

Tears of joy are rolling down my cheeks. I'm so happy and thrilled. (A)If I were a bird, I would fly. I look around. The other members in my orchestra are hugging one another. Our concert has just finished and everyone is standing and ⓐgiving us _______ _______ _______. None of us ever expected that this day would come. It has been a long journey.

01 위 글의 밑줄 친 ⓐgiving us 다음에 이어지는 빈칸에 알맞은 세 단어를 넣어, 다음과 같은 뜻이 되도록 하시오.

> clapping his or her hands loudly and enthusiastically

➡ giving us _______ _______ _______

중요

02 위 글의 밑줄 친 (A)를 직설법 문장으로 고치시오.

➡ ______________________________

03 위 글의 내용을 다음과 같이 정리하고자 한다. 빈칸 (A)와 (B)에 들어갈 알맞은 단어를 본문에서 찾아 쓰시오.

> The concert has just finished and the writer is weeping for (A)_______. The audience is applauding and (B)_______ of the members in the orchestra ever expected that this day would come.

[04~06] 다음 글을 읽고 물음에 답하시오.

My name is Andrea and I'm a violinist in the Recycled Orchestra. Why is it called the Recycled Orchestra? It's because our musical instruments are made of objects from a landfill. ⓐ그것이 오케스트라가 Landfill Harmonic Orchestra로도 알려진 이유이다.

ⓑMost of us in the orchestra is from Cateura, a small town in Paraguay. There is a huge landfill in our town. Some people even say that Cateura itself is a giant landfill. Many of us are poor. There weren't many hopes and dreams in our town. Everything began to change, however, when we met Favio Chávez.

고난이도

04 위 글의 밑줄 친 ⓐ의 우리말에 맞게 주어진 어휘를 이용하여 10 단어로 영작하시오.

> why, also, as

➡ ______________________________
____

05 위 글의 밑줄 친 ⓑ에서 어법상 틀린 부분을 찾아 고치시오.

______________ ➡ ______________

06 위 글의 내용을 다음과 같이 정리하고자 한다. 빈칸 (A)와 (B)에 들어갈 알맞은 단어를 본문에서 찾아 쓰시오.

> People call the orchestra (A)_______ _______ _______ or the Landfill Harmonic Orchestra because their musical instruments are made of objects from (B)_______ _______.

[07~10] 다음 글을 읽고 물음에 답하시오.

Favio was an environmental educator and a musician. He wanted to teach us music, but there was a big problem. There were only a few musical instruments in the whole town. We couldn't afford to buy new ones. But Favio didn't give up. He said that we could make musical instruments with objects from the landfill. A talented man ____ⓐ____ Nicholas was able to put ⓑthis idea into practice. He made violins from oil drums. He turned water pipes into flutes.

중요

07 위 글의 빈칸 ⓐ에 name을 알맞은 형태로 쓰시오.

➡ ____________________

08 위 글의 밑줄 친 ⓑthis idea가 가리키는 것을 본문에서 찾아 쓰시오.

➡ ____________________________________

____

고난이도

09 What objects did Nicholas use to make violins and flutes? Fill in the blanks (A) and (B) with suitable words.

He made violins from (A)________ ________ and flutes from (B)________ ________.

10 다음 빈칸 (A)와 (B)에 알맞은 단어를 넣어 Favio와 Nicholas에 대한 소개를 완성하시오.

Favio was an environmental educator and a musician who had an idea of making (A)________ ________ with objects from the landfill, and Nicholas was a (B)________ man who was able to put Favio's idea into practice.

[11~13] 다음 글을 읽고 물음에 답하시오.

We had another problem. No one knew how to play musical instruments. ⓐWe didn't even know how to read music. Favio taught us with great patience. Step by step, we began to make some sounds on our instruments. I still remember the first piece of music that we played. It was very short and mostly out of tune. But it was the most beautiful music to us. We felt a new hope in our hearts. From then on, we gathered to practice every day. One day, Favio told us ⓑ some great news. We were going to have a concert, a real concert!

ⓒAnd here we are now in front of hundred of people. They love our music. The world sends us trash, but we send back music!

*We: the children of Cateura

중요

11 위 글의 밑줄 친 ⓐ를 다음과 같이 바꿔 쓸 때 빈칸에 들어갈 알맞은 말을 두 단어로 쓰시오.

We didn't even know how ________ ________ read music.

12 위 글의 밑줄 친 ⓑsome great news가 가리키는 것을 본문에서 찾아 쓰시오.

➡ ____________________________________

13 위 글의 밑줄 친 ⓒ에서 어법상 어색한 것을 고치시오.

____________ ➡ ____________

교과서

구석구석

After You Read B

Reporter: Congratulations! How do you feel now?

Andrea: I feel thrilled. We just performed our first concert.
감정을 나타내는 동사는 수식받는 명사가 감정을 느끼게 되는 경우에 과거분사를 씀.

Reporter: Why is the orchestra called the Recycled Orchestra?

Andrea: That's because our musical instruments are made of objects from a landfill.
그것은 ~ 때문이다

Reporter: That's amazing.
감정을 나타내는 동사는 감정을 유발할 때 현재분사를 씀.

Andrea: Yeah. None of us knew how to play musical instruments, but Favio taught us with great patience.
우리들 중 아무도 ~ 않다
with patience = patiently: 인내심 있게

Reporter: That is a wonderful story.

구문해설 • thrilled: 황홀해하는, 아주 신이 난 • orchestra: 오케스트라, 관현악단 • musical instrument: 악기 • landfill: 쓰레기 매립지 • amazing: 놀라운

해석

리포터: 축하합니다! 지금 기분이 어떠세요?
Andrea: 나는 아주 황홀해요. 우리는 막 첫 번째 공연을 했어요.
리포터: 오케스트라가 왜 Recycled Orchestra라고 불립니까?
Andrea: 그것은 우리의 악기들이 쓰레기 매립지에서 나온 물건들로 만들어지기 때문입니다.
리포터: 그것은 놀랍군요.
Andrea: 네, 우리들 중 아무도 악기를 연주할 줄 몰랐지만, Favio 선생님은 엄청난 인내심으로 우리를 가르치셨어요.
리포터: 멋있는 이야기입니다.

Think and Write

Dear Admiral Yi Sun-sin,

I'm Sumin. I really respect you because you never gave up in difficult situations. You saved the country and the people. It was amazing that you won the battle with only 12 ships. If I had a time machine, I would go to meet you! I'd like to ask you how to make geobukseon. You're my hero. Thank you.

존경하다 / 이유를 나타내는 접속사 / give up: 포기하다 / save: 구하다 / ⇩ 가정법과거를 사용하여 현재 사실과 반대되는 것을 상상하여 말할 수 있다.
가정법과거의 형태는 'if+주어+과거동사, 주어+조동사의 과거형+동사원형'으로, '~하다면 …할 텐데.'라고 해석한다.
how to 동사원형: ~하는 방법

Sincerely yours,

Sumin

구문해설 • admiral: 장군 • situation: 상황 • battle: 전투

이순신 장군님께,

저는 수민이에요. 저는 당신이 어려운 상황에서 결코 포기하지 않았기 때문에 당신을 정말 존경해요. 당신은 나라와 국민을 구했어요. 단지 12척의 배로 전투를 이긴 것은 놀라웠어요. 제게 타임 머신이 있다면, 저는 당신을 만나러 갈 텐데요! 저는 당신에게 거북선을 어떻게 만드는지를 묻고 싶어요. 당신은 제 영웅이에요. 감사합니다.

존경을 담아,
수민이가

Project Step 3

This is a bottle shaker. To make it, you need a bottle and buttons. Clean the bottle and put the buttons in the bottle. Close the bottle and decorate it. You can also put different things like rice or sand in it. Different items make different sounds. Listen to my group's bottle shaker.

부사적 용법(목적) / 명령문 / Clean과 병렬 / = the bottle / = such as / = the bottle

구문해설 • shaker: 흔드는 데 쓰는 용기, 셰이커 • decorate: 장식하다

이것은 병 셰이커야. 그것을 만들려면 너는 병 하나와 단추들이 필요해. 병을 씻고 단추들을 병 속에 넣어. 병을 닫고 그것을 장식해. 너는 또한 쌀이나 모래 같은 다른 것들을 안에 넣을 수 있어. 다른 물건들은 다른 소리들을 만들어 내. 내 모둠의 병 셰이커 소리를 들어 봐.

영역별 핵심문제

Words & Expressions

[01~02] 다음 빈칸에 가장 알맞은 말을 고르시오.

01

She is a[an] ________ musician as well as a photographer.

① talented ② effective
③ accountable ④ extensive
⑤ individual

02

They ________ for their favorite teams and players.

① apply ② discourage
③ cheer ④ ensure
⑤ prevent

03 두 문장이 같은 의미가 되도록 빈칸을 채우시오.

They expected him to participate in the ceremony.
= They expected him to ________ ________ in the ceremony.

04 다음 빈칸에 공통으로 들어갈 말을 쓰시오.

• They're not ________ of stone the way ancient Greek temples were.
• Her bestseller is soon to be ________ into a television mini-series.
• Many products are ________ from machinery rather than by hand.

Conversation

[05~07] 다음 대화를 읽고 물음에 답하시오.

B: Hey, Bora. Welcome to our rock band.
G: Thanks. I'm looking forward (A)to playing in a concert with you.
B: We're (B)excite to have a new guitar player.
G: Yeah. See you on Friday.

05 밑줄 친 (A)와 성격이 다른 하나를 고르시오.

① What do you say to eating out tonight?
② I prefer walking to climbing.
③ What is to be used to clean the sinks?
④ It took her a while to adjust to living alone.
⑤ I'm a real coward when it comes to going to the dentist.

06 위 대화의 밑줄 친 (B)를 알맞은 형으로 고치시오.

➡ ____________________

07 위 대화의 내용으로 보아 알 수 없는 것은?

① Bora can play the guitar.
② They are going to meet on Friday.
③ Their rock band will play in a concert.
④ Bora is a new member of the rock band.
⑤ Bora has once played the guitar in a concert.

[08~09] 다음 대화를 읽고 물음에 답하시오.

G: Jiho, what are you reading?
B: I'm reading a book about baseball player named Jim Abbott. (①)
G: Oh, 오른손이 없이 태어난 그 사람? (②)
B: That's right. (③) He tried really hard and even won the MVP award.
G: Yeah. His story was made into a movie. I'm going to watch it this Saturday.
B: Really? What's the title?
G: *Our Hero*. (④) I'm really looking forward to watching it.
B: Can I join you?
G: Sure. (⑤)

08 위 대화의 ①~⑤ 중 주어진 문장이 들어갈 곳은?

See you on Saturday.

① ② ③ ④ ⑤

09 밑줄 친 우리말을 조건에 맞게 영작하시오.

보기
• 전치사와 관계대명사를 사용할 것.
• bear를 사용할 것. (형태 변화 가능)

➡ ______________________________

[10~12] 다음 대화를 읽고 물음에 답하시오.

G: Alex, I'm going to __(A)__ part in a singing contest next Monday. (①)
B: That's great, Sumin!
G: You know how to play the guitar, right?
B: Yes, I __(B)__ the guitar for 3 years. (②)
G: Great. (③) Can you play the guitar __(C)__ I sing in the contest?
B: I'd love to, but I can't. (④)
G: Oh! I'm sorry to hear that. (⑤)
B: Thanks. But I'll be there to cheer for you.

10 위 대화의 ①~⑤ 중 주어진 문장이 들어갈 곳은?

I hurt my hand in gym class yesterday.

① ② ③ ④ ⑤

11 빈칸 (A)에 들어갈 말로 적절한 것을 고르시오

① make ② do ③ have
④ be ⑤ take

12 빈칸 (B)와 (C)에 들어갈 말로 알맞게 짝지어진 것은?

	(B)		(C)
①	played	–	if
②	played	–	when
③	have played	–	while
④	have played	–	although
⑤	have been played	–	when

13 다음 대화가 자연스럽게 연결되도록 (A)~(D)를 순서대로 배열하시오.

(A) I'd love to, but I can't. I have to visit my grandparents.
(B) I'm going to play soccer. Do you want to join me?
(C) What are you going to do this afternoon?
(D) Okay, then next time.

➡ ____________________

Grammar

14 다음 중 밑줄 친 if의 쓰임이 나머지와 다른 하나를 고르시오.

① I would put it in the living room, if I were you.
② What would you do if you could win the lottery?
③ I wasn't sure if I could handle such a powerful car.
④ If he studied hard, he could pass the exam.
⑤ I would be happy if I could cut out junk food, like candy and potato chips.

15 다음 중 어법상 어색한 문장은?

① Would you tell me where to park the car?
② Could you tell me how to get to City Hall?
③ I'm hesitating about who to invite.
④ She asked her mother when to make spaghetti.
⑤ The writer couldn't decide what to wear the dress.

16 다음 주어진 문장을 가정법으로 바르게 고친 것은?

As it doesn't rain, I won't use my umbrella.

① If it rained, I won't use my umbrella.
② If it rained, I would use my umbrella.
③ If it rained, I wouldn't use my umbrella.
④ If it had rained, I would use my umbrella.
⑤ If it hadn't rained, I wouldn't use my umbrella.

[17~18] 우리말에 맞게 주어진 어휘를 이용하여 빈칸에 알맞은 말을 쓰시오.

17

내 문제는 모든 사람에게 어떻게 연락할지였다. = My problem was _______ _______ _______ everyone. (contact)

18

내가 한국의 대통령이라면, 우리나라를 더 아름답게 만들 텐데. = If I _______ the president of Korea, I _______ _______ my country more beautiful. (be, make)

19 다음 괄호 안에 주어진 단어를 어법에 맞게 빈칸에 쓰시오.

(1) We didn't even know how _______ _______ _______ music. (read)
(2) Please tell me what _______ _______ _______. (do)
(3) I don't have any idea who _______ _______. (contact)
(4) They didn't decide when _______ _______ for the station. (leave)
(5) If you ask three people _______ bus _______ _______ to reach a given place, you are sure to get three different answers. (take)

20 다음 그림을 보고, 괄호 안에 주어진 단어를 빈칸에 알맞게 채우시오.

If we ________ the music as we have practiced, we ________ ________ the contest. (play, win)

21 두 문장의 의미가 같도록 빈칸에 알맞은 말을 쓰시오.

(1) Please tell me when I can take out the eggs.
= Please tell me ____________________ the eggs.

(2) It's hard to choose which dress I should wear to the party.
= It's hard to choose ________________ to the party.

(3) Did you decide whom you should meet at the meeting?
= Did you decide ________________ at the meeting?

Reading

[22~23] 다음 글을 읽고 물음에 답하시오.

My name is Andrea and I'm a violinist in the Recycled Orchestra. Why is ①it called ②the Recycled Orchestra? ③It's because our musical instruments are made of objects from a landfill. That's why ④it's also known as ⑤the Landfill Harmonic Orchestra.

Most of us in the orchestra are from Cateura, a small town in Paraguay. There is a ⓐhuge landfill in our town. Some people even say that Cateura itself is a giant landfill. Many of us are poor. There weren't many hopes and dreams in our town. Everything began to change, however, when we met Favio Chávez.

22 밑줄 친 ①~⑤ 중에서 가리키는 대상이 나머지 넷과 다른 것은?

① ② ③ ④ ⑤

23 위 글의 밑줄 친 ⓐhuge의 반의어를 고르시오.

① giant
② tiny
③ little
④ large
⑤ rare

[24~26] 다음 글을 읽고 물음에 답하시오.

Favio was an environmental educator and a musician. He wanted to teach us music, but there was a big problem. ⓐ온 마을에 악기가 단지 몇 개뿐이었다. (①) We couldn't afford to buy new ones. (②) He said that we could make musical instruments with objects from the landfill. (③) A talented man named Nicholas was able to put this idea into practice. (④) He made violins from oil drums. (⑤) He turned water pipes into flutes.

*We: the children of Cateura

24 위 글의 흐름으로 보아, 주어진 문장이 들어가기에 가장 적절한 곳은?

But Favio didn't give up.

① ② ③ ④ ⑤

25 밑줄 친 ⓐ의 우리말에 맞게 주어진 어휘를 이용하여 11 단어로 영작하시오.

there, only, whole town

➡ ______________________________

____

26 According to the passage, which is NOT true?

① Favio was an environmental educator and a musician.
② The children of Cateura couldn't afford to buy new musical instruments.
③ Favio didn't give up teaching music to the children of Cateura.
④ Nicholas was able to put Favio's idea into practice.
⑤ Nicholas made flutes from oil drums and violins from water pipes.

[27~29] 다음 글을 읽고 물음에 답하시오.

We had another problem. No one knew (A) how to play musical instruments. We didn't even know how to read music. Favio taught us with great patience. Step by step, we began to make some sounds on our instruments. I still remember the first piece of music that we played. It was very short and mostly out of tune. But it was the most beautiful music to us. We felt a new hope in our hearts. From then (B)on, we gathered to practice every day. One day, Favio told us some great news. We were going to have a concert, a real concert!

And here we are now in front of hundreds of people. They love our music. The world sends us trash, but we send back ___ⓐ___!

27 위 글의 빈칸 ⓐ에 들어갈 알맞은 말을 고르시오.

① dance ② music
③ stories ④ garbage
⑤ pictures

28 위 글의 밑줄 친 (A)how to play와 to부정사의 용법이 같은 것을 모두 고르시오.

① To hear him talk, you would think him a foreigner.
② I think it wrong to tell a lie.
③ I want something to write with.
④ He decided to buy new shoes.
⑤ I am sorry to give you much trouble.

29 위 글의 밑줄 친 (B)on과 같은 의미로 쓰인 것을 고르시오.

① Put it down on the table.
② He came on Sunday.
③ He worked on without a break.
④ On arriving home I discovered they had gone.
⑤ He is a reporter on the New York Times staff.

단원별 예상문제

출제율 95%

01 다음 단어들의 관계가 다른 하나를 고르시오.

① bored : thrilled
② award : prize
③ journey : trip
④ mostly : mainly
⑤ take care of : look after

[02~03] 다음 빈칸에 알맞은 말을 고르시오.

출제율 95%

02

It was time to ________ their suggestion into practice.

① keep ② make ③ set
④ put ⑤ bring

출제율 90%

03

Would you please ________ them a big hand?

① give ② find ③ take
④ do ⑤ get

출제율 100%

04 다음 중 밑줄 친 부분의 뜻풀이가 바르지 않은 것은?

① Can we afford a new car? (~을 살[가질] 형편이 되다)
② I'll buy a few things at the store. (거의 없는)
③ The ball rolled into the net. (굴러갔다)
④ They discussed environmental issues. (환경의)
⑤ He had a scar running down his left cheek. (뺨)

[05~08] 다음 대화를 읽고 물음에 답하시오.

Linda: Hi, Tony! ________(A)________
Tony: (①) I'm going to watch the musical, *Billy Elliot*.
Linda: *Billy Elliot*? (②) ________(B)________
Tony: It's about a boy ⓐ[who / what / how / why / that] became a famous dancer. I'm looking forward to watching it. (③)
Linda: Sounds interesting. ________(C)________
Tony: Jason Kim. He's a great dancer. (④)
Linda: He's my favorite actor. I ⓑ[watched / played / have watched / have played] his musical last year.
Tony: Oh, really? ________(D)________
Linda: (⑤) I have volunteer work this weekend.
Tony: Okay. Maybe next time!

출제율 90%

05 빈칸 (A)~(D)에 들어가지 않는 말을 고르시오.

① What is it about?
② What's the title?
③ Do you want to join me?
④ What are you going to do this weekend?
⑤ Who is the main actor?

출제율 100%

06 ①~⑤ 중 주어진 문장이 들어갈 곳은?

I'd love to, but I can't.

① ② ③ ④ ⑤

출제율 90%

07 위 대화에서 다음 영영풀이에 해당하는 어구를 찾아 쓰시오.

> to want it to happen because you think you will enjoy it

➡ ____________________

출제율 100%

08 위 대화의 괄호 ⓐ와 ⓑ에서 적절한 것을 고르시오.

ⓐ ____________ ⓑ ____________

출제율 95%

09 다음 대화의 빈칸에 기대를 표현하는 말을 주어진 단어를 이용하여 완성하시오.

> A: You look happy today. What's going on?
> B: I'm so excited. I'm going to learn to fly a drone.
> A: That sounds great!
> B: Yes. ______________________________
> (the park, really, forward, in)

➡ ________________________________
____________ (11 단어)

출제율 100%

10 주어진 문장 이후에 올 대화의 순서를 바르게 배열하시오.

> Minho, did you finish the math homework?

> (A) Then can you help me with my math homework?
> (B) Not yet. Math is difficult.
> (C) I'd love to, but I can't. I have to take care of my brother.
> (D) Yes, but it's interesting, too.

➡ ____________________

[11~12] 다음 대화를 읽고 물음에 답하시오.

> G: Jiho, what are you reading?
> B: I'm reading a book about baseball player named Jim Abbott.
> G: Oh, the man who was born without a right hand?
> B: That's right. He tried really hard and even won the MVP award.
> G: Yeah. His story was made into a movie. I'm going to watch it this Saturday.
> B: Really? What's the title?
> G: *Our Hero*. __________(A)__________ (it, forward, really, looking, watching, to, I'm)
> B: Can I join you?
> G: Sure. See you on Saturday.

출제율 90%

11 위 대화에서 다음 영영풀이에 해당하는 단어를 찾아 쓰시오.

> a prize or certificate that a person is given for doing something well

➡ ____________________

출제율 95%

12 빈칸 (A)를 괄호 안에 주어진 단어를 알맞게 배열하여 채우시오.

➡ ________________________________

출제율 95%

13 다음 중 어법상 올바른 문장은?

① If I knew the truth, I will tell it to you.
② If there were no corn, there will be no frozen pizza.
③ Without your help, I could not succeed.
④ If were it not for trade unions, wages would not be so high as they are.
⑤ But for his idleness, he will be a good man.

출제율 90%

14 다음 우리말을 괄호 안에 주어진 조건대로 영작하시오.

(1) 그녀가 날아다니는 양탄자를 가지고 있다면, 전 세계를 여행할 수 있을 텐데. (if로 시작) (같은 뜻을 as로 시작)

➡ ______________________

____

____

(2) 만약 눈이 많이 내린다면, 나는 산에서 스키를 탈 텐데. (if로 시작) (같은 뜻을 since로 시작)

➡ ______________________

____

____

(3) 그는 우리에게 그 기계를 어떻게 사용해야 할지 가르쳐 주었다. (to부정사 이용) (should 이용)

➡ ______________________

____

출제율 100%

15 다음 중 어법상 어색한 것을 모두 고르시오.

① He showed me how to open the safe.

② We must come to a decision about what to do next by tomorrow.

③ The message will tell you whom contacting.

④ Do you want to know what to make friends?

⑤ I am not sure where to put the key.

[16~18] 다음 글을 읽고 물음에 답하시오.

My name is Andrea and I'm a violinist in the Recycled Orchestra. Why is it called the Recycled Orchestra? It's because our musical instruments are made of ⓐ objects from a landfill. That's why it's also known as the Landfill Harmonic Orchestra.

Most of us in the orchestra are from Cateura, a small town in Paraguay. There is a huge landfill in our town. Some people even say that Cateura itself is a giant landfill. Many of us are poor. There weren't many hopes and dreams in our town. Everything began to change, however, when we met Favio Chávez.

출제율 90%

16 Why do they call it the Recycled Orchestra? Answer in English beginning with "Because".

➡ ______________________

____

출제율 95%

17 위 글의 밑줄 친 ⓐobjects와 같은 의미로 쓰인 것을 고르시오.

① His objects in life are success and fame.

② She objects to your opinion.

③ He bought everyday objects such as cups and pots.

④ I learned about two kinds of objects in today's grammar class.

⑤ You must care for the objects of consideration.

출제율 100%

18 According to the passage, which is NOT true?

① Andrea is a violinist in the Recycled Orchestra.

② Andrea's violin is made of objects from a landfill.

③ The Recycled Orchestra is also known as the Landfill Harmonic Orchestra.

④ Cateura is a huge landfill.

⑤ There weren't many hopes and dreams in Cateura.

[19~20] 다음 글을 읽고 물음에 답하시오.

Favio was an ⓐenvironment educator and a musician. He wanted to teach us music, but there was a big problem. There were only a few musical instruments in the whole town. We couldn't afford to buy new ⓑones. But Favio didn't give up. He said that we could make musical instruments with objects from the landfill. A talented man named Nicholas was able to put this idea into practice. He made violins from oil drums. He turned water pipes into flutes.

출제율 95%

19 위 글의 밑줄 친 ⓐ를 알맞은 어형으로 고치시오.

➡ ____________________

출제율 90%

20 위 글의 밑줄 친 ⓑones가 가리키는 것을 본문에서 찾아 쓰시오.

➡ ____________________

[21~23] 다음 글을 읽고 물음에 답하시오.

We had another problem. ⓐ아무도 악기를 연주할 줄 몰랐다. We didn't even know how to read music. (①) Favio taught us with great patience. (②) I still remember the first piece of music ⓑthat we played. (③) It was very short and mostly out of tune. (④) But it was the most beautiful music to us. (⑤) We felt a new hope in our hearts. From then on, we gathered to practice every day. One day, Favio told us some great news. We were going to have a concert, a real concert!

And here we are now in front of hundreds of people. They love our music. The world sends us trash, but we send back music!

출제율 95%

21 위 글의 흐름으로 보아, 주어진 문장이 들어가기에 가장 적절한 곳은?

> Step by step, we began to make some sounds on our instruments.

① ② ③ ④ ⑤

출제율 90%

22 위 글의 밑줄 친 ⓐ의 우리말에 맞게 주어진 어휘를 알맞게 배열하시오.

> musical instruments / how / no one / to play / knew

➡ ____________________

출제율 100%

23 위 글의 밑줄 친 ⓑthat과 문법적 쓰임이 같은 것을 모두 고르시오.

① The people that I spoke to were very helpful.
② The fact that he's older than me is not true.
③ I was living with my parents at that time.
④ There was no hope that she would recover her health.
⑤ It's the best movie that I've ever watched.

서술형 실전문제

01 다음 대화의 밑줄 친 문장 중 흐름상 또는 어법상 어색한 것을 찾아 바르게 고치시오.

G: Jiho, what are you reading?
B: (a)I'm reading a book about baseball player named Jim Abbott.
G: Oh, the man who was born without a right hand?
B: (b)That's right. He tried really hard and even won the MVP award.
G: Yeah. (c)His story was made into a movie. (d)I'm going to watch it this Saturday.
B: Really? What's the title?
G: (e)*Our Hero*. I'm really looking forward to watching it.
B: Can I join you?
G: (f)I'd love to, but I can't. See you on Saturday.

➡ ______________________

[02~03] 밑줄 친 우리말과 일치하도록 주어진 단어를 사용하여 영작하시오.

02

A: You look happy today. What's going on?
B: I'm so excited. I'm going to travel to Jeju-do.
A: That sounds great!
B: Yes. 나는 말 타기를 정말 고대하고 있어.

(1) ______________________
(look)

(2) ______________________
(wait)

03

A: What are you going to do this afternoon?
B: I'm going to ride my bike. Do you want to join me?
A: 그러고 싶지만, 안 돼. I have to do my homework.
B: Okay, then next time.

(1) ______________________
(can, love)

(2) ______________________
(sorry, can)

04 다음 문장을 주어진 어휘를 이용하여 바꿔 쓰시오.

(1) If I had a time machine, I would go back in time and meet King Sejong. (as)
➡ ______________________

(2) If I had a better camera, I could take better photos. (so)
➡ ______________________

(3) As she is working, she can't go to a movie with Jack. (if)
➡ ______________________

(4) Since he is not in Seoul today, he won't come to my house. (were)
➡ ______________________

(5) There could be no government if there were no people to be governed. (without)
➡ ______________________

05 다음 문장을 주어진 조건대로 바꿔 쓰시오.

(1) They want to know how people decide how much to eat. (can 이용)

➡ ______________________________

____

(2) I don't know which one to say first. (should 이용)

➡ ______________________________

(3) The most important grammar rule to master is when we should use "I" and when we should use "me." (to부정사 이용)

➡ ______________________________

____

[06~08] 다음 글을 읽고 물음에 답하시오.

My name is Andrea and I'm a violinist in the Recycled Orchestra. ⓐWhy is it called the Recycled Orchestra? It's (A)[because / why] our musical instruments are made of (B)[objects / subjects] from a landfill. That's (C)[because / why] it's also known as the Landfill Harmonic Orchestra.

Most of us in the orchestra are from Cateura, a small town in Paraguay. There is a huge landfill in our town. Some people even say that Cateura ___ⓑ___ is a giant landfill. Many of us are poor. There weren't many hopes and dreams in our town. Everything began to change, however, when we met Favio Chávez.

06 위 글의 밑줄 친 ⓐ를 능동태로 고치시오.

➡ ______________________________

____

07 위 글의 빈칸 ⓑ에 it을 알맞은 형태로 쓰시오.

➡ ______________________________

08 위 글의 괄호 (A)~(C)에서 문맥이나 어법상 알맞은 낱말을 골라 쓰시오.

(A) ________ (B) ________ (C) ________

[09~10] 다음 글을 읽고 물음에 답하시오.

We had another problem. No one knew how to play musical instruments. We didn't even know how to read music. Favio taught us with great patience. Step by step, we began to make some sounds on our instruments. I still remember the first piece of music that we played. ⓐIt was very short and mostly out of tune. But it was the most beautiful music to us. We felt a new hope in our hearts. From then on, ⓑwe gathered to practice every day. One day, Favio told us some great news. We were going to have a concert, a real concert!

And here we are now in front of hundreds of people. They love our music. The world sends us trash, but we send back music!

*We: the children of Cateura

09 위 글의 밑줄 친 ⓐIt이 가리키는 것을 본문에서 찾아 쓰시오.

➡ ______________________________

10 위 글의 밑줄 친 ⓑ를 다음과 같이 바꿔 쓸 때 빈칸에 들어갈 알맞은 말을 쓰시오.

we gathered ________ ________ we ________ practice every day 혹은 we gathered ________ ________ ________ we ________ practice every day

창의사고력 서술형 문제

01 다음은 Kate의 가족이 이번 주말에 할 계획이다. 이에 대한 정보와 주어진 <조건>에 맞게 글을 완성하시오.

조건
- 기대 표현하기, 거절하기의 표현을 각각 1번씩 사용한다.
- 주어진 단어를 이용하여 문장을 만든다.

A: ______________________ this weekend. (look)
B: Why? Do you have any special plans?
A: I'm going to go to the music festival. Do you want to join me?
B: ______________________ (can, love) I should study for the test.

02 다음 문장을 가정법을 사용하여 같은 의미가 되도록 바꿔 쓰시오.

(1) As he doesn't have enough time, he doesn't visit us.
➡ ____

(2) It's rainy, so I will not go swimming.
➡ ____

(3) Since I don't have a car, I have to walk.
➡ ____

(4) Flights are delayed because of the fog.
➡ ____

03 다음 대화를 읽고 대화의 내용과 일치하도록 빈칸을 완성하시오.

Q1. Who is the person you respect most?
A: Admiral Yi Sun-sin.
Q2. Why do you respect that person?
A: He never gave up in difficult situations.
Q3. What did that person do?
A: He saved the country and the people. He won the battle with only 12 ships.
Q4. What would you like to ask/tell that person?
A: I'd like to ask him how to make geobukseon.

Dear (A)______________,
I'm Sumin. I really respect you because (B)______________________________. You (C)______________ the country and the people. It was amazing that you won the battle (D)______________. If I had a time machine, I would go to meet you! I'd like to ask you (E)______________________. You're my hero. Thank you.

Sincerely yours,
Sumin

단원별 모의고사

01 밑줄 친 부분과 바꿔 쓸 수 있는 말을 고르시오.

> I've always been frightened of dogs.

① bored ② excited
③ angry ④ worried
⑤ scared

02 빈칸 (A)와 (B)에 들어갈 말로 알맞은 것끼리 짝지어진 것을 고르시오.

> • Simon loves you – that's ___(A)___ he wants to be with you.
> • Do you know ___(B)___ to use the coffee machine?

	(A)		(B)
①	why	–	how
②	why	–	what
③	why	–	why
④	how	–	how
⑤	how	–	what

03 다음 빈칸을 <보기>에 있는 어휘를 이용하여 채우시오. (형태 변형 가능)

> 보기
> afford look take turn

(1) I am _______ forward to working with him.
(2) The prince was _______ into a frog by the witch.
(3) We can't _______ to buy a new computer because it is too costly.
(4) I'm not worried about her — she can _______ care of herself.

04 다음 우리말에 맞도록 빈칸에 알맞은 말을 쓰시오. (철자가 주어진 경우 주어진 철자로 시작할 것.)

(1) 고래와 돌고래는 사람들이 말하면서 의사소통하는 것과 똑같이 서로 의사소통한다.
➡ Whales and dolphins communicate with o_______ _______ just like humans do – by talking.
(2) 한 팀이 이기도록 응원하는 것은 즐겁다.
➡ It is fun to c_______ _______ one team to win.
(3) 그녀는 키가 나보다 몇 인치 더 크다.
➡ She's a _______ inches taller than me.
(4) 그들은 경주에 참가할 것이다.
➡ They will _______ _______ in the race.
(5) 너 올 수 있겠니?
➡ Will you be _______ _______ come?
(6) 이 흥미로운 발견을 한 소년에게 큰 박수를 보내주세요!
➡ Let's _______ the boy _______ _______ _______ for this interesting discocery.

05 대화가 자연스럽게 연결되도록 (A)~(D)를 순서대로 배열하시오.

> (A) I'm so excited. I'm going to see Jackson's concert.
> (B) You look happy today. What's going on?
> (C) Yes. I'm really looking forward to watching Jackson's performance.
> (D) That sounds great!

➡ _______________

[06~08] 다음 대화를 읽고 물음에 답하시오.

G: Jiho, what are you reading?
B: I'm reading a book about baseball player ⓐ named Jim Abbott. (①)
G: Oh, the man who ⓑwas born without a right hand?
B: That's right. (②) He tried really hard and even ⓒwas won the MVP award.
G: Yeah. His story ⓓwas made into a movie. I'm going ⓔto watch it this Saturday. (③)
B: Really? (④)
G: *Our Hero*. (⑤) (A)I'm really looking forward to watching it.
B: Can I join you?
G: Sure. See you on Saturday.

06 ①~⑤ 중 주어진 문장이 들어갈 곳은?

What's the title?

① ② ③ ④ ⑤

07 ⓐ~ⓔ 중 흐름상 또는 어법상 어색한 것을 고르시오.

① ⓐ ② ⓑ ③ ⓒ ④ ⓓ ⑤ ⓔ

08 밑줄 친 (A)와 바꿔 쓸 수 있는 문장을 주어진 단어를 이용하여 쓰시오.

➡ ______________________________
(to, wait)

[09~11] 다음 대화를 읽고 물음에 답하시오.

G: Alex, I'm going to take part ___(A)___ a singing contest next Monday.
B: That's great, Sumin!
G: You know how to play the guitar, right?
B: Yes, I've played the guitar ___(B)___ 3 years.
G: Great. Can you play the guitar while I sing in the contest?
B: ______(C)______ I hurt my hand in gym class yesterday.
G: Oh! I'm sorry to hear that.
B: Thanks. But I'll be there to cheer for you.

09 빈칸 (A)와 (B)에 들어갈 전치사를 쓰시오.

(A) __________ (B) __________

10 빈칸 (C)에 들어갈 말로 알맞은 것을 고르시오.

① Okay, then next time.
② Yes. I'm really looking forward to it.
③ Yeah. See you next Monday.
④ I'd love to, but I can't.
⑤ Sure, I can.

11 위 대화를 읽고 답할 수 없는 질문을 고르시오.

① Is Alex able to play the guitar?
② What time is Alex going to go to the contest to cheer for Sumin?
③ How long has Alex played the guitar?
④ What contest is Sumin going to participate in?
⑤ Why can't Alex play the guitar in the contest?

12 빈칸 (A)와 (B)에 들어갈 말로 알맞은 것끼리 짝지어진 것을 고르시오.

A: What are you going to do first?
B: I'm going to watch a parade at 10:30. ____(A)____
A: Sounds fun.
B: Do you want to join me?
A: ____(B)____ I'm going to get my face painted at that time.

① I'm really looking forward to watching it. – Yes, I'd love to.
② I'm really looking forward to watching it. – I'd love to, but I can't.
③ I'm really looking forward to watching it. – I'm afraid I can.
④ I'm really looking forward to watch it. – I'd love to, but I can't.
⑤ I'm really looking forward to watch it. – I'm afraid I can.

13 다음 문장의 뜻이 나머지 넷과 다른 것은?

① If I were a doctor, I could help sick people.
② Were I a doctor, I could help sick people.
③ Since I am a doctor, I can help sick people.
④ As I am not a doctor, I can't help sick people.
⑤ I am not a doctor, so I can't help sick people.

14 다음 문장을 조동사를 이용하여 바꿔 쓰시오.

(1) Please tell me where to park my car.
➡ ____________________

(2) He hasn't decided when to leave for America.
➡ ____________________
____

(3) I'm trying to decide what to take with me.
➡ ____________________

15 다음 중 밑줄 친 부분의 쓰임이 다른 것은?

① I don't know what she'd do if it rained.
② I had no idea if it would be possible or not.
③ If it were not for her mom, she would be in big trouble.
④ If I were a scientist, I would try to invent new medicines.
⑤ I could buy a house if I had one billion won.

16 다음 중 <보기>의 밑줄 친 부분과 바꿔 쓸 수 없는 것은?

보기
If there were no tests, I wouldn't study hard.

① If it were not for tests
② Without tests
③ But for tests
④ Had there no tests
⑤ Were it not for tests

17 다음 문장을 의문사나 조동사를 이용하여 바꿔 쓰시오.

(1) 그녀가 어른이라면, 전 세계를 여행할 텐데. (an adult, travel, all around)

➡ ______________________

____

(2) 만약 내가 왕이라면, 나는 사람들에게 선물을 줄 텐데. (people, presents, give)

➡ ______________________

(3) 어떻게 시작해야 할지가 전체에서 가장 중요한 부분이다. (start, part of all)

➡ ______________________

(4) 나는 건물에서 화재가 발생하면 무엇을 해야 할지 모르겠어. (know, a fire, to do, if, there)

➡ ______________________

____

(5) 어디에 주차해야 할지 말해 주시겠습니까? (could, tell, park)

➡ ______________________

[18~19] 다음 글을 읽고 물음에 답하시오.

My name is Andrea and I'm a violinist in the Recycled Orchestra. Why is it called the Recycled Orchestra? It's because our musical instruments are made of objects from ___ⓐ___. That's why it's also known ⓑas the Landfill Harmonic Orchestra.

18 위 글의 빈칸 ⓐ에 들어갈 알맞은 말을 고르시오.

① a factory ② a marketplace
③ a workshop ④ a landfill
⑤ a shop for musical instruments

19 위 글의 밑줄 친 ⓑas와 같은 의미로 쓰인 것을 고르시오.

① As he is honest, he is trusted by everyone.
② Some animals, as the fox and the squirrel, have bushy tails.
③ This is twice as large as that.
④ As one grows older, one becomes more silent.
⑤ He was famous as a statesman.

[20~22] 다음 글을 읽고 물음에 답하시오.

Favio was an environmental educator and a musician. He wanted to teach us music, but there was a big problem. There were only a few musical instruments in the whole town. We couldn't afford (A)to buy new ones. But Favio didn't give up. He said that we could make musical instruments with objects ___ⓐ___ the landfill. A talented man named Nicholas was able to put this idea into practice. He made violins ___ⓑ___ oil drums. He turned water pipes into flutes.

*We: the children of Cateura

20 위 글의 빈칸 ⓐ와 ⓑ에 공통으로 들어갈 알맞은 전치사를 고르시오.

① on ② from ③ for
④ by ⑤ into

21 위 글의 밑줄 친 (A)to buy와 to부정사의 용법이 다른 것을 모두 고르시오.

① He is too young to read the book.
② I don't know where to go.
③ She has many children to look after.
④ He cannot be rich to ask you for some money.
⑤ It is difficult to know oneself.

22 본문의 내용과 일치하도록 다음 빈칸 (A)~(C)에 알맞은 단어를 쓰시오.

> Though there were (A)_______ _______ _______ musical instruments in the whole town and the children of Cateura couldn't afford to buy new ones, they could have musical instruments like (B)_______ and (C)_______ thanks to Favio and Nicholas.

[23~25] 다음 글을 읽고 물음에 답하시오.

> We had another problem. No one knew how to play musical instruments. We didn't even know how to read music. Favio taught us with great patience. Step by step, we began to make some sounds on our instruments. I still remember the first piece of music that we played. It was very short and mostly out of tune. But it was the most beautiful music to us. We felt a new hope in our hearts. From then on, we gathered to practice every day. One day, Favio told us some great news. We were going to have a concert, a real concert!
>
> And here we are now in front of hundreds of people. They love our music. ⓐ세상은 우리에게 쓰레기를 보내지만, 우리는 음악을 돌려보낸다!
>
> *We: the children of Cateura

23 위 글에 어울리는 속담으로 알맞지 않은 것을 고르시오.

① No pains, no gains.
② Sweet after bitter.
③ A stitch in time saves nine.
④ April showers bring May flowers.
⑤ Pain is gone, and pleasure is come.

24 위 글의 밑줄 친 ⓐ의 우리말에 맞게 주어진 어휘를 이용하여 10 단어로 영작하시오.

trash, but, send back

➡ ________________________________
____

25 According to the passage, which is NOT true?

① There was no one that knew how to play musical instruments.
② The children of Cateura didn't even know how to read music.
③ Step by step, the children of Cateura began to make some sounds on their instruments.
④ The first piece of music that they played was very short but in tune.
⑤ Favio told them that they were going to have a real concert.

MEMO

교과서 파헤치기

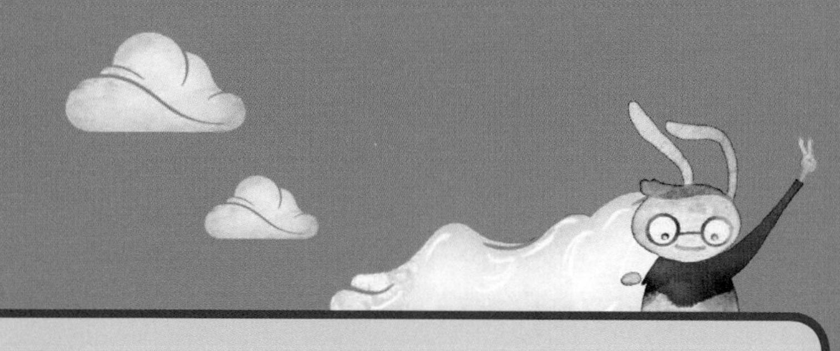

Lesson 3 **Heal the World**

Lesson 4 **Open a Book, Open Your Mind**

Lesson 5 **Believe in Yourself**

단어 Test

Step1

※ 다음 영어를 우리말로 쓰시오.

01 later ____________
02 location ____________
03 vote ____________
04 wall painting ____________
05 background ____________
06 bake ____________
07 rewarding ____________
08 neighborhood ____________
09 spot ____________
10 prepare ____________
11 nursing home ____________
12 select ____________
13 deliver ____________
14 site ____________
15 experience ____________
16 friendly ____________
17 shelf ____________
18 fur ____________
19 pack ____________
20 apply ____________
21 recycling bin ____________
22 arrange ____________
23 remove ____________
24 divide ____________
25 clearly ____________
26 matter ____________
27 neat ____________
28 politely ____________
29 donation ____________
30 manager ____________
31 plant ____________
32 reply ____________
33 suggest ____________
34 volunteer ____________
35 pick up ____________
36 get along with ~ ____________
37 be proud of ~ ____________
38 get together ____________
39 keep ~ in mind ____________
40 take a break ____________
41 make sure ~ ____________
42 be on time ____________
43 give ~ a hand ____________

단어 Test

Step2

※ 다음 우리말을 영어로 쓰시오.

01 배경 ____________
02 운영자, 관리자 ____________
03 짐을 꾸리다 ____________
04 물감 ____________
05 기부, 기증 ____________
06 문제되다, 중요하다 ____________
07 깨끗한 ____________
08 현장, 장소 ____________
09 보람 있는 ____________
10 놀이 공원 ____________
11 경험 ____________
12 지원하다 ____________
13 분명하게 ____________
14 재활용 쓰레기통 ____________
15 배열하다 ____________
16 투표하다 ____________
17 선택하다, 선정하다 ____________
18 (특정한) 장소, 자리 ____________
19 벽화 ____________
20 양로원 ____________
21 예의 바르게 ____________
22 책꽂이 ____________
23 배달하다 ____________
24 근처, 이웃 ____________
25 준비하다 ____________
26 없애다, 제거하다 ____________
27 나누다 ____________
28 제안하다 ____________
29 자원봉사; 자원봉사하다 ____________
30 마을 ____________
31 응답하다 ____________
32 날개 ____________
33 나누다, 공유하다 ____________
34 칠판 ____________
35 치우다, 줍다 ____________
36 ~을 자랑스러워하다 ____________
37 줄서다 ____________
38 목욕시키다 ____________
39 휴식을 취하다 ____________
40 모이다 ____________
41 제 시간에 도착하다 ____________
42 ~와 사이좋게 지내다 ____________
43 ~에게 도움을 주다 ____________

단어 Test

Step3

※ 다음 영영풀이에 알맞은 단어를 <보기>에서 골라 쓴 후, 우리말 뜻을 쓰시오.

1 __________: to be important: __________

2 __________: a particular place: __________

3 __________: to put a seed, flower, or plant in the ground: __________

4 __________: to take something to a person or place: __________

5 __________: to put things into cases, bags, etc. ready for a trip: __________

6 __________: to move or take something away from a place: __________

7 __________: a picture that you draw with a pencil, pen, etc.: __________

8 __________: a person who does a job without being paid: __________

9 __________: to cook something using dry heat, in an oven: __________

10 __________: something that you give to help a person or organization: __________

11 __________: to separate or make something separate into parts: __________

12 __________: to put a group of things or people in a particular order or position: __________

13 __________: the area that is behind the main thing that you are looking at: __________

14 __________: to choose someone or something from a group of people or things: __________

15 __________: a large park with many machines that you can ride on, such as roller coasters: __________

16 __________: someone whose job is to manage part or all of a company or other organization: __________

보기

manager	arrange	divide	location
pack	bake	donation	select
amusement park	volunteer	background	matter
deliver	remove	drawing	plant

대화문 Test

Step1

※ 다음 우리말과 일치하도록 빈칸에 알맞은 말을 쓰시오.

Listen and Speak 1 A

B: ________ are all these boxes and books ________?

G: I'm ________ the books for the ________ center. Can you ________ ________ ________ hand?

B: Sure. What do you ________ me ________ do?

G: Please ________ the ________ ________ the boxes.

B: No ________.

B: 이 박스와 책들은 다 무엇에 쓰려는 거니?
G: 기부 센터에 보내려고 책을 싸고 있어. 도와줄래?
B: 물론이야. 내가 무엇을 하길 원하니?
G: 박스에 주소를 좀 써 줘.
B: 그래.

Listen and Speak 1 B

B: What is ________ ________?

G: I'm ________ cookies.

B: ________ are you ________ so ________ cookies?

G: ________ ________ the people at the ________ ________.

B: That's very ________ ________ you.

G: ________ ________ ________ me a ________?

B: Sure. What ________ ________ ________ ________ to do?

G: Please ________ the cookies in the ________ ________. Three cookies in ________ box.

B: Okay.

B: 이 엉망진창은 뭐니?
G: 쿠키를 굽고 있어.
B: 왜 이렇게 많은 쿠키를 굽고 있니?
G: 쿠키는 양로원에 계신 분들을 위한 거야.
B: 정말 착하구나.
G: 도와줄래?
B: 물론이야. 내가 무엇을 하길 원하니?
G: 선물 상자에 쿠키를 좀 넣어 줘. 상자 하나에 쿠키 3개씩.
B: 알겠어.

Listen and Speak 1 C

1. A: What are you ________?

   B: I'm ________ ________ my ________ tomorrow. ________ ________ ________ me?

   A: Sure. ________ ________ ________ ________ me ________ ________?

   B: Please ________ ________ ________ ________ the box.

   A: No problem.

2. A: What ________ you ________?

   B: I'm ________ ________ my ________ tomorrow. ________ ________ ________ ________?

   A: Sure. What do you ________ ________ ________ ________?

   B: Please ________ the chairs ________.

   A: No problem.

1. A: 너 뭐 하고 있니?
   B: 내일 이사를 위해 짐을 싸는 중이야. 도와줄래?
   A: 물론이지. 내가 무엇을 하길 원하니?
   B: 옷을 상자 안에 넣어 줘.
   A: 그래.

2. A: 너 뭐 하고 있니?
   B: 내일 이사를 위해 짐을 싸는 중이야. 도와줄래?
   A: 물론이지. 내가 무엇을 하길 원하니?
   B: 의자를 밖으로 옮겨 줘.
   A: 그래.

3. A: ________ ________ ________ ________?

B: I'm ________ ________ my ________ tomorrow. ________ ________ ________ ________?

A: Sure. ________ ________ ________ ________ ________ ________ ________?

B: Please ________ ________the trach.

A: No problem.

3. A: 너 뭐 하고 있니?
B: 내일 이사를 위해 짐을 싸는 중이야. 도와줄래?
A: 물론이지. 내가 무엇을 하길 원하니?
B: 쓰레기를 밖에 갖다 버려 줘.
A: 그래.

Listen and Speak 2 A

B: ________ the concert, Mom.

W: Okay, I ________. Thanks. Your dinner ________ ________ the table.

B: All right. ________ ________ ________ me.

W: ________ ________ ________ ________ the dog ________ you have dinner.

B: Okay. Mom, you ________ go now. Dad is waiting in the car.

B: 콘서트 재미있게 보세요, 엄마.
W: 그래. 고마워. 저녁은 식탁에 있어.
B: 알겠어요. 저는 걱정 마세요.
W: 저녁 먹은 후에 개 밥 주는 거 명심해라.
B: 알겠어요. 엄마, 이제 가셔야 해요. 아빠가 차에서 기다리고 계셔요.

Listen and Speak 2 B

B: Hello, class. ________ ________ ________ four people and ________ around the tables. Today we're going ________ ________ bacon and egg sandwiches. ________ ________ ________ two rules for our class. First, ________ ________ you wash your hands ________ ________ ________. ________, be careful ________ you use a knife. All right, ________ start.

B: 안녕하세요, 여러분. 4명씩 모둠을 만들어 탁자에 둘러앉으세요. 오늘 우리는 베이컨 달걀 샌드위치를 만들 거예요. 우리 수업의 두 가지 규칙에 유의하세요. 첫째, 시작하기 전에 손을 씻는 것을 명심하세요. 둘째, 칼을 사용할 때 조심하세요. 좋아요, 시작해 봐요.

Listen and Speak 2 C

1. A: It's time ________ ________ home.

B: Yes. ________ ________ you ________ the doors.

A: Okay, I will. ________ else?

B: No, ________ it. See you tomorrow.

2. A: It's ________ ________ go home.

B: Yes. ________ ________ ________ ________ the board.

A: Okay, I will. ________ ________?

B: No, that's it. See you tomorrow.

3. A: ________ ________ ________ ________ home.

B: Yes. ________ ________ you ________ ________ ________.

A: Okay, I ________. Anything ________?

B: No, that's it. See you tomorrow.

1. A: 집에 갈 시간이야.
B: 응. 문 잠그는 거 명심해.
A: 알겠어, 그렇게 할게. 또 다른 건?
B: 없어, 그게 전부야. 내일 보자.

2. A: 이제 집에 갈 시간이야.
B: 응. 칠판 닦는 거 명심해.
A: 알겠어, 그렇게 할게. 또 다른 건?
B: 없어, 그게 전부야. 내일 보자.

3. A: 이제 집에 갈 시간이야.
B: 응. 식물에 물 주는 거 명심해.
A: 알겠어, 그렇게 할게. 또 다른 건?
B: 없어, 그게 전부야. 내일 보자.

Real Life Talk Watch a Video

Woman: Good morning. ________ ________ ________ ________ for you?

Tony: Hi. I'm ________ ________ the ________ ________.

Woman: Oh, you ________ ________ Tony.

Tony: That's right. ________ ________ ________ ________ ________ ________ ________ today?

Woman: Please ________ this book ________ ________ ________ in the ________ ________.

Tony: No problem. ________ I ________ in now?

Woman: Yes. Please ________ ________ Room 7.

Tony: Okay. Is there ________ ________ ________ ________ mind?

Woman: Yes. ________ ________ ________ read ________ ________ ________.

Tony: Okay. I'll ________ ________ ________.

Woman: 안녕하세요. 무엇을 도와드릴까요?
Tony: 안녕하세요. 저는 봉사 활동을 하러 왔어요.
Woman: 오, Tony군요.
Tony: 맞아요. 오늘 제가 무엇을 하길 원하세요?
Woman: 녹음실에서 시각 장애인들을 위해 이 책을 읽어 주세요.
Tony: 알겠어요. 지금 들어가야 하나요?
Woman: 네. 7번 방으로 들어가 주세요.
Tony: 네. 명심해야 할 것이 있나요?
Woman: 네. 천천히 그리고 명확하게 읽어야 하는 것을 명심하세요.
Tony: 네. 최선을 다할게요.

Real Life Talk Step 3

1. **A:** Hi, I'm Minsu. ________ ________ ________ the volunteer work.
   B: Thanks ________ ________, Minsu.
   A: What ________ ________ ________ ________ ________ ________ today?
   B: Please ________ the dog ________ ________.
   A: Okay. ________ ________ ________ to ________ ________ ________?
   B: Yes. ________ ________ you ________ the ________ first.
   A: Okay, I will.
2. **A:** Hi, I'm Tony. ________ ________ ________ ________ ________.
   B: ________ ________ coming, Tony.
   A: ________ ________ ________ ________ ________ ________ ________ today?
   B: Please record a book ________ ________ ________.
   A: Okay. ________ ________ ________ ________ ________ ________ ________?
   B: Yes. Make ________ you read ________ and ________.
   A: Okay, I will.

1. A: 안녕하세요. 저는 민수예요. 저는 봉사 활동을 하러 왔어요.
   B: 민수 군, 와 주셔서 감사합니다.
   A: 오늘 제가 무엇을 하길 원하세요?
   B: 개를 목욕시켜 주세요.
   A: 네. 명심해야 할 것이 있나요?
   B: 네. 털을 먼저 빗길 것을 명심하세요.
   A: 네. 그렇게 할게요.
2. A: 안녕하세요. 저는 Tony예요. 저는 봉사 활동을 하러 왔어요.
   B: Tony 군, 와 주셔서 감사합니다.
   A: 오늘 제가 무엇을 하길 원하세요?
   B: 시각 장애인들을 위해 책을 녹음해 주세요.
   A: 네. 유념해야 할 것이 있나요?
   B: 네. 천천히 그리고 명확하게 읽어야 하는 것을 명심하세요.
   A: 네. 그렇게 할게요.

대화문 Test

※ 다음 우리말에 맞도록 대화를 영어로 쓰시오.

Listen and Speak 1 A

B: ______________________________

G: ______________________________

B: ______________________________

G: ______________________________

B: ______________________________

B: 이 박스와 책들은 다 무엇에 쓰려는 거니?
G: 기부 센터에 보내려고 책을 싸고 있어. 도와줄래?
B: 물론이야. 내가 무엇을 하길 원하니?
G: 박스에 주소를 좀 써 줘.
B: 그래.

Listen and Speak 1 B

B: ______________________________

G: ______________________________

B: ______________________________

G: ______________________________

B: ______________________________

G: ______________________________

B: ______________________________

G: ______________________________

B: ______________________________

B: 이 엉망진창은 뭐니?
G: 쿠키를 굽고 있어.
B: 왜 이렇게 많은 쿠키를 굽고 있니?
G: 쿠키는 양로원에 계신 분들을 위한 거야.
B: 정말 착하구나.
G: 도와줄래?
B: 물론이야. 내가 무엇을 하길 원하니?
G: 선물 상자에 쿠키를 좀 넣어 줘. 상자 하나에 쿠키 3개씩.
B: 알겠어.

Listen and Speak 1 C

1. A: ______________________________

   B: ______________________________

   A: ______________________________

   B: ______________________________

   A: ______________________________

2. A: ______________________________

   B: ______________________________

   A: ______________________________

   B: ______________________________

   A: ______________________________

1. A: 너 뭐 하고 있니?
   B: 내일 이사를 위해 짐을 싸는 중이야. 도와줄래?
   A: 물론이지. 내가 무엇을 하길 원하니?
   B: 옷을 상자 안에 넣어 줘.
   A: 그래.

2. A: 너 뭐 하고 있니?
   B: 내일 이사를 위해 짐을 싸는 중이야. 도와줄래?
   A: 물론이지. 내가 무엇을 하길 원하니?
   B: 의자를 밖으로 옮겨 줘.
   A: 그래.

3. A:

B:

A:

B:

A:

3. A: 너 뭐 하고 있니?
B: 내일 이사를 위해 짐을 싸는 중이야. 도와줄래?
A: 물론이지. 내가 무엇을 하길 원하니?
B: 쓰레기를 밖에 갖다 버려 줘.
A: 그래.

Listen and Speak 2 A

B:

W:

B:

W:

B:

B: 콘서트 재미있게 보세요, 엄마.
W: 그래. 고마워. 저녁은 식탁에 있어.
B: 알겠어요. 저는 걱정 마세요.
W: 저녁 먹은 후에 개 밥 주는 거 명심해라.
B: 알겠어요. 엄마, 이제 가셔야 해요. 아빠가 차에서 기다리고 계셔요.

Listen and Speak 2 B

B:

B: 안녕하세요, 여러분. 4명씩 모둠을 만들어 탁자에 둘러앉으세요. 오늘 우리는 베이컨 달걀 샌드위치를 만들 거예요. 우리 수업의 두 가지 규칙에 유의하세요. 첫째, 시작하기 전에 손을 씻는 것을 명심하세요. 둘째, 칼을 사용할 때 조심하세요. 좋아요, 시작해 봐요.

Listen and Speak 2 C

1. A:

B:

A:

B:

2. A:

B:

A:

B:

3. A:

B:

A:

B:

1. A: 집에 갈 시간이야.
B: 응. 문 잠그는 거 명심해.
A: 알겠어, 그렇게 할게. 또 다른 건?
B: 없어, 그게 전부야. 내일 보자.

2. A: 이제 집에 갈 시간이야.
B: 응. 칠판 닦는 거 명심해.
A: 알겠어, 그렇게 할게. 또 다른 건?
B: 없어, 그게 전부야. 내일 보자.

3. A: 이제 집에 갈 시간이야.
B: 응. 식물에 물 주는 거 명심해.
A: 알겠어, 그렇게 할게. 또 다른 건?
B: 없어, 그게 전부야. 내일 보자.

Real Life Talk Watch a Video

Woman: ______________________________

Tony: ______________________________

Woman: ______________________________

Tony: ______________________________

Woman: ______________________________

Tony: ______________________________

Woman: ______________________________

Tony: ______________________________

Woman: ______________________________

Tony: ______________________________

Woman: 안녕하세요. 무엇을 도와드릴까요?
Tony: 안녕하세요. 저는 봉사 활동을 하러 왔어요.
Woman: 오, Tony군요.
Tony: 맞아요. 오늘 제가 무엇을 하길 원하세요?
Woman: 녹음실에서 시각 장애인들을 위해 이 책을 읽어 주세요.
Tony: 알겠어요. 지금 들어가야 하나요?
Woman: 네. 7번 방으로 들어가 주세요.
Tony: 네. 명심해야 할 것이 있나요?
Woman: 네. 천천히 그리고 명확하게 읽어야 하는 것을 명심하세요.
Tony: 네. 최선을 다할게요.

Real Life Talk Step 3

1. A: ______________________________
   B: ______________________________
   A: ______________________________
   B: ______________________________
   A: ______________________________
   B: ______________________________
   A: ______________________________
2. A: ______________________________
   B: ______________________________
   A: ______________________________
   B: ______________________________
   A: ______________________________
   B: ______________________________
   A: ______________________________

1. A: 안녕하세요. 저는 민수예요. 저는 봉사 활동을 하러 왔어요.
   B: 민수 군, 와 주셔서 감사합니다.
   A: 오늘 제가 무엇을 하길 원하세요?
   B: 개를 목욕시켜 주세요.
   A: 네. 명심해야 할 것이 있나요?
   B: 네. 털을 먼저 빗길 것을 명심하세요.
   A: 네. 그렇게 할게요.
2. A: 안녕하세요. 저는 Tony예요. 저는 봉사 활동을 하러 왔어요.
   B: Tony 군, 와 주셔서 감사합니다.
   A: 오늘 제가 무엇을 하길 원하세요?
   B: 시각 장애인들을 위해 책을 녹음해 주세요.
   A: 네. 유념해야 할 것이 있나요?
   B: 네. 천천히 그리고 명확하게 읽어야 하는 것을 명심하세요.
   A: 네. 그렇게 할게요.

본문 Test

Step1

※ 다음 우리말과 일치하도록 빈칸에 알맞은 것을 골라 쓰시오.

1 ________ a ________ ________
A. Tomorrow B. Paint C. Better

2 Hi. ________ ________ ________ Homin.
A. is B. name C. my

3 ________ is me in ________ of the ________ painting.
A. front B. wall C. this

4 The wings are ________ pretty, ________ ________?
A. they B. so C. aren't

5 Many people like to ________ pictures in ________ of wall ________.
A. paintings B. take C. front

6 They make ________ ________ ________ and new.
A. bright B. neighborhoods C. old

7 ________ month, I visited a ________ ________ wall paintings in Yeosu.
A. with B. last C. village

8 As I was taking a picture, a ________ ________ ________ in my ________.
A. head B. went C. light D. on

9 I ________, "I'm ________ the school ________ club.
A. in B. art C. thought

10 ________ ________ ________ do wall paintings ________ these?"
A. we B. why C. like D. don't

11 I ________ this ________ at the next club ________, and the members loved it.
A. meeting B. suggested C. idea

12 We ________ a ________ ________ project ________ the Internet.
A. teen B. found C. on D. volunteer

13 The project was ________ do a ________ ________ in our ________.
A. to B. neighborhood C. painting D. wall

14 We ________ ________ it, and two weeks ________, our club was ________!
A. for B. selected C. applied D. later

15 The ________ of the project ________ ________.
A. came B. day C. finally

16 The project manager ________ ________ ________ at the painting ________ at 9 a.m.
A. site B. meet C. had D. us

17 The wall was ________ very ________ ________.
A. poor B. condition C. in

1 더 나은 내일을 그려라

2 안녕. 내 이름은 호민이야.

3 벽화 앞에 있는 사람이 나야.

4 날개가 예뻐, 그렇지 않니?

5 많은 사람들이 벽화 앞에서 사진 찍는 것을 좋아해.

6 벽화는 오래된 마을을 밝고 새롭게 만들어.

7 지난달에 나는 여수에 있는 벽화 마을을 방문했어.

8 내가 사진을 찍을 때 머릿속에 좋은 생각이 떠올랐어.

9 나는 생각했어. "나는 학교 미술 동아리에 있잖아.

10 우리가 이것처럼 벽화를 그리면 어떨까?

11 나는 이 아이디어를 다음 동아리 모임에서 제안했고, 동아리 부원들은 그것을 아주 좋아했어.

12 우리는 인터넷에서 청소년 봉사 프로젝트를 찾았어.

13 그 프로젝트는 우리 마을에 벽화를 그리는 것이었어.

14 우리는 거기에 지원했고, 2주 후에 우리 동아리가 선택되었어!

15 마침내 프로젝트 날이 되었어.

16 프로젝트 책임자는 우리를 오전 9시에 그림 그리는 곳에서 만나게 했어.

17 벽은 상태가 별로 좋지 않았어.

18 There were _______ _______ and _______ on some _______.
A. writings B. parts C. strange D. drawings

19 _______ _______ had old posters _______ them.
A. on B. parts C. other

20 We _______ the posters first and painted _______ the writings and drawings _______ white _______.
A. with B. removed C. paint D. over

21 The manager _______ _______ _______ anything we wanted.
A. us B. let C. paint

22 We _______ to paint _______ _______ because the wall was _______ an elementary school.
A. cute B. near C. something D. decided

23 We _______ _______ three groups and _______ painting.
A. into B. divided C. began

24 I _______ _______ the _______ Minsu and Jiwon.
A. with B. in C. group D. was

25 I _______ my _______ and started to _______ my favorite movie _______.
A. character B. chose C. paint D. spot

26 Minsu _______ some flowers and Jiwon _______ some _______ _______.
A. background B. did C. drawings D. painted

27 Our club painted _______ _______ five _______.
A. hours B. for C. about

28 _______ we _______, we got _______ and _______ the day's experiences.
A. shared B. together C. finished D. after

29 Minsu _______ _______ _______ _______ his flower painting.
A. of B. was C. proud D. very

30 He said, "My flower is _______ real _______ a bee _______ _______ it."
A. landed B. so C. that D. on

31 I said, "Drawing on a wall was _______ _______ _______ _______ on paper."
A. than B. drawing C. harder D. much

32 We all _______ that our wall painting _______ _______.
A. perfect B. agreed C. wasn't

33 _______ it _______ _______.
A. matter B. but C. didn't

34 We made our neighborhood _______ _______ _______ and _______.
A. brighter B. a C. happier D. little

35 We were _______ _______ _______.
A. of B. proud C. ourselves

36 We _______ _______ _______ pictures _______ a wall that day.
A. just B. didn't C. paint D. on

37 It was _______ _______ _______ that we _______.
A. better B. tomorrow C. a D. painted

18 몇 군데에는 이상한 낙서와 그림이 있었어.

19 다른 부분에는 오래된 포스터들이 붙어 있었어.

20 우리는 먼저 포스터들을 제거하고 낙서와 그림을 흰 페인트로 덧칠했어.

21 책임자는 우리가 원하는 어떤 것이든 그리게 했어.

22 우리는 그 벽이 초등학교 근처에 있어서 귀여운 뭔가를 그리기로 했어.

23 우리는 세 그룹으로 나뉘어 그리기 시작했어.

24 나는 민수와 지원이와 같은 그룹이었어.

25 나는 내 구역을 정해서 가장 좋아하는 영화 캐릭터를 그리기 시작했어.

26 민수는 몇 송이의 꽃을 그렸고 지원이는 배경 그림을 그렸어.

27 우리 동아리는 약 다섯 시간 동안 그림을 그렸어.

28 끝난 후에 우리는 모여서 그날의 경험을 함께 이야기했어.

29 민수는 자신이 그린 꽃 그림을 정말 자랑스러워했어.

30 그는 "내 꽃이 정말 진짜 같아서 벌이 꽃에 앉았어."라고 말했어.

31 나는 "벽에 그리는 것이 종이에 그리는 것보다 훨씬 힘들었어."라고 말했어.

32 우리 모두는 우리 벽화가 완벽하지는 않다는 것에 동의했어.

33 하지만 그것은 중요하지 않았어.

34 우리는 동네를 조금 더 밝고 행복하게 만들었어.

35 우리는 우리 자신이 자랑스러웠어.

36 우리는 그날 벽에 그림만 그린 게 아니었어.

37 우리가 그린 것은 바로 더 나은 내일이었어.

※ 다음 우리말과 일치하도록 빈칸에 알맞은 말을 쓰시오.

1 Paint a ________ ________

더 나은 내일을 그려라

2 Hi. ________ ________ ________ Homin.

안녕. 내 이름은 호민이야.

3 ________ ________ ________ in ________ of the wall painting.

벽화 앞에 있는 사람이 나야.

4 The wings are so pretty, ________ ________?

날개가 예뻐, 그렇지 않니?

5 Many people like to ________ ________ in front of ________ ________.

많은 사람들이 벽화 앞에서 사진 찍는 것을 좋아해.

6 They make ________ ________ ________ and new.

벽화는 오래된 마을을 밝고 새롭게 만들어.

7 ________ ________, I visited a village ________ ________ ________ in Yeosu.

지난달에 나는 여수에 있는 벽화 마을을 방문했어.

8 ________ I was taking a picture, ________ ________ ________ ________ ________ ________ ________.

내가 사진을 찍을 때 머릿속에 좋은 생각이 떠올랐어.

9 I ________, "________ ________ the school art club.

나는 생각했어. "나는 학교 미술 동아리에 있잖아.

10 ________ ________ ________ do wall paintings ________ these?"

우리가 이것처럼 벽화를 그리면 어떨까?

11 I ________ ________ ________ at the next club meeting, and the members loved it.

나는 이 아이디어를 다음 동아리 모임에서 제안했고, 동아리 부원들은 그것을 아주 좋아했어.

12 We ________ a teen volunteer project ________ ________ ________.

우리는 인터넷에서 청소년 봉사 프로젝트를 찾았어.

13 The project was ________ ________ ________ ________ ________ in our neighborhood.

그 프로젝트는 우리 마을에 벽화를 그리는 것이었어.

14 We ________ ________ it, and two weeks ________, our club ________ ________!

우리는 거기에 지원했고, 2주 후에 우리 동아리가 선택되었어!

15 The day of the project ________ ________.

마침내 프로젝트 날이 되었어.

16 The project manager ________ ________ ________ at the ________ ________ at 9 a.m.

프로젝트 책임자는 우리를 오전 9시에 그림 그리는 곳에서 만나게 했어.

17 The wall ________ ________ ________ ________ ________.

벽은 상태가 별로 좋지 않았어.

18 There were ________ ________ ________ ________ on some parts.

19 ________ ________ had old posters on them.

20 We removed the posters first and ________ ________ the writings and drawings ________ ________ ________.

21 The manager ________ ________ ________ anything we wanted.

22 We ________ ________ paint ________ ________ because the wall was near an elementary school.

23 We ________ ________ three groups and began painting.

24 I ________ ________ ________ ________ with Minsu and Jiwon.

25 I ________ ________ ________ and started to paint my favorite ________ ________.

26 Minsu ________ some flowers and Jiwon ________ some ________ ________.

27 Our club painted ________ ________ five hours.

28 After we ________, we ________ ________ and ________ the day's ________.

29 Minsu ________ ________ ________ ________ his flower painting.

30 He said, "My flower is ________ real ________ a bee ________ ________ it."

31 I said, "________ on a wall was ________ ________ ________ drawing on paper."

32 We all agreed that our wall painting ________ ________.

33 But it didn't ________.

34 We made our neighborhood ________ ________ ________ ________ ________.

35 We ________ ________ ________ ________.

36 We ________ ________ ________ pictures on a wall that day.

37 It was ________ ________ ________ that we painted.

18 몇 군데에는 이상한 낙서와 그림이 있었어.

19 다른 부분에는 오래된 포스터들이 붙어 있었어.

20 우리는 먼저 포스터들을 제거하고 낙서와 그림을 흰 페인트로 덧칠했어.

21 책임자는 우리가 원하는 어떤 것이든 그리게 했어.

22 우리는 그 벽이 초등학교 근처에 있어서 귀여운 뭔가를 그리기로 했어.

23 우리는 세 그룹으로 나뉘어 그리기 시작했어.

24 나는 민수와 지원이와 같은 그룹이었어.

25 나는 내 구역을 정해서 가장 좋아하는 영화 캐릭터를 그리기 시작했어.

26 민수는 몇 송이의 꽃을 그렸고 지원이는 배경 그림을 그렸어.

27 우리 동아리는 약 다섯 시간 동안 그림을 그렸어.

28 끝난 후에 우리는 모여서 그날의 경험을 함께 이야기했어.

29 민수는 자신이 그린 꽃 그림을 정말 자랑스러워했어.

30 그는 "내 꽃이 정말 진짜 같아서 벌이 꽃에 앉았어."라고 말했어.

31 나는 "벽에 그리는 것이 종이에 그리는 것보다 훨씬 힘들었어."라고 말했어.

32 우리 모두는 우리 벽화가 완벽하지는 않다는 것에 동의했어.

33 하지만 그것은 중요하지 않았어.

34 우리는 동네를 조금 더 밝고 행복하게 만들었어.

35 우리는 우리 자신이 자랑스러웠어.

36 우리는 그날 벽에 그림만 그린 게 아니었어.

37 우리가 그린 것은 바로 더 나은 내일이었어.

본문 Test

Step3

※ 다음 문장을 우리말로 쓰시오.

1 Paint a Better Tomorrow

➡ ____________________

2 Hi. My name is Homin.

➡ ____________________

3 This is me in front of the wall painting.

➡ ____________________

4 The wings are so pretty, aren't they?

➡ ____________________

5 Many people like to take pictures in front of wall paintings.

➡ ____________________

6 They make old neighborhoods bright and new.

➡ ____________________

7 Last month, I visited a village with wall paintings in Yeosu.

➡ ____________________

8 As I was taking a picture, a light went on in my head.

➡ ____________________

9 I thought, "I'm in the school art club.

➡ ____________________

10 Why don't we do wall paintings like these?"

➡ ____________________

11 I suggested this idea at the next club meeting, and the members loved it.

➡ ____________________

12 We found a teen volunteer project on the Internet.

➡ ____________________

13 The project was to do a wall painting in our neighborhood.

➡ ____________________

14 We applied for it, and two weeks later, our club was selected!

➡ ____________________

15 The day of the project finally came.

➡ ____________________

16 The project manager had us meet at the painting site at 9 a.m.

➡ ____________________

17 The wall was in very poor condition.

➡ ____________________

18 There were strange writings and drawings on some parts.
➡ ______________________________

19 Other parts had old posters on them.
➡ ______________________________

20 We removed the posters first and painted over the writings and drawings with white paint.
➡ ______________________________

21 The manager let us paint anything we wanted.
➡ ______________________________

22 We decided to paint something cute because the wall was near an elementary school.
➡ ______________________________

23 We divided into three groups and began painting.
➡ ______________________________

24 I was in the group with Minsu and Jiwon.
➡ ______________________________

25 I chose my spot and started to paint my favorite movie character.
➡ ______________________________

26 Minsu painted some flowers and Jiwon did some background drawings.
➡ ______________________________

27 Our club painted for about five hours.
➡ ______________________________

28 After we finished, we got together and shared the day's experiences.
➡ ______________________________

29 Minsu was very proud of his flower painting.
➡ ______________________________

30 He said, "My flower is so real that a bee landed on it."
➡ ______________________________

31 I said, "Drawing on a wall was much harder than drawing on paper."
➡ ______________________________

32 We all agreed that our wall painting wasn't perfect.
➡ ______________________________

33 But it didn't matter.
➡ ______________________________

34 We made our neighborhood a little brighter and happier.
➡ ______________________________

35 We were proud of ourselves.
➡ ______________________________

36 We didn't just paint pictures on a wall that day.
➡ ______________________________

37 It was a better tomorrow that we painted.
➡ ______________________________

본문 Test

Step4

※ 다음 괄호 안의 단어들을 우리말에 맞도록 바르게 배열하시오.

1 (a / Paint / Tomorrow / Better)

➡ ______________________________

1 더 나은 내일을 그려라

2 (hi. // name / my / Homin. / is)

➡ ______________________________

2 안녕. 내 이름은 호민이야.

3 (is / this / in / me / of / front / wall / the / painting.)

➡ ______________________________

3 벽화 앞에 있는 사람이 나야.

4 (wings / the / so / are / pretty, / they? / aren't)

➡ ______________________________

4 날개가 예뻐, 그렇지 않니?

5 (people / many / to / like / pictures / take / front / in / wall / of / paintings.)

➡ ______________________________

5 많은 사람들이 벽화 앞에서 사진 찍는 것을 좋아해.

6 (make / they / neighborhoods / old / new. / and / bright)

➡ ______________________________

6 벽화는 오래된 마을을 밝고 새롭게 만들어.

7 (month, / last / visited / I / village / a / wall / with / paintings / Yeosu. / in)

➡ ______________________________

7 지난달에 나는 여수에 있는 벽화 마을을 방문했어.

8 (I / as / taking / was / picture, / a / light / a / in / went / on / head. / my)

➡ ______________________________

8 내가 사진을 찍을 때 머릿속에 좋은 생각이 떠올랐어.

9 (thought, / I / in / "I'm / the / art / school / club.)

➡ ______________________________

9 나는 생각했어. "나는 학교 미술 동아리에 있잖아.

10 (don't / why / do / we / paintings / wall / these?" / like)

➡ ______________________________

10 우리가 이것처럼 벽화를 그리면 어떨까?

11 (suggested / I / idea / this / the / at / next / meeting, / club / and / members / the / it. / loved)

➡ ______________________________

____

11 나는 이 아이디어를 다음 동아리 모임에서 제안했고, 동아리 부원들은 그것을 아주 좋아했어.

12 (found / we / teen / a / volunteer / on / project / Internet. / the)

➡ ______________________________

12 우리는 인터넷에서 청소년 봉사 프로젝트를 찾았어.

13 (project / the / to / was / do / painting / wall / a / our / in / neighborhood.)

➡ ______________________________

13 그 프로젝트는 우리 마을에 벽화를 그리는 것이었어.

14 (applied / we / it, / for / two / and / later, / weeks / club / our / selected! / was)

➡ ______________________________

15 (day / the / of / project / the / came. / finally)

➡ ______________________________

16 (project / the / had / manager / us / at / meet / the / site / painting / 9 / a.m. / at)

➡ ______________________________

17 (wall / the / in / was / very / condition. / poor)

➡ ______________________________

18 (were / there / writings / strange / and / on / drawings / parts. / some)

➡ ______________________________

19 (parts / other / old / had / on / posters / them.)

➡ ______________________________

20 (removed / we / posters / the / and / first / over / painted / writings / the / and / drawings / white / with / paint.)

➡ ______________________________

____

21 (manager / the / us / let / anything / paint / wanted. / we)

➡ ______________________________

22 (decided / we / paint / to / cute / something / the / because / wall / near / was / elementary / school. / an)

➡ ______________________________

____

23 (divided / we / three / into / and / groups / painting. / began)

➡ ______________________________

24 (was / I / the / in / group / with / Jiwon. / and / Minsu)

➡ ______________________________

25 (chose / I / spot / my / and / to / started / my / paint / movie / favorite / character.)

➡ ______________________________

14 우리는 거기에 지원했고, 2주 후에 우리 동아리가 선택되었어!

15 마침내 프로젝트 날이 되었어.

16 프로젝트 책임자는 우리를 오전 9시에 그림 그리는 곳에서 만나게 했어.

17 벽은 상태가 별로 좋지 않았어.

18 몇 군데에는 이상한 낙서와 그림이 있었어.

19 다른 부분에는 오래된 포스터들이 붙어 있었어.

20 우리는 먼저 포스터들을 제거하고 낙서와 그림을 흰 페인트로 덧칠했어.

21 책임자는 우리가 원하는 어떤 것이든 그리게 했어.

22 우리는 그 벽이 초등학교 근처에 있어서 귀여운 뭔가를 그리기로 했어.

23 우리는 세 그룹으로 나뉘어 그리기 시작했어.

24 나는 민수와 지원이와 같은 그룹이었어.

25 나는 내 구역을 정해서 가장 좋아하는 영화 캐릭터를 그리기 시작했어.

26 (painted / Minsu / flowers / some / and / did / Jiwon / background / some / drawings.)

➡ ____________________

27 (club / our / painted / about / for / hours. / five)

➡ ____________________

28 (we / after / finished, / got / we / together / shared / and / the / experiences. / day's)

➡ ____________________

29 (was / Minsu / proud / very / his / of / painting. / flower)

➡ ____________________

30 (said, / he / flower / "my / so / is / real / a / that / bee / on / it." / landed)

➡ ____________________

31 (said, / I / on / "drawing / wall / a / was / harder / much / drawing / than / paper." / on)

➡ ____________________

32 (all / we / that / agreed / our / painting / wall / perfect. / wasn't)

➡ ____________________

33 (it / but / matter. / didn't)

➡ ____________________

34 (made / we / neighborhood / our / little / a / happier. / and / brighter)

➡ ____________________

35 (were / we / of / proud / ourselves.)

➡ ____________________

36 (didn't / we / paint / just / on / pictures / wall / a / day. / that)

➡ ____________________

37 (was / it / better / a / that / tomorrow / painted. / we)

➡ ____________________

26 민수는 몇 송이의 꽃을 그렸고 지원이는 배경 그림을 그렸어.

27 우리 동아리는 약 다섯 시간 동안 그림을 그렸어.

28 끝난 후에 우리는 모여서 그날의 경험을 함께 이야기했어.

29 민수는 자신이 그린 꽃 그림을 정말 자랑스러워했어.

30 그는 "내 꽃이 정말 진짜 같아서 벌이 꽃에 앉았어."라고 말했어.

31 나는 "벽에 그리는 것이 종이에 그리는 것보다 훨씬 힘들었어."라고 말했어.

32 우리 모두는 우리 벽화가 완벽하지는 않다는 것에 동의했어.

33 하지만 그것은 중요하지 않았어.

34 우리는 동네를 조금 더 밝고 행복하게 만들었어.

35 우리는 우리 자신이 자랑스러웠어.

36 우리는 그날 벽에 그림만 그린 게 아니었어.

37 우리가 그린 것은 바로 더 나은 내일이었어.

본문 Test

※ 다음 우리말을 영어로 쓰시오.

1. 더 나은 내일을 그려라
➡ ______________________________

2. 안녕. 내 이름은 호민이야.
➡ ______________________________

3. 벽화 앞에 있는 사람이 나야.
➡ ______________________________

4. 날개가 예뻐, 그렇지 않니?
➡ ______________________________

5. 많은 사람들이 벽화 앞에서 사진 찍는 것을 좋아해.
➡ ______________________________

6. 벽화는 오래된 마을을 밝고 새롭게 만들어.
➡ ______________________________

7. 지난달에 나는 여수에 있는 벽화 마을을 방문했어.
➡ ______________________________

8. 내가 사진을 찍을 때 머릿속에 좋은 생각이 떠올랐어.
➡ ______________________________

9. 나는 생각했어. "나는 학교 미술 동아리에 있잖아.
➡ ______________________________

10. 우리가 이것처럼 벽화를 그리면 어떨까?"
➡ ______________________________

11. 나는 이 아이디어를 다음 동아리 모임에서 제안했고, 동아리 부원들은 그것을 아주 좋아했어.
➡ ______________________________

12. 우리는 인터넷에서 청소년 봉사 프로젝트를 찾았어.
➡ ______________________________

13. 그 프로젝트는 우리 마을에 벽화를 그리는 것이었어.
➡ ______________________________

14. 우리는 거기에 지원했고, 2주 후에 우리 동아리가 선택되었어!
➡ ______________________________

15. 마침내 프로젝트 날이 되었어.
➡ ______________________________

16. 프로젝트 책임자는 우리를 오전 9시에 그림 그리는 곳에서 만나게 했어.
➡ ______________________________

17. 벽은 상태가 별로 좋지 않았어.
➡ ______________________________

18 몇 군데에는 이상한 낙서와 그림이 있었어.
➡ ______

19 다른 부분에는 오래된 포스터들이 붙어 있었어.
➡ ______

20 우리는 먼저 포스터들을 제거하고 낙서와 그림을 흰 페인트로 덧칠했어.
➡ ______

21 책임자는 우리가 원하는 어떤 것이든 그리게 했어.
➡ ______

22 우리는 그 벽이 초등학교 근처에 있어서 귀여운 뭔가를 그리기로 했어.
➡ ______

23 우리는 세 그룹으로 나뉘어 그리기 시작했어.
➡ ______

24 나는 민수와 지원이와 같은 그룹이었어.
➡ ______

25 나는 내 구역을 정해서 가장 좋아하는 영화 캐릭터를 그리기 시작했어.
➡ ______

26 민수는 몇 송이의 꽃을 그렸고 지원이는 배경 그림을 그렸어.
➡ ______

27 우리 동아리는 약 다섯 시간 동안 그림을 그렸어.
➡ ______

28 끝난 후에 우리는 모여서 그날의 경험을 함께 이야기했어.
➡ ______

29 민수는 자신이 그린 꽃 그림을 정말 자랑스러워했어.
➡ ______

30 그는 “내 꽃이 정말 진짜 같아서 벌이 꽃에 앉았어.”라고 말했어.
➡ ______

31 나는 “벽에 그리는 것이 종이에 그리는 것보다 훨씬 힘들었어.”라고 말했어.
➡ ______

32 우리 모두는 우리 벽화가 완벽하지는 않다는 것에 동의했어.
➡ ______

33 하지만 그것은 중요하지 않았어.
➡ ______

34 우리는 동네를 조금 더 밝고 행복하게 만들었어.
➡ ______

35 우리는 우리 자신이 자랑스러웠어.
➡ ______

36 우리는 그날 벽에 그림만 그린 게 아니었어.
➡ ______

37 우리가 그린 것은 바로 더 나은 내일이었어.
➡ ______

구석구석 지문 Test

Step1

※ 다음 우리말과 일치하도록 빈칸에 알맞은 말을 쓰시오.

After You Read B

1. Project: ________ a ________ ________
2. ________: ________ 15
3. ________ ________: 9 a.m.
4. Do you ________ ________?
5. Do you want to ________ ________ ________ ________?
6. ________ ________, the wall is in very ________ ________.
7. You ________ ________ ________ the old posters and ________ ________ the strange writings ________ ________ ________.
8. You can paint ________ ________ ________!
9. ________: volunteer@1365.go.kr

1. 프로젝트: 더 나은 내일을 그려라
2. 날짜: 4월 15일
3. 만나는 시간: 오전 9시
4. 당신은 그림 그리기를 좋아하십니까?
5. 당신의 동네를 더 밝게 만들기를 원합니까?
6. 지금, 벽은 상태가 별로 좋지 않습니다.
7. 당신은 먼저 오래된 포스터들을 제거하고 이상한 낙서를 흰 페인트로 덧칠할 필요가 있습니다.
8. 당신은 원하는 어떤 것이든 그릴 수 있습니다!
9. 이메일: volunteer@1365.go.kr

Word Power

1. Sally ________ ________ early and ________ ________ school.
2. She ________ ________ ________ her mom.
3. Her mom said, "________ ________ ________ ________ ________ your friends and ________ ________."
4. Sally ________, "Okay, I will," and ________ ________ the school bus.

1. Sally는 일찍 일어나서 학교 갈 준비를 했다.
2. 그녀는 엄마에게 작별인사를 했다.
3. 엄마는 "친구들과 잘 지내고 즐거운 시간을 보내라."라고 말했다.
4. Sally는 "그럴게요."라고 대답하고 스쿨 버스를 탔다.

Think and Write

1. ________ ________ Diary
2. I ________ at Dream ________.
3. I ________ English books ________ ________.
4. I ________ ________ read ________ a ________ ________.
5. The ________ manager ________ me ________ the books ________ ________ ________.
6. The books were ________ heavy ________ I had to ________ ________ ________ ________ 30 ________.
7. ________ I ________, the shelves ________ very ________.
8. I ________ very ________.
9. It was a fun and ________ ________.

1. 봉사 활동 일기
2. 나는 Dream 도서관에서 자원봉사를 했다.
3. 나는 아이들에게 영어책을 읽어 줬다.
4. 나는 성우처럼 읽으려고 노력했다.
5. 자원봉사 책임자는 내게 책을 책장에 정리하라고 했다.
6. 책이 너무 무거워서 나는 30분마다 쉬어야 했다.
7. 끝난 후에는 책장이 아주 깔끔해 보였다.
8. 나는 매우 자랑스러움을 느꼈다.
9. 재미있고 보람된 경험이었다.

구석구석 지문 Test

Step2

※ 다음 우리말을 영어로 쓰시오.

After You Read B

1. 프로젝트: 더 나은 내일을 그려라
➡ ____________________
2. 날짜: 4월 15일
➡ ____________________
3. 만나는 시간: 오전 9시
➡ ____________________
4. 당신은 그림 그리기를 좋아하십니까?
➡ ____________________
5. 당신의 동네를 더 밝게 만들기를 원합니까?
➡ ____________________
6. 지금, 벽은 상태가 별로 좋지 않습니다.
➡ ____________________
7. 당신은 먼저 오래된 포스터들을 제거하고 이상한 낙서를 흰 페인트로 덧칠할 필요가 있습니다.
➡ ____________________
8. 당신은 원하는 어떤 것이든 그릴 수 있습니다!
➡ ____________________
9. 이메일: volunteer@1365.go.kr
➡ ____________________

Word Power

1. Sally는 일찍 일어나서 학교 갈 준비를 했다.
➡ ____________________
2. 그녀는 엄마에게 작별인사를 했다.
➡ ____________________
3. 엄마는 "친구들과 잘 지내고 즐거운 시간을 보내라."라고 말했다.
➡ ____________________
4. Sally는 "그럴게요."라고 대답하고 스쿨 버스를 탔다.
➡ ____________________

Think and Write

1. 봉사 활동 일기
➡ ____________________
2. 나는 Dream 도서관에서 자원봉사를 했다.
➡ ____________________
3. 나는 아이들에게 영어책을 읽어 줬다.
➡ ____________________
4. 나는 성우처럼 읽으려고 노력했다.
➡ ____________________
5. 자원봉사 책임자는 내게 책을 책장에 정리하라고 했다.
➡ ____________________
6. 책이 너무 무거워서 나는 30분마다 쉬어야 했다.
➡ ____________________
7. 끝난 후에는 책장이 아주 깔끔해 보였다.
➡ ____________________
8. 나는 매우 자랑스러움을 느꼈다.
➡ ____________________
9. 재미있고 보람된 경험이었다.
➡ ____________________

단어 Test

Step1

※ 다음 영어를 우리말로 쓰시오.

01 shiny ____________
02 dirt ____________
03 adventure ____________
04 brain ____________
05 dig ____________
06 beat ____________
07 brush ____________
08 wide ____________
09 assign ____________
10 convenient ____________
11 cruel ____________
12 bone ____________
13 acting ____________
14 detective ____________
15 skip ____________
16 driverless ____________
17 helpful ____________
18 convenience ____________
19 steal ____________
20 hole ____________
21 light ____________
22 marry ____________
23 summary ____________
24 muscle ____________
25 awake ____________
26 raise ____________
27 return ____________
28 scene ____________
29 character ____________
30 bottom ____________
31 unfortunately ____________
32 carefully ____________
33 suddenly ____________
34 object ____________
35 put down ____________
36 be full of ____________
37 stand for ____________
38 pick up ____________
39 end up ____________
40 at the bottom of ____________
41 look up ____________
42 belong to ____________
43 fall in love with ____________

단어 Test

Step2

※ 다음 우리말을 영어로 쓰시오.

01 훔치다 ____________
02 (구멍 등을) 파다 ____________
03 모험 ____________
04 근육 ____________
05 품성, 인격 ____________
06 흙 ____________
07 머리, 지능 ____________
08 갑자기 ____________
09 털다 ____________
10 (사람을) 배치하다 ____________
11 구덩이, 구멍 ____________
12 요약, 개요 ____________
13 조심스럽게 ____________
14 뼈 ____________
15 장면 ____________
16 폭넓은, 폭이 ~인 ____________
17 빛나는, 반짝거리는 ____________
18 졸리는 ____________
19 편리, 편의 ____________
20 실제로 ____________
21 형사, 탐정 ____________
22 (일을) 거르다, 빼먹다 ____________
23 고함치다 ____________
24 가벼운 ____________
25 잠들지 않은, 깨어 있는 ____________
26 (심장이) 고동치다, 때리다 ____________
27 불행히도 ____________
28 키우다, 기르다 ____________
29 맨 아래, 바닥 ____________
30 편리한 ____________
31 돌려주다, 반품하다 ____________
32 잔혹한, 잔인한 ____________
33 (연극, 영화에서의) 연기 ____________
34 인기 있는 ____________
35 ~와 사랑에 빠지다 ____________
36 사실 ____________
37 ~을 의미하다 ____________
38 휴일, 쉬는 날 ____________
39 내려놓다 ____________
40 결국 ~이 되다 ____________
41 깨어 있다 ____________
42 ~의 바닥에서 ____________
43 찾아보다 ____________

단어 Test

Step3

※ 다음 영영풀이에 알맞은 단어를 <보기>에서 골라 쓴 후, 우리말 뜻을 쓰시오.

1 __________: not sleeping: ______________

2 __________: measured from side to side: __________

3 __________: the lowest part of something: __________

4 __________: smooth and bright: ____________

5 __________: an empty space in something solid: __________

6 __________: to pass over or not do something: ____________

7 __________: a day when you do not go to work, school, etc.: __________

8 __________: a thing that you can see and touch but is not alive: __________

9 __________: to remove something with a brush or with your hand: __________

10 __________: to move soil, sand, snow, etc., in order to create a hole: __________

11 __________: a body tissue that can contract and produce movement: __________

12 __________: a long and empty object that is usually round, like a pipe: __________

13 __________: the activity or profession of performing in plays, movies, etc.: ______________

14 __________: to send someone to a particular group or place as part of a job: ____________

15 __________: to take something that does not belong to you in a way that is wrong or illegal: __________

16 __________: to shout loudly, for example because you are angry, excited, frightened, or in pain: __________

보기

yell	steal	muscle	acting
awake	hole	shiny	object
brush	dig	assign	tube
day off	bottom	wide	skip

※ 다음 우리말과 일치하도록 빈칸에 알맞은 말을 쓰시오.

Listen and Speak 1 A

B: Hi, Amy. ________ ________ Korea.

G: ________ time ________ see, Minho. ________ have you ________?

B: Great. ________ did you come ________ ________ the airport?

G: I came here ________ ________.

B: ________ do you ________ ________ the subway in Korea?

G: I think it's very ________.

B: 안녕, Amy. 한국에 온 걸 환영해.
G: 오랜만이야, 민호야. 어떻게 지냈니?
B: 잘 지냈어. 공항에서 여기에 어떻게 왔니?
G: 여기까지 지하철을 타고 왔어.
B: 한국 지하철에 관해 어떻게 생각하니?
G: 매우 깨끗하다고 생각해.

Listen and Speak 1 B

G: Brian, ________did you ________ the news?

B: ________ news?

G: We ________ use smartphones ________ ________ ________ next week.

B: Yes, I ________ that.

G: ________ do you ________ about it?

B: I think it will be very ________. I can ________ ________ ________ ________ ________ ________.

G: Yeah. We ________ ________ ________ information on the Internet.

B: Right. It will be very ________.

G: Brian, 너 그 소식 들었니?
B: 어떤 소식?
G: 우리는 다음 주부터 수업 중에 스마트폰을 사용할 수 있어.
B: 응, 그 소식을 들었어.
G: 넌 그것에 관해 어떻게 생각하니?
B: 매우 유용할 거라고 생각해. 모르는 단어들을 찾아볼 수 있잖아.
G: 그래. 우리는 또한 인터넷으로 정보를 찾을 수도 있어.
B: 맞아. 매우 도움이 될 거야.

Listen and Speak 1 C

1. A: ________ ________ ________ you a difficult question?
   B: Sure. I'll ________ my ________.
   A: ________ do you ________ about the ________ food diet?
   B: I think it's ________ but ________.
2. A: Can I ________ you a ________ question?
   B: Sure. I'll ________ my best.
   A: ________ ________ ________ ________ about the AI robot?
   B: I think it's ________ ________ ________.
3. A: ________ ________ ________ ________ a difficult question?
   B: Sure. I'll ________ ________ ________.
   A: ________ ________ ________ ________ ________ animal testing?
   B: I think it's ________ ________ ________.

1. A: 어려운 질문을 해도 될까?
   B: 물론이지. 최선을 다할게.
   A: 싱글 푸드 다이어트에 대해 어떻게 생각하니?
   B: 쉽지만 건강에 해롭다고 생각해.
2. A: 어려운 질문을 해도 될까?
   B: 물론이지. 최선을 다할게.
   A: AI 로봇에 대해 어떻게 생각하니?
   B: 도움이 되지만 무섭다고 생각해.
3. A: 어려운 질문을 해도 될까?
   B: 물론이지. 최선을 다할게.
   A: 동물 실험에 대해 어떻게 생각하니?
   B: 도움이 되지만 잔인하다고 생각해.

Listen and Speak 2 A

B: ________ ________ ________ the movie?

G: Yes, I liked it ________ ________.

B: ________ ________ ________ ________ ________ about it?

G: The ________ ________ so great.

B: I'm ________ ________ ________ that.

B: 그 영화 재미있었니?
G: 응, 아주 좋았어.
B: 무엇이 가장 좋았니?
G: 연기가 아주 멋졌어.
B: 나도 그 점에 동의해.

Listen and Speak 2 B

B: Hey, Jessica. ________ are you ________ ________ energy drinks?

G: Because they ________ ________ ________ ________.

B: ________ ________ ________ ________ that, but they have ________ ________ ________.

G: Well, they ________ ________ ________ ________ my studies.

B: Did you ________ ________ ________ ________ ________ can hurt your bones?

G: Oh, I didn't know that.

B: I think you ________ ________ energy drinks ________ ________.

G: ________ you're right. Thanks, Tom.

B: 얘, Jessica, 너는 왜 늘 에너지 음료를 마시니?
G: 에너지 음료가 깨어 있는 데 도움이 되기 때문이야.
B: 그 점에는 동의하지만, 에너지 음료에는 카페인이 너무 많아.
G: 음, 공부에 집중하는 데 도움이 돼.
B: 너무 많은 카페인은 뼈를 다치게 할 수 있다는 것을 알고 있었니?
G: 아, 그건 몰랐어.
B: 내 생각에 넌 에너지 음료를 덜 자주 마셔야 해.
G: 네 말이 맞는 거 같아. 고마워, Tom.

Listen and Speak 2 C

1. A: ________ ________ ________ ________ ________ ________ books on a smartphone?
   B: I think it's good. We can read ________.
   A: I'm ________ ________ ________ ________. / I don't agree. It's ________ ________ ________ our eyes.
2. A: ________ ________ ________ ________ ________ ________ breakfast?
   B: I think it's good. We can sleep ________.
   A: ________ ________ ________ ________ ________. / I don't agree. Our brain ________ ________ ________ well.
3. A: ________ ________ ________ ________ ________ ________ fast food?
   B: I think it's bad. Fast food has ________ ________ ________ ________.
   A: ________ ________ ________ ________ ________. / ________ ________ ________. We ________ ________ time.

1. A: 스마트폰으로 책 읽는 것에 대해 어떻게 생각하니?
   B: 좋다고 생각해. 언제든지 읽을 수 있잖아.
   A: 동의해. / 동의하지 않아. 그것은 우리의 눈에 나빠.
2. A: 아침을 건너뛰는 것을 어떻게 생각하니?
   B: 좋다고 생각해. 우리는 잠을 더 잘 수 있어.
   A: 동의해. / 나는 동의하지 않아. 우리의 뇌가 잘 작동하지 않을 수 있어.
3. A: 패스트 푸드를 먹는 것에 대해 어떻게 생각하니?
   B: 나쁘다고 생각해. 패스트 푸드는 많은 지방을 가지고 있어.
   A: 동의해. / 나는 동의하지 않아. 우리는 시간을 절약할 수 있어.

Real Life Talk Watch a Video

Tony: ________ are all these boxes, Suji?
Suji: ________ ________ ________ ________ online.
Tony: You like shopping on the Internet, ________ ________?
Suji: Yes, I do. ________ ________ ________ ________ ________ online shopping, Tony?
Tony: I don't like it ________ ________.
Suji: Why?
Tony: It's very ________ ________ ________ ________ an item ________ ________ ________.
Suji: I'm ________ ________ ________ that.
Tony: It's also ________ ________ ________ an item if you don't like it.
Suji: You're ________, but I think it's very ________.
Tony: Well, ________ isn't ________.

Tony: 이 상자들은 전부 뭐니, 수지야?
수지: 내가 온라인으로 주문한 물건들이야.
Tony: 너 인터넷으로 쇼핑하는 걸 좋아하는구나, 그렇지 않니?
수지: 응, 그래. 넌 온라인 쇼핑에 관해 어떻게 생각하니, Tony?
Tony: 난 전혀 좋아하지 않아.
수지: 왜?
Tony: 물건이 실제로 어떻게 생겼는지 알기가 매우 어렵거든.
수지: 그 점에는 동의해.
Tony: 만약 물건이 마음에 들지 않으면 물건을 돌려보내는 것도 어려워.
수지: 네 말이 맞지만, 온라인 쇼핑은 매우 편리하다고 생각해.
Tony: 음, 편리함이 전부는 아니야.

Real Life Talk Step 2

1. **A:** How do you ________ ________ ________ on the Internet?
   B: I like it ________ ________.
   A: ________ ________ ________ ________ the reason?
   B: I can ________ ________ I want.
   A: ________ ________ ________ on that.
2. **A:** ________ ________ ________ ________ ________ ________ pets?
   B: I don't like it.
   A: Can you ________ ________ the ________?
   B: It's a lot of ________ ________ ________ ________ ________ them.
   A: I ________ ________. They're so ________ and ________ ________ ________.

1. A: 인터넷에서 쇼핑하는 것을 어떻게 생각해?
   B: 나는 아주 좋아해.
   A: 이유를 말해 줄 수 있니?
   B: 내가 원할 때마다 쇼핑할 수 있어.
   A: 나도 동의해.
2. A: 애완동물을 기르는 것을 어떻게 생각해?
   B: 나는 좋아하지 않아.
   A: 이유를 말해 줄 수 있니?
   B: 애완동물을 돌보기 위해 할 일이 많아.
   A: 나는 동의하지 않아. 그들은 아주 귀엽고, 우리를 기쁘게 해줘.

Check up Dialogue Champion

A: ________ ________ ________ ________ ________ ________ smartphones ________ ________?
B: I think smartphones are ________ in class. We can ________ ________ ________ on them.
A: I'm ________ ________ ________ ________.

A: 수업 시간에 스마트폰을 사용하는 것에 대해 어떻게 생각해?
B: 수업 시간에 스마트폰은 유용하다고 생각해. 우리는 스마트폰으로 정보를 찾을 수 있어.
A: 나는 그 점에 동의해.

대화문 Test

※ 다음 우리말에 맞도록 대화를 영어로 쓰시오.

Listen and Speak 1 A

B: ______________________

G: ______________________

B: ______________________

G: ______________________

B: ______________________

G: ______________________

B: 안녕, Amy. 한국에 온 걸 환영해.
G: 오랜만이야, 민호야. 어떻게 지냈니?
B: 잘 지냈어. 공항에서 여기에 어떻게 왔니?
G: 여기까지 지하철을 타고 왔어.
B: 한국 지하철에 관해 어떻게 생각하니?
G: 매우 깨끗하다고 생각해.

Listen and Speak 1 B

G: ______________________

B: ______________________

G: ______________________

B: ______________________

G: ______________________

B: ______________________

G: ______________________

B: ______________________

G: Brian, 너 그 소식 들었니?
B: 어떤 소식?
G: 우리는 다음 주부터 수업 중에 스마트폰을 사용할 수 있어.
B: 응, 그 소식을 들었어.
G: 넌 그것에 관해 어떻게 생각하니?
B: 매우 유용할 거라고 생각해. 모르는 단어들을 찾아볼 수 있잖아.
G: 그래. 우리는 또한 인터넷으로 정보를 찾을 수도 있어.
B: 맞아. 매우 도움이 될 거야.

Listen and Speak 1 C

1. A: ______________________
   B: ______________________
   A: ______________________
   B: ______________________
2. A: ______________________
   B: ______________________
   A: ______________________
   B: ______________________
3. A: ______________________
   B: ______________________
   A: ______________________
   B: ______________________

1. A: 어려운 질문을 해도 될까?
   B: 물론이지. 최선을 다할게.
   A: 싱글 푸드 다이어트에 대해 어떻게 생각하니?
   B: 쉽지만 건강에 해롭다고 생각해.

2. A: 어려운 질문을 해도 될까?
   B: 물론이지. 최선을 다할게.
   A: AI 로봇에 대해 어떻게 생각하니?
   B: 도움이 되지만 무섭다고 생각해.

3. A: 어려운 질문을 해도 될까?
   B: 물론이지. 최선을 다할게.
   A: 동물 실험에 대해 어떻게 생각하니?
   B: 도움이 되지만 잔인하다고 생각해.

Listen and Speak 2 A

B: ______________________________
G: ______________________________
B: ______________________________
G: ______________________________
B: ______________________________

B: 그 영화 재미있었니?
G: 응, 아주 좋았어.
B: 무엇이 가장 좋았니?
G: 연기가 아주 멋졌어.
B: 나도 그 점에 동의해.

Listen and Speak 2 B

B: ______________________________
G: ______________________________
B: ______________________________
G: ______________________________
B: ______________________________
G: ______________________________
B: ______________________________
G: ______________________________

B: 얘, Jessica. 너는 왜 늘 에너지 음료를 마시니?
G: 에너지 음료가 깨어 있는 데 도움이 되기 때문이야.
B: 그 점에는 동의하지만, 에너지 음료에는 카페인이 너무 많아.
G: 음, 공부에 집중하는 데 도움이 돼.
B: 너무 많은 카페인은 뼈를 다치게 할 수 있다는 것을 알고 있었니?
G: 아, 그건 몰랐어.
B: 내 생각에 넌 에너지 음료를 덜 자주 마셔야 해.
G: 네 말이 맞는 거 같아. 고마워, Tom.

Listen and Speak 2 C

1. A: ______________________________
   B: ______________________________
   A: ______________________________
2. A: ______________________________
   B: ______________________________
   A: ______________________________
3. A: ______________________________
   B: ______________________________
   A: ______________________________

1. A: 스마트폰으로 책 읽는 것에 대해 어떻게 생각하니?
   B: 좋다고 생각해. 언제든지 읽을 수 있잖아.
   A: 동의해. / 동의하지 않아. 그것은 우리의 눈에 나빠.
2. A: 아침을 건너뛰는 것을 어떻게 생각하니?
   B: 좋다고 생각해. 우리는 잠을 더 잘 수 있어.
   A: 동의해. / 나는 동의하지 않아. 우리의 뇌가 잘 작동하지 않을 수 있어.
3. A: 패스트 푸드를 먹는 것에 대해 어떻게 생각하니?
   B: 나쁘다고 생각해. 패스트 푸드는 많은 지방을 가지고 있어.
   A: 동의해. / 나는 동의하지 않아. 우리는 시간을 절약할 수 있어.

Real Life Talk Watch a Video

Tony: ____________________

Suji: ____________________

Tony: ____________________

Suji: ____________________

Tony: ____________________

Suji: ____________________

Tony: ____________________

Suji: ____________________

Tony: ____________________

Suji: ____________________

Tony: ____________________

Tony: 이 상자들은 전부 뭐니, 수지야?
수지: 내가 온라인으로 주문한 물건들이야.
Tony: 너 인터넷으로 쇼핑하는 걸 좋아하는구나, 그렇지 않니?
수지: 응, 그래. 넌 온라인 쇼핑에 관해 어떻게 생각하니, Tony?
Tony: 난 전혀 좋아하지 않아.
수지: 왜?
Tony: 물건이 실제로 어떻게 생겼는지 알기가 매우 어렵거든.
수지: 그 점에는 동의해.
Tony: 만약 물건이 마음에 들지 않으면 물건을 돌려보내는 것도 어려워.
수지: 네 말이 맞지만, 온라인 쇼핑은 매우 편리하다고 생각해.
Tony: 음, 편리함이 전부는 아니야.

Real Life Talk Step 2

1. A: ____________________
   B: ____________________
   A: ____________________
   B: ____________________
   A: ____________________
2. A: ____________________
   B: ____________________
   A: ____________________
   B: ____________________
   A: ____________________

1. A: 인터넷에서 쇼핑하는 것을 어떻게 생각해?
   B: 나는 아주 좋아해.
   A: 이유를 말해 줄 수 있니?
   B: 내가 원할 때마다 쇼핑할 수 있어.
   A: 나도 동의해.

2. A: 애완동물을 기르는 것을 어떻게 생각해?
   B: 나는 좋아하지 않아.
   A: 이유를 말해 줄 수 있니?
   B: 애완동물을 돌보기 위해 할 일이 많아.
   A: 나는 동의하지 않아. 그들은 아주 귀엽고, 우리를 기쁘게 해줘.

Check up Dialogue Champion

A: ____________________

B: ____________________

____

A: ____________________

A: 수업 시간에 스마트폰을 사용하는 것에 대해 어떻게 생각해?
B: 수업 시간에 스마트폰은 유용하다고 생각해. 우리는 스마트폰으로 정보를 찾을 수 있어.
A: 나는 그 점에 동의해.

※ 다음 우리말과 일치하도록 빈칸에 알맞은 것을 골라 쓰시오.

HOLES

1 "________ ________, Stanley!
A. harder B. dig

2 The ________ you dig, ________ ________ you'll finish!" ________ Mr. Sir.
A. yelled B. the C. harder D. faster

3 Stanley Yelnats couldn't dig any ________ ________ every single ________ ________.
A. muscle B. harder C. hurt D. since

4 He was ________ and ________.
A. hungry B. thirsty

5 He wanted ________ ________ ________.
A. home B. go C. to

6 Unfortunately, Stanley's home ________ the next 18 months ________ ________ right here, ________ Camp Green Lake.
A. be B. for C. at D. would

7 Camp Green Lake was ________ ________ ________.
A. terrible B. name C. a

8 It wasn't green and ________ ________ ________ ________.
A. no B. there C. lake D. was

9 Camp Green Lake was ________ and ________ ________ ________.
A. full B. hot C. sand D. of

10 ________ ________, it wasn't ________ a camp.
A. fact B. even C. in

11 It was a ________ ________ ________ boys.
A. for B. place C. bad

12 Then ________ was a good boy ________ Stanley ________ here?
A. like B. what C. doing

13 He was ________ to the camp for ________ a ________ ________ sneakers.
A. stealing B. sent C. of D. pair

14 Stanley ________ ________ ________ a pair of sneakers.
A. really B. didn't C. steal

15 He was just ________ the wrong ________ ________ the ________ time.
A. at B. place C. in D. wrong

16 One day, he was ________ ________ ________ ________.
A. home B. walking C. school D. from

17 ________, a ________ of old sneakers ________ ________ the sky.
A. fell B. suddenly C. from D. pair

18 The sneakers ________ ________ the ________.
A. on B. hit C. head D. him

구덩이

1 "더 열심히 파, Stanley!

2 네가 열심히 파면 팔수록, 너는 더 빨리 끝낼 거야!" Sir 씨가 소리를 질렀다.

3 Stanley Yelnats는 모든 근육 하나하나가 아팠기 때문에 더 열심히 팔 수가 없었다.

4 그는 목이 마르고 배가 고팠다.

5 그는 집에 가고 싶었다.

6 불행히도, 앞으로 18개월 동안 Stanley의 집은 바로 여기 Green Lake 캠프가 될 것이었다.

7 Green Lake 캠프는 형편없는 이름이었다.

8 그곳은 초록색도 아니었고 호수도 없었다.

9 Green Lake 캠프는 뜨거웠고 온통 모래였다.

10 사실 그곳은 캠프조차 아니었다.

11 그곳은 나쁜 소년들을 위한 곳이었다.

12 그렇다면 Stanley 같이 착한 소년이 여기서 무엇을 하고 있었을까?

13 그는 운동화 한 켤레를 훔쳤다는 이유로 캠프에 보내졌다.

14 Stanley가 정말로 운동화 한 켤레를 훔친 것은 아니었다.

15 그는 그저 잘못된 시간에 잘못된 장소에 있었다.

16 어느 날, 그는 학교에서 집으로 걸어가고 있었다.

17 갑자기, 낡은 운동화 한 켤레가 하늘에서 떨어졌다.

18 그 운동화는 그의 머리에 맞았다.

19 He started running ________ the sneakers to ________ his father ________ ________.
A. happened B. what C. tell D. with

20 A ________ minutes later, the police ________ Stanley and asked him ________ he was ________.
A. stopped B. why C. running D. few

21 Unfortunately ________ Stanley, the sneakers ________ ________ a ________ baseball player, Clyde Livingstone.
A. belonged B. famous C. for D. to

22 That was ________ Stanley ________ ________ ________ Camp Green Lake.
A. up B. why C. at D. ended

23 Stanley ________ ________ ________ Group D in the camp.
A. was B. to C. assigned

24 ________ were ________ ________ ________ in Stanley's group.
A. other B. there C. boys D. six

25 They all ________ ________ ________ ________ X-Ray, Zigzag and Zero.
A. cool B. had C. like D. names

26 ________ boy ________ to ________ one ________ every day.
A. dig B. each C. hole D. had

27 It had ________ be ________ 150cm ________ and 150cm ________.
A. deep B. about C. wide D. to

28 Mr. Sir said, "You are ________ ________ ________ ________."
A. build B. digging C. to D. character

29 The ________ Stanley ________, the ________ he ________.
A. stronger B. more C. became D. dug

30 It ________ ________ time to ________ his hole ________ day.
A. less B. each C. took D. finish

31 In his second week, as Stanley was ________ his hole, he saw ________ ________ in the ________.
A. dirt B. shiny C. finishing D. something

32 Stanley's ________ ________ ________.
A. faster B. heart C. beat

33 He heard that anyone who found ________ ________ would be ________ the day ________.
A. given B. intersting C. off D. something

34 He carefully ________ ________ the shiny object and ________ ________ the dirt.
A. off B. picked C. brushed D. up

35 It was a ________ ________ ________.
A. tube B. gold C. small

36 But it ________ ________ real gold ________ it was too ________.
A. be B. light C. since D. couldn't

37 ________ were two ________, *KB*, at the ________ of the ________.
A. letters B. tube C. there D. bottom

38 What ________ KB ________ ________?
A. stand B. did C. for

39 Stanley's heart ________ ________ ________.
A. even B. beat C. faster

---

19 그는 그의 아버지에게 무슨 일이 일어났는지 말하기 위해 운동화를 가지고 달리기 시작했다.

20 몇 분 후에, 경찰이 Stanley를 멈춰 세웠고 그가 왜 달리고 있었는지를 그에게 물었다.

21 Stanley에게는 불행히도, 그 운동화는 유명한 야구 선수인 Clyde Livingstone의 것이었다.

22 그것이 Stanley가 Green Lake 캠프에 오게 된 이유였다.

23 Stanley는 캠프에서 D 그룹에 배치되었다.

24 Stanley의 그룹에는 6명의 다른 소년들이 있었다.

25 그들은 모두 X-Ray, Zigzag, Zero와 같은 멋진 이름을 가지고 있었다.

26 각 소년은 매일 구덩이 하나를 파야 했다.

27 그것은 150cm 정도 깊이와 150cm 정도 너비여야 했다.

28 Sir 씨는 "너희들은 인격을 수양하기 위해 구덩이를 파고 있는 것이야."라고 말했다.

29 Stanley는 많이 파면 팔수록, 더 힘이 세졌다.

30 하루하루 구덩이를 끝내는 데 시간이 덜 걸렸다.

31 그가 온 지 두 번째 주, Stanley가 자기 구덩이를 끝내 가고 있었을 때, 그는 흙 속에서 빛나는 뭔가를 봤다.

32 Stanley의 심장은 더 빨리 뛰었다.

33 그는 흥미로운 뭔가를 발견한 사람은 그 날을 쉬게 된다고 들었다.

34 그는 조심스럽게 그 빛나는 물체를 집어 흙을 털어 냈다.

35 그것은 작은 금색 통이었다.

36 그러나 그것은 너무 가벼웠기 때문에 진짜 금일 리가 없었다.

37 그 통의 바닥에는 KB라는 두 글자가 있었다.

38 KB는 무엇을 의미할까?

39 Stanley의 심장은 훨씬 더 빨리 뛰었다.

※ 다음 우리말과 일치하도록 빈칸에 알맞은 말을 쓰시오.

HOLES

1 "________ ________, Stanley!

2 ________ ________ you dig, ________ ________ you'll finish!" ________ Mr. Sir.

3 Stanley Yelnats couldn't dig ________ ________ ________ every single muscle ________.

4 He was ________ and ________.

5 He wanted to ________ ________.

6 ________, Stanley's home ________ the next 18 months ________ ________ right here, at Camp Green Lake.

7 Camp Green Lake was ________ ________ ________.

8 It wasn't green and ________ was ________ ________.

9 Camp Green Lake was ________ and ________ ________ ________.

10 ________ ________, it wasn't ________ a camp.

11 It was ________ ________ ________ ________ ________.

12 Then what was a good boy ________ Stanley ________ here?

13 He ________ ________ to the camp ________ ________ a pair of sneakers.

14 Stanley ________ ________ ________ a pair of sneakers.

15 He was just ________ ________ ________ ________ at the ________ ________.

16 One day, he was ________ ________ ________ ________.

17 Suddenly, ________ ________ ________ old sneakers ________ ________ the sky.

18 The sneakers ________ ________ ________ ________ ________.

구덩이

1 "더 열심히 파, Stanley!

2 네가 열심히 파면 팔수록, 너는 더 빨리 끝낼 거야!" Sir 씨가 소리를 질렀다.

3 Stanley Yelnats는 모든 근육 하나하나가 아팠기 때문에 더 열심히 팔 수가 없었다.

4 그는 목이 마르고 배가 고팠다.

5 그는 집에 가고 싶었다.

6 불행히도, 앞으로 18개월 동안 Stanley의 집은 바로 여기 Green Lake 캠프가 될 것이었다.

7 Green Lake 캠프는 형편없는 이름이었다.

8 그곳은 초록색도 아니었고 호수도 없었다.

9 Green Lake 캠프는 뜨거웠고 온통 모래였다.

10 사실 그곳은 캠프조차 아니었다.

11 그곳은 나쁜 소년들을 위한 곳이었다.

12 그렇다면 Stanley 같이 착한 소년이 여기서 무엇을 하고 있었을까?

13 그는 운동화 한 켤레를 훔쳤다는 이유로 캠프에 보내졌다.

14 Stanley가 정말로 운동화 한 켤레를 훔친 것은 아니었다.

15 그는 그저 잘못된 시간에 잘못된 장소에 있었다.

16 어느 날, 그는 학교에서 집으로 걸어가고 있었다.

17 갑자기, 낡은 운동화 한 켤레가 하늘에서 떨어졌다.

18 그 운동화는 그의 머리에 맞았다.

19 He started running _______ the sneakers to tell his father _______ _______.

20 _______ _______ _______ later, the police _______ Stanley and asked him _______ _______ _______ _______.

21 Unfortunately _______ Stanley, the sneakers _______ _______ a famous baseball player, Clyde Livingstone.

22 _______ _______ _______ Stanley _______ _______ at Camp Green Lake.

23 Stanley _______ _______ _______ Group D in the camp.

24 There were _______ _______ _______ in Stanley's group.

25 They all had _______ names _______ X-Ray, Zigzag and Zero.

26 Each boy had to dig _______ _______ _______ _______.

27 It had to be _______ 150cm _______ and 150cm _______.

28 Mr. Sir said, "You are digging _______ _______ _______."

29 _______ _______ Stanley dug, _______ _______ he became.

30 _______ _______ less time _______ _______ his hole _______ _______.

31 In his second week, as Stanley was finishing his hole, he saw _______ _______ _______ _______ _______.

32 Stanley's heart _______ _______.

33 He heard that _______ _______ found something interesting would _______ _______ _______ _______ _______.

34 He carefully _______ _______ the shiny object and _______ _______ the dirt.

35 It was a _______ _______ _______.

36 But it _______ _______ real gold _______ it was too light.

37 There were two _______, *KB*, _______ _______ _______ _______ the tube.

38 What did KB _______ _______?

39 Stanley's heart _______ _______ _______.

19 그는 그의 아버지에게 무슨 일이 일어났는지 말하기 위해 운동화를 가지고 달리기 시작했다.

20 몇 분 후에, 경찰이 Stanley를 멈춰 세웠고 그가 왜 달리고 있었는지를 그에게 물었다.

21 Stanley에게는 불행히도, 그 운동화는 유명한 야구 선수인 Clyde Livingstone의 것이었다.

22 그것이 Stanley가 Green Lake 캠프에 오게 된 이유였다.

23 Stanley는 캠프에서 D 그룹에 배치되었다.

24 Stanley의 그룹에는 6명의 다른 소년들이 있었다.

25 그들은 모두 X-Ray, Zigzag, Zero와 같은 멋진 이름을 가지고 있었다.

26 각 소년은 매일 구덩이 하나를 파야 했다.

27 그것은 150cm 정도 깊이와 150cm 정도 너비여야 했다.

28 Sir 씨는 "너희들은 인격을 수양하기 위해 구덩이를 파고 있는 것이야."라고 말했다.

29 Stanley는 많이 파면 팔수록, 더 힘이 세졌다.

30 하루하루 구덩이를 끝내는 데 시간이 덜 걸렸다.

31 그가 온 지 두 번째 주, Stanley가 자기 구덩이를 끝내 가고 있었을 때, 그는 흙 속에서 빛나는 뭔가를 봤다.

32 Stanley의 심장은 더 빨리 뛰었다.

33 그는 흥미로운 뭔가를 발견한 사람은 그 날을 쉬게 된다고 들었다.

34 그는 조심스럽게 그 빛나는 물체를 집어 흙을 털어 냈다.

35 그것은 작은 금색 통이었다.

36 그러나 그것은 너무 가벼웠기 때문에 진짜 금일 리가 없었다.

37 그 통의 바닥에는 KB라는 두 글자가 있었다.

38 KB는 무엇을 의미할까?

39 Stanley의 심장은 훨씬 더 빨리 뛰었다.

본문 Test

Step3

※ 다음 문장을 우리말로 쓰시오.

HOLES

1 "Dig harder, Stanley!

➡ ______

2 The harder you dig, the faster you'll finish!" yelled Mr. Sir.

➡ ______

3 Stanley Yelnats couldn't dig any harder since every single muscle hurt.

➡ ______

4 He was thirsty and hungry.

➡ ______

5 He wanted to go home.

➡ ______

6 Unfortunately, Stanley's home for the next 18 months would be right here, at Camp Green Lake.

➡ ______

7 Camp Green Lake was a terrible name.

➡ ______

8 It wasn't green and there was no lake.

➡ ______

9 Camp Green Lake was hot and full of sand.

➡ ______

10 In fact, it wasn't even a camp.

➡ ______

11 It was a place for bad boys.

➡ ______

12 Then what was a good boy like Stanley doing here?

➡ ______

13 He was sent to the camp for stealing a pair of sneakers.

➡ ______

14 Stanley didn't really steal a pair of sneakers.

➡ ______

15 He was just in the wrong place at the wrong time.

➡ ______

16 One day, he was walking home from school.

➡ ______

17 Suddenly, a pair of old sneakers fell from the sky.

➡ ______

18 The sneakers hit him on the head.

➡ ______

19 He started running with the sneakers to tell his father what happened.
➡ ______________________________

20 A few minutes later, the police stopped Stanley and asked him why he was running.
➡ ______________________________

21 Unfortunately for Stanley, the sneakers belonged to a famous baseball player, Clyde Livingstone.
➡ ______________________________

22 That was why Stanley ended up at Camp Green Lake.
➡ ______________________________

23 Stanley was assigned to Group D in the camp.
➡ ______________________________

24 There were six other boys in Stanley's group.
➡ ______________________________

25 They all had cool names like X-Ray, Zigzag and Zero.
➡ ______________________________

26 Each boy had to dig one hole every day.
➡ ______________________________

27 It had to be about 150cm deep and 150cm wide.
➡ ______________________________

28 Mr. Sir said, "You are digging to build character."
➡ ______________________________

29 The more Stanley dug, the stronger he became.
➡ ______________________________

30 It took less time to finish his hole each day.
➡ ______________________________

31 In his second week, as Stanley was finishing his hole, he saw something shiny in the dirt.
➡ ______________________________

32 Stanley's heart beat faster.
➡ ______________________________

33 He heard that anyone who found something interesting would be given the day off.
➡ ______________________________

34 He carefully picked up the shiny object and brushed off the dirt.
➡ ______________________________

35 It was a small gold tube.
➡ ______________________________

36 But it couldn't be real gold since it was too light.
➡ ______________________________

37 There were two letters, *KB*, at the bottom of the tube.
➡ ______________________________

38 What did KB stand for?
➡ ______________________________

39 Stanley's heart beat even faster.
➡ ______________________________

본문 Test

Step4

※ 다음 괄호 안의 단어들을 우리말에 맞도록 바르게 배열하시오.

HOLES

1 (harder, / "dig / Stanley!)

➡ ______________________

2 (harder / the / dig, / you / faster / the / finish!" / you'll / Mr. / yelled / Sir.)

➡ ______________________

3 (Yelnats / Stanley / dig / couldn't / harder / any / every / since / single / hurt. / muscle)

➡ ______________________

4 (was / he / hungry. / and / thirsty)

➡ ______________________

5 (wanted / he / go / to / home.)

➡ ______________________

6 (Stanley's / unfortunately, / home / for / next / the / months / 18 / be / would / here, / right / Camp / at / Lake. / Green)

➡ ______________________

____

7 (Green / Camp / was / Lake / a / name. / terrible)

➡ ______________________

8 (wasn't / it / and / green / was / there / lake. / no)

➡ ______________________

9 (Green / Camp / Lake / hot / was / full / and / sand. / of)

➡ ______________________

10 (fact, / in / wasn't / it / a / even / camp.)

➡ ______________________

11 (was / it / place / a / bad / for / boys.)

➡ ______________________

12 (what / then / was / good / a / like / boy / doing / Stanley / here?)

➡ ______________________

13 (was / he / to / sent / camp / the / stealing / for / pair / of / sneakers. / a)

➡ ______________________

구덩이

1 "더 열심히 파, Stanley!

2 네가 열심히 파면 팔수록, 너는 더 빨리 끝낼 거야!" Sir 씨가 소리를 질렀다.

3 Stanley Yelnats는 모든 근육 하나하나가 아팠기 때문에 더 열심히 팔 수가 없었다.

4 그는 목이 마르고 배가 고팠다.

5 그는 집에 가고 싶었다.

6 불행히도, 앞으로 18개월 동안 Stanley의 집은 바로 여기 Green Lake 캠프가 될 것이었다.

7 Green Lake 캠프는 형편없는 이름이었다.

8 그곳은 초록색도 아니었고 호수도 없었다.

9 Green Lake 캠프는 뜨거웠고 온통 모래였다.

10 사실 그곳은 캠프조차 아니었다.

11 그곳은 나쁜 소년들을 위한 곳이었다.

12 그렇다면 Stanley 같이 착한 소년이 여기서 무엇을 하고 있었을까?

13 그는 운동화 한 켤레를 훔쳤다는 이유로 캠프에 보내졌다.

14 (didn't / Stanley / steal / really / pair / a / sneakers. / of)

➡ ______________________________

15 (was / he / in / just / the / place / wrong / the / at / time. / wrong)

➡ ______________________________

16 (day, / one / he / was / walking / from / home / school.)

➡ ______________________________

17 (a / suddenly, / of / pair / sneakers / old / from / fell / sky. / the)

➡ ______________________________

18 (sneakers / the / him / hit / the / on / head.)

➡ ______________________________

19 (started / he / with / running / sneakers / the / tell / to / father / his / happened. / what)

➡ ______________________________

20 (few / a / later, / minutes / police / the / Stanley / stopped / asked / and / why / him / he / running. / was)

➡ ______________________________

____

21 (for / unfortunately / Stanley, / sneakers / the / belonged / a / to / baseball / famous / player. / Livingstone. / Clyde)

➡ ______________________________

____

22 (was / that / Stanley / why / up / ended / Camp / at / Lake. / Green)

➡ ______________________________

23 (was / Stanley / assigned / Group / to / in / D / camp. / the)

➡ ______________________________

24 (were / there / other / six / in / boys / group. / Stanley's)

➡ ______________________________

25 (all / they / cool / had / like / names / Zigzag / X-Ray / Zero. / and)

➡ ______________________________

14 Stanley가 정말로 운동화 한 켤레를 훔친 것은 아니었다.

15 그는 그저 잘못된 시간에 잘못된 장소에 있었다.

16 어느 날, 그는 학교에서 집으로 걸어가고 있었다.

17 갑자기, 낡은 운동화 한 켤레가 하늘에서 떨어졌다.

18 그 운동화는 그의 머리에 맞았다.

19 그는 그의 아버지에게 무슨 일이 일어났는지 말하기 위해 운동화를 가지고 달리기 시작했다.

20 몇 분 후에, 경찰이 Stanley를 멈춰 세웠고 그가 왜 달리고 있었는지를 그에게 물었다.

21 Stanley에게는 불행히도, 그 운동화는 유명한 야구 선수인 Clyde Livingstone의 것이었다.

22 그것이 Stanley가 Green Lake 캠프에 오게 된 이유였다.

23 Stanley는 캠프에서 D 그룹에 배치되었다.

24 Stanley의 그룹에는 6명의 다른 소년들이 있었다.

25 그들은 모두 X-Ray, Zigzag, Zero와 같은 멋진 이름을 가지고 있었다.

26 (boy / each / to / had / one / dig / every / hole / day.)

➡ ______________________________

27 (had / it / be / to / 150cm / about / and / deep / wide. / 150cm)

➡ ______________________________

28 (Sir / Mr. / said, / are / "you / digging / build / to / character.")

➡ ______________________________

29 (more / the / dug, / Stanely / stronger / the / became. / he)

➡ ______________________________

30 (took / it / time / less / finish / to / hole / his / day. / each)

➡ ______________________________

31 (his / in / week, / second / Stanley / as / finishing / was / hole, / his / saw / he / shiny / something / in / dirt. / the)

➡ ______________________________

____

32 (heart / Stanley's / faster. / beat)

➡ ______________________________

33 (heard / he / anyone / that / found / who / interesting / something / be / would / the / given / off. / day)

➡ ______________________________

____

34 (carefully / he / up / picked / shiny / the / and / object / off / brushed / dirt. / the)

➡ ______________________________

35 (was / it / a / gold / small / tube.)

➡ ______________________________

36 (it / but / be / couldn't / gold / real / it / since / too / was / light.)

➡ ______________________________

37 (were / there / letters, / two / at / *KB*, / the / of / bottom / tube. / the)

➡ ______________________________

38 (did / what / stand / KB / for?)

➡ ______________________________

39 (heart / Stanley's / beat / faster. / even)

➡ ______________________________

26 각 소년은 매일 구덩이 하나를 파야 했다.

27 그것은 150cm 정도 깊이와 150cm 정도 너비여야 했다.

28 Sir 씨는 "너희들은 인격을 수양하기 위해 구덩이를 파고 있는 것이야."라고 말했다.

29 Stanley는 많이 파면 팔수록, 더 힘이 세졌다.

30 하루하루 구덩이를 끝내는 데 시간이 덜 걸렸다.

31 그가 온 지 두 번째 주, Stanley가 자기 구덩이를 끝내 가고 있었을 때, 그는 흙 속에서 빛나는 뭔가를 봤다.

32 Stanley의 심장은 더 빨리 뛰었다.

33 그는 흥미로운 뭔가를 발견한 사람은 그 날을 쉬게 된다고 들었다.

34 그는 조심스럽게 그 빛나는 물체를 집어 흙을 털어 냈다.

35 그것은 작은 금색 통이었다.

36 그러나 그것은 너무 가벼웠기 때문에 진짜 금일 리가 없었다.

37 그 통의 바닥에는 KB라는 두 글자가 있었다.

38 KB는 무엇을 의미할까?

39 Stanley의 심장은 훨씬 더 빨리 뛰었다.

본문 Test

※ 다음 우리말을 영어로 쓰시오.

HOLES

1 "더 열심히 파, Stanley!
➡ ________________

2 네가 열심히 파면 팔수록, 너는 더 빨리 끝낼 거야!" Sir 씨가 소리를 질렀다.
➡ ________________

3 Stanley Yelnats는 모든 근육 하나하나가 아팠기 때문에 더 열심히 팔 수가 없었다.
➡ ________________

4 그는 목이 마르고 배가 고팠다.
➡ ________________

5 그는 집에 가고 싶었다.
➡ ________________

6 불행히도, 앞으로 18개월 동안 Stanley의 집은 바로 여기 Green Lake 캠프가 될 것이었다.
➡ ________________

7 Green Lake 캠프는 형편없는 이름이었다.
➡ ________________

8 그곳은 초록색도 아니었고 호수도 없었다.
➡ ________________

9 Green Lake 캠프는 뜨거웠고 온통 모래였다.
➡ ________________

10 사실 그곳은 캠프조차 아니었다.
➡ ________________

11 그곳은 나쁜 소년들을 위한 곳이었다.
➡ ________________

12 그렇다면 Stanley 같이 착한 소년이 여기서 무엇을 하고 있었을까?
➡ ________________

13 그는 운동화 한 켤레를 훔쳤다는 이유로 캠프에 보내졌다.
➡ ________________

14 Stanley가 정말로 운동화 한 켤레를 훔친 것은 아니었다.
➡ ________________

15 그는 그저 잘못된 시간에 잘못된 장소에 있었다.
➡ ________________

16 어느 날, 그는 학교에서 집으로 걸어가고 있었다.
➡ ________________

17 갑자기, 낡은 운동화 한 켤레가 하늘에서 떨어졌다.
➡ ________________

18 그 운동화는 그의 머리에 맞았다.
➡ ________________

19 그는 그의 아버지에게 무슨 일이 일어났는지 말하기 위해 운동화를 가지고 달리기 시작했다.
➡ ______________________________

20 몇 분 후에, 경찰이 Stanley를 멈춰 세웠고 그가 왜 달리고 있었는지를 그에게 물었다.
➡ ______________________________

21 Stanley에게는 불행히도, 그 운동화는 유명한 야구 선수인 Clyde Livingstone의 것이었다.
➡ ______________________________

22 그것이 Stanley가 Green Lake 캠프에 오게 된 이유였다.
➡ ______________________________

23 Stanley는 캠프에서 D 그룹에 배치되었다.
➡ ______________________________

24 Stanley의 그룹에는 6명의 다른 소년들이 있었다.
➡ ______________________________

25 그들은 모두 X-Ray, Zigzag, Zero와 같은 멋진 이름을 가지고 있었다.
➡ ______________________________

26 각 소년은 매일 구덩이 하나를 파야 했다.
➡ ______________________________

27 그것은 150cm 정도 깊이와 150cm 정도 너비여야 했다.
➡ ______________________________

28 Sir 씨는 “너희들은 인격을 수양하기 위해 구덩이를 파고 있는 것이야.”라고 말했다.
➡ ______________________________

29 Stanley는 많이 파면 팔수록, 더 힘이 세졌다.
➡ ______________________________

30 하루하루 구덩이를 끝내는 데 시간이 덜 걸렸다.
➡ ______________________________

31 그가 온 지 두 번째 주, Stanley가 자기 구덩이를 끝내 가고 있었을 때, 그는 흙 속에서 빛나는 뭔가를 봤다.
➡ ______________________________

32 Stanley의 심장은 더 빨리 뛰었다.
➡ ______________________________

33 그는 흥미로운 뭔가를 발견한 사람은 그 날을 쉬게 된다고 들었다.
➡ ______________________________

34 그는 조심스럽게 그 빛나는 물체를 집어 흙을 털어 냈다.
➡ ______________________________

35 그것은 작은 금색 통이었다.
➡ ______________________________

36 그러나 그것은 너무 가벼웠기 때문에 진짜 금일 리가 없었다.
➡ ______________________________

37 그 통의 바닥에는 KB라는 두 글자가 있었다.
➡ ______________________________

38 KB는 무엇을 의미할까?
➡ ______________________________

39 Stanley의 심장은 훨씬 더 빨리 뛰었다.
➡ ______________________________

구석구석 지문 Test

Step1

※ 다음 우리말과 일치하도록 빈칸에 알맞은 말을 쓰시오.

After You Read B

1. Monday, ________ ________
2. ________, the camp isn't green and ________ ________ ________ ________.
3. I'm ________ Group D. My group members ________ ________ ________ ________ X-Ray, Zigzag and Zero.
4. We ________ ________ ________ one hole ________ 150cm ________ and 150cm ________.
5. The good news is this: ________ ________ finds ________ ________ can ________ ________ ________ ________.
6. I ________ I ________ ________ the one.

1. 8월 5일, 월요일
2. 불행히도, 캠프는 초록색도 아니고 호수도 없다.
3. 나는 D 그룹에 있다. 나의 그룹 멤버들은 X-Ray, Zigzag, Zero와 같은 멋진 이름들을 가지고 있다.
4. 우리는 150cm 정도 깊이와 150cm 정도 너비의 구덩이 하나를 파야 한다.
5. 좋은 소식은 다음과 같다: 흥미로운 뭔가를 발견한 사람은 그 날을 쉴 수 있다.
6. 내가 그 사람이기를 바란다.

Word Power

1. She ________ ________ ________ ________ ________ ________ 15 dollars.

2 I ________ ________ ________ ________ ________ under the chair.

3 He ________ ________ ________ ________ ________ in his bag.

1. 그녀는 구두 한 켤레를 15달러에 샀다.

2 나는 의자 아래에서 안경 한 개를 찾았다.

3 그는 가방에 청바지 세 벌을 쌌다.

Think and Write

1. Kate Barlow ________ ________ ________ ________ Green Lake.
2. She ________ ________ ________.
3. ________ ________ ________ in the town wanted ________ ________ ________.
4. But Kate ________ ________ ________ ________ Sam, a ________ ________.
5. The rich men ________ ________ ________ Sam.
6. ________, Sam was ________ ________. Kate ________ ________ and ________ the town.

1. Kate Barlow는 그린 레이크 마을의 교사였다.
2. 그녀는 매우 인기가 있었다.
3. 마을의 많은 부유한 남자들이 그녀와 결혼하고 싶어했다.
4. 그러나 Kate는 가난한 남자인 Sam과 사랑에 빠졌다.
5. 부유한 남자들은 Sam을 다치게 하려고 했다.
6. 나중에 Sam은 죽은 채로 발견되었다. Kate는 슬퍼서 마을을 떠났다.

구석구석 지문 Test

Step2

※ 다음 우리말을 영어로 쓰시오.

After You Read B

1. 8월 5일, 월요일
➡ ____________________
2. 불행히도, 캠프는 초록색도 아니고 호수도 없다.
➡ ____________________
3. 나는 D 그룹에 있다. 나의 그룹 멤버들은 X-Ray, Zigzag, Zero와 같은 멋진 이름들을 가지고 있다.
➡ ____________________
4. 우리는 150cm 정도 깊이와 150cm 정도 너비의 구덩이 하나를 파야 한다.
➡ ____________________
5. 좋은 소식은 다음과 같다: 흥미로운 뭔가를 발견한 사람은 그 날을 쉴 수 있다.
➡ ____________________
6. 내가 그 사람이기를 바란다.
➡ ____________________

Word Power

1. 그녀는 구두 한 켤레를 15달러에 샀다.
➡ ____________________
2. 나는 의자 아래에서 안경 한 개를 찾았다.
➡ ____________________
3. 그는 가방에 청바지 세 벌을 쌌다.
➡ ____________________

Think and Write

1. Kate Barlow는 그린 레이크 마을의 교사였다.
➡ ____________________
2. 그녀는 매우 인기가 있었다.
➡ ____________________
3. 마을의 많은 부유한 남자들이 그녀와 결혼하고 싶어했다.
➡ ____________________
4. 그러나 Kate는 가난한 남자인 Sam과 사랑에 빠졌다.
➡ ____________________
5. 부유한 남자들은 Sam을 다치게 하려고 했다.
➡ ____________________
6. 나중에 Sam은 죽은 채로 발견되었다. Kate는 슬퍼서 마을을 떠났다.
➡ ____________________

단어 Test

Step1

※ 다음 영어를 우리말로 쓰시오.

01 none ____________
02 ocean ____________
03 afford ____________
04 talented ____________
05 bored ____________
06 roll ____________
07 scared ____________
08 worried ____________
09 excited ____________
10 cheer ____________
11 speech ____________
12 journey ____________
13 landfill ____________
14 mostly ____________
15 appear ____________
16 surprised ____________
17 thrilled ____________
18 battle ____________
19 tune ____________
20 educator ____________
21 environmental ____________
22 patience ____________
23 award ____________
24 musical instrument ____________
25 performance ____________
26 respect ____________
27 giant ____________
28 cheek ____________
29 stick ____________
30 title ____________
31 trash ____________
32 gym ____________
33 drone ____________
34 orchestra ____________
35 cheer for ____________
36 from then on ____________
37 take care of ____________
38 give up ____________
39 take part in ____________
40 one another ____________
41 give a big hand ____________
42 put ~ into practice ____________
43 out of tune ____________

단어 Test

Step2

※ 다음 우리말을 영어로 쓰시오.

01 무인 항공기 ______________

02 교육자 ______________

03 공연 ______________

04 존경하다 ______________

05 거대한 ______________

06 쓰레기 매립지 ______________

07 대부분, 일반적으로 ______________

08 ~할 형편이 되다 ______________

09 나타나다 ______________

10 아무도 ~않다 ______________

11 볼, 뺨 ______________

12 상 ______________

13 전쟁, 전투 ______________

14 바이올린 연주자 ______________

15 황홀해하는, 아주 신이 난 ______________

16 걱정하는 ______________

17 놀란, 놀라는 ______________

18 재능 있는 ______________

19 지루해하는 ______________

20 쓰레기 ______________

21 인내심 ______________

22 붙이다 ______________

23 구르다, 굴러가다 ______________

24 무서워하는, 겁먹은 ______________

25 환경의 ______________

26 응원하다 ______________

27 신이 난, 흥분한 ______________

28 연설 ______________

29 아직도, 여전히 ______________

30 곡, 곡조, 선율 ______________

31 체육 수업 ______________

32 여행 ______________

33 퍼레이드, 가두 행진 ______________

34 악기 ______________

35 포기하다 ______________

36 ~로 알려지다 ______________

37 ~에 참가하다 ______________

38 응원하다 ______________

39 그때부터 ______________

40 서로 ______________

41 ~로 만들어지다 ______________

42 ~을 돌보다 ______________

43 ~을 실행에 옮기다 ______________

단어 Test

Step3

※ 다음 영영풀이에 알맞은 단어를 <보기>에서 골라 쓴 후, 우리말 뜻을 쓰시오.

1 __________: able or skillful: __________

2 __________: to be able to pay for something: _____________

3 __________: very excited and happy: _______________

4 __________: in a gradual manner: _______________

5 __________: either side of the face below the eyes: __________

6 __________: action rather than ideas: __________

7 __________: frightened of someone or something: _____________

8 __________: to move along a surface by turning over and over: _____________

9 __________: an area where waste is buried under the ground: __________

10 __________: things that you throw away because you no longer want or need them: __________

11 __________: a prize or certificate that a person is given for doing something well: __________

12 __________: to want it to happen because you think you will enjoy it: _______________

13 __________: the ability to stay calm and accept a delay or suffering without complaining: __________

14 __________: a series of musical notes that make a pleasing sound when played together: __________

15 __________: a large group of people who play various musical instruments together, led by a conductor: _____________

16 __________: to feel tired and impatient because you have lost interest in something or because you have nothing to do: __________

보기

tune	roll	scared	patience
trash	thrilled	afford	step by step
practice	orchestra	award	talented
landfill	look forward to	bored	cheek

대화문 Test

Step1

※ 다음 우리말과 일치하도록 빈칸에 알맞은 말을 쓰시오.

Listen and Speak 1 A

B: Hey, Bora. ________ ________ our rock band.
G: Thanks. I'm ________ ________ ________ ________ in a concert with you.
B: We're ________ ________ have a new guitar player.
G: Yeah. ________ ________ ________ Friday.

B: 얘, 보라야. 우리 록 밴드에 온 걸 환영해.
G: 고마워. 공연에서 너희들과 함께 연주할 게 기대돼.
B: 우리는 새로운 기타 연주자를 갖게 되어서 신나.
G: 잘됐다. 금요일에 봐.

Listen and Speak 1 B

G: Jiho, ________ ________ you ________?
B: I'm ________ a book ________ baseball player ________ Jim Abbott.
G: Oh, the man ________ ________ ________ ________ a right hand?
B: That's right. He tried really hard and ________ ________ the MVP award.
G: Yeah. His story ________ ________ ________ a movie. I'm ________ ________ ________ it this Saturday.
B: Really? What's the ________?
G: *Our Hero*. ________ ________ ________ ________ ________ ________ it.
B: Can I ________ you?
G: Sure. See you ________ Saturday.

G: 지호야, 뭘 읽고 있니?
B: Jim Abbott이라는 이름의 야구 선수에 관한 책을 읽고 있어.
G: 오, 오른손이 없이 태어난 사람?
B: 맞아. 그는 정말 열심히 노력해서 최우수 선수상까지 받았어.
G: 그래. 그의 이야기가 영화로 만들어졌어. 난 이번 주 토요일에 그 영화를 볼 거야.
B: 정말? 제목이 뭐니?
G: 'Our Hero'야. 그 영화를 볼 게 정말 기대돼.
B: 나도 너와 함께해도 될까?
G: 물론이지. 토요일에 봐.

Listen and Speak 1 C

1. A: You look happy today. ________ going ________?
   B: I'm so ________. ________ ________ ________ ________ to Jeju-do.
   A: That ________ great!
   B: Yes. I'm ________ ________ ________ ________ riding a horse.

2. A: You ________ ________ today. What's going on?
   B: I'm so ________. I'm going to ________ ________ ________ a drone.
   A: That sounds great!
   B: Yes. ________ ________ ________ forward ________ ________ a drone in the park.

3. A: You ________ ________ today. What's ________ ________?
   B: I'm ________ ________. ________ ________ to see Jackson's concert.
   A: That sounds great!
   B: Yes. I'm really ________ ________ ________ ________ Jackson's ________.

1. A: 너 오늘 행복해 보인다. 무슨 일이야?
   B: 나는 아주 신나. 제주도로 여행을 갈 거야.
   A: 좋겠다!
   B: 응, 나는 말 타기를 정말 고대하고 있어.

2. A: 너 오늘 행복해 보인다. 무슨 일이야?
   B: 나는 아주 신나. 드론을 날리는 것을 배울 거야.
   A: 좋겠다!
   B: 응. 공원에서 드론을 날리는 것이 정말 기대돼.

3. A: 너 오늘 행복해 보인다. 무슨 일이야?
   B: 나는 아주 신나. Jackson의 콘서트를 볼 거야.
   A: 좋겠다!
   B: 응. Jackson의 공연을 보는 것이 정말 기대돼.

Listen and Speak 2 A

G: Minho, did you ________ the ________ ________?
B: Not yet. Math is ________.
G: Yes, but it's ________, ________.
B: Then can you ________ ________ ________ my math homework?
G: ________ ________ ________, but I can't. I ________ ________ ________ ________ ________ my brother.

G: 민호야, 너 수학 숙제 끝냈니?
B: 아직. 수학은 어려워.
G: 맞아, 그렇지만 재미있기도 해.
B: 그럼 내 수학 숙제 좀 도와줄래?
G: 그러고 싶지만, 안 돼. 내 남동생을 돌봐야 해.

Listen and Speak 2 B

G: Alex, I'm ________ ________ ________ ________ ________ a singing contest next Monday.
B: That's great, Sumin!
G: You know ________ ________ ________ the guitar, ________?
B: Yes, ________ ________ the guitar ________ 3 years.
G: Great. ________ ________ ________ the guitar ________ I sing in the contest?
B: I'd love to, ________ ________ ________. I ________ my hand in ________ ________ yesterday.
G: Oh! I'm ________ ________ ________ that.
B: Thanks. But I'll be there to ________ ________ you.

G: Alex, 나 다음 월요일에 노래 대회에 참가할 거야.
B: 대단하다, 수민아!
G: 너 기타 칠 줄 알지, 그렇지?
B: 응, 3년 동안 기타를 쳤어.
G: 잘됐다. 내가 대회에서 노래하는 동안 기타를 쳐 줄 수 있니?
B: 그러고 싶지만, 안 돼. 어제 체육 수업 중에 손을 다쳤어.
G: 오! 유감이다.
B: 고마워. 하지만 너를 응원하러 거기에 갈게.

Listen and Speak 2 C

1. A: What are you ________ ________ ________ this afternoon?
   B: I'm going to ride my bike. Do you ________ ________ join me?
   A: I'd love to, ________ ________ ________. I ________ ________ do my homework.
   B: Okay, then ________ ________.

2. A: What ________ ________ ________ ________ do this afternoon?
   B: I'm ________ ________ play soccer. Do you want to ________ ________?
   A: ________ ________ ________, but I can't. I have ________ ________ my grandparents.
   B: Okay, then ________ ________.

1. A: 오후에 뭐 할 거니?
   B: 나는 자전거를 탈 거야. 같이 할래?
   A: 그러고 싶지만, 안 돼. 나는 숙제를 해야 해.
   B: 알겠어, 다음에 하자.

2. A: 오후에 뭐 할 거니?
   B: 나는 축구를 할 거야. 같이 할래?
   A: 그러고 싶지만, 안 돼. 나는 조부모님 댁을 방문해야 해.
   B: 알겠어, 다음에 하자.

Real Life Talk Watch a Video

Linda: Hi, Tony! ________ ________ ________ ________ to do this weekend?

Tony: I'm ________ ________ ________ the musical, *Billy Elliot*.

Linda: *Billy Elliot*? What is ________ ________?

Tony: It's ________ ________ ________ ________ ________ a famous dancer. I'm ________ ________ ________ ________ it.

Linda: Sounds ________. Who is the ________ ________?

Tony: Jason Kim. He's a great dancer.

Linda: He's my favorite actor. I ________ his musical ________ ________.

Tony: Oh, really? Do you ________ ________ ________ me?

Linda: I'd love to, ________ ________ ________. I have ________ work this weekend.

Tony: Okay. Maybe ________ time!

Linda: 안녕, Tony! 이번 주말에 뭐 할 거니?
Tony: 나는 뮤지컬 'Billy Elliot'를 볼 거야.
Linda: 'Billy Elliot'? 무슨 내용이니?
Tony: 유명한 무용수가 된 한 소년에 관한 내용이야. 그 뮤지컬을 볼 게 기대돼.
Linda: 재미있겠다. 주연 배우가 누구니?
Tony: Jason Kim이야. 그는 훌륭한 무용수야.
Linda: 그는 내가 가장 좋아하는 배우야. 작년에 그의 뮤지컬을 봤어.
Tony: 오, 정말? 나와 함께 가고 싶니?
Linda: 그러고 싶지만, 안 돼. 이번 주말에 자원봉사 활동이 있어.
Tony: 알겠어. 다음에 같이 가자!

Real Life Talk Step 2

1. A: What ________ you ________ ________ do first?
   B: ________ ________ ________ ________ a parade at 10:30. I'm really ________ ________ ________ ________ it.
   A: Sounds ________.
   B: Do you want to join me?
   A: Yes, I'd ________ ________. / I'd love to, ________ ________ ________. I'm going to get ________ ________ ________ at that time.

2. A: What are you ________ ________ ________ ________?
   B: I'm going to play a water balloon game ________ 12:30. ________ ________ ________ ________ to ________ ________.
   A: ________ fun.
   B: Do you want ________ ________ me?
   A: Yes, I'd love to. / ________ ________ ________, ________ I can't. I'm going to have the ________ hot dog at that time.

1. A: 처음에 무엇을 할 거니?
   B: 10시 30분에 퍼레이드를 볼 거야. 퍼레이드 보는 것이 정말 기대돼.
   A: 재미있겠다.
   B: 너도 같이 할래?
   A: 응, 그래. / 그러고 싶지만, 안 돼. 나는 그 때 얼굴에 페이스 페인팅을 할 거야.

2. A: 다음에 무엇을 할 거니?
   B: 물풍선 게임을 12시 30분에 할 거야. 나는 그것을 하는 것이 정말 기대돼.
   A: 재미있겠다.
   B: 너도 같이 할래?
   A: 응, 그래. / 그러고 싶지만, 안 돼. 나는 그 때 가장 긴 핫도그를 먹을 거야.

대화문 Test

※ 다음 우리말에 맞도록 대화를 영어로 쓰시오.

Listen and Speak 1 A

B: ______________________________
G: ______________________________
B: ______________________________
G: ______________________________

B: 얘, 보라야. 우리 록 밴드에 온 걸 환영해.
G: 고마워. 공연에서 너희들과 함께 연주할 게 기대돼.
B: 우리는 새로운 기타 연주자를 갖게 되어서 신나.
G: 잘됐다. 금요일에 봐.

Listen and Speak 1 B

G: ______________________________
B: ______________________________
G: ______________________________
B: ______________________________
G: ______________________________
B: ______________________________
G: ______________________________
B: ______________________________
G: ______________________________

G: 지호야, 뭘 읽고 있니?
B: Jim Abbott이라는 이름의 야구 선수에 관한 책을 읽고 있어.
G: 오, 오른손이 없이 태어난 사람?
B: 맞아. 그는 정말 열심히 노력해서 최우수 선수상까지 받았어.
G: 그래. 그의 이야기가 영화로 만들어졌어. 난 이번 주 토요일에 그 영화를 볼 거야.
B: 정말? 제목이 뭐니?
G: 'Our Hero'야. 그 영화를 볼 게 정말 기대돼.
B: 나도 너와 함께해도 될까?
G: 물론이지. 토요일에 봐.

Listen and Speak 1 C

1. A: ______________________________
   B: ______________________________
   A: ______________________________
   B: ______________________________
2. A: ______________________________
   B: ______________________________
   A: ______________________________
   B: ______________________________
3. A: ______________________________
   B: ______________________________
   A: ______________________________
   B: ______________________________

1. A: 너 오늘 행복해 보인다. 무슨 일이야?
   B: 나는 아주 신나. 제주도로 여행을 갈 거야.
   A: 좋겠다!
   B: 응, 나는 말 타기를 정말 고대하고 있어.

2. A: 너 오늘 행복해 보인다. 무슨 일이야?
   B: 나는 아주 신나. 드론을 날리는 것을 배울 거야.
   A: 좋겠다!
   B: 응. 공원에서 드론을 날리는 것이 정말 기대돼.

3. A: 너 오늘 행복해 보인다. 무슨 일이야?
   B: 나는 아주 신나. Jackson의 콘서트를 볼 거야.
   A: 좋겠다!
   B: 응. Jackson의 공연을 보는 것이 정말 기대돼.

Listen and Speak 2 A

G: ______________________

B: ______________________

G: ______________________

B: ______________________

G: ______________________

G: 민호야, 너 수학 숙제 끝냈니?
B: 아직. 수학은 어려워.
G: 맞아, 그렇지만 재미있기도 해.
B: 그럼 내 수학 숙제 좀 도와줄래?
G: 그러고 싶지만, 안 돼. 내 남동생을 돌봐야 해.

Listen and Speak 2 B

G: ______________________

B: ______________________

G: ______________________

B: ______________________

G: ______________________

B: ______________________

G: ______________________

B: ______________________

G: Alex, 나 다음 월요일에 노래 대회에 참가할 거야.
B: 대단하다, 수민아!
G: 너 기타 칠 줄 알지, 그렇지?
B: 응, 3년 동안 기타를 쳤어.
G: 잘됐다. 내가 대회에서 노래하는 동안 기타를 쳐 줄 수 있니?
B: 그러고 싶지만, 안 돼. 어제 체육 수업 중에 손을 다쳤어.
G: 오! 유감이다.
B: 고마워. 하지만 너를 응원하러 거기에 갈게.

Listen and Speak 2 C

1. A: ______________________
   B: ______________________
   A: ______________________
   B: ______________________

2. A: ______________________
   B: ______________________
   A: ______________________
   B: ______________________

1. A: 오후에 뭐 할 거니?
   B: 나는 자전거를 탈 거야. 같이 할래?
   A: 그러고 싶지만, 안 돼. 나는 숙제를 해야 해.
   B: 알겠어, 다음에 하자.

2. A: 오후에 뭐 할 거니?
   B: 나는 축구를 할 거야. 같이 할래?
   A: 그러고 싶지만, 안 돼. 나는 조부모님 댁을 방문해야 해.
   B: 알겠어, 다음에 하자.

Real Life Talk Watch a Video

Linda: ______________________

Tony: ______________________

Linda: ______________________

Tony: ______________________

____

Linda: ______________________

Tony: ______________________

Linda: ______________________

Tony: ______________________

Linda: ______________________

Tony: ______________________

Linda: 안녕, Tony! 이번 주말에 뭐 할 거니?
Tony: 나는 뮤지컬 'Billy Elliot'를 볼 거야.
Linda: 'Billy Elliot'? 무슨 내용이니?
Tony: 유명한 무용수가 된 한 소년에 관한 내용이야. 그 뮤지컬을 볼 게 기대돼.
Linda: 재미있겠다. 주연 배우가 누구니?
Tony: Jason Kim이야. 그는 훌륭한 무용수야.
Linda: 그는 내가 가장 좋아하는 배우야. 작년에 그의 뮤지컬을 봤어.
Tony: 오, 정말? 나와 함께 가고 싶니?
Linda: 그러고 싶지만, 안 돼. 이번 주말에 자원봉사 활동이 있어.
Tony: 알겠어. 다음에 같이 가자!

Real Life Talk Step 2

1. A: ______________________

B: ______________________

____

A: ______________________

B: ______________________

A: ______________________

____

2. A: ______________________

B: ______________________

____

A: ______________________

B: ______________________

A: ______________________

____

1. A: 처음에 무엇을 할 거니?
B: 10시 30분에 퍼레이드를 볼 거야. 퍼레이드 보는 것이 정말 기대돼.
A: 재미있겠다.
B: 너도 같이 할래?
A: 응, 그래. / 그러고 싶지만, 안 돼. 나는 그 때 얼굴에 페이스 페인팅을 할 거야.

2. A: 다음에 무엇을 할 거니?
B: 물풍선 게임을 12시 30분에 할 거야. 나는 그것을 하는 것이 정말 기대돼.
A: 재미있겠다.
B: 너도 같이 할래?
A: 응, 그래. / 그러고 싶지만, 안 돼. 나는 그 때 가장 긴 핫도그를 먹을 거야.

본문 Test

Step1

※ 다음 우리말과 일치하도록 빈칸에 알맞은 것을 골라 쓰시오.

1 From _______ _______ _______

A. Music B. to C. Trash

2 _______ of _______ are _______ _______ my cheeks.

A. down B. joy C. rolling D. tears

3 I'm _______ _______ and _______.

A. happy B. so C. thrilled

4 If I _______ a bird, I _______ _______.

A. would B. were C. fly

5 I _______ _______.

A. around B. look

6 The _______ members in my orchestra are _______ _______ _______.

A. another B. other C. hugging D. one

7 Our concert _______ just _______ and everyone is standing and _______ us a big _______.

A. finished B. hand C. has D. giving

8 _______ of us _______ _______ that this day _______ come.

A. expected B. none C. ever D. would

9 It _______ _______ a _______ _______.

A. journey B. long C. been D. has

10 My _______ is Andrea and I'm _______ _______ _______ the Recycled Orchestra.

A. in B. violinist C. name D. a

11 _______ _______ _______ _______ the Recycled Orchestra?

A. it B. why C. called D. it

12 It's _______ our musical instruments are _______ _______ objects _______ a landfill.

A. made B. because C. from D. of

13 That's _______ it's _______ _______ _______ the Landfill Harmonic Orchestra.

A. as B. why C. known D. also

14 _______ of _______ in the orchestra _______ _______ Cateura, a small town in Paraguay.

A. most B. from C. us D. are

1 쓰레기를 음악으로

2 기쁨의 눈물이 내 볼에 흘러내리고 있다.

3 나는 정말 기쁘고 황홀하다.

4 내가 새라면, 날아오를 텐데.

5 나는 주변을 본다.

6 우리 오케스트라의 다른 단원들은 서로 껴안고 있다.

7 우리의 공연은 이제 막 끝났고 모든 사람들이 서서 우리에게 큰 박수를 보내고 있다.

8 우리 중 아무도 이 날이 올 거라고 예상하지 못했다.

9 긴 여정이었다.

10 내 이름은 Andrea이고 나는 Recycled Orchestra의 바이올리니스트이다.

11 오케스트라가 왜 Recycled Orchestra라고 불리냐고?

12 그것은 우리의 악기들이 쓰레기 매립지에서 나온 물건들로 만들어지기 때문이다.

13 그것이 오케스트라가 Landfill Harmonic Orchestra로도 알려진 이유이다.

14 오케스트라의 우리들 대부분은 파라과이의 작은 마을인 카테우라 출신이다.

15 _______ is a _______ _______ in our _______.

A. landfill B. huge C. town D. there

16 Some people _______ say that Cateura _______ is a _______ _______.

A. itself B. giant C. even D. landfill

17 _______ of _______ are _______.

A. us B. many C. poor

18 There _______ _______ _______ and _______ in our town.

A. many B. dreams C. hopes D. weren't

19 Everything _______ to _______, _______, when we _______ Favio Chávez.

A. change B. met C. began D. however

20 Favio was _______ _______ _______ and a _______.

A. environment B. musician C. educator D. an

21 He wanted to _______ _______ _______, but there was a big _______.

A. teach B. problem C. music D. us

22 There were _______ a _______ musical _______ in the _______ town.

A. whole B. few C. only D. instruments

23 We _______ _______ _______ buy new _______.

A. to B. afford C. couldn't D. ones

24 But Favio _______ _______ _______.

A. give B. didn't C. up

25 He said that we could make musical instruments _______ _______ _______ the _______.

A. objects B. landfill C. with D. from

26 A talented man _______ Nicholas was able to _______ this idea _______ _______.

A. put B. practice C. named D. into

27 He _______ violins _______ oil _______.

A. from B. made C. drums

15 우리 마을에는 거대한 쓰레기 매립지가 있다.

16 몇몇 사람들은 심지어 카테우라 자체가 거대한 쓰레기 매립지라고 말한다.

17 우리들 중 많은 이들이 가난하다.

18 우리 마을에는 꿈과 희망이 많지 않았다.

19 그러나 우리가 Favio Chávez 선생님을 만났을 때 모든 것이 바뀌기 시작했다.

20 Favio 선생님은 환경 교육가이자 음악가였다.

21 그는 우리에게 음악을 가르치고 싶어 했지만, 큰 문제가 있었다.

22 온 마을에 악기가 단지 몇 개뿐이었다.

23 우리는 새 악기를 살 형편도 아니었다.

24 그러나 Favio 선생님은 포기하지 않았다.

25 그는 우리가 쓰레기 매립지의 물건들로 악기를 만들 수 있다고 말했다.

26 재능이 많은 Nicholas 아저씨가 이 생각을 실행에 옮길 수 있었다.

27 그는 기름통으로 바이올린을 만들었다.

28 He _______ water pipes _______ _______.
A. into B. turned C. flutes

29 We _______ _______ _______.
A. problem B. had C. another

30 _______ one knew _______ _______ _______ musical instruments.
A. no B. to C. how D. play

31 We didn't _______ know _______ _______ _______ music.
A. to B. even C. read D. how

32 Favio taught us _______ _______ _______.
A. great B. with C. patience

33 Step _______ _______, we began to make some _______ on our _______.
A. sounds B. step C. by D. instruments

34 I still _______ the first _______ of _______ that we _______.
A. piece B. played C. remember D. music

35 It was very _______ and _______ _______ of _______.
A. tune B. mostly C. short D. out

36 But it was _______ _______ _______ _______ to us.
A. beautiful B. the C. music D. most

37 We _______ a _______ _______ in our _______.
A. hearts B. new C. hope D. felt

38 _______ _______ _______, we _______ to practice every day.
A. gathered B. then C. from D. on

39 _______ day, Favio told us _______ _______ _______.
A. great B. one C. news D. some

40 We _______ _______ _______ _______ a concert, a real concert!
A. have B. going C. were D. to

41 And here we are now in _______ of _______ _______ _______.
A. front B. of C. people D. hundreds

42 They _______ _______ _______.
A. our B. love C. music

43 The world _______ _______ _______, but we send _______ music!
A. trash B. back C. us D. sends

28 그는 수도관을 플루트로 바꾸었다.

29 우리에게 또 다른 문제가 있었다.

30 아무도 악기를 연주할 줄 몰랐다.

31 우리는 심지어 악보를 읽는 방법도 알지 못했다.

32 Favio 선생님은 엄청난 인내심으로 우리를 가르쳤다.

33 점차로, 우리는 악기로 어떤 소리를 만들어 내기 시작했다.

34 나는 아직도 우리가 연주했던 첫 곡을 기억한다.

35 그 곡은 매우 짧고 대부분은 음이 맞지 않았다.

36 그러나 그것은 우리에게 가장 아름다운 곡이었다.

37 우리는 마음속에 새로운 희망을 느꼈다.

38 그때부터, 우리는 매일 연습을 하기 위해 모였다.

39 어느 날, Favio 선생님은 우리에게 엄청난 소식을 말해 줬다.

40 우리는 공연을, 진짜 공연을 하게 될 것이었다!

41 그리고 여기 우리는 지금 수백 명의 사람들 앞에 있다.

42 그들은 우리의 음악을 사랑한다.

43 세상은 우리에게 쓰레기를 보내지만, 우리는 음악을 돌려보낸다!

본문 Test

※ 다음 우리말과 일치하도록 빈칸에 알맞은 것을 골라 쓰시오.

1 From ________ to ________

2 ________ ________ ________ are ________ ________ my cheeks.

3 I'm so happy and ________.

4 If I ________ a bird, I ________ ________.

5 I ________ ________.

6 ________ ________ ________ in my orchestra are hugging ________ ________.

7 Our concert ________ ________ ________ and everyone is standing and ________ ________ ________ ________ ________.

8 ________ of us ________ ________ that this day would come.

9 ________ ________ ________ a long ________.

10 My name is Andrea and ________ ________ ________ in the Recycled Orchestra.

11 ________ ________ ________ ________ the Recycled Orchestra?

12 It's ________ our musical instruments ________ ________ ________ objects ________ a ________.

13 ________ ________ it's also ________ ________ the Landfill Harmonic Orchestra.

14 ________ ________ us in the orchestra ________ ________ Cateura, a small town in Paraguay.

1 쓰레기를 음악으로

2 기쁨의 눈물이 내 볼에 흘러내리고 있다.

3 나는 정말 기쁘고 황홀하다.

4 내가 새라면, 날아오를 텐데.

5 나는 주변을 본다.

6 우리 오케스트라의 다른 단원들은 서로 껴안고 있다.

7 우리의 공연은 이제 막 끝났고 모든 사람들이 서서 우리에게 큰 박수를 보내고 있다.

8 우리 중 아무도 이 날이 올 거라고 예상하지 못했다.

9 긴 여정이었다.

10 내 이름은 Andrea이고 나는 Recycled Orchestra의 바이올리니스트이다.

11 오케스트라가 왜 Recycled Orchestra라고 불리냐고?

12 그것은 우리의 악기들이 쓰레기 매립지에서 나온 물건들로 만들어지기 때문이다.

13 그것이 오케스트라가 Landfill Harmonic Orchestra로도 알려진 이유이다.

14 오케스트라의 우리들 대부분은 파라과이의 작은 마을인 카테우라 출신이다.

15 There is _______ _______ _______ in our town.

16 Some people even say that Cateura _______ is a _______ _______.

17 _______ _______ _______ are _______.

18 There weren't _______ _______ _______ _______ in our town.

19 Everything _______ _______ _______, _______, when we met Favio Chávez.

20 Favio was _______ _______ _______ and a _______.

21 He wanted to _______ _______ _______, but there was a big problem.

22 There were _______ _______ _______ musical instruments in the _______ _______.

23 We _______ _______ _______ buy new ones.

24 But Favio didn't _______ _______.

25 He said that we could make musical instruments _______ _______ _______ _______ _______.

26 A talented man _______ Nicholas _______ _______ _______ _______ this idea _______ _______.

27 He _______ violins _______ oil drums.

15 우리 마을에는 거대한 쓰레기 매립지가 있다.

16 몇몇 사람들은 심지어 카테우라 자체가 거대한 쓰레기 매립지라고 말한다.

17 우리들 중 많은 이들이 가난하다.

18 우리 마을에는 꿈과 희망이 많지 않았다.

19 그러나 우리가 Favio Chávez 선생님을 만났을 때 모든 것이 바뀌기 시작했다.

20 Favio 선생님은 환경 교육가이자 음악가였다.

21 그는 우리에게 음악을 가르치고 싶어 했지만, 큰 문제가 있었다.

22 온 마을에 악기가 단지 몇 개뿐이었다.

23 우리는 새 악기를 살 형편도 아니었다.

24 그러나 Favio 선생님은 포기하지 않았다.

25 그는 우리가 쓰레기 매립지의 물건들로 악기를 만들 수 있다고 말했다.

26 재능이 많은 Nicholas 아저씨가 이 생각을 실행에 옮길 수 있었다.

27 그는 기름통으로 바이올린을 만들었다.

28 He _______ water pipes _______ flutes.

29 We had _______ _______.

30 No one knew _______ _______ _______ musical instruments.

31 We didn't even know _______ _______ _______ music.

32 Favio _______ us _______ _______ _______.

33 _______ _______ _______, we began to make some sounds on our instruments.

34 I still remember _______ _______ _______ _______ _______ that we _______.

35 It was very short and _______ _______ _______ _______.

36 But it was _______ _______ _______ _______ to us.

37 We _______ _______ _______ _______ in our hearts.

38 _______ _______ _______, we _______ _______ _______ every day.

39 One day, Favio told us _______ _______ _______.

40 We _______ _______ _______ _______ a concert, a real concert!

41 And here we are now in _______ of _______ _______ _______.

42 They love _______ _______.

43 The world _______ _______ _______, but we _______ _______ _______!

28 그는 수도관을 플루트로 바꾸었다.

29 우리에게 또 다른 문제가 있었다.

30 아무도 악기를 연주할 줄 몰랐다.

31 우리는 심지어 악보를 읽는 방법도 알지 못했다.

32 Favio 선생님은 엄청난 인내심으로 우리를 가르쳤다.

33 점차로, 우리는 악기로 어떤 소리를 만들어 내기 시작했다.

34 나는 아직도 우리가 연주했던 첫 곡을 기억한다.

35 그 곡은 매우 짧고 대부분은 음이 맞지 않았다.

36 그러나 그것은 우리에게 가장 아름다운 곡이었다.

37 우리는 마음속에 새로운 희망을 느꼈다.

38 그때부터, 우리는 매일 연습을 하기 위해 모였다.

39 어느 날, Favio 선생님은 우리에게 엄청난 소식을 말해 줬다.

40 우리는 공연을, 진짜 공연을 하게 될 것이었다!

41 그리고 여기 우리는 지금 수백 명의 사람들 앞에 있다.

42 그들은 우리의 음악을 사랑한다.

43 세상은 우리에게 쓰레기를 보내지만, 우리는 음악을 돌려보낸다!

본문 Test

Step3

※ 다음 문장을 우리말로 쓰시오.

1 From Trash to Music

➡ ______________________________

2 Tears of joy are rolling down my cheeks.

➡ ______________________________

3 I'm so happy and thrilled.

➡ ______________________________

4 If I were a bird, I would fly.

➡ ______________________________

5 I look around.

➡ ______________________________

6 The other members in my orchestra are hugging one another.

➡ ______________________________

7 Our concert has just finished and everyone is standing and giving us a big hand.

➡ ______________________________

8 None of us ever expected that this day would come.

➡ ______________________________

9 It has been a long journey.

➡ ______________________________

10 My name is Andrea and I'm a violinist in the Recycled Orchestra.

➡ ______________________________

11 Why is it called the Recycled Orchestra?

➡ ______________________________

12 It's because our musical instruments are made of objects from a landfill.

➡ ______________________________

13 That's why it's also known as the Landfill Harmonic Orchestra.

➡ ______________________________

14 Most of us in the orchestra are from Cateura, a small town in Paraguay.

➡ ______________________________

15 There is a huge landfill in our town.

➡ ______________________________

16 Some people even say that Cateura itself is a giant landfill.

➡ ______________________________

17 Many of us are poor.

➡ ______________________________

18 There weren't many hopes and dreams in our town.

➡ ______________________________

19 Everything began to change, however, when we met Favio Chávez.

➡ ______________________________

20 Favio was an environmental educator and a musician.

➡ ______________________________

21 He wanted to teach us music, but there was a big problem.

➡ ______________________________

22 There were only a few musical instruments in the whole town.

➡ ______________________________

23 We couldn't afford to buy new ones.

➡ ______________________________

24 But Favio didn't give up.

➡ ______________________________

25 He said that we could make musical instruments with objects from the landfill.

➡ ______________________________

26 A talented man named Nicholas was able to put this idea into practice.

➡ ______________________________

27 He made violins from oil drums.

➡ ______________________________

28 He turned water pipes into flutes.

➡ ______________________________

29 We had another problem.

➡ ______________________________

30 No one knew how to play musical instruments.

➡ ______________________________

31 We didn't even know how to read music.

➡ ______________________________

32 Favio taught us with great patience.

➡ ______________________________

33 Step by step, we began to make some sounds on our instruments.

➡ ______________________________

34 I still remember the first piece of music that we played.

➡ ______________________________

35 It was very short and mostly out of tune.

➡ ______________________________

36 But it was the most beautiful music to us.

➡ ______________________________

37 We felt a new hope in our hearts.

➡ ______________________________

38 From then on, we gathered to practice every day.

➡ ______________________________

39 One day, Favio told us some great news.

➡ ______________________________

40 We were going to have a concert, a real concert!

➡ ______________________________

41 And here we are now in front of hundreds of people.

➡ ______________________________

42 They love our music.

➡ ______________________________

43 The world sends us trash, but we send back music!

➡ ______________________________

본문 Test

※ 다음 괄호 안의 단어들을 우리말에 맞도록 바르게 배열하시오.

1 (Trash / From / Music / to)
➡ ____________________

2 (of / tears / are / joy / down / rolling / cheeks. / my)
➡ ____________________

3 (so / I'm / thrilled. / and / happy)
➡ ____________________

4 (I / if / were / bird, / a / would / I / fly.)
➡ ____________________

5 (look / I / around.)
➡ ____________________

6 (other / the / in / members / orchestra / my / hugging / are / another. / one)
➡ ____________________

7 (concert / our / just / as / finished / and / is / everyone / standing / giving / and / a / us / hand. / big)
➡ ____________________
____

8 (of / none / us / expected / ever / this / that / day / come. / would)
➡ ____________________

9 (has / it / a / been / journey. / long)
➡ ____________________

10 (name / my / Andrea / is / and / a / I'm / in / violinist / the / Orchestra. / Recycled)
➡ ____________________

11 (is / why / called / it / Recycled / the / Orchestra?)
➡ ____________________

12 (because / it's / musical / our / are / instruments / of / made / from / objects / landfill. / a)
➡ ____________________

13 (why / that's / also / it's / as / known / the / Harmonic / Landfill / Orchestra.)
➡ ____________________

14 (of / most / in / us / the / are / orchestra / Cateura, / from / small / a / town / Paraguay. / in)
➡ ____________________

1 쓰레기를 음악으로

2 기쁨의 눈물이 내 볼에 흘러내리고 있다.

3 나는 정말 기쁘고 황홀하다.

4 내가 새라면, 날아오를 텐데.

5 나는 주변을 본다.

6 우리 오케스트라의 다른 단원들은 서로 껴안고 있다.

7 우리의 공연은 이제 막 끝났고 모든 사람들이 서서 우리에게 큰 박수를 보내고 있다.

8 우리 중 아무도 이 날이 올 거라고 예상하지 못했다.

9 긴 여정이었다.

10 내 이름은 Andrea이고 나는 Recycled Orchestra의 바이올리니스트이다.

11 오케스트라가 왜 Recycled Orchestra라고 불리냐고?

12 그것은 우리의 악기들이 쓰레기 매립지에서 나온 물건들로 만들어지기 때문이다.

13 그것이 오케스트라가 Landfill Harmonic Orchestra로도 알려진 이유이다.

14 오케스트라의 우리들 대부분은 파라과이의 작은 마을인 카테우라 출신이다.

15 (is / there / huge / a / landfill / our / in / town.)

➡ ______________________________

16 (people / some / say / even / that / itself / Cateura / a / is / landfill. / giant)

➡ ______________________________

17 (of / many / us / poor. / are)

➡ ______________________________

18 (weren't / there / hopes / many / and / in / dreams / town. / our)

➡ ______________________________

19 (began / everything / change, / to / however, / we / when / Favio / met / Chávez)

➡ ______________________________

20 (Favio / an / was / educator / environmental / and / musician. / a)

➡ ______________________________

21 (wanted / he / teach / to / music, / us / there / but / a / was / problem. / big)

➡ ______________________________

22 (were / there / a / only / musical / few / in / instruments / the / town. / whole)

➡ ______________________________

23 (couldn't / we / to / afford / new / buy / ones.)

➡ ______________________________

24 (Favio / but / give / didn't / up.)

➡ ______________________________

25 (said / he / we / that / make / could / instruments / musical / objects / with / the / from / landfill.)

➡ ______________________________

____

26 (talented / a / named / man / was / Nicholas / to / able / put / idea / this / practice. / into)

➡ ______________________________

27 (made / he / from / violins / drums. / oil)

➡ ______________________________

15 우리 마을에는 거대한 쓰레기 매립지가 있다.

16 몇몇 사람들은 심지어 카테우라 자체가 거대한 쓰레기 매립지라고 말한다.

17 우리들 중 많은 이들이 가난하다.

18 우리 마을에는 꿈과 희망이 많지 않았다.

19 그러나 우리가 Favio Chávez 선생님을 만났을 때 모든 것이 바뀌기 시작했다.

20 Favio 선생님은 환경 교육가이자 음악가였다.

21 그는 우리에게 음악을 가르치고 싶어 했지만, 큰 문제가 있었다.

22 온 마을에 악기가 단지 몇 개뿐이었다.

23 우리는 새 악기를 살 형편도 아니었다.

24 그러나 Favio 선생님은 포기하지 않았다.

25 그는 우리가 쓰레기 매립지의 물건들로 악기를 만들 수 있다고 말했다.

26 재능이 많은 Nicholas 아저씨가 이 생각을 실행에 옮길 수 있었다.

27 그는 기름통으로 바이올린을 만들었다.

28 (turned / he / pipes / water / flutes. / into)

➡ ______________________________

29 (had / we / problem. / another)

➡ ______________________________

30 (one / no / how / knew / play / to / instruments. / musical)

➡ ______________________________

31 (didn't / we / know / even / to / how / music. / read)

➡ ______________________________

32 (taught / Favio / with / us / patience. / great)

➡ ______________________________

33 (by / step / we / step, / to / began / make / sounds / some / our / on / instruments.)

➡ ______________________________

34 (still / I / the / remember / piece / first / music / of / we / that / played.)

➡ ______________________________

35 (was / it / short / very / and / out / mostly / tune. / of)

➡ ______________________________

36 (it / but / the / was / beautiful / most / music / us. / to)

➡ ______________________________

37 (felt / we / new / a / in / hope / hearts. / our)

➡ ______________________________

38 (then / from / on, / gathered / we / practice / to / day. / every)

➡ ______________________________

39 (day, / one / told / Favio / some / us / news. / great)

➡ ______________________________

40 (were / we / to / going / a / have / concert, / real / a / concert!)

➡ ______________________________

41 (here / and / are / we / in / now / front / hundreads / of / people. / of)

➡ ______________________________

42 (love / they / music. / our)

➡ ______________________________

43 (world / the / us / sends / trash, / we / but / back / send / music!)

➡ ______________________________

28 그는 수도관을 플루트로 바꾸었다.

29 우리에게 또 다른 문제가 있었다.

30 아무도 악기를 연주할 줄 몰랐다.

31 우리는 심지어 악보를 읽는 방법도 알지 못했다.

32 Favio 선생님은 엄청난 인내심으로 우리를 가르쳤다.

33 점차로, 우리는 악기로 어떤 소리를 만들어 내기 시작했다.

34 나는 아직도 우리가 연주했던 첫 곡을 기억한다.

35 그 곡은 매우 짧고 대부분은 음이 맞지 않았다.

36 그러나 그것은 우리에게 가장 아름다운 곡이었다.

37 우리는 마음속에 새로운 희망을 느꼈다.

38 그때부터, 우리는 매일 연습을 하기 위해 모였다.

39 어느 날, Favio 선생님은 우리에게 엄청난 소식을 말해 줬다.

40 우리는 공연을, 진짜 공연을 하게 될 것이었다!

41 그리고 여기 우리는 지금 수백 명의 사람들 앞에 있다.

42 그들은 우리의 음악을 사랑한다.

43 세상은 우리에게 쓰레기를 보내지만, 우리는 음악을 돌려보낸다!

※ 다음 우리말을 영어로 쓰시오.

1 쓰레기를 음악으로

➡ ______________________

2 기쁨의 눈물이 내 볼에 흘러내리고 있다.

➡ ______________________

3 나는 정말 기쁘고 황홀하다.

➡ ______________________

4 내가 새라면, 날아오를 텐데.

➡ ______________________

5 나는 주변을 본다.

➡ ______________________

6 우리 오케스트라의 다른 단원들은 서로 껴안고 있다.

➡ ______________________

7 우리의 공연은 이제 막 끝났고 모든 사람들이 서서 우리에게 큰 박수를 보내고 있다.

➡ ______________________

8 우리 중 아무도 이 날이 올 거라고 예상하지 못했다.

➡ ______________________

9 긴 여정이었다.

➡ ______________________

10 내 이름은 Andrea이고 나는 Recycled Orchestra의 바이올리니스트이다.

➡ ______________________

11 오케스트라가 왜 Recycled Orchestra라고 불리냐고?

➡ ______________________

12 그것은 우리의 악기들이 쓰레기 매립지에서 나온 물건들로 만들어지기 때문이다.

➡ ______________________

13 그것이 오케스트라가 Landfill Harmonic Orchestra로도 알려진 이유이다.

➡ ______________________

14 오케스트라의 우리들 대부분은 파라과이의 작은 마을인 카테우라 출신이다.

➡ ______________________

15 우리 마을에는 거대한 쓰레기 매립지가 있다.

➡ ______________________________

16 몇몇 사람들은 심지어 카테우라 자체가 거대한 쓰레기 매립지라고 말한다.

➡ ______________________________

17 우리들 중 많은 이들이 가난하다.

➡ ______________________________

18 우리 마을에는 꿈과 희망이 많지 않았다.

➡ ______________________________

19 그러나 우리가 Favio Chávez 선생님을 만났을 때 모든 것이 바뀌기 시작했다.

➡ ______________________________

20 Favio 선생님은 환경 교육가이자 음악가였다.

➡ ______________________________

21 그는 우리에게 음악을 가르치고 싶어 했지만, 큰 문제가 있었다.

➡ ______________________________

22 온 마을에 악기가 단지 몇 개뿐이었다.

➡ ______________________________

23 우리는 새 악기를 살 형편도 아니었다.

➡ ______________________________

24 그러나 Favio 선생님은 포기하지 않았다.

➡ ______________________________

25 그는 우리가 쓰레기 매립지의 물건들로 악기를 만들 수 있다고 말했다.

➡ ______________________________

26 재능이 많은 Nicholas 아저씨가 이 생각을 실행에 옮길 수 있었다.

➡ ______________________________

27 그는 기름통으로 바이올린을 만들었다.

➡ ______________________________

28 그는 수도관을 플루트로 바꾸었다.

➡ ____________________

29 우리에게 또 다른 문제가 있었다.

➡ ____________________

30 아무도 악기를 연주할 줄 몰랐다.

➡ ____________________

31 우리는 심지어 악보를 읽는 방법도 알지 못했다.

➡ ____________________

32 Favio 선생님은 엄청난 인내심으로 우리를 가르쳤다.

➡ ____________________

33 점차로, 우리는 악기로 어떤 소리를 만들어 내기 시작했다.

➡ ____________________

34 나는 아직도 우리가 연주했던 첫 곡을 기억한다.

➡ ____________________

35 그 곡은 매우 짧고 대부분은 음이 맞지 않았다.

➡ ____________________

36 그러나 그것은 우리에게 가장 아름다운 곡이었다.

➡ ____________________

37 우리는 마음속에 새로운 희망을 느꼈다.

➡ ____________________

38 그때부터, 우리는 매일 연습을 하기 위해 모였다.

➡ ____________________

39 어느 날, Favio 선생님은 우리에게 엄청난 소식을 말해 줬다.

➡ ____________________

40 우리는 공연을, 진짜 공연을 하게 될 것이었다!

➡ ____________________

41 그리고 여기 우리는 지금 수백 명의 사람들 앞에 있다.

➡ ____________________

42 그들은 우리의 음악을 사랑한다.

➡ ____________________

43 세상은 우리에게 쓰레기를 보내지만, 우리는 음악을 돌려보낸다!

➡ ____________________

※ 다음 우리말과 일치하도록 빈칸에 알맞은 말을 쓰시오.

After You Read B

1. Reporter: Congratulations! How do you ________ now?
2. Andrea: I ________ ________. We ________ ________ our ________ ________.
3. Reporter: ________ is the orchestra ________ the Recycled Orchestra?
4. Andrea: ________ ________ our ________ ________ ________ ________ ________ objects ________ ________ ________.
5. Reporter: That's ________.
6. Andrea: Yeah. ________ ________ us knew ________ ________ ________ ________ ________, but Favio taught us ________ ________ ________.
7. Reporter: That is a ________ ________.

1. 리포터: 축하합니다. 지금 기분이 어떠세요?
2. Andrea: 나는 아주 황홀해요. 우리는 막 첫 번째 공연을 했어요.
3. 리포터: 오케스트라가 왜 Recycled Orchestra라고 불립니까?
4. Andrea: 그것은 우리의 악기들이 쓰레기 매립지에서 나온 물건들로 만들어지기 때문입니다.
5. 리포터: 그것은 놀랍군요.
6. Andrea: 네, 우리들 중 아무도 악기를 연주할 줄 몰랐지만, Favio 선생님은 엄청난 인내심으로 우리를 가르치셨어요.
7. 리포터: 멋있는 이야기입니다.

Think and Write

1. ________ ________ Yi Sun-sin,
2. I'm Sumin. I really ________ you ________ you never ________ ________ ________ ________ ________.
3. You ________ the ________ and the people.
4. ________ was amazing ________ you ________ the battle ________ ________ ________ ________.
5. ________ I ________ a time machine, I ________ ________ ________ ________ you!
6. I'd ________ ________ ________ you ________ ________ ________ geobukseon.
7. You're ________ ________. Thank you.
8. ________ yours,

Sumin

1. 이순신 장군님께,
2. 저는 수민이에요. 저는 당신이 어려운 상황에서 결코 포기하지 않았기 때문에 당신을 정말 존경해요.
3. 당신은 나라와 국민을 구했어요.
4. 단지 12척의 배로 전투를 이긴 것은 놀라웠어요.
5. 제게 타임머신이 있다면, 저는 당신을 만나러 갈 텐데요!
6. 저는 당신에게 거북선을 어떻게 만드는지를 묻고 싶어요.
7. 당신은 제 영웅이에요. 감사합니다.
8. 존경을 담아,

수민이가

Project Step 3

1. This is a ________ ________.
2. ________ ________ it, you need ________ ________ and ________.
3. ________ the bottle and ________ the buttons ________ ________ ________.
4. ________ the bottle and ________ ________.
5. You ________ ________ ________ ________ ________ ________ rice or sand in ________.
6. ________ items make ________ ________.
7. ________ ________ my ________ ________ ________.

1. 이것은 병 셰이커야.
2. 그것을 만들려면 너는 병 하나와 단추들이 필요해.
3. 병을 씻고 단추들을 병 속에 넣어.
4. 병을 닫고 그것을 장식해.
5. 너는 또한 쌀이나 모래 같은 다른 것들을 안에 넣을 수 있어.
6. 다른 물건들은 다른 소리들을 만들어 내.
7. 내 모둠의 병 셰이커 소리를 들어 봐.

구석구석 지문 Test

Step2

※ 다음 우리말을 영어로 쓰시오.

After You Read B

1. 리포터: 축하합니다. 지금 기분이 어떠세요?
➡
2. Andrea: 나는 아주 황홀해요. 우리는 막 첫 번째 공연을 했어요.
➡
3. 리포터: 오케스트라가 왜 Recycled Orchestra라고 불립니까?
➡
4. Andrea: 그것은 우리의 악기들이 쓰레기 매립지에서 나온 물건들로 만들어지기 때문입니다.
➡
5. 리포터: 그것은 놀랍군요.
➡
6. Andrea: 네, 우리들 중 아무도 악기를 연주할 줄 몰랐지만, Favio 선생님은 엄청난 인내심으로 우리를 가르치셨어요.
➡
7. 리포터: 멋있는 이야기입니다.
➡

Think and Write

1. 이순신 장군님께,
➡
2. 저는 수민이에요. 저는 당신이 어려운 상황에서 결코 포기하지 않았기 때문에 당신을 정말 존경해요.
➡
3. 당신은 나라와 국민을 구했어요.
➡
4. 단지 12척의 배로 전투를 이긴 것은 놀라웠어요.
➡
5. 제게 타임머신이 있다면, 저는 당신을 만나러 갈 텐데요!
➡
6. 저는 당신에게 거북선을 어떻게 만드는지를 묻고 싶어요.
➡
7. 당신은 제 영웅이에요. 감사합니다.
➡
8. 존경을 담아, 수민이가
➡

Project Step 3

1. 이것은 병 셰이커야.
➡
2. 그것을 만들려면 너는 병 하나와 단추들이 필요해.
➡
3. 병을 씻고 단추들을 병 속에 넣어.
➡
4. 병을 닫고 그것을 장식해.
➡
5. 너는 또한 쌀이나 모래 같은 다른 것들을 안에 넣을 수 있어.
➡
6. 다른 물건들은 다른 소리들을 만들어 내.
➡
7. 내 모둠의 병 셰이커 소리를 들어 봐.
➡

MEMO

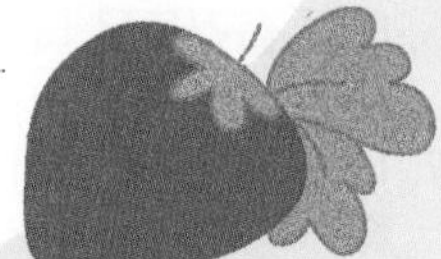

영어 기출 문제집

적중100

1학기

정답 및 해설

동아 | 이병민

중3

적중100

영어 기출 문제집

적중100

1학기

정답 및 해설

동아 | 이병민

중3

적중100

Lesson 3

Heal the World

시험대비 실력평가 p.08

01 ② 02 ④ 03 ② 04 ③
05 ① 06 ②

01 rewarding: 보람 있는 satisfying: 만족시키는

02 be on time: 제시간에 도착하다 / 또 늦었구나. 시간 약속을 지키는 것은 중요하단다.

03 ① give, give a bath: 목욕시키다 / 내가 아기를 목욕시킬 동안 편안하게 있어. ② keep ~ in mind: ~을 명심하다 / 너는 그의 충고를 명심해야 한다. ③ doing, do one's best: 최선을 다하다 / 가장 중요한 것은 최선을 다하는 것이다. ④ prepare, prepare for ~: ~을 준비하다 / Joe는 내가 시험 준비하는 것을 도와주었다. ⑤ having, have fun: 즐거운 시간을 보내다 / 그 아이들은 서로의 그림자를 쫓으며 재미있게 놀고 있었다.

04 ① 너의 가방들을 꾸리는 게 좋겠다. 우리는 한 시간 뒤에 떠날 거야. ② 비누와 차가운 물은 대부분의 음식 얼룩을 제거할 것이다. ③ matter: 문제되다 / 깔끔하게 보인다면, 무엇을 입던 문제가 되지 않는다. ④ 의자에 온통 고양이 털이 있다. ⑤ 심지어 아무리 작은 기부라도 한 아이의 인생에 큰 차이를 만들 수 있다.

05 suggest: 제안하다 take a rest: 휴식하다

06 (A) get together: 모이다 / 그는 그녀를 위한 파티를 계획하기 위해 몇몇 친구들과 모였다. (B) keep in mind: 명심하다 / 바닥 타일은 청소하기 힘들 수 있다. 그것은 새로운 바닥을 고를 때 기억할 가치가 있다. (C) make sure ~: 꼭 ~하다, 확실하게 ~하다 / 매끼 식사 후에 이 약을 꼭 드세요.

서술형 시험대비 p.09

01 (r)emoved
02 (1) up (2) together (3) on (4) along
03 to introduce
04 up
05 plant
06 (1) (l)anded (2) (n)eat (3) the (e)lderly (4) (s)pot
07 (1) They must be so proud of themselves.
(2) This situation matters a lot.
(3) I'll give a hand if I finish early.

01 remove: 제거하다 / 어떤 것을 한 장소에서 옮기거나 치우다 / 불법 주차 차량들은 치워진다.

02 (1) get up: (잠자리에서) 일어나다 / 첫 기차에 늦지 않게 일찍 일어나라. (2) get together: 모이다 / 그들은 수요일마다 모여서 수학을 공부한다. (3) get on: (탈것에) 타다 / 우리는 Lime Street역에서 기차를 탔다. (4) get along with ~: ~와 잘 지내다 / 나는 반 친구들과 잘 지낸다.

03 It's time to 동사원형 ~: ~해야 할 시간이다 (= It's time for (동)명사 ~.) / 자기 소개를 할 시간이다.

04 pick up: 치우다, 줍다 / 쓰레기를 줍는 게 어떨까? line up: 줄서다 / 자동차들이 줄을 지어 배에 타려고 기다리고 있었다.

05 plant: 식물; 심다 / 식물에 물 주는 것을 잊지 말아라. 우리는 토마토와 당근을 정원에 심을 것이다.

06 (1) land: 착륙하다 (2) neat: 깨끗한 (3) the elderly (people): 나이 든 사람들 (4) spot: 장소, 지점

07 (1) be proud of ~: ~을 자랑스러워하다 (2) matter: 문제가 되다, 중요하다 (3) give ~ a hand ~에게 도움을 주다

교과서

Conversation

핵심 Check p.10~11

1 What do you want me to do?
2 Make sure you lock the door.
3 (B) → (A) → (C) → (D)

교과서 대화문 익히기

Check(√) True or False p.12~13

1 T 2 T 3 T 4 F 5 T 6 F 7 T 8 F

교과서 확인학습 p.15~17

Listen and Speak 1 A

What, for / packing, donation, give me a / want, to / address on

Listen and Speak 1 B

this mess / baking / Why, many / They're for / nice of / Can you give / do you want me / put, each

Listen and Speak 1 C

1. doing / packing for, Can you help / What do you want / put the clothes into
2. packing for, move, Can you help me / move, outside
3. What are you doing / packing for, move, Can you help me / What do you want me to do / take out

Listen and Speak 2 A

Enjoy / will, is on / worry about / Make sure you feed, after / should

Listen and Speak 2 B

Make groups of, sit, to make, Keep in mind, make sure, before you start, Second, when, let's

Listen and Speak 2 C

1. to go / Make sure / Anything / that's
2. time to / Make sure you clean / Anything else
3. It's time to go / Make sure, water the plants / will

Real Life Talk Watch a Video

What can I do / here for / must be / What do you want me to do / read, for the blind / go into / anything to keep in / Make sure you read, slowly and clearly / do my best

Real Life Talk Step 3

1. I'm here for / for / do you want me to do / give, a bath / Is there anything / Make sure
2. I'm here for the volunteer / Thanks for / What do you want me to do / for the blind / Is there anything to keep in mind /sure

시험대비 기본평가 p.18

01 ④ 02 ⑤
03 (C) → (E) → (A) → (B) → (D)

01 'What do you want me to do?'는 '너는 내가 무엇을 해 주기를 원하니?'라는 뜻으로 상대방이 원하는 행동이 무엇인지를 물어보는 표현이다. me는 want의 목적어이고 to do는 목적격보어이다.

02 빈칸에는 무엇을 해 주기를 원하는지 묻는 말에 대한 대답으로 어떠한 것을 해달라고 요청하는 말이 어울린다.

03 엉망진창이 된 상황을 보고 무슨 일인지 남자아이가 질문하자 (C) 쿠키를 굽고 있다고 대답한다. (E) 많은 쿠키를 굽는 이유를 물어보고 (A) 양로원에 계신 분들을 위한 것이라고 대답한다. (B) 착하다고 말하자 (D) 여자아이는 남자아이에게 도움을 요청한다. 남자아이는 승낙하고 무엇을 도울지 물어본다.

시험대비 실력평가 p.19~20

01 ②	02 ⑤	03 ④	04 ②
05 ②	06 ①	07 ③	08 ①
09 ④	10 ④	11 ③	

01 빈칸에는 도움을 요청하는 말에 상대방이 구체적으로 무엇을 원하는지 묻는 말인 'What do you want me to do?(제가 무엇을 하기를 원하십니까?)'가 어울린다.

02 주어진 문장은 아빠가 차에서 기다리고 있다는 말로, 남자아이가 엄마가 가셔야 한다고 말하는 내용과 연결되는 것이 적절하다.

03 상대방이 꼭 하기를 원하는 내용을 말하기 위해서 'make sure'를 사용한다. 'make sure'는 '꼭 ~해라, 확실하게 ~해라'의 의미를 가지고 있다.

04 ① 남자아이는 저녁 먹은 후에 무엇을 해야 하는가? (개 밥을 줘야 한다.) ② 남자아이는 무엇을 걱정하는가? ③ 남자아이의 저녁식사는 어디에 있는가? (식탁 위에) ④ 아빠는 어디에 있는가? (차 안에) ⑤ 엄마는 어디를 갈 것인가? (콘서트)

05 주어진 문장은 '도와줄래?'의 의미로 상대방에게 도움을 요청할 때 사용하는 표현이다. 'Sure.(물론이야.)'라고 요청에 대한 대답을 하는 것과 어울리므로 ②에 들어가야 적절하다.

06 'What are all these boxes and books for?(이 박스와 책들은 다 무엇에 쓰려는 거니?)'와 'Please write the address on the boxes.(박스에 주소를 좀 써 줘.)' 두 문장에서 책을 포장하고 있다는 것을 알 수 있다. pack: 짐을 꾸리다

07 ① 남자아이는 여자아이를 도울 것인가? (네) ② 여자아이는 지금 무엇을 하는 중인가? (책을 싸고 있다.) ③ 여자아이는 얼마나 많은 책들을 기부 센터에 보낼 것인가? ④ 책은 무엇에 쓰려는 것인가? (기부 센터에 보내기 위한 책들이다.) ⑤ 대화가 끝나고 남자아이는 무엇을 할 것인가? (박스에 주소를 쓸 것이다.)

08 노인들에게 식사를 배달하는데 'Is there anything to keep in mind?(유념해야 할 것이 있나요?)'라고 묻고 있다. greet: 인사하다 politely: 예의 바르게

09 영화 시작이 7시인데 반드시 7시 30분 이후에 가라고 당부하는 것은 어색하다.

10 keep in mind: 명심하다. 두 가지 규칙을 명심하라고 얘기하고 그 두 가지가 무엇인지 구체적으로 말하는 것이 적절하다.

11 ① 무엇을 만들 것인가? (베이컨 달걀 샌드위치) ② 무슨 수업인가? (요리 수업) ③ 베이컨 달걀 샌드위치를 만드는 데 몇 시간이 걸리는가? ④ 수업 시간에 얼마나 많은 유의해야 할 규칙이 있는가? (2 개) ⑤ 몇 명이 한 그룹을 만드는가? (4명)

서술형 시험대비 p.21

01 ⓐ in ⓑ do
02 What do you want me to do today?

03 blind → the blind
04 (A) give (B) want
05 (A) to go (B) lock
06 What would you like me to do?

01 ⓐ keep in mind: 명심하다 ⓑ do one's best: 최선을 다하다

02 'What do you want me to do?'는 '제가 무엇을 하길 원하세요?'라는 뜻으로 상대방이 원하는 것이 무엇인지 물어보는 표현이다.

03 'the+형용사'는 복수 보통명사로 여기서 the blind는 blind people을 의미한다. 책을 시각 장애인들을 위해 읽어 주는 것이므로 the blind가 어울린다.

04 (A) 'give ~ a hand'는 '~를 돕다'라는 관용적 표현으로, 이 표현을 이용해 'Can you give me a hand?'라고 하면, '너 나 좀 도와줄래?'의 의미로 상대방에게 도움을 요청할 때 사용하는 표현이다. (B) 'What do you want to me to do?'는 '너는 내가 무엇을 하기를 원하니?'로 상대방이 원하는 것이 무엇인지 묻는 표현이다.

05 (A) It's time to 동사원형 ~: ~해야 할 시간이다 (B) 'Make sure (that) 주어+동사 ~' 구문으로 상대방이 잊어버리지 않도록 중요한 일에 대해 강한 당부 또는 경고하는 의미를 나타낼 수 있다. '~을 확실히 하라, ~을 반드시 하라'의 뜻이다.

06 'What do you want me to ~?'와 'What would you like me to ~?'는 '너는 내가 무엇을 하기를 원하니?'의 의미로 상대방이 원하는 행동을 물어볼 때 사용하는 표현이다.

교과서

Grammar

핵심 Check

p.22~23

1 (1) know (2) feel
2 (1) that (2) It (3) whom

시험대비 기본평가

p.24

01 ① 02 ④ 03 ⑤
04 (1) Mr. Brown let his son go to the party.
(2) The project manager had us meet at 9 a.m.
(3) They made me repeat the whole story.
(4) She helped me to complete this assignment.

01 사역동사 have 뒤의 목적보어 자리에는 원형부정사를 쓴다.

02 'It ~ that 강조 구문'은 'It is/was ~ that ...'의 형태로, 강조하고자 하는 부분을 It is/was와 that 사이에 넣고, 나머지 부분을 that 뒤에 써서 주어, 목적어, 부사(구/절) 등을 강조한다. 공통으로 that이 들어가는 것이 적절하다.

03 It was Jim who[that] I met again. 강조되는 어구가 사람일 때는 that 대신에 who[whom]를 쓸 수 있다.

04 (1) let+목적어+원형부정사(go) (2) have+목적어+원형부정사(meet) (3) make+목적어+원형부정사(repeat) (4) help+목적어+to부정사(원형부정사 / to complete) 등에 유의하여 영작한다.

시험대비 실력평가

p.25~27

01 ① 02 ② 03 ⓐ, ⓓ
04 ④ 05 ②, ⑤ 06 ③ 07 ③
08 ④ 09 ② 10 ① 11 ⑤
12 ③
13 (1) paint → painted (2) to play → play
(3) escaping → escape[to escape]
(4) which → that (5) what → that[which]
(6) which → that
14 (1) feel, smaile (2) fixed (3) to remain
(4) that (5) who
15 ⑤ 16 ⑤ 17 ③ 18 ④

01 He let me finish playing the piano. 사역동사 let의 목적보어로 동사원형이 적절하다.

02 ① which → that[who] ③ That → It ④ which → that ⑤ what → that

03 <보기>와 ⓐ, ⓓ는 목적보어로 동사원형이 사용된 사역동사 make이다 ⓑ 4형식 동사(수여동사) ⓒ (어느 방향으로) 나아가다(자동사) ⓔ 3형식 동사

04 '사역동사 had+목적어+목적보어 draw'와 관계대명사 what을 이용한다.

05 'a better tomorrow'를 강조하는 것이므로 which나 that을 써야 한다.

06 made가 사역동사이므로 목적보어로 동사원형이 온다.

07 <보기>와 ③번은 강조구문의 that이다. ① 지시부사 ② 지시대명사 ④ 접속사 ⑤ 지시형용사

08 (A) 사역동사 let 뒤의 목적보어로 동사원형, (B) the paper가 복사되는 것이므로 수동의 의미를 갖는 과거분사, (C) get은 사역동사가 아니므로 목적보어로 to부정사를 받는다.

09 ②번은 'It: 가주어, that절: 진주어'이고 나머지는 모두 It ~

that 강조구문으로 쓰였다.

10 (A) 주어가 복수이므로 give, (B)에는 사역동사 make의 목적보어로 원형부정사가 적절하다. (C)에는 사역동사 have의 목적보어로 원형부정사가 적절하다.

11 ① goes → go ② cleaned → clean ③ make → makes ④ draw → to draw

12 ① which → that ② which → that ④ which → that ⑤ which → that

13 (1) 목적어와 목적격보어의 관계가 수동이므로 목적격보어로 과거분사를 쓰는 것이 적절하다. (2) 목적어와 관계가 능동이므로 목적격보어로 동사원형이 적절하다. (3) help는 준사역동사로 목적격보어로 원형부정사나 to부정사를 받으므로 escaping을 escape나 to escape로 고쳐야 한다. (4) last week을 강조하는 것으로 전치사가 없어서 last week을 선행사처럼 생각할 수 있지만 여기서는 last week이 부사구이므로 that이 적절하다. (5) 강조하는 것이 his smartphone이므로 what을 that이나 which로 고치는 것이 적절하다. (6) in this school을 강조하는 것으로 school을 선행사로 생각하면 안 된다. which를 that으로 고친다.

14 (1) 사역동사는 목적격보어로 동사원형이 나온다. (2) get의 목적격보어로 수동의 의미가 필요하므로 과거분사가 적절하다. (3) ask는 목적격보어로 to부정사가 나온다. (4) 강조하는 것이 yesterday이므로 that이 적절하다. (5) 강조하는 것이 Tom이므로 who가 적절하다.

15 get은 사역동사의 뜻으로 쓰일 때 목적어와 목적격보어의 관계가 능동일 경우 목적격 보어로 to부정사를 쓴다.

16 'my favorite movie character'를 강조하는 것으로 'It was ~ that[which] ...'가 적절하다.

17 get은 사역동사의 뜻으로 쓰일 때 목적어와 목적격보어의 관계가 능동일 경우 목적격보어로 to부정사를 쓴다.

18 사역동사 make는 수동태에서 목적격보어가 to부정사로 바뀐다.

서술형 시험대비

p.28~29

01 (1) The project manager let us paint anything we wanted.
(2) She wasn't happy with our work and made us start over.
(3) They immediately had the meeting cancelled.
(4) When you cut them into pieces, let them be marinated.
(5) You in this country helped us (to) become free.
(6) It was Susan that(who/whom) I had a date with at the park last Saturday.
(7) It was in the train that Kimberly lost her wallet.
(8) It was last Friday that Mina flew a drone at the school.

02 (1) He let me play the piano with him.
(2) She had her computer fixed.

03 (1) It was Mina that[who] found a deer behind a tree.
(2) It was a deer that[which] Mina found behind a tree.
(3) It was behind a tree that Mina found a deer.

04 (1) I had my sister bring my gym uniform.
(2) Ashley got me to fix dinner.
(3) He made me wash his car.
(4) The doctor let her return to work.

05 (1) It was I that[who] bought this nice jacket at the store last Sunday.
(2) I did buy this nice jacket at the store last Sunday.
(3) It was this nice jacket that[which] I bought at the store last Sunday.
(4) It was at the store that I bought this nice jacket last Sunday.
(5) It was last Sunday that I bought this nice jacket at the store.

06 taken

07 (1) Peter sometimes lets his dog sleep on his bed.
(2) My dad makes me read lots of books.
(3) Where do you want me to hang this picture?
(4) It was the novel that[which] John borrowed from a library last week.
(5) It was in 2014 that I met her for the first time.

01 (1) 사역동사 let 뒤에 원형부정사를 쓴다. (2) 사역동사 make 뒤에 원형부정사를 쓴다. (3) 회의가 취소되는 수동이므로 과거분사로 바꾼다. (4) 목적어와의 관계가 수동일 경우 let은 목적격보어로 'be p.p.' 형태를 쓴다. (5) help는 목적격보어로 동사원형이나 to부정사가 나온다. (6) 강조하는 것이 'Susan'이므로 that이나 who 또는 whom을 쓰는 것이 적절하다. (7) which 다음에 완전한 절이 나오므로 the train을 강조하는 것으로 볼 수 없다. 'in the train'을 강조하는 것으로 that을 쓰는 것이 적절하다. (8) 강조하는 것이 'last Friday'이므로 that을 쓰는 것이 적절하다.

02 (1) 'allowed ~ to부정사'는 사역동사 let을 이용한다. (2) 목적어와 목적격보어의 관계가 수동일 경우 사역동사의 목적격보어로 과거분사를 쓴다.

03 It was와 that 사이에 강조하고자 하는 부분을 넣고, that 대신에 사람이면 who, 사물이나 동물이면 which를 쓸 수도 있다.

04 (1), (3), (4) 사역동사 have, make, let의 목적격보어로 목적

어와의 관계가 능동일 경우 원형부정사를 쓴다. (2) get은 목적어와 목적격보어의 관계가 능동일 경우 목적격보어로 to부정사를 쓴다.

05 과거시제이므로 강조하고자 하는 부분을 It was와 that 사이에 넣고, 나머지 부분을 that 뒤에 쓴다. 이때 that 대신에 사람이면 who, 사물이면 which를 사용할 수 있다. 또한 'It is[was] ~ that ...' 구문은 동사를 강조할 수 없으므로 동사는 동사 앞에 do/does/did를 사용하여 강조한다.

06 사역동사의 목적격보어로 '아들이 병원으로 데려가지는' 수동의 의미가 필요하므로 과거분사가 적절하다.

07 (1), (2) '사역동사+목적어+원형부정사'에 유의한다. (3) want는 목적격보어로 to부정사가 나온다. (4), (5) 강조하고자 하는 부분을 It was와 that 사이에 넣고, 나머지 부분을 that 뒤에 쓴다. 이때 that 대신에 사물이면 which를 사용할 수 있다.

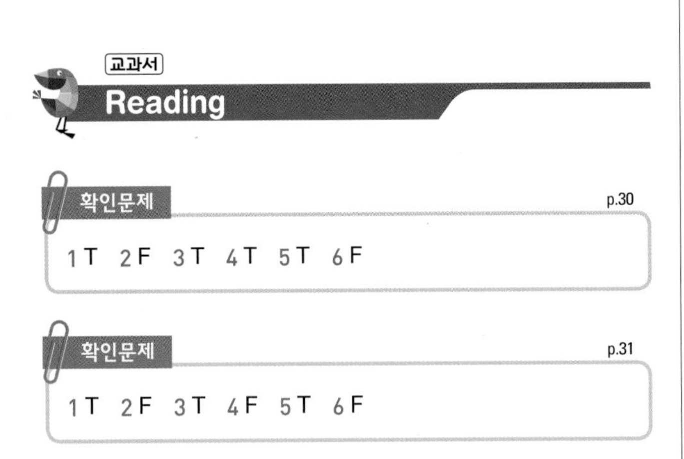

교과서

Reading

확인문제 p.30

1 T 2 F 3 T 4 T 5 T 6 F

확인문제 p.31

1 T 2 F 3 T 4 F 5 T 6 F

교과서 확인학습 A p.32~33

01 Better Tomorrow
02 My name is
03 This is me
04 aren't they
05 take pictures
06 old neighborhoods
07 with wall paintings
08 a light went on in my head
09 I'm in
10 Why don't we
11 suggested this idea
12 on the Internet
13 to do a wall painting
14 applied for, was selected
15 finally came
16 had us meet
17 was in very poor condition
18 strange writings and drawings
19 Other parts 20 with white paint
21 let us paint
22 something cute
23 divided into
24 was in the group
25 chose my spot
26 did, background drawings
27 for about 28 got together, shared
29 was very proud of
30 so, that 31 much harder
32 wasn't perfect
33 matter
34 a little brighter and happier
35 ourselves 36 didn't just paint
37 a better tomorrow

교과서 확인학습 B p.34~35

1 Paint a Better Tomorrow
2 Hi. My name is Homin.
3 This is me in front of the wall painting.
4 The wings are so pretty, aren't they?
5 Many people like to take pictures in front of wall paintings.
6 They make old neighborhoods bright and new.
7 Last month, I visited a village with wall paintings in Yeosu.
8 As I was taking a picture, a light went on in my head.
9 I thought, "I'm in the school art club.
10 Why don't we do wall paintings like these?"
11 I suggested this idea at the next club meeting, and the members loved it.
12 We found a teen volunteer project on the Internet.
13 The project was to do a wall painting in our neighborhood.
14 We applied for it, and two weeks later, our club was selected!
15 The day of the project finally came.
16 The project manager had us meet at the painting site at 9 a.m.
17 The wall was in very poor condition.
18 There were strange writings and drawings on some parts.
19 Other parts had old posters on them.
20 We removed the posters first and painted over

the writings and drawings with white paint.
21 The manager let us paint anything we wanted.
22 We decided to paint something cute because the wall was near an elementary school.
23 We divided into three groups and began painting.
24 I was in the group with Minsu and Jiwon.
25 I chose my spot and started to paint my favorite movie character.
26 Minsu painted some flowers and Jiwon did some background drawings.
27 Our club painted for about five hours.
28 After we finished, we got together and shared the day's experiences.
29 Minsu was very proud of his flower painting.
30 He said, "My flower is so real that a bee landed on it."
31 I said, "Drawing on a wall was much harder than drawing on paper."
32 We all agreed that our wall painting wasn't perfect.
33 But it didn't matter.
34 We made our neighborhood a little brighter and happier.
35 We were proud of ourselves.
36 We didn't just paint pictures on a wall that day.
37 It was a better tomorrow that we painted.

시험대비 실력평가

p.36~39

01 isn't it → aren't they 02 ②
03 Why don't we do wall paintings like these?
04 ⑤ 05 ② 06 ②, ⑤
07 The wall was in very poor condition. 08 ③
09 (A) taking a picture (B) wall paintings
10 여수에 있는 벽화 마을의 벽화들 11 ③
12 ⑤ 13 ④
14 ①번 → for, ②번 → that, ③번 → a little[또는 much/even/still/far/a lot], ④번 → ourselves, ⑤번 → that[which]
15 bad 16 so → because(as/since) 17 ⑤
18 was selected 19 ①, ⑤ 20 ①
21 ⑤
22 (A) to meet → meet, 또는 had → got
(B) to paint → paint 또는 let → allowed 23 ③

01 주어가 The wing이 아니라 The wings이므로, aren't they로 고치는 것이 적절하다.

02 주어진 문장의 'a light went on in my head'에 주목한다. ②번 다음 문장의 내용을 가리키므로 ②번이 적절하다.

03 '우리가 이것처럼 벽화를 그리면 어떨까?'라는 생각을 가리킨다.

04 호민이의 학교 미술 동아리가 청소년 봉사 프로젝트에 선택된 것은 '그 프로젝트에 지원한지' 2주 후(two weeks after it applied for the project)였다.

05 오래된 포스터들이 붙어 있던 것을 '제거했다'고 하는 것이 적절하다. ① 보호했다, ③ 막았다, 예방했다, ④ 유지했다, ⑤ 파괴했다

06 '마침내' 프로젝트 날이 왔다고 하는 것이 적절하다. finally = at last = in the end: 마침내, ①, ④: 무엇보다도, 특히, ③ 적어도[최소한]

07 be in poor[bad] condition: 보존 상태가 나쁘다, 건강이 좋지 않다

08 ⓐ on the Internet: 인터넷 상에서, ⓑ apply for: ~에 신청하다, ~에 지원하다

09 호민이는 여수에 있는 벽화 마을에서 '사진을 찍는' 동안 어떤 아이디어가 떠올라서, 미술 동아리 부원들에게 그것처럼 '벽화'를 그리자고 제안했다.

10 'wall paintings at a village with wall paintings in Yeosu'를 가리킨다.

11 ⓐ와 ③: 중요하다, 문제가 되다(동사), ①, ④: 문제, 일, 사건, ② (쓰인·인쇄된) 것, 우편물, ⑤ 물질

12 이 글은 '동아리 부원들이 벽화를 그린 후, 자신들이 그날 벽에 그린 것은 단지 그림만이 아니라 더 나은 내일을 그린 것이라며 스스로를 대견하게 생각하는' 내용의 글이므로, 제목으로는 ⑤번 '우리가 무엇을 그렸냐고? 더 나은 내일!'이 적절하다. ① incredible: 믿을 수 없는, ③ So what?: 그래서 어쩌라는 거야?

13 matter = count = be important = be of importance = be significant: 중요하다, ④ make a difference: 변화를 가져오다, 중요하다

14 ① 'for+숫자', 'during+기간을 나타내는 명사', ② so ~ that ...: 너무 ~해서 …하다, ③ very는 형용사나 부사의 원급을 강조하는 말이므로, 비교급을 강조하는 말로 고치는 것이 적절하다. 다만 'a little'은 '약간'이라는 뜻이고, 'much/even/still/far/a lot'은 '훨씬'이라는 뜻이다. ④ 주어와 목적어가 같으므로 재귀대명사로 고치는 것이 적절하다. ⑤ painted의 목적어에 해당하는 'a better tomorrow'를 강조하는 것이므로 that이나 which로 고치는 것이 적절하다.

15 be in poor[bad] condition: 보존 상태가 나쁘다, 건강이 좋지 않다

16 '그 벽이 초등학교 근처에 있어서 귀여운 뭔가를 그리기로 했다'고 해야 하므로, 이유를 나타내는 접속사로 고치는 것이 적절하다.

17 호민이가 가장 좋아하는 영화 캐릭터가 무엇인지는 대답할 수

없다. ① They met at 9 a.m. ② No. right away: 곧바로, 즉시, ③ No. The manager let them paint anything they wanted. ④ Yes. They decided to paint something cute because the wall was near an elementary school. subject matter: 소재

18 동아리가 '선택된' 것이므로 수동태로 쓰는 것이 적절하다.

19 (A) 와 ①, ⑤: 명사적 용법, ②, ④ 형용사적 용법, ③: 부사적 용법

20 이 글은 '글쓴이가 여수에 있는 벽화 마을을 방문하고 나서 학교 미술 동아리 부원들에게 벽화를 그리자고 제안한 다음, 청소년 봉사 프로젝트에 지원해서 선택되는' 내용이므로, 제목으로는 ①번 '이것들처럼 벽화를 그리면 어떨까?'가 적절하다.

21 some ~, others(other+복수명사) ~: 어떤 것[사람]들은 ~, 다른 것[사람]들은 ~, ⓑ 뒤에 명사가 있으므로 Others가 아니라 Other를 쓰는 것이 적절하다. each+단수명사, another+단수명사, the other: 둘 중 다른 하나

22 (A) have+목적어+원형부정사 = get+목적어+to부정사, (B) let+목적어+원형부정사 = allow+목적어+to부정사

23 이 글은 '벽화 그리기 위한 프로젝트를 행하는 과정'을 설명하는 글이므로, 주제로는 ③번 '벽화를 그리기 위한 과정'이 적절하다. ④ subject matter: 소재, ⑤ effectively: 효과적으로

서술형 시험대비

p.40~41

01 aren't they
02 (A) This is (B) so (C) bright and new
03 wall paintings
04 a light went on in my head
05 (A) idea (B) project
06 school art club
07 **몇 군데에는 이상한 낙서와 그림이 있었고, 다른 부분에는 오래된 포스터들이 붙어 있었다.**
08 whatever
09 (1) **먼저 포스터들을 제거했다.**
(2) **낙서와 그림을 흰 페인트로 덧칠했다.**
(3) **호민이는 자신의 구역을 정해서 가장 좋아하는 영화 캐릭터를 그리기 시작했다.**
(4) **민수는 몇 송이의 꽃을 그렸다.**
(5) **지원이는 배경 그림을 그렸다.**
10 (1) enough (2) We painted a better tomorrow.
11 (A) imperfect (B) pride
12 shared
13 (1) as[so], as (2) less

01 주어가 The wings이므로, aren't they가 적절하다.

02 (A) 가까이 있는 사람을 소개할 때 'This is'를 사용한다. (B) 'so+형용사[부사]', 'such+a+형용사+명사'이므로 so가 적절하다. (C) 목적격보어로 형용사를 써야 하므로 bright and new가 적절하다.

03 '벽화'를 가리킨다. 'Many people'이라고 하지 않도록 조심해야 한다.

04 a light went on in my head: 머릿속에 좋은 생각이 떠올랐다

05 ⓑ 이 '아이디어', ⓒ 우리 마을에 벽화를 그리는 '프로젝트'를 가리킨다.

06 호민이가 봉사활동으로 하필이면 벽화를 그리자고 제안한 이유는 그가 '학교 미술 동아리'에 있기 때문이었다. of all things: 하필이면

07 뒤에 이어지는 문장의 내용을 쓰는 것이 적절하다.

08 anything (that) = whatever: (~하는) 것은 무엇이든지

09 그들은 먼저 별로 좋지 않았던 벽의 상태를 정리하고, 벽화 작업을 했다.

10 (1) so ~ that... = enough to 동사원형, to부정사나 전치사의 목적어가 주어와 같으면 생략한다. (2) 강조되었던 목적어를 동사 뒤에 쓰는 것이 적절하다.

11 (A) wasn't perfect = was imperfect, (B) be proud of = take pride in

12 share ~ = have ~ in common

13 A 비교급 than B = B not as(so) ~ as A = B less 원급 than A

영역별 핵심문제

p.43~47

01 ⑤	02 ④	03 (n)eat	04 take
05 ④	06 ③	07 ⑤	08 ②
09 ④	10 volunteer	11 ①	12 ②

13 (1) follow (2) ask (3) be taken (4) written
14 ⑤
15 (1) It was I that[who] played hide and seek with my friends in the park yesterday.
(2) I did play hide and seek with my friends in the park yesterday.
(3) It was hide and seek that[which] I played with my friends in the park yesterday.
(4) It was with my friends that I played hide and seek in the park yesterday.
(5) It was in the park that I played hide and seek with my friends yesterday.
(6) It was yesterday that I played hide and seek with my friends in the park.
16 ① 17 ③
18 It was, that[which]
19 (1) open (2) read (3) be taken (4) that
(5) which (6) that

20 (1) Mr. Brown made the students line up at the gym.
(2) It was a bird that broke the window yesterday.
21 ③ 22 ①, ④ 23 volunteer project
24 ② 25 ① 26 ③
27 ⓐ my flower ⓒ our wall painting wasn't perfect
28 ②
29 We made our neighborhood a little brighter and happier.
30 It took for about five hours (for them to do it).

01 prepare: 준비하다 / 나는 엄마가 아침에 쉬실 수 있도록 아침을 준비하려고 했었다.

02 as: ~할 때, ~ 때문에 ① 내가 과학 보고서를 쓰고 있을 때, 그가 나에게 전화했다. ② 내가 집에 도착했을 때, 나의 남동생이 울고 있었다. ③ 너는 들어갈 때 표를 보여 줘야 한다. ④ 엘리베이터가 고장 났기 때문에, 우리는 계단으로 올라가야 했다. ⑤ 내가 버스에서 내릴 때 Peter를 봤다.

03 neat: 단정한, 말쑥한 / 그의 옷은 항상 단정하고 깨끗했다.

04 take a break: 휴식을 취하다 / 10분 휴식을 취하자. take a picture: 사진을 찍다 / 제가 사진 찍어 드릴까요?

05 주어진 문장은 상대방이 원하는 행동이 무엇인지 물어보는 표현으로, 도움을 요청한 G에게 B가 수락하고 이어서 '내가 무엇을 하길 원하니?'라고 묻자 G는 B에게 박스에 주소를 써 달라고 얘기한다.

06 ③은 상대방에게 도움을 제안하는 표현이고, 나머지 보기들은 상대방에게 도움을 요청하는 표현들이다.

07 ⓒ는 자신에 대해서 걱정하지 말라는 의미이므로, worry가 아니라 don't worry가 어울린다. ⓐ Enjoy ⓑ will ⓒ Don't worry ⓓ Make ⓔ have

08 무엇을 하고 있는지 묻자 (B) 이사를 위해 짐을 싸는 중이라 대답하며 상대방에게 도움을 요청한다. (C) 요청을 수락하며, 무엇을 도와줘야 하는지 묻자 (A) 테이프로 상자를 묶어달라고 얘기하고 (D) 알았다고 대답한다.

09 주어진 문장은 '지금 들어가야 하나요?'의 의미로 'Yes. Please go into Room 7.(네. 7번 방으로 들어가 주세요.)'에 대한 질문이 될 수 있으므로 ④에 들어가는 것이 적절하다.

10 volunteer: 자원봉사자 / 대가를 기대하지 않고 어떤 일을 하는 사람

11 대화의 must는 '~임에 틀림없다'의 의미로 사용되었다. ①은 '~임에 틀림없다'로 강한 추측을 나타낼 때 사용한다. 이외의 보기들은 의무를 나타내는 '~해야 한다'의 의미로 사용되었다.

12 ① Tony는 책을 읽을 때 무엇을 명심해야 하는가?(천천히 그리고 명확하게 읽어야 한다.) ② Tony는 봉사활동을 전에 한 경험이 있는가? ③ Tony는 녹음을 위해 몇 번 방으로 갈 것인가?(7번) ④ 누구를 위해 Tony는 책을 녹음할 것인가?(시각 장애인들) ⑤ Tony는 시각 장애인들을 위해 무엇을 할 예정인가?(책을 읽을 것이다.)

13 사역동사의 목적격보어로 목적어와의 관계가 능동일 경우 동사원형이 나오며, 수동일 경우 make, have는 목적격보어로 과거분사를 쓰고, let은 'be p.p.' 형태를 쓴다.

14 'It is[was] ~ that ...' 강조 구문에서 that 대신에 강조하는 것이 사람이면 who, 사물이면 which를 쓸 수 있다.

15 강조하고자 하는 부분을 It is[was]와 that 사이에 넣고, 나머지 부분을 that 뒤에 쓴다. that 대신에 강조하는 것이 사람이면 who, 사물이면 which를 쓸 수 있다. 하지만 'It is[was] ~ that ...' 구문은 동사를 강조할 수는 없고 동사는 동사 앞에 do/does/did를 사용하여 강조한다.

16 사역동사의 목적어와 목적격보어의 관계가 능동일 경우 동사원형이 나오며, 수동의 관계에 있을 경우 목적격보어로 과거분사를 쓴다. let은 'be p.p.' 형태를 쓴다. get은 목적격보어로 to부정사를 쓴다.

17 ① My sister always helps me (to) clean the garden. ② Ms. Parker made them water the plants. ④ I remember hearing him come[coming] in. ⑤ He advised her not to smoke.

18 'It is[was] ~ that ...' 구문은 강조하고자 하는 부분을 It is[was]와 that 사이에 넣고, 나머지 부분을 that 뒤에 쓰며. 강조하는 것이 사물이나 동물이면 that 대신에 which를 쓸 수 있다.

19 (1)~(3) 사역동사의 목적격보어로 목적어와의 관계가 능동일 경우 동사원형이 나오며, 수동의 관계에 있을 경우 과거분사를 쓴다. (4)~(6) 'It is[was] ~ that …' 구문에서 that 대신에 강조하는 것이 사람이면 who, 사물이나 동물이면 which를 쓸 수 있다.

20 (1) 사역동사의 목적격보어로 원형부정사를 쓴다. (2) 강조하고자 하는 부분을 It is[was]와 that 사이에 넣고, 나머지 부분을 that 뒤에 쓴다.

21 ③ be lost in a daydream: '공상에 잠기다[빠지다]', ⓐ와 나머지는 다 '좋은 생각이 떠올랐다', a light went on in my head: 머릿속에 좋은 생각이 떠올랐다

22 호민이가 여수에 있는 벽화 마을을 방문하고 나서 학교 미술 동아리 부원들에게 벽화를 그리자고 제안한 다음, 청소년 봉사 프로젝트에 지원하는 것으로 보아, '적극적'이고 '사려 깊은' 성격이라고 하는 것이 적절하다. ① 활동적인, 적극적인, ② 소극적인, 수동적인, ③ 이기적인, ④ 사려 깊은, (남을) 배려하는, ⑤ 거만한

23 호민이와 학교 미술 동아리 부원들은 벽화를 그리기를 원했기 때문에 '봉사 프로젝트'에 참여하기로 결정했다.

24 ②번 다음 문장의 'strange writings and drawings'에 주목한다. 주어진 문장의 'very poor condition'의 구체적인 예에 해당하므로 ②번이 적절하다.

25 이 글은 '호민이와 친구들이 벽화 그리는 프로젝트를 위해 만나서 벽화를 그리는' 내용의 글이므로, 제목으로는 ①번 '마침내 프로젝트를 위한 D-day가 되었어!'가 적절하다. D-day: 작전 행동 개시일, 중요한 작전·변화가 예정된 날

26 그들은 먼저 포스터들을 제거하고 낙서와 그림을 흰 페인트로 덧칠했다.

27 ⓐ '내 꽃', ⓒ '우리의 벽화가 완벽하지는 않다'는 것을 가리킨다.

28 ⓐ와 ②, ③: 동명사, ①, ④, ⑤: 현재분사

29 형용사의 비교급 앞에 a little을 붙여서 목적격보어로 쓰는 것이 적절하다.

30 동아리 부원들이 벽화를 그리는 데 약 다섯 시간이 걸렸다.

단원별 예상문제

p.48-51

01 ② 02 so, that 03 ③ 04 ②
05 ① 06 ③, ⑤ 07 make
08 Keep in mind two rules for our class.
09 ① 10 ① 11 give 12 ④
13 ④ 14 ③, ⑤
15 (1) It was what he said that worried me.
(2) It was with my friends that I played soccer after school.
(3) It was my club members that[who] planted flowers in the garden on April 5th.
16 ⑤ 17 ②
18 (A) suggestion (B) teen volunteer project
19 ③ 20 ④ 21 ③ 22 ①
23 ②, ⑤ 24 ②
25 (A) minutes (B) neat (C) rewarding 26 ④

01 ① get, get up: (잠자리에서) 일어나다 / 그 소년들은 일어나서 화장실에 간다. ② turn, turn off: 끄다 / 내가 잘 수 있도록 불을 꺼주세요. ③ get, get on: (탈것에) 타다 / 지하철 타는 데가 어디입니까? ④ get, get together: 모이다 / 많은 친척들이 거실에 모일 수 있다. ⑤ get, get along with ~: ~와 잘 지내다 / 우리가 친구들과 잘 어울리는 것은 좋다.

02 so ~ that ...: 너무 ~해서 …하다 / 그 컴퓨터는 너무 비싸서 나는 살 수 없다.

03 apply: 지원하다, 신청하다 / 나는 4개의 대학에 지원했고, 모든 대학에서 받아들여졌다.

04 a light went on in the head: 머릿속에 좋은 생각이 떠올랐다 / 그것은 마치 그들에게 좋은 생각이 떠오른 것 같았다.

05 주어진 문장은 '내일 이사를 위해 짐을 싸는 중이야.'로 무엇을 하고 있는 중인지 묻는 'What are you doing?'의 대답이다.

06 'What do you want me to ~?'로 상대방이 원하는 행동을 물어볼 때 동사 'want, would like'를 이용해 대답할 수 있다. ②는 '나는 옷을 상자 안에 넣고 싶다.'의 의미로 맞지 않는다.

07 (A), (B) make: 만들다 (C) make sure ~: 꼭 ~해라, 확실하게 ~해라

08 keep in mind: 명심하다 rule: 규칙

09 주어진 문장은 '저는 봉사 활동을 하러 왔어요.'의 의미로, 자신이 온 목적을 말할 때 사용하는 표현이다.

10 Thanks 뒤에 for를 쓰는 경우, for 뒤에 감사의 이유를 적는다.

11 give a bath: 목욕시키다

12 봉사를 하러 온 A와 봉사 내용과 주의 사항을 가르쳐 주고 있는 B를 볼 때, 자원봉사자와 자원봉사 관리자의 관계임을 알 수 있다.

13 통증이 무엇을 줄이는 것이 아니라 줄어드는 것으로 목적어와의 관계가 수동이므로 과거분사가 적절하다.

14 ① 사역동사 let의 목적보어로 원형부정사, ② 목적어와의 관계가 수동이므로 과거분사, ④ 사역동사 make의 목적보어로 원형부정사, ⑥ that 다음에 나오는 절이 완전하고 Bob이 화장실을 떨어뜨릴 수는 없으므로 in을 the toilet 앞에 넣어 장소를 강조하는 문장으로 만들어야 한다. ⑦ a drone을 강조하는 것이므로 that이나 which를 써야 한다.

15 강조하고자 하는 부분을 It is[was]와 that 사이에 넣고, 나머지 부분을 that 뒤에 쓴다.

16 ⓐ와 ⑤: ~와 (똑)같이, ~처럼(전치사), ①, ④: 좋아하다(동사), ② 비슷한(형용사), ③ 비슷한 것(명사)

17 이 글은 '호민이와 학교 미술 동아리 부원들이 자원봉사 활동으로 벽화를 그리기로 결정하는 것'에 관한 글이므로, 주제로는 ②번 '자원봉사 활동으로 벽화를 그리기'가 적절하다.

18 학교 미술 동아리 부원들이 호민이의 '제안'을 수락한 뒤, 그들은 인터넷을 검색해서 그들 마을에 벽화를 그리는 '청소년 봉사 프로젝트'에 지원했다. 2주 후에 그들의 동아리가 선택되었다.

19 ⓐ be in poor[bad] condition: 보존 상태가 나쁘다, 건강이 좋지 않다, ⓑ divide into: ~으로 나뉘다

20 ⓒ와 ④: (소설 등의) 등장인물, (연극의) 역(役), (만화의) 캐릭터, leading character: 주역, ① 인격, 품성, ② 특성, 특질, 특색, ③ 글자, 부호, ⑤ (개인·국민의) 성격, 성질, 기질

21 책임자는 그들이 원하는 어떤 것이든 그리게 했다.

22 주어진 문장의 it에 주목한다. ①번 앞 문장의 'our wall painting wasn't perfect'를 받고 있으므로 ①번이 적절하다.

23 ① 실망, ② 만족감, ③ 우울함, ④ 수치심, ⑤ 자부심

24 호민이에게는 '벽'에 그리는 것이 '종이'에 그리는 것보다 훨씬 힘들었다.

25 (A) every 30 minutes: 30분마다, every+기수+복수명사: (빈도를 나타내어) 매~[~마다], (B) 감각동사 look의 보어이므로 형용사 neat이 적절하다. (C) 경험이 '보람을 받는' 것이 아니라 '보람을 주는' 것이므로 rewarding이 적절하다. rewarding: 보람 있는, 보람을 주는

26 얼마나 오래 봉사를 했는지는 알 수 없다.

서술형 실전문제 p.52~53

01 What do you want me to do? /
What would you like me to do?
02 to keeping → to keep
03 Be sure to read slowly and clearly. /
Don't forget to read slowly and clearly. /
Please remember to read slowly and clearly.
04 (1) He let us take pictures of his artwork.
(2) It is a white bear that I am drawing now.
(3) How much would it cost to have the camera cleaned?
05 (1) My mom made me prepare dinner.
(2) My boss let the work be done by tomorrow.
(3) Linda had her wallet stolen on her way home.
(4) It was at[in] the restaurant that I saw Juliet calling her friend.
(5) It is because they have no jobs that they cannot afford to buy them.
06 applied
07 (1) How[What] about (2) shall we
08 They found it on the Internet.
09 (A) poor (B) to paint (C) near
10 other parts
11 They had to remove the posters first and paint over the writings and drawings with white paint.

01 What would you like me to ~?'와 'What do you want me to ~?'는 '너는 내가 무엇을 하기를 원하니?'의 의미로 상대방이 원하는 행동을 물어볼 때 사용하는 표현이다.

02 to keep in mind는 앞의 대명사 anything을 수식하고 있다. (to부정사의 형용사적 용법) keep in mind: 명심하다

03 상대방이 꼭 하기를 원하는 내용을 강조하기 위해서 make sure를 사용한다. make sure는 '꼭 ~해라, 확실하게 ~해라'의 의미를 가지고 있다. 상대방에게 '꼭 ~해라', '~할 것을 잊지 말아라, ~할 것을 기억해라'라고 당부할 때는 'Be sure to 동사원형', 'Don't forget to 동사원형 ~'이나 'Remember to 동사원형 ~'으로 나타내기도 한다.

04 (1) 사역동사 let의 목적격보어로 동사원형이 나와야 한다. (2) It is와 that 사이에 a white bear를 넣어 강조한다. (3) 카메라가 청소되는 것이므로 수동의 의미를 나타내는 과거분사를 이용한다. 가격을 나타내는 비인칭주어 it을 써야 함에 주의한다.

05 (1) 사역동사 make의 목적격보어로 동사원형이 나와야 한다. (2) 목적어와의 관계가 수동일 경우 let은 목적격보어로 'be p.p.' 형태를 쓴다. (3) 지갑을 도난당한 것이므로 수동의 의미를 나타내는 과거분사를 써야 한다. (4) that 다음에 나오는 절이 완전하므로 'the restaurant'을 'at[in] the restaurant'으로 고쳐야 한다. (5) which 다음에 나오는 절이 완전하므로 which를 that으로 고쳐 부사절을 강조하는 문장으로 만들어야 한다.

06 apply: 신청하다, 지원하다, 과거시제로 쓰는 것이 적절하다, <영영풀이: 공식적으로 어떤 것을 요청하기 위해 편지를 쓰거나 양식에 기입하다>

07 Why don't we 동사원형? = How[What] about ~ing? = Let's 동사원형, shall we?: ~하는 게 어때?

08 호민이와 학교 미술 동아리 부원들이 청소년 봉사 프로젝트를 '찾은 곳은 인터넷에서'였다.

09 (A) 벽은 상태가 별로 '좋지 않았다'고 해야 하므로 poor가 적절하다. be in poor[bad] condition: 보존 상태가 나쁘다, 건강이 좋지 않다 (B) decide는 목적어로 to부정사를 써야 하므로 to paint가 적절하다. (C) 벽이 초등학교 '근처에' 있다고 해야 하므로 near가 적절하다. near: 가까운; 가까이, nearly: 거의

10 '다른 부분들'을 가리킨다.

11 그들은 먼저 포스터들을 제거하고 낙서와 그림을 흰 페인트로 덧칠해야 했다.

창의사고력 서술형 문제 p.54

|모범답안|
01 B: Make sure that you take an umbrella
02 (1) It is the magician that[who] shows magic to children.
(2) It is a pigeon that[which] the magician holds in his hands.
(3) It is John that[who] is surprised at the magic.
(4) It is Sam that[who] points at the pigeon.
03 (A) Friday, May 3rd (B) Dream Library
(C) English books (D) arrange the books
(E) very proud

01 상대방에게 '꼭 ~해라. 반드시 ~해라.'라고 당부할 때는 'Make sure ~.'라고 한다. Make sure 뒤에는 '주어+동사'의 형태가 나온다.

02 강조하고자 하는 부분을 It is[was]와 that 사이에 넣고, 나머지 부분을 that 뒤에 쓴다.

단원별 모의고사 p.55~58

01 (s)pot 02 ① 03 ③
04 background 05 (A) to (B) out
06 to sit → sit, after → before
07 ⑤ 08 ④ 09 ④
10 Make sure you turn off the lights. 11 for
12 ① 13 Is there anything to keep in mind?
14 handed in on time
15 (1) It was we that[who] found a teen volunteer project

on the Internet.

(2) It was something cute that[which] we decided to paint because the wall was near an elementary school.

(3) It was two weeks later that our club was selected.

(4) It was near the park that Mike built a tree house.

16 ③ 17 ②, ③, ⑥, ⑦ 18 ④

19 founded → found 20 ②

21 Drawing on a wall was much harder than drawing on paper

22 a better tomorrow 23 ③ 24 ⑤

25 a text message → an email

01 주어진 단어들은 동의어 관계이다. neat: 깨끗한 tidy: 깔끔한 location: 장소 spot: 장소, 지점

02 (A) line up: 줄서다 / 줄을 서서 기다려 주세요. (B) be proud of ~: ~을 자랑스러워하다 / 그녀는 틀림없이 자신이 아주 자랑스러울 것이다. (C) on time: 제시간에 / 버스는 정확히 제시간에 왔다.

03 ① selected, select: 선택하다 / 우리는 인터뷰를 위해서 4명의 지원자를 선택했다. ② plant, plant: 심다 / 그들은 내가 나무를 심는 것을 도왔다. ③ suggested, suggest: 제안하다 / 그녀의 엄마는 그녀가 병원에 가기를 제안했다. ④ replied, reply: 응답하다 / '오늘 Simon을 봤니?' '물론이지' Nathalie가 웃으며 대답했다. ⑤ share, share: 나누다, 공유하다 / 나와 튀김을 같이 먹을래?

04 background: 배경 / 보고 있는 주된 것 뒤에 있는 영역 / 다른 배경 출신의 사람들을 이해하는 것은 중요하다.

05 (A) 'What do you want to me to do?'는 '너는 내가 무엇을 하기를 원하니?'로 상대방이 원하는 것이 무엇인지 묻는 표현이다. 여기서 want는 5형식 동사로 'me'는 목적어, 'to do'가 목적격보어로 사용되었다. (B) take out: 가지고 나가다 trash: 쓰레기

06 접속사 and로 make와 sit이 병렬로 연결되어 있다. 그러므로 sit은 to sit이 아니라 sit이 적절하다. 요리를 시작하기 전에 손을 닦는 것이 문맥상 어울리므로 after를 before로 고쳐야 한다.

07 주어진 문장은 '제가 무엇을 하기를 원하십니까?'이므로 상대방인 어떤 것을 도와주기를 원한다는 대답인 'Please put the cookies in the gift boxes.(선물 상자에 쿠키를 좀 넣어 줘.)'의 앞이 어울린다.

08 ⓓ는 양로원에 계신 분들을 위해 쿠키를 굽고 있는 것을 의미하고 나머지는 모두 쿠키를 의미한다.

09 ① 소년은 소녀를 도울 것인가? (네) ② 왜 소녀는 그토록 많은 쿠키를 굽고 있는가? (양로원에 계신 분들에게 주기 위해서) ③ 소년은 상자 하나에 몇 개의 쿠키를 넣을 것인가? (3개) ④ 얼마나 많은 쿠키를 소녀는 구웠는가? ⑤ 소녀는 지금 무엇을 하고 있는가? (쿠키를 굽고 있다.)

10 make sure ~: 꼭 ~해라, 확실하게 ~해라 turn off: 끄다

11 'I'm here for ~.'는 '나는 ~을 위해[~하러] 왔어요.'의 의미로 온 목적에 대해 말할 때 사용할 수 있다.

12 빈칸은 동사인 read를 수식하고 있으므로 부사가 어울리며, 시각 장애인들을 위한 책을 읽어 녹음하고 있으므로 내용상 'slowly and clearly(천천히 그리고 명확하게)'가 어울린다.

13 to keep in mind는 anything을 수식하고 있다.(to부정사의 형용사적 용법) keep in mind: 명심하다

14 보고서(report)가 제출되는 것이므로 과거분사로 쓰는 것이 적절하다.

15 강조하고자 하는 부분을 시제에 맞춰 It is[was]와 that 사이에 넣고, 나머지 부분을 that 뒤에 쓴다. 이때 that 대신에 사람이면 who, 사물이면 which를 쓸 수 있다.

16 ③번은 4형식으로 쓰였고 나머시는 모두 목석어와 목적격보어가 있는 5형식이다.

17 ② '가방들이 검사를 당하는 것'이므로 수동의 의미를 나타내는 'have+목적어+과거분사'가 적절하다. ③ 사역동사 have의 목적보어로 동사원형이 나오고, help는 동사원형이나 to부정사가 나온다. ⑥, ⑦ 'It ~ that ...' 강조 구문은 동사나 양태 부사를 강조하는 데 쓰이지 않는다.

18 ⓐ와 ④: ~할 때(접속사), ① [보통 as ~ as ...로 형용사·부사 앞에서] …와 같은 정도로, (as ~ as ...에서, 앞의 as가 지시부사, 뒤의 as는 접속사), ② ~와 같이(접속사), ③ ~이므로, ~이기 때문에(접속사), ⑤ ~이라고, ~처럼(전치사)

19 인터넷에서 청소년 봉사 프로젝트를 '찾았다'고 해야 하므로 found로 고치는 것이 적절하다. find-found-found: 찾다, 발견하다, found-founded-founded: 설립하다

20 호민이가 그곳에서 몇 장의 사진을 찍었는지는 알 수 없다. ① A village with wall paintings in Yeosu. ③ The school art club. ④ Yes. ⑤ A teen volunteer project to do a wall painting in their neighborhood.

21 much를 보충하면 된다.

22 우리가 그날 벽에 그린 것은 단지 그림이 아니라, 오히려 더 나은 내일이었다. rather: 오히려, 'rather+a+형용사+명사' 또는 'a+rather +형용사+명사'의 순서로 쓴다.

23 이 글은 '동아리 부원들이 벽화를 그린 후, 자신들이 그날 벽에 그린 것은 단지 그림만이 아니라 더 나은 내일을 그린 것이라며 스스로를 대견하게 생각하는' 내용의 글이므로, 주제로는 ③번 '보람 있는 자원봉사 일에 의해 얻어진 자부심'이 적절하다. self-esteem: 자부심, rewarding: 보람 있는, ① laborious: (많은 시간과 노력을 요하는) 힘든, ④ carry out: 수행하다, ⑤ convenient: 편리한

24 위 글은 자원봉사자를 모집하는 '광고'이다. ① (신문 • 잡지의) 글, 기사, ② 수필, ③ 요약, 개요, ④ (책 • 연극 • 영화 등에 대한) 논평[비평], 감상문

25 이 프로젝트에 관심이 있으면, '이메일'을 보내어 신청할 수 있다.

Lesson 4

Open a Book, Open Your Mind

시험대비 실력평가 p.62

01 ⑤	02 ③	03 ③	04 ④
05 ④	06 ④	07 ②	

01 assign: (사람을) 배치하다 / 새로운 선생님이 과학 실험실 로 배치되었다.

02 ① 사실, Kobe는 너무 바빠서 창밖을 보는 시간을 가지지 못했다. ② 그 돈은 그의 소유이다. ③ look up: (사전·참고 자료·컴퓨터 등에서 정 보를) 찾아보다 / 많은 사람들은 사전에서 이 단어의 의미를 찾아봐야 한다. ④ 난 그 책을 내려놓을 수가 없어서 앉은 자리에서 다 읽었다. ⑤ 강과 호수 의 바닥에 있는 진흙 역시 식량과 은신처를 제공한다.

03 hole: 구덩이, 구멍 / 무언가 단단한 것에 비어 있는 공간

04 beat: ~을 치다, 두드리다, (심장이) 고동치다

05 stand for: ~을 의미하다

06 쌍으로 이루어진 것, 2개의 비슷한 것이 하나의 물건을 이 룰 때 'a pair of+복수 명사'의 형태로 쓴다. ① a pair of sneakers: 운동화 한 켤레 / 그는 운동화 한 켤레를 샀다. ② a pair of glasses: 안경 한 개 / 그가 필요한 것은 안 경 하나였다. ③ a pair of scissors: 가위 하나 / 식탁 위 에 가위 하나가 있었다. ④ The, 그 옷들은 의자 위에 높이 쌓여 있었다. ⑤ A pair of gloves: 장갑 한 켤레 / 한 켤레 의 장갑은 좋은 선물이다.

07 (A) fall in love with: ~와 사랑에 빠지다 / 나는 그의 착 한 성품 때문에 그와 사랑에 빠졌다. (B) build character: 덕성 을 기르다, 인성을 키우다 / 좋은 책을 읽는 것은 인격 형성에 도움 이 된다. (C) stay awake: 깨어 있다 / 나는 너무 피곤해서 깨어 있기가 어렵다.

서술형 시험대비 p.63

01 up
02 since
03 Unfortunately
04 They were assigned to design a Space settlement.
05 (1) wide (2) driverless (3) convenient (4) detective
06 (1) (e)nded up (2) (h)it me on (3) takes, to
(4) The higher, the colder (5) was why

01 pick up: ~을 집다 / 그녀는 장갑을 주우려고 몸을 굽혔다. look up: (사전·참고 자료·컴퓨터 등에서 정보를) 찾아보다 / 웹사이트에서 개장[개점] 시간을 찾아볼 수 있니? end up: 결국 ~이 되다, 결국 (어떤 처지)에 처하게 되다 / 온라인 쇼핑이야말로 내 돈을 다 써버리고 마는 이유야.

02 since: ~이기 때문에, ~한 이후로 / 나는 그녀가 태어난 이래로 Joanna를 안다. 아무도 신경 쓰지 않았기 때문에 그들은 그의 취미에 대해 몰랐다.

03 fortunate: 운 좋은 unfortunately: 불행히도 / 불행히도 저는 그 회의에 참석할 수 없을 거예요.

04 assign: 맡기다, 부과하다 be assigned to 동사원형: ~하도록 맡겨지다

05 (1) wide: 폭넓은, 폭이 ~인 / 그것은 음식 준비를 위해 충분한 공간이 허락되어져야 한다. (2) driverless: 운전자가 없는 / 구글은 운전자 없는 자동차가 사람이 운전하는 자동차보다 안전하다고 말하고 있다. (3) convenient: 편리한 / 그 가족은 부엌에서 먹기가 더 편하다고 생각했다. (4) detective: 형사 / 그녀는 딸을 찾기 위해서 사립 탐정을 고용했다.

06 (1) end up: 결국 ~이 되다, 결국 (어떤 처지)에 처하게 되다 (2) hit+사람+on the+신체 부위: ~의 …을 때리다 (3) It+takes+시간+to부정사: ~하는 데 (…의) 시간이 걸리다 (4) The+비교급(+주어+동사) ~, the+비교급(+주어+동사) …: ~할수록 (점점) 더 …하다 (5) That was why ~: 그것이 ~한 이유였다

교과서

Conversation

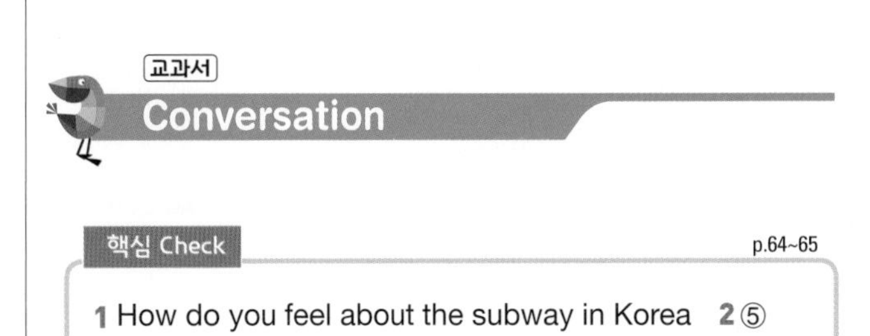

핵심 Check p.64~65

1 How do you feel about the subway in Korea 2 ⑤

교과서 대화문 익히기

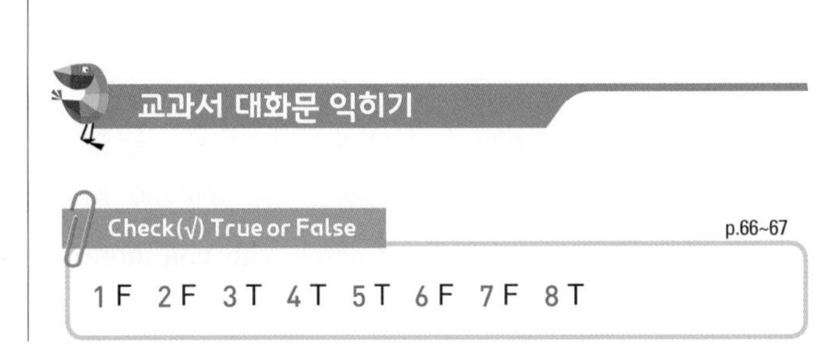

Check(√) True or False p.66~67

1 F 2 F 3 T 4 T 5 T 6 F 7 F 8 T

교과서 확인학습 p.69~71

Listen and Speak 1 A

to / Long, no, How, been / How, here from / by / How, about / clean

Listen and Speak 1 B

did, hear / What / can, during, from / heard / How / useful, look up words I don't know / find / helpful

Listen and Speak 1 C

1. Can I ask / best / How, feel, single / unhealthy
2. ask, difficult / try / How do you feel / helpful but
3. Can I ask you / try my best / How do you feel about / helpful but cruel

Listen and Speak 2 A

Did you enjoy / a / What did you like / was / with you on

Listen and Speak 2 B

Why, always drinking / help me stay / I'm with you on, too / help me focus on / know that too much caffeine / should drink, less

Listen and Speak 2 C

1. How do you feel about reading / anytime / with you on that, not good for
2. How do you feel about / more / I'm with you on that
3. How do you feel about / I'm with you on that / I don't agree

Real Life Talk Watch a Video

What / They're items I ordered / How do you feel about / at all / difficult to know what, like / difficult to return / convenient / convenience

Real Life Talk Step 2

1. feel about shopping / Can you tell me / shop whenever / I'm with you
2. How do you feel about raising / work to take care of / don't agree, make us happy

Check up Dialogue Champion

How do you feel about using / useful, search for / with you on that

시험대비 기본평가 p.72

01 ③ 02 ② 03 ⑤

01 'I'm with you on that.'은 '나는 그 말에 동의해.'라는 뜻으로 상대방의 의견에 동의할 때 사용할 수 있는 표현이다. 바꿔 쓸 수 있는 표현으로 'I couldn't agree with you more.', 'That's exactly how I feel.', 'No doubt about it.', 'You are absolutely right.', 'You have a point there.' 등이 있다. 동의하지 않을 때는 'I don't agree.' 또는 'I don't think so.' 등으로 표현할 수 있다.

02 빈칸 이후에 수업 중에 스마트폰을 사용하는 것에 대한 소년의 생각이 나오고 있으므로 빈칸에는 이에 대한 상대방의 의견을 묻는 것이 적절하다. 'How do you feel about ~?'은 '~에 관해 어떻게 생각하세요?'라는 뜻으로 상대방의 의견을 물을 때 사용할 수 있다.

03 (C) 어려운 질문을 해도 되는지 질문하자 (D) 괜찮다고 대답하면서, 최선을 다하겠다고 말한다. (B) 동물 실험에 대한 상대방의 의견을 묻자 (A) 도움이 되지만 잔인하다고 생각한다고 대답한다.

시험대비 실력평가 p.73~74

01 ②	02 ④	03 ⑤	04 ②
05 ②	06 ⑤	07 ①	
08 ②, ③, ⑤	09 ①, ⑤		

01 주어진 문장은 '어떻게 지냈니?'의 의미로 상대방의 안부를 물을 때 사용하는 표현이다. 안부를 묻는 질문에 민호가 'Great.(잘 지냈어.)'라고 대답하는 것이 어울리므로 ②가 적절하다.

02 Amy가 한국에 와 본 경험이 있는지 없는지는 위의 대화에서 알 수 없다. ① Amy는 한국의 지하철이 깨끗하다고 생각한다. ② Amy는 공항에서 여기에 지하철을 타고 왔다. ③ 민호와 Amy는 오랜 시간 동안 보지 못했다. ④ Amy는 한국에 전에 와 본 적이 없다. ⑤ 민호는 잘 지냈다.

03 상대방에게 왜 에너지 음료를 늘 마시는지 묻고 있으므로, 이유에 대해 설명하는 ⑤가 적절하다.

04 Tom은 에너지 음료가 깨어 있는 데 도움이 된다는 것에 동의하고 있지만 공부에 집중하는 데 도움이 된다는 Jessica의 말에는 동의하는 말은 하지 않았다.

05 소식을 들었는지 묻는 질문에 어떤 소식이냐고 묻고 (B) 다음 주부터 수업 중에 스마트폰을 사용할 수 있다고 이야기한다. (C) 그 소식을 들었다고 대답하자 (A) 그에 대한 의견을 묻는다. (D) B는 그것이 유용할 거라고 생각한다고 이야기하며 수업 시간에 모르는 단어들을 찾아볼 수 있다고 말한다.

06 'I'm with you on that.'은 '나는 그 말에 동의해.'라는 뜻으로 상대방의 의견에 동의할 때 사용할 수 있는 표현이다. 바꿔 쓸 수 있는 표현으로 'I couldn't agree with you more.', 'That's exactly how I feel.', 'No doubt about it.', 'You

are absolutely right.', 'You have a point there.' 등이 있다. 동의하지 않을 때는 'I don't agree.' 또는 'I don't think so.' 등으로 표현할 수 있다.

07 'How do you feel about ~?'은 '~에 관해 어떻게 생각하세요?'라는 뜻으로 상대방의 의견을 물을 때 사용하는 표현이다.

08 B는 학생들이 수업 시간에 게임을 할 수 있어서 수업 시간에 핸드폰을 이용하는 것에 반대를 하지만 A는 스마트폰으로 정보를 찾을 수 있다고 얘기하는 것으로 보아 둘은 반대되는 의견을 가지고 있다. 상대방의 의견에 동의하지 않을 때, 'I don't think so.', 'I totally disagree.', 'I'm not sure about that.' 등을 사용할 수 있다.

09 ① 영화가 재미있다고 말하며 그렇지 않은지 묻는 말에 대한 대답으로 재미있지 않다고 말하며 이야기가 좋았다고 대답하는 것은 어울리지 않는다. ⑤ 학교 점심에 대한 의견을 묻는 말에 '그렇게 생각하지 않아.'라고 동의하지 않는 말을 하는 것은 어색하다.

서술형 시험대비 p.75

01 How do you feel about it?
02 up
03 They are items I ordered online.
04 ⓐ with ⓑ on
05 convenient
06 How do you feel about eating fast food?
07 I don't agree.

01 'How do you feel about ~?'은 '~에 관해 어떻게 생각하세요?'라는 뜻으로 상대방의 의견을 물을 때 사용하는 표현이다.

02 look up: (사전·참고 자료·컴퓨터 등에서 정보를) 찾아보다

03 items와 I ordered online 사이에 목적격 관계대명사 which나 that이 생략되어 있다. order: 주문하다

04 'I'm with you on that.'은 '나는 그 말에 동의해.'라는 뜻으로 상대방의 의견에 동의할 때 사용할 수 있는 표현이다.

05 Tony가 편리함이 전부가 아니라고 말한 것으로 보아, 수지는 온라인으로 쇼핑하는 것이 편리하다고 말한 것을 유추할 수 있다. convenience: 편리, 편의 convenient: 편리한

06 'How do you feel about ~?'은 '~에 관해 어떻게 생각하세요?'라는 뜻으로 상대방의 의견을 물을 때 사용하는 표현이다.

07 상대방의 의견에 동의하지 않을 때는 'I don't agree.', 'I don't think so.', 'I totally disagree.', 'Absolutely not.', 'I'm not sure about that.' 등으로 표현할 수 있다.

Grammar

핵심 Check p.76~77

1 (1) longer (2) more
2 (1) since (2) since (3) Because

시험대비 기본평가 p.78

01 ④ 02 ③ 03 ②
04 (1) The more Stanley dug, the stronger he became.
(2) The more I heard about him, the more sympathetic I felt for him.
(3) Since he was sick, he couldn't go to school.

01 the 비교급+주어+동사 ~, the 비교급+주어+동사 …: ~할수록 …하다

02 첫 번째 빈칸에는 뒤에 나오는 주절에 대한 이유가 나오는 것이 적절하고, 두 번째 빈칸에는 앞에 나온 주절에 대한 이유가 나오는 것이 적절하다. 그러므로 이유를 나타내는 부사절을 이끄는 since가 적절하다.

03 ② The long → The longer / the 비교급+주어+동사 ~, the 비교급+주어+동사 …: ~할수록 …하다

04 (1), (2) 'the 비교급+주어+동사 ~, the 비교급+주어+동사 …'의 형태로 '~할수록 …하다'라는 뜻으로, 점점 더해지거나 덜해지는 것을 표현할 때 사용한다. (3) since는 이유를 나타내는 접속사로 쓰여, '~이기 때문에'의 뜻으로 이유를 나타내는 부사절을 이끈다.

시험대비 실력평가 p.79~81

01 ② 02 ① 03 ④ 04 ⑤
05 ③, ⑤ 06 ③, ⑤ 07 ④ 08 ②
09 ① 10 ①, ④
11 (1) The colder it is, the larger and deeper the hole becomes.
(2) The stronger will you have, the more you will learn.
12 ②
13 (1) This book is the better of the two.
(2) The harder he tried to get out, the deeper he went.
(3) The less people spend, the slower the economy growth becomes.

14 ③ 15 ⑤
16 (1) Though → Since[Because/As]
(2) if → since[because/as]
(3) because → because of
17 (1) The more, the more (2) The closer, the happier
(3) The bigger, the better (4) Because
(5) because of 18 ①
19 ②, ⑤

01 the 비교급+주어+동사 ~, the 비교급+주어+동사 …: ~할수록 …하다 The more sugar in the orange juice, the shorter the shelf life.

02 ② though → since[because, as] ③ because → since ④ Unless → Since[Because, As] ⑤ before → since

03 'the 비교급+주어+동사 ~, the 비교급+주어+동사 …: ~할수록 …하다' 구문은 'As+주어+동사+비교급 ~, 주어+동사+비교급 …'으로 바꿔 쓸 수 있다.

04 이유를 나타내는 접속사로 쓰인 since는 because나 as로 바꿔 쓸 수 있다.

05 the 비교급+주어+동사 ~, the 비교급+주어+동사 … = As+주어+동사+비교급 ~, 주어+동사+비교급 …: ~할수록 …하다

06 '~이기 때문에'의 뜻으로 이유를 나타내는 부사절을 이끄는 since[because]를 쓰는 것이 적절하다.

07 the 비교급+주어+동사 ~, the 비교급+주어+동사 …: ~할수록 …하다

08 <보기>와 ②번은 '이유'의 접속사이다. ① 전치사 ③ '시간'의 접속사 ④ 전치사 ⑤ 부사

09 the 비교급+주어+동사 ~, the 비교급+주어+동사 …: ~할수록 …하다

10 빈칸에는 이유를 나타내는 접속사로 쓰인 since, because나 as가 적절하다.

11 (1) the 비교급+주어+동사 ~, the 비교급+주어+동사 … = As+주어+동사+비교급 ~, 주어+동사+비교급 …: ~할수록 …하다 (2) '더 강한 의지를 갖는다면, 더 많이 배울 것이다.'라는 의미이므로 비교급을 이용하여 바꿔 쓰면, '강한 의지를 가질수록 더 많이 배울 것이다.'라고 쓸 수 있다.

12 ②번은 '이유'의 접속사이고 나머지는 모두 '시간'의 접속사로 쓰였다.

13 (1) 비교급에는 the를 사용하지 않는 것이 원칙이지만 문장 속에 'of the two'와 같이 비교의 대상이 명확히 둘인 경우 'the+비교급'으로 쓴다. (2), (3) the 비교급+주어+동사 ~, the 비교급+주어+동사 …: ~할수록 …하다

14 ① pretty → prettier ② more safe → safer ④ Smaller → The smaller ⑤ dark and dark → darker and darker

15 ① until → since ② because of → because ③ while → since[because, as] ④ though → since[because, as]

16 (1) Though는 양보절을 이끄는 접속사이므로 Though를 Since[Because/As]로 고치는 것이 적절하다. (2) if는 조건절을 이끄는 접속사이므로 if를 since[because/as]로 고치는 것이 적절하다. (3) because of는 전치사처럼 절이 아닌 구가 나오고, because는 접속사로 다음에 절이 나와야 한다.

17 (1)~(3) the 비교급+주어+동사 ~, the 비교급+주어+동사 …: ~할수록 …하다 (4) 이유를 나타내는 부사절을 이끄는 접속사 Because가 적절하다. (5) 뒤에 명사구가 이어지므로 because of가 적절하다.

18 the merrier로 쓰는 것이 적절하다.

19 이유를 나타내는 접속사 because는 since나 as로 바꿔 쓸 수 있다.

서술형 시험대비 p.82~83

01 (1) The younger you are, the easier it is to learn.
(2) The larger the picture is, the longer it will take for people to download.
02 (1) The older he grew, the poorer his memory became.
(2) I think the harder I work, the more I move up in the world.
(3) Ann is the taller and the more beautiful of the two sisters.
(4) This dictionary is a lot the better of the two.
(5) The plan failed because of lack of money.
(6) The accident happened because[as, since] nobody paid attention to the warning signs.
(7) They've been best friends since they were children.
(8) She had only spoken to him once since the party.
03 (1) The hotter, the more exhausted
(2) The more, the more thirsty
04 (1) Since I was hungry, I had a whole pizza.
(2) I didn't enjoy the book since I couldn't identify with any of the main characters.
05 (1) The more books you read, the more things you will know.
(2) The earlier you start, the sooner you arrive there.

(3) The more arguments you win, the fewer friends you'll have.
(4) The healthier one's mind is, the healthier one's body will be.
06 (1) the better you do
(2) the more water you drink
(3) the less holiday time they have
07 (1) The older we grow, the wiser we become.
(2) The higher you climb, the farther you see.
(3) The less you spend, the more you save.
(4) I couldn't buy anything to eat since I had no money.
(5) She has written many books since she left college.

01 the 비교급+주어+동사 ~, the 비교급+주어+동사 …: ~할수록 …하다

02 (1)~(2) the 비교급+주어+동사 ~, the 비교급+주어+동사 …: ~할수록 …하다 (3)~(4) 비교급에는 the를 사용하지 않는 것이 원칙이지만 문장 속에 'of the two'와 같이 비교의 대상이 명확히 둘인 경우 'the+비교급'으로 쓴다. (5) because+주어+동사, because of+명사(구) (6) 'because of' 다음에는 명사(구)가 나와야 하므로 since나 because를 쓰는 것이 적절하다. (7) 의미상 before가 아니라 since가 적절하다. 현재완료 시제임에 유의한다. (8) though는 접속사이므로 다음에 절이 나와야 한다. 현재완료 시제이므로 since가 적절하다.

03 the 비교급+주어+동사 ~, the 비교급+주어+동사 …: ~할수록 …하다

04 since는 '~이기 때문에'의 뜻으로 이유를 나타내는 부사절을 이끌므로 이유를 나타내는 절에 since를 넣어 연결한다.

05 (1) '많은 책을 읽으면, 많은 것을 알게 될 것이다.'를 비교급을 이용하여 '더 많은 책을 읽을수록 더 많은 것을 알게 될 것이다.'라고 쓸 수 있다. (2) '일찍 출발하면, 그곳에 빨리 도착할 것이다.'를 비교급을 이용하여 '더 일찍 출발할수록 더 빨리 도착할 것이다.'라고 쓸 수 있다. (3), (4) the 비교급+주어+동사 ~, the 비교급+주어+동사 … = As+주어+동사+비교급 ~, 주어+동사+비교급 …: ~할수록 …하다

06 the 비교급+주어+동사 ~, the 비교급+주어+동사 …: ~할수록 …하다

07 (1)~(3) the 비교급+주어+동사 ~, the 비교급+주어+동사 …: ~할수록 …하다 (4) since를 '~이기 때문에'의 뜻으로 이유를 나타내는 접속사로 이용한다. (5) since를 '~ 이후로'의 뜻으로 시간의 부사절을 이끄는 접속사로 이용한다.

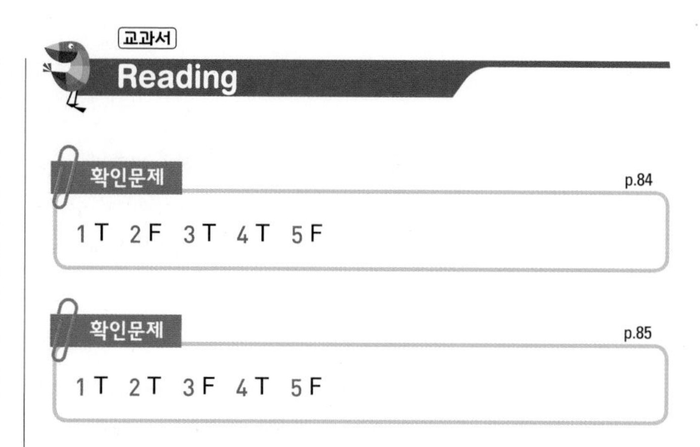

교과서 Reading

확인문제 p.84

1 T 2 F 3 T 4 T 5 F

확인문제 p.85

1 T 2 T 3 F 4 T 5 F

교과서 확인학습 A p.86~87

01 harder
02 harder, the faster
03 any harder
04 thirsty, hungry
05 go home
06 would be
07 terrible
08 no lake
09 full of sand
10 In fact, even
11 a place for bad boys
12 like
13 for stealing
14 didn't really steal
15 in the wrong place
16 from school
17 fell from
18 hit him on the head
19 what happened
20 stopped, why he was running
21 for, belonged to
22 That was why
23 was assigned to
24 six other boys
25 cool, like
26 one hole every day
27 about, deep, wide
28 to build character
29 The more, the stronger
30 It took, to finish
31 something shiny
32 beat faster
33 anyone who, be given the day off
34 brushed off
35 small gold tube
36 couldn't be, since
37 at the bottom of
38 stand for
39 even

교과서 확인학습 B p.88~89

1 "Dig harder, Stanley!
2 The harder you dig, the faster you'll finish!" yelled Mr. Sir.
3 Stanley Yelnats couldn't dig any harder since every single muscle hurt.
4 He was thirsty and hungry.
5 He wanted to go home.
6 Unfortunately, Stanley's home for the next 18 months would be right here, at Camp Green Lake.
7 Camp Green Lake was a terrible name.
8 It wasn't green and there was no lake.
9 Camp Green Lake was hot and full of sand.
10 In fact, it wasn't even a camp.
11 It was a place for bad boys.
12 Then what was a good boy like Stanley doing here?
13 He was sent to the camp for stealing a pair of sneakers.
14 Stanley didn't really steal a pair of sneakers.
15 He was just in the wrong place at the wrong time.
16 One day, he was walking home from school.
17 Suddenly, a pair of old sneakers fell from the sky.
18 The sneakers hit him on the head.
19 He started running with the sneakers to tell his father what happened.
20 A few minutes later, the police stopped Stanley and asked him why he was running.
21 Unfortunately for Stanley, the sneakers belonged to a famous baseball player, Clyde Livingstone.
22 That was why Stanley ended up at Camp Green Lake.
23 Stanley was assigned to Group D in the camp.
24 There were six other boys in Stanley's group.
25 They all had cool names like X-Ray, Zigzag and Zero.
26 Each boy had to dig one hole every day.
27 It had to be about 150cm deep and 150cm wide.
28 Mr. Sir said, "You are digging to build character."
29 The more Stanley dug, the stronger he became.
30 It took less time to finish his hole each day.
31 In his second week, as Stanley was finishing his hole, he saw something shiny in the dirt.
32 Stanley's heart beat faster.
33 He heard that anyone who found something interesting would be given the day off.
34 He carefully picked up the shiny object and brushed off the dirt.
35 It was a small gold tube.
36 But it couldn't be real gold since it was too light.
37 There were two letters, *KB*, at the bottom of the tube.
38 What did KB stand for?
39 Stanley's heart beat even faster.

시험대비 실력평가 p.90~93

01 for 02 ④ 03 ③
04 The more Stanley dug, the stronger he became.
05 finishing → to finish
06 ④ 07 ② 08 ④ 09 ④
10 ⑤
11 the more → more, the stronger → stronger
12 Because he heard that anyone who found something interesting would be given the day off.
13 ④ 14 ④
15 (A) depth (B) width 16 ② 17 ①, ③
18 They were Clyde Livingstone's.
19 ② 20 was sent
21 The harder you dig, the faster you'll finish!
22 He couldn't dig any harder since every single muscle hurt.
23 assigned
24 one hundred and fifty centimeters
25 ①

01 ⓐ for: ~을 위한, ⓑ for: ~라는 이유로

02 (A)와 ④: 이유나 원인을 나타내는 절을 이끄는 접속사, ①, ③ ~한 이후로(접속사), ② ~부터[이후](전치사), ⑤ 그(때) 이후로(부사)

03 'It wasn't green and there was no lake.'라고 되어 있다. be named after: ~을 따서 명명되다

04 The+비교급(+주어+동사) ~, the+비교급(+주어+동사): ~할수록, (점점) 더 …하다

05 It+takes+시간+to부정사구: ~하는 데 (…의) 시간이 걸리다

06 very는 형용사나 부사의 원급을 강조하는 말이고, 나머지는 다 비교급을 강조하는 말이다.

07 정말로 운동화 한 켤레를 훔친 것이 아니었는데 Green Lake 캠프에 오게 되었으므로, '부당한' 심경을 느꼈을 것이라고 하는 것이 적절하다. unfair: 부당한, 불공평한, ① 부끄러운, ③ 흥분한, ⑤ 지루한

08 suddenly = all at once = abruptly = all of a sudden = unexpectedly: 갑자기, ④ urgently: 급히

09 운동화 한 켤레가 왜 하늘에서 떨어졌는지는 알 수 없다. ① No. ② He was walking home from school. ③ The sneakers hit Stanley on the head. ⑤ A few minutes after he started running with the sneakers.

10 ⑤는 빛나는 '물체의 바닥에 쓰여 있는 글자'를 가리키고, 나머지는 다 '빛나는 물체'를 가리킨다.

11 As로 시작하면 the를 삭제한 비교급을 본래의 자리에 쓰는 것이 적절하다.

12 그는 흥미로운 뭔가를 발견한 사람은 그 날을 쉬게 된다고 들었기 때문이다.

13 이 글은 'Stanley의 그룹에 속한 소년들이 매일 구덩이 하나를 파야 했다'는 내용의 글이므로, 주제로는 ④번 'D 그룹의 소년들이 매일 해야 했던 의무'가 적절하다.

14 ⓐ와 ②: 부사적 용법, ①, ④: 명사적 용법, ③, ⑤: 형용사적 용법

15 구덩이의 '깊이'는 150cm 정도였고 '너비'도 150cm 정도였다. depth: 깊이, width: 폭, 너비

16 이 글은 'Stanley가 정말로 운동화 한 켤레를 훔친 것이 아니었는데 Green Lake 캠프에 오게 되었다'는 내용의 글이므로, 제목으로는 ②번 '억울하게 누명을 쓴 Stanley'가 적절하다. accuse: 고발[기소/비난]하다

17 ⓐ와 ①, ③: 부사적 용법, ②, ⑤: 형용사적 용법, ④: 명사적 용법

18 그 운동화는 Clyde Livingstone의 것이었다.

19 ② 앞의 내용을 추가해서 설명하고 있으므로 In fact가 가장 적절하다. ③ 그에 반해서, 그와 대조적으로, ⑤ 비슷하게, 마찬가지로

20 캠프에 '보내진' 것이므로 수동태로 쓰는 것이 적절하다.

21 The+비교급(+주어+동사) ~, the+비교급(+주어+동사): ~할수록, (점점) 더 …하다

22 Stanley는 모든 근육 하나하나가 아팠기 때문에 더 열심히 팔 수가 없었다.

23 어떤 사람을 특정한 장소에서 또는 그 사람을 위해 일하도록, 특정한 장소나 그룹 또는 사람에게 보내는 것 / 수동태로 써야 하므로 과거분사 형태로 쓰는 것이 적절하다. assign: (사람을) 배치하다

24 cm를 읽을 때 앞에 복수가 있으면 centimeters로 읽는 것이 적절하다.

25 ⓒ와 ①: 품성, 인격, ② (책·영화 등의) 등장인물, ③, ⑤: 특징, 특질, ④ 문자

서술형 시험대비

p.94~95

01 be given
02 (A) less (B) since (C) for
03 right place → wrong place, right time → wrong time
04 That was why Stanley ended up at Camp Green Lake.
05 could[might] tell
06 six → seven
07 It had to be about 150cm deep and 150cm wide.
08 finishing
09 symbolize 또는 represent
10 As you dig harder, you'll finish faster!
11 such as
12 (A) a camp (B) green (C) sand

01 흥미로운 뭔가를 발견한 사람은 그 날을 '쉴 수 있게 되는 것'이므로, 수동태로 쓰는 것이 적절하다.

02 (A) Stanley는 많이 파면 팔수록, 더 힘이 세져 갔다고 했으므로, 하루하루 구덩이를 끝내는 데 시간이 '덜' 걸렸다고 하는 것이 적절하므로 less가 옳다. (B) 너무 가벼웠기 '때문에' 진짜 금일 리가 없었다고 해야 하므로, 원인이나 이유를 나타내는 부사절을 이끄는 접속사 since를 쓰는 것이 적절하다. (C) 'KB는 무엇을 의미할까'라고 해야 하므로 for가 옳다. stand by: (방관, 좌시하며) 가만히 있다, stand for: ~을 상징하다

03 Stanley는 학교에서 집으로 걸어가고 있다가 하늘에서 떨어진 낡은 운동화 한 켤레에 머리를 맞은 것 때문에 Green Lake 캠프에 오게 된 것이므로, 그는 그저 '잘못된 시간'에 '잘못된 장소'에 있었다고 하는 것이 적절하다.

04 That was why: 그것이 ~한 이유였다, end up+특정 장소나 상황: 결국 (어떤 처지)에 처하게 되다

05 그는 그의 아버지에게 무슨 일이 일어났는지 '말하기 위해' 운동화를 가지고 달리기 시작했다. '~하기 위해서'라는 뜻의 목적을 나타내는 부사적 용법의 to부정사는 'in order that 주어 can[may]'을 사용하여 복문으로 고치는 것이 가능하다.

06 D 그룹에는 Stanley를 포함하여 '7명'의 소년들이 있었다.

07 had to be: ~이어야 했다

08 spend+시간+~ing

09 stand for = symbolize = represent: ~을 상징하다

10 As로 시작하면 the를 삭제한 비교급을 본래의 자리에 쓰는 것이 적절하다.

11 like = such as: (예를 들어) ~ 같은

12 Green Lake 캠프는 '캠프'가 아니라 나쁜 소년들을 위한 곳이었다. 그것의 이름과는 달리 그곳은 '초록색'도 아니었고 호수도 없었다. 사실, 그곳은 뜨거웠고 온통 '모래'였다.

영역별 핵심문제

p.97~101

01 bottom 02 ④ 03 ②
04 (1) why (2) look like (3) look up
05 ② 06 How
07 (A) during (B) useful

08 I can look up words I don't know. 09 ③
10 ⑤ 11 I'm with you on that. 12 ②, ④
13 ③ 14 ⑤ 15 ①, ④
16 (1) The more, the more tired
(2) The more, the more sleepy 17 ①
18 (1) The fresher the fruit is
(2) Since[As/Because] the sunlight was very strong
19 (1) The nearer, the longer
(2) warmer and warmer
(3) because of (4) since (5) As
20 ④ 21 ②, ③
22 Then what was a good boy like Stanley doing here?
23 ⑤ 24 ④
25 were belonged → belonged 26 ②
27 ④ 28 ①
29 (A) home (B) the (C) why
30 ②

01 (1) 주어진 단어들은 반의어 관계를 가지고 있다. asleep: 잠이 든 awake: 깨어 있는 bottom: 맨 아래 top: 꼭대기

02 character: 품성, 인격 / 어떤 사람의 인격은 그가 나누는 대화를 통해 알 수 있다.

03 skip: (일을) 거르다, 빼먹다 / 수업 시간에 그 주제를 다루었으면 다음 장은 건너뛰어도 된다.

04 (1) That is why ~: 그것이 ~한 이유이다 (2) look like: ~처럼 보이다 (3) look up: (사전·참고 자료·컴퓨터 등에서 정보를) 찾아보다

05 (A) to, Welcome to ~: ~에 온 것을 환영해 (B) from, from: ~에서 부터 (C) by, by+교통수단: 교통수단을 이용해, 교통수단으로 (D) about, How do you feel about ~?: ~에 관해 어떻게 생각하니?

06 ⓐ 'How have you been?'은 '어떻게 지냈니?'의 의미로 상대방의 안부를 묻는 표현이다. ⓑ 'How do you feel about ~?'은 '~에 관해 어떻게 생각하니?'라는 뜻으로 상대방의 의견을 묻는 표현이다.

07 (A) during은 '~ 동안에'의 의미로, 전치사이기 때문에 뒤에 명사가 온다. (B) useful: 유용한

08 look up: (사전·참고 자료·컴퓨터 등에서 정보를) 찾아보다 words와 I don't know 사이에 목적격 관계대명사 which나 that이 생략되어 있다.

09 'How do you feel about ~?'은 '~에 관해 어떻게 생각하세요?'라는 뜻으로 상대방의 의견을 물을 때 사용하는 표현이다. 여기서는 온라인 쇼핑에 관한 상대방의 의견을 물어보고, Tony가 '전혀 좋아하지 않아.'라고 대답하는 것이 어울리므로 ③이 적절하다.

10 return: 돌려주다, 반품하다

11 'I'm with you on that.'은 상대방의 의견에 동의할 때 사용할 수 있는 표현이다.

12 ① Tony는 인터넷으로 쇼핑하는 것을 좋아하지 않는다. ② 수지는 Tony의 인터넷 쇼핑에 대한 생각에 동의하지 않는다. (동의하고 있다.) ③ 수지는 온라인 쇼핑으로 물품을 주문했다. ④ Tony는 온라인 쇼핑이 많은 이점을 가지고 있다고 생각한다. (물건이 실제로 어떻게 생겼는지 알기가 어렵고, 마음에 들지 않으면 물건을 돌려보내는 것도 어렵다고 말하고 있다.) ⑤ 수지는 온라인 쇼핑을 좋아한다.

13 ① The angrier Judy got, the more loudly she yelled. ② The higher the expectation, the greater the disappointment. ④ The more technology develops, the more people seem to miss traditional forms of communication. ⑤ The more you exercise, the healthier you get.

14 the 비교급+주어+동사 ~, the 비교급+주어+동사 …: ~할수록 …하다

15 '~이기 때문에'의 뜻으로 이유를 나타내는 부사절을 이끄는 since는 because나 as로 바꿔 쓸 수 있다.

16 the 비교급+주어+동사 ~, the 비교급+주어+동사 …: ~할수록 …하다

17 since로 이어지는 절이므로 적절한 이유를 나타내는 문장을 찾는다.

18 (1) the 비교급+주어+동사 ~, the 비교급+주어+동사 …: ~할수록 …하다 (2) 이유를 나타내는 접속사 since를 이용한다. 이때 since 대신에 as나 because를 쓸 수 있다.

19 (1) the 비교급+주어+동사 ~, the 비교급+주어+동사 …: ~할수록 …하다 (2) '비교급 and 비교급'은 '점점 더 …하다'의 뜻이다. (3) because+주어+동사, because of+명사(구) (4) 의미상 '이유'를 나타내는 since가 적절하다. (5) as가 '이유'를 나타내는 부사절을 이끌고 있는 문장이다.

20 ④는 '일반적인 캠프'를 가리키고, 나머지는 다 'Green Lake 캠프'를 가리킨다.

21 in fact = actually = as a matter of fact = to tell the truth: 사실, ② thus: 따라서 ③ reasonably: 합리적으로, 타당[적정]하게

22 like: (예를 들어) ~ 같은

23 선행사를 포함하는 관계대명사 what을 쓰는 것이 적절하다.

24 주어진 문장의 The sneakers에 주목한다. ④번 앞 문장의 a pair of old sneakers를 받고 있으므로 ④번이 적절하다.

25 belong은 자동사라서 수동태로 쓸 수 없으므로 were belonged를 belonged로 고치는 것이 적절하다.

26 ⓐ와 ②: 멋진, ① 차분한, 침착한, ③ 시원한, 서늘한, ④ ~을 서늘하게 하다, 식히다(동사), ⑤ 냉담한, 열의 없는

27 그룹의 소년들이 협동하여 구덩이를 판 것이 아니라, 각 소년이 매일 구덩이 하나를 파야 했다. cooperate: 협동하다

28 ⓐ Unfortunately for: ~에게 불행하게도, ⓑ belong to: ~의 소유이다〔것이다〕

29 (A) home이 부사로 쓰여 '~에, ~로'라는 뜻이므로, 전치사 없이 home으로 쓰는 것이 적절하다. (B) hit+사람+on+the+신체 부위: ~의 …을 때리다, (C) That was why ~: 그것이 ~한 이유였다

30 '낡은' 운동화 한 켤레가 하늘에서 떨어졌다. awesome: 경탄할 만한, 어마어마한, 엄청난

단원별 예상문제

p.102~105

01 ③
02 (1) ordering (2) raise (3) brushes (4) dig
03 (e)ven 04 (s)ince 05 ①
06 (A) eating (B) bad (C) save 07 ③
08 ⑤ 09 awake 10 ⑤
11 How do you feel about online shopping
12 ④ 13 ② 14 ③, ⑤
15 (1) The better the chair is, the more comfortable you feel.
(2) Since Tom was tired, he stopped working.
16 was assigned
17 Each boy had to dig one hole every day.
18 ②, ③, ⑤ 19 marry with → marry
20 ② 21 a pair of
22 ⑤ 23 ④ 24 day off 25 ③

01 (A) try one's best: 최선을 다하다 / 그것은 그녀의 잘못이 아니었지만, 그녀는 돕는 데 최선을 다했다. (B) focus on: ~에 집중하다 / 더 수익성 있는 상품 개발에 주력하는 편이 좋다.

02 (1) order: (물건, 음식을) 주문하다 / 의류를 주문할 때에는 잊지 말고 치수를 명시하세요.(2) raise: 키우다, 기르다 / 그녀는 아이를 양육하기에 참 위험한 세상이라고 말했다. (3) brush off: 털다, 털어 내다 / 진흙은 마르면 잘 털린다. (4) dig: (구멍 등을) 파다 / 인부가 기계로 구멍을 파고 있다.

03 even: ~조차도, (비교급 강조) 훨씬, 더욱 / 그는 문도 열 수 없었다. 암컷 흰긴수염고래는 수컷 흰긴수염고래보다 훨씬 더 크다.

04 since: ~이기 때문에, ~한 이후로 / 7살 이후로 나는 독립해서 살았다. 세제는 호수와 개울을 오염시킬 수 있기 때문에 가급적 사용하지 않는 것이 좋습니다.

05 (A) 원할 때 언제든지 쇼핑을 한다는 대답으로 보아 B는 온라인 쇼핑을 하는 것을 좋아한다. (B) reason: 이유

06 (A) 전치사 다음에는 명사나 동명사가 올 수 있다. (B) 패스트푸드가 많은 지방을 가지고 있다고 말하고 있으므로, 패스트푸드에 대해 안 좋다는 생각을 가지고 있다. (C) A는 B의 의견에 동의하지 않았으므로 패스트 푸드의 장점을 말하는 save(절약하다)가 spend(쓰다, 소비하다)보다 어울린다.

07 동의할 때 사용할 수 있는 표현이 적절하다. 'I couldn't agree with you more.', 'You are absolutely right.', 'No doubt about it.'

08 ⓐ drinking, 부사 always, all the time 등과 현재진행형(be+동사ing)을 사용해 습관적인 행동을 표현할 수 있다. ⓑ stay, help의 목적격 보어로는 동사원형과 to부정사 모두 올 수 있다. ⓒ much, caffeine은 셀 수 없는 명사로 much의 수식을 받을 수 있다. ⓓ on, focus on: ~에 집중하다

09 awake: 잠들지 않은, 깨어 있는 / 잠자고 있지 않은

10 주어진 문장은 '편리함이 전부는 아니야.'의 뜻으로 수지가 말하는 'I think it's very convenient.(온라인 쇼핑은 매우 편리하다고 생각해.)'에 대해 말할 수 있는 내용이다.

11 'How do you feel about ~?'은 '~에 관해 어떻게 생각하니?'라는 뜻으로 상대방의 의견을 물을 때 사용하는 표현이다.

12 ⓐ online shopping ⓑ 가주어 ⓒ 가주어 ⓓ an item ⓔ online shopping

13 ① The more you chew bread, the sweeter it tastes. ③ Since the lamp was very dirty, the mother began to clean it. ④ He bought two pairs of sneakers and a cap at the store. ⑤ Since[Because, As] he had a headache, Jack went to see the doctor.

14 ① The harder you study, the better you will do. ② This is because the hotter it is, the more energy it has. ④ As he was sleepy, Mr. Smith went to bed early. ⑥ Because he was sick, he couldn't go to school. ⑦ Ann drank two glasses of water since she was thirsty.

15 (1) the 비교급+주어+동사 ~, the 비교급+주어+동사 …: ~할수록 …하다 (2) since로 '이유'를 나타내는 부사절을 이끌도록 하고 stop은 동명사를 목적어로 받으므로 working으로 쓴다.

16 D 그룹에 '배치되었다'고 해야 하므로 수동태로 쓰는 것이 적절하다.

17 must의 과거 had to를 사용하는 것이 적절하다.

18 about = roughly = around = approximately: 대략, ①, ④: 정확히

19 marry는 타동사이므로, 전치사 없이 바로 목적어를 쓰는 것이

적절하다.

20 Kate Barlow가 왜 인기가 많았는지는 알 수 없다. ① In Green Lake. ③ With Sam. ④ They tried to hurt Sam. ⑤ Somewhere in Green Lake.

21 sneakers와 같이 짝을 이루는 명사를 셀 때는 'a pair of'를 사용하는 것이 적절하다.

22 (A)와 ⑤: 정확히, 바로(부사), ① 오른쪽으로(부사), ② (상태가) 좋은[정상인](형용사), ③ (법적, 도덕적) 권리[권한](명사), ④ 오른쪽(명사)

23 ④번 다음 문장의 Then에 주목한다. 주어진 문장의 내용에 대한 논리적인 결과를 나타내는 말이므로 ④번이 적절하다.

24 비록 근무일이지만 일하러 가지 않는 날, day off: (근무·일을) 쉬는 날

25 위 글은 '일기'이다. ② 수필, ④ (책•연극•영화 등에 대한) 논평[비평], 감상문, ⑤ (신문•잡지의) 글, 기사

서술형 실전문제 p.106~107

01 ④ more → less
02 I'm with you on that. → I don't agree.
03 I couldn't agree with you more
04 (1) I think the older she grows, the smarter she becomes.
(2) Ann drank a lot of water since[as/because] she was thirsty.
(3) He closed the window because the wind was blowing outside.
(4) Venus is hot since[as/because] it is near the sun.
05 (1) The harder you dig, the faster you'll finish.
(2) The higher we go up, the colder it becomes.
06 though → since[because, as]
07 a half, a half
08 stole
09 was he → he was
10 reason
11 (A) on the head (B) ended up

01 너무 많은 카페인은 뼈를 다치게 할 수 있다는 것을 얘기하면서 상대방에게 에너지 음료를 더 자주 마셔야 한다고 말하는 것은 어색하므로 more를 less로 바꿔야 한다.

02 스마트폰으로 책을 읽는 것에 대해 A는 눈에 좋지 않다고 얘기하고 있으므로, 언제든지 책을 읽을 수 있다는 장점을 이야기하고 있는 B와는 반대의 의견을 가지고 있다. 그러므로 상대방의 의견에 반대하는 표현인 'I don't agree.'가 어울린다. be good for: ~에 좋다

03 'I'm with you on that.'은 '나는 그 말에 동의해.'라는 뜻으로 상대방의 의견에 동의할 때 사용할 수 있는 표현이다. 바꿔 쓸 수 있는 표현으로 'I couldn't agree with you more.', 'That's exactly how I feel.', 'No doubt about it.', 'You are absolutely right.', 'You have a point there.' 등이 있다.

04 (1) the 비교급+주어+동사 ~, the 비교급+주어+동사 …: ~할수록 …하다 (2), (4) 다음에 나오는 절이 '이유'를 나타내므로 though를 since[as/because]로 고쳐야 한다. (3) because+주어+동사, because of+명사(구)

05 the 비교급+주어+동사 ~, the 비교급+주어+동사 … = As+주어+동사+비교급 ~, 주어+동사+비교급 …: ~할수록 …하다

06 though를 이유나 원인을 나타내는 절을 이끄는 접속사 since[because, as]로 고치는 것이 적절하다.

07 eighteen months = one and a half years = one year and a half: 1년 반

08 그는 운동화 한 켤레를 훔쳤다는 이유로 Green Lake 캠프에 보내졌다.

09 asked의 직접목적어로 간접의문문을 써야 하므로, why he was running의 순서로 고치는 것이 적절하다.

10 That was (the reason) why는 For that reason으로 바꿔 쓰는 것이 적절하다. That was (the reason) why ~: '그것이 ~한 이유였다

11 어느 날, 낡은 운동화 한 켤레가 하늘에서 떨어져서 Stanley의 '머리에' 맞았다. 그는 단지 그의 아버지에게 무슨 일이 일어났는지 말하기 위해 운동화를 가지고 달렸지만 그 운동화 때문에 결국 Green Lake 캠프에 '오게 되었다.' end up: 결국 ~이 되다

창의사고력 서술형 문제 p.108

|모범답안|

01 do you feel about it? / I'm with you on that. / Because it's very delicious and healthy.
02 (1) They can't have lunch at the restaurant since it is closed.
(2) They had to go back home since the cafe was closed.
03 (A) a pair of sneakers (B) running home
(C) Camp Green Lake (D) one hole every day
(E) at the bottom

01 How do you feel about ~?: ~에 관해 어떻게 생각하니?
02 '이유'를 나타내는 since를 이용하여 어법에 맞게 쓴다.

단원별 모의고사

p.109~112

01 assigned 02 ② 03 ①
04 (1) hour later (2) stay awake (3) like, at all
05 ④
06 We can search for information on them.
07 How do you feel about using smartphones in class?
08 I'm with you on that, but they have too much caffeine.
09 (A) Why (B) that
10 they help me focus on my studies 11 ④
12 What do you think about the subway in Korea? / What's your opinion on the subway in Korea?
13 (1) you fear something, the bigger it will appear to be
(2) the top of a tower is, the finer view it commands
14 (1) The angrier the chameleon is, the brighter its color becomes.
(2) The harder you study, the better grades you can get.
(3) Because of the sneakers, he was sent to Camp Green Lake.
(4) Everything has changed so much since last summer.
15 ⑤
16 ②, ④, ⑥ 17 ⑤ 18 ③
19 The sneakers hit him on the head.
20 was happened → happened 21 ②
22 ⑤ 23 One hole
24 (1) in order to (2) in order that, may[can]

01 assign (사람을) 배치하다 / 누군가를 일의 일부로 특정 집단이나 장소로 보내다 / 어떤 사람이 자기 능력 밖의 자리에 배치된다면, 성공을 기대하기가 더 힘들 것이다.

02 ②는 반의어, 나머지 보기들은 동의어이다. ① dangerous: 위험한 risky: 위험한 ② useful: 유용한 useless: 쓸모없는 ③ cruel: 잔혹한 brutal: 잔혹한 ④ focus: 집중하다 concentrate: 집중하다 ⑤ assign: 배치하다 allocate: 할당하다, 배치하다

03 (A) be full of: ~로 가득 차다 / 내 가방에는 책이 가득 들어 있었다. (B) stand for: ~을 의미하다 / 왕관은 왕의 위엄을 의미한다[상징한다].

04 (1) 시간+later: ~ 시간이 지난 후에 (2) stay awake: 자지 않고 깨어 있다 (3) look like: ~처럼 보이다 not ~ at all: 전혀 ~ 않다

05 주어진 문장에서 'How do you feel about ~?(~에 대해 어떻게 생각하세요?)'는 의견을 묻는 표현으로, 인터넷 쇼핑하는 것을 어떻게 생각하는지 상대방의 의견을 묻고 있다. (C) 좋아한다고 대답하고 (B) 왜 좋아하는지 이유를 말해달라고 한다. (A) 원할 때마다 쇼핑을 할 수 있다고 대답하고 (D) 상대방도 이 의견에 동의한다.

06 search for: ~을 찾다

07 'How do you feel about ~?'은 '~에 관해 어떻게 생각하니?'라는 뜻으로 상대방의 의견을 물을 때 사용하는 표현이다.

08 'I'm with you on that.'은 '나는 그 말에 동의해.'라는 뜻으로 상대방의 의견에 동의할 때 사용할 수 있는 표현이다. 접속사 but이 두 문장을 연결하고 있다. caffeine: 카페인

09 (A) Jessica의 대답이 Because로 시작하는 것으로 볼 때, 이유에 관해서 질문하고 있다. (B) know의 목적어로 명사절이 나와야 한다. 이 명사절을 접속사 that이 연결하고 있다.

10 help는 뒤에 목적어와 목적격 보어가 와서 '(목적어)가 ~하는 것을 돕다'의 의미를 나타낸다. 이때 목적격 보어로는 동사원형과 to부정사 모두 올 수 있다. focus on: ~에 집중하다

11 주어진 문장은 공항에서 여기까지 어떻게 왔는지를 묻고 있으므로, 전철을 타고 왔다는 대답과 어울린다.

12 'How do you feel about ~?'은 '~에 관해 어떻게 생각하니?'라는 뜻으로 상대방의 의견을 물을 때 사용하는 표현이다. about 뒤에는 명사(구)나 동명사(구)를 넣어 말한다. 비슷한 표현으로 'What do you think about ~?', 'What's your opinion on ~?', 'Can you give me your thoughts on ~?', 'Do you have any opinions on/about ~?' 등이 있다.

13 'the 비교급, the 비교급' 구문은 'As+주어+동사+비교급 ~, 주어+동사+비교급 …'으로 바꿔 쓸 수 있다.

14 (1), (2) the 비교급+주어+동사 ~, the 비교급+주어+동사 …: ~할수록 …하다 (3) because of+명사(구) (4) since가 전치사로 'since+명사(구)'의 형태로 쓰여 '~ 이후'의 뜻을 갖는다.

15 the 비교급+주어+동사 ~, the 비교급+주어+동사 …: ~할수록 …하다 sweater는 명사이므로 적절하지 않다. sweeter로 쓰면 적절하다.

16 ② The earlier they start, the sooner they will arrive. ④ We didn't go on a picnic since[as/because] it rained a lot. ⑥ Mina went home early since[because, as] she felt very tired.

17 Green Lake 캠프는 초록색도 아니었고 호수도 없었고 뜨거웠고 온통 모래였다고 했으므로, Green Lake 캠프는 '끔찍한' 이름이었다고 하는 것이 적절하다. ① 멋진, ② 아주 좋은, 멋진, ③ 타당한, 합리적인, ④ 경탄할 만한

18 ⓑ와 ③: (예를 들어) ~와 같은(전치사), ① ~와 비슷한(전치사), ② …을 좋아하다(동사), ④ ~처럼(전치사), ⑤ 마치 ~인 것처럼(접속사)

19 hit+사람+on+the+신체 부위: ~의 …을 때리다

20 happen은 자동사라서 수동태로 쓸 수 없으므로, happened로 고치는 것이 적절하다.

21 ②번 다음 문장의 내용에 주목한다. 주어진 문장의 결과로 심장이 더 빨리 뛰게 된 것이므로 ②번이 적절하다.

22 There were two letters, *KB*, at the 'bottom' of the tube.

23 '구덩이 하나'를 가리킨다.

24 '~하기 위해서'라는 뜻의 목적을 나타내는 부사적 용법의 to부정사는 'in order that 주어 can[may]'을 사용하여 복문으로 고치는 것이 가능하다. (1) 'so as to'도 가능하다. (2) 'so that ~ may[can]'도 가능하다.

Lesson 5

Believe in Yourself

시험대비 실력평가 p.116

01 ③ 02 ③ 03 ④ 04 ⑤
05 ② 06 ①

01 ③에는 'ing'가, 나머지 보기의 빈칸에는 'ed'가 어울린다. 감정을 나타내는 동사의 형용사형으로 주어가 감정을 느끼는 주체일 경우에는 과거분사 형태를 쓰고, 주어가 감정의 대상인 경우에는 현재분사(동사원형-ing) 형태를 쓴다. ① 그들은 뱀을 무서워했다. ② 그녀는 뉴스를 듣고 충격을 받았다. ③ 그의 이야기는 항상 흥미롭다. ④ 나는 그를 직접 봐서 신이 난다. ⑤ 그는 시험 결과에 실망했다.

02 ① surprised: 놀란, 놀라는 / 나는 그가 경기에서 이겨서 놀랐다. ② bored: 지루해하는 / 그녀는 음악뿐만 아니라 미술에도 지루해한다. ③ scared: 무서워하는, 겁먹은 → thrilled: 아주 신이 난 / 그들이 금메달을 따냈다는 소식에 모두들 신이 났다. ④ worried: 걱정하는 / 나는 내일 영어 시험이 걱정된다. ⑤ excited: 신이 난 , 흥분한 / 아이들은 선물에 신이 나 있었다.

03 ④ 는 비교급 강조 부사로 '한층'의 뜻이다.

04 look after: ~를 돌보다, 살피다 take care of: ~를 돌보다 / 당신이 없을 때 아이들은 누가 돌볼 것인가요?

05 '매우 신이 나고 행복한'을 나타내는 단어는 thrilled(황홀해하는, 아주 신이 난)이다.

06 (A) turn A into B: A를 B로 바꾸다 / 그는 곧 그의 꿈을 현실로 바꿨다. (B) take part in: ~에 참가하다 / 그들은 부산 국제 영화제에 참석하기 위해 부산에 갔다.

서술형 시험대비 p.117

01 ⓑ going → go, ⓒ work → working
02 (1) boring (2) shocking (3) amazing (4) scared
03 into
04 (1) step by step (2) known as (3) out, (t)une
(4) (F)rom then on, take (5) patience (6) (j)ourney
05 afford

01 ⓐ how to 동사원형: ~하는 방법, 어떻게 ~할지 / 그것을 어떻게 하는지 내게 보여 줄 수 있니? ⓑ can't afford to 동사원형: ~을 할 형편이 못되다 / 우리가 올 여름에는 해외로 갈 형편이 안 된다. ⓒ look forward to (동)명사: ~를 기대하다, 고대하다 / 나는 너와 일하기를 기대하고 있다.

02 감정을 나타내는 동사의 형용사형으로 주어가 감정을 느끼는 주체일 경우에는 과거분사 형태를 쓰고, 주어가 감정의 대상인 경우에는 현재분사(동사원형-ing) 형태를 쓴다. (1) boring: 재미없는, 지루한 / 그 쇼는 아주 지루했다. (2) shocking: 충격적인 / 그 소식은 모든 사람들에게 충격적이었다. (3) amazing: 놀라운 / 그의 새로운 책은 정말 놀랍다! (4) scared: 무서워하는, 겁먹은 / Mike는 너무 겁먹어서 번지 점프를 할 수 없었다.

03 be made into ~: ~로 만들어지다 / 소설 '미녀와 야수'가 영화로 만들어졌다. turn A into B: A를 B로 바꾸다 / 서울 도심에 위치한 광화문 광장이 스케이트장으로 바뀌었다. put ~ into practice: ~을 실행에 옮기다 / 그녀는 자신의 새 아이디어를 실행에 옮기기로 결심했다.

04 (1) step by step: 점차로, 차근차근, 하나씩 (2) be known as: ~로 알려지다 (3) out of tune: 음이 맞지 않는 (4) from then on: 그때부터 계속 take care of: ~를 돌보다 (5) patience: 인내심 (6) journey: 여행

05 afford: ~할 형편이 되다 / 어떤 것의 비용을 지불할 수 있는 / 나는 그들이 어떻게 그렇게 비싼 휴일을 보낼 형편이 되었는지 모르겠다.

교과서

Conversation

핵심 Check p.118~119

1 looking forward to
2 going
3 (B) → (A) → (C)
4 I'd love to, but I have to do my homework.
5 love to, but I can't
6 (D) → (B) → (C) → (A)

교과서 대화문 익히기

Check(√) True or False p.120~121

1 T 2 F 3 F 4 F 5 F 6 T 7 F 8 T

교과서 확인학습 p.123~125

Listen and Speak 1 A

to, looking forward, excited to, See you on

Listen and Speak 1 B

what are / reading, about, named / who was born without / even won / was made into, going to / I'm really looking forward to / on

Listen and Speak 1 C

1. What's / excited, I'm going to travel / really looking forward to
2. look happy / learn to fly / I'm really looking, to flying
3. going on / so excited, I'm going / looking forward to watching

Listen and Speak 2 A

finish / difficult / interesting, too / help me with / I'd love to, have to take care of

Listen and Speak 2 B

take part in / how to play / I've played / Can you play / but I can't / sorry to hear / cheer for

Listen and Speak 2 C

1. going to do / want to / but I can't, have to / next time
2. are you going to / join me / I'd love to, to visit / next time

Real Life Talk Watch a Video

What are you going / watch / it about / about a boy who became / looking forward to watching / interesting / watched / want to join / but I can't, volunteer / next

Real Life Talk Step 2

1. I'm going to watch, to watching / fun / love to, but I can't, my face painted
2. going to do next / at, I'm really looking, playing it / Sounds / I'd love to, but

시험대비 기본평가 p.126

01 ①	02 ②	03 ②, ④

01 숙제를 도와달라는 B의 요청에 G가 거절하면서, 남동생을 돌봐야 한다고 이유를 말하고 있다. 그러므로 빈칸에는 거절하는 표현인 'I'd love to, but I can't.'가 들어가는 것이 적절하다.

02 B는 드론을 날리는 것을 배우는 것에 대해 신나하고 있으므로, 이에 대한 기대를 표현하는 ②가 빈칸에 들어가는 것이 적절하다. be interested in: ~에 흥미가 있다 look forward to (동)명사: ~를 기대하다, 고대하다 be good at: ~을 잘하다

03 'I'm looking forward to (동)명사 ~.'는 '나는 ~하기를 기대한다.'라는 뜻으로, 기대를 나타낼 때 사용하는 표현이다. 'I'm looking forward to (동)명사 ~.' 대신 쓸 수 있는 표현으로, 'I can't wait to 동사원형 ~.', 'I'm excited about (동)명사 ~.' 등이 있다.

시험대비 실력평가 p.127~128

01 ④	02 ④, ⑤	03 ①, ③	04 ③
05 ③	06 ②	07 ⑤	08 ③
09 ②	10 watch → watching		

01 주어진 문장은 '그의 이야기가 영화로 만들어졌어.'란 의미이다. 이후에 그 영화의 제목을 물어보는 'What's the title?'이 나와야 하므로 ④에 들어가는 것이 적절하다.

02 'I'm looking forward to (동)명사 ~.'는 '나는 ~하기를 기대한다.'라는 뜻으로, 기대를 나타낼 때 사용하는 표현이다. to는 전치사로 뒤에 명사 또는 동명사(-ing)를 쓴다. 'I'm looking forward to (동)명사 ~.' 대신 쓸 수 있는 표현으로, 'I can't wait to ~.'가 있는데 'can't wait to' 다음에는 동사원형을 써야 한다.

03 ② 여자아이는 영화 제목을 알고 있었다. ④ 지호는 토요일에 Jim Abbott에 관한 영화를 볼 것이다. ⑤ 여자아이는 Jim Abbott이 오른손이 없이 태어난 사람이라고 대답했다.

04 help A with B: A가 B하는 것을 돕다

05 ⓐ에는 수학이 어렵다는 말에 동의를 하고 이어서 흥미롭다는 말을 하고 있으므로 역접을 나타내는 but이 어울린다. ⓑ 'I'd love to, but I can't.'는 '그러고 싶지만, 할 수 없어.'라는 뜻으로 상대방의 제안을 거절할 때 사용할 수 있는 표현이다.

06 ① 민호는 남동생이 있다. (소녀는 남동생이 있다.) ② 소녀는 민호가 숙제하는 것을 도울 수 없다. ③ 민호는 수학이 쉽다고 생각한다. (민호는 수학이 어렵다고 생각한다.) ④ 소녀는 수학이 재미있지 않고 어렵다고 생각한다. (소녀는 수학이 어렵지만 재미있다고 생각한다.) ⑤ 민호는 수학 숙제를 끝냈다. (못 끝냈다.)

07 인사동에 같이 가자고 제안하는 말에 'Sure.'로 수락한 다음에 곧바로 'I'd love to, but I can't.'로 거절하는 말을 하는 것은 어색하다.

08 ⓐ, ⓑ, ⓔ, ⓕ가 빈칸에 들어갈 수 있다. 빈칸 (A)에는 뮤지컬을 같이 보러 가자고 제안하는 말에, 거절하며 주말에 자원봉사 활동이 있다고 말하는 것이 어울린다. 상대방의 제안을 거절할 때 사용할 수 있는 표현으로는 'I'd love to, but I can't.', 'I'm sorry, but I can't.', 'I'm afraid I can't.', 'I'll take a rain check.', 'I wish I could, but I have to ~.', 'Your suggestion sounds great, but ~.' 등이 있다.

09 ① 뮤지컬 Billy Elliot은 무엇에 관한 내용인가?(유명한 무용수가 된 한 소년에 관한 내용이다.) ② 얼마나 오래 Linda

는 자원봉사 활동을 했는가? ③ Jason Kim이 나온 뮤지컬을 Linda는 언제 보았는가?(작년) ④ 이번 주말에 Tony는 무엇을 할 것인가?(뮤지컬 Billy Elliot을 볼 것이다.) ⑤ Billy Elliot에서 누가 주연 배우인가?(Jason Kim)

10 'I'm looking forward to (동)명사 ~.'에서 to는 전치사로 뒤에 명사 또는 동명사(-ing)를 쓴다.

서술형 시험대비

p.129

01 (A) named (B) to watching
02 but I can't
03 of
04 (E), I'd love to, but I can't.
05 I'm looking forward to watching it.

01 (A) named는 동사 name(이름 짓다)의 과거분사형으로 '이름이 ~인'의 의미를 가지며, 앞의 명사 baseball player를 수식하고 있다. (B) 'I'm looking forward to ~.'는 앞으로 일어날 일에 대한 기대를 표현할 때 사용하는 표현으로, '나는 ~하기를 기대한다'라는 의미이며 to 뒤에는 명사나 동명사가 온다.

02 'I'd love to, but I can't.'는 '그러고 싶지만, 할 수 없어.'라는 뜻으로 상대방의 제안을 거절할 때 사용할 수 있는 표현이다.

03 take care of: ~를 돌보다

04 뮤지컬을 보러 가자는 말에, 이번 주말에 자원봉사 활동이 있다고 말했으므로, 거절하는 것이 어울린다. 그러므로 'Of course.(물론이지.)'라는 제안에 승낙하는 말을 'I'd love to, but I can't.(그러고 싶지만, 할 수 없어.)'로 바꾸는 것이 적절하다.

05 'I'm looking forward to (동)명사 ~.'는 '나는 ~하기를 기대한다.'라는 뜻으로, 기대를 나타낼 때 사용하는 표현이다. to는 전치사로 뒤에 명사 또는 동명사(-ing)를 쓴다.

교과서

Grammar

핵심 Check

p.130~131

1 If I were you, I would wait a little longer.
2 (1) how to use
(2) where to park

시험대비 기본평가

p.132

01 (1) have → had (2) will → would
(3) know → knew (4) will → would
02 ③ 03 ④
04 I did not know whom I should thank for the gift.

01 문제에서 모든 문장이 가정법 문장이라고 했고, 모든 문장의 구조는 '가정법과거' 형태이므로, 조건절의 동사를 과거로, 주절의 조동사도 과거형으로 고치는 것이 적절하다.

02 'why+to부정사'는 쓰이지 않으므로 'I can't find the reason why I should stay here.' 정도로 쓰는 것이 적절하다.

03 주절에 조동사의 과거형이 나왔으므로, 가정법 문장이다. 내용상 be동사의 과거형이 필요한데, 일반적으로 가정법과거에서 be동사의 과거형은 were를 쓴다.

04 '의문사+to부정사'는 '의문사+주어+should[can]+동사원형'으로 바꿔 쓸 수 있다. 내용상 should가 적절하다.

시험대비 실력평가

p.133~135

01 ④	02 ①	03 ②	04 ⑤
05 ③	06 ①	07 ③	08 ②

09 (1) were (2) had (3) how (4) to go 10 ④
11 (1) how they should[can] write
(2) when I should[can] bring
(3) what I should[can] do

12 ⑤	13 ②, ④	14 ②	15 ③

16 (1) If it snowed all night, I would not leave tomorrow morning.
(2) My mom taught me how to bake cookies.
17 (1) will → would (2) what → how

01 가정법 문장이라면 will을 would로, 직설법 문장이라면 occurred를 occurrs로 쓰는 것이 적절하다.

02 'cook the eggs'로 목적어가 나와 있으므로 목적어로 쓰일 수 있는 것은 적절하지 않으며 'why to부정사'는 쓰지 않는다.

03 주절에 would가 나와 있고 내용상 가정법으로 보아야 하므로 have를 had로 고치는 것이 적절하다.

04 목적어 it이 있으므로 what이 아니라 how나 where 등이 나와야 하거나 it을 삭제해야 한다.

05 ①번과 ④번은 가정법 전환이 잘못된 이상한 문장이며, ②번은 과거의 상황이므로 가정법 과거완료가 필요하고, ⑤번은 직설법의 인과관계가 반대로 표현되었다.

06 ①번은 부사적 용법으로 쓰였고 주어진 문장과 나머지는 명사적 용법으로 쓰였다.

07 가정법과거 시제의 문장으로 쓴다. 'If I had a time machine'으로 종속절을 쓰고 주절에 조동사의 과거형 could를 쓰는 것에 유의한다.

08 'where to buy(어디에서 사야 할지)'가 found out의 목적어가 되도록 한다.

09 (1), (2) 주절에 조동사의 과거형이 나왔으므로, 가정법 문장이다. (3) ride의 목적어로 'a bicycle'이 있으므로 what을 쓸 수 없다. (4) '의문사+to부정사'가 적절하다.

10 가정법과거의 문장들이다. If절에는 동사의 과거형을, 주절에는 조동사의 과거형을 쓰는 것이 적절하다. Were it not for water and air = If there were no water and air = Without water and air = But for water and air

11 '의문사+to부정사'는 '의문사+주어+should/can+동사원형'으로 바꾸어 쓸 수 있다.

12 가정법과거 문장은 현재시제의 직설법으로 바꿔 쓸 수 있다. 가정법은 반대로 가정하는 것이므로 부정하는 것이 서로 바뀌는 것에 주의한다.

13 내용상 그들이 만나는 것이므로 목적어가 필요 없어 what과 which는 적절하지 않고 'why+to부정사'는 쓰지 않는다.

14 옳은 문장은 ⓒ, ⓔ 2개이다. ⓐ have → had, ⓑ will → would, ⓓ going → to go ⓕ exciting → excited ⓖ scare → scared

15 '~가 없다면'이라는 가정법 표현은 'If there were no ~'로 나타낸다. If there were no computers = If it were not for computers = Were it not for computers = Without computers = But for computers

16 (1) 주절에 would가 있는 가정법과거 문장이다. snows를 snowed로 고치는 것이 적절하다. (2) '의문사+to부정사'의 어순이 적절하다.

17 (1) 가정법과거는 'If+주어+were/동사의 과거형 ~, 주어+조동사의 과거형(would/should/could/might)+동사원형 …'의 형태이다. will을 would로 고치는 것이 적절하다. (2) play의 목적어로 chess가 나와 있으므로 what을 쓸 수 없고 내용상 how로 고치는 것이 적절하다.

서술형 시험대비

p.136~137

01 If he knew my address, he would send me a letter.

02 I told him when to feed the dog.

03 (1) If it were not for
(2) Were it not for
(3) If there were no
(4) But for
(5) As there is

04 which guitar to buy

05 sang

06 where to go

07 spoke, could be

08 (1) If I were[was] Superman, I would save people in danger.
(2) If he didn't have a cold, he could go shopping with me.
(3) No one knew how to play musical instruments.
(4) Can you tell me which train to take?

09 amazed → amazing / am → were[was] / will → would

10 (1) If I were a bird, I would fly.
(2) If it rained, I would put on the boots.
(3) If she had enough eggs, she could bake bread for her family.
(4) If I had a magic carpet, I would travel all around the world.

11 (1) where I should put the eggs
(2) how I can use this camera
(3) when they should take action

12 (1) has → had
(2) taking → to take

01 가정법과거 시제의 문장으로 쓴다. 'If he knew my address'로 종속절을 쓰고 주절에 조동사의 과거형 would를 쓰는 것에 유의한다.

02 'when to feed(언제 먹이를 줄지)'가 told의 직접목적어가 되도록 한다.

03 '불의가 없다면 인간은 정의를 알지 못할 것이다.(헤라클레이토스)'라는 뜻이다. 가정법 과거의 경우, Without = If it were not for = Were it not for = If there were no = But for이다.

04 의문사 which가 의문형용사로 쓰여 '의문형용사+명사+to부정사' 형태로 사용된 경우이다.

05 가정법과거는 'If+주어+were/동사의 과거형 ~, 주어+조동사의 과거형(would/should/could/might)+동사원형 …'의 형태이다.

06 '의문사+to부정사'를 이용한다.

07 가정법과거는 현재 사실과 반대되는 가정을 나타낼 때 사용하므로 직설법 문장을 가정법으로 나타낼 수 있다.

08 (1), (2) '가정법과거'를 이용한다. (3) '의문사+to부정사'를 이용한다. (4) 의문사 which를 의문형용사로 사용하여 'which+명사+to부정사' 형태를 이용한다.

09 주어가 It이므로 amazing이 되어야 하며 내용상 가정법과거가 되어야 하므로 'If+주어+were/동사의 과거형 ~, 주어+조동사의 과거형(would/should/could/might)+동사원형 …'의 형태로 나타내야 한다.

10 직설법현재 문장을 가정법과거 문장으로 바꿀 때, 종속절에는 동사의 과거형을, 주절에는 '조동사의 과거형+동사원형'을 쓰는 것에 유의한다.

11 '의문사+to부정사'는 '의문사+주어+should[can]+동사원형'으로 바꿔 쓸 수 있다.

12 (1) 가정법과거에서 종속절에는 동사의 과거형을 쓴다. (2) '의문사+to부정사' 형태가 적절하다.

확인문제 p.138

1 T 2 F 3 T 4 F 5 T 6 F

확인문제 p.139

1 T 2 F 3 T 4 F 5 T 6 F

교과서 확인학습 A p.140~141

01 Trash, Music
02 Tears of joy
03 thrilled
04 were, would fly
05 look around
06 The other members
07 has just finished, giving us a big hand
08 ever expected
09 It has been
10 I'm a violinist
11 Why is it called
12 are made of, from
13 That's why
14 are from
15 a huge landfill
16 itself
17 Many of us
18 many hopes and dreams
19 began to change
20 an environmental educator
21 teach us music
22 only a few
23 couldn't afford to
24 give up
25 with objects from the landfill
26 named, put, into practice
27 made, from
28 turned, into
29 another problem
30 how to play
31 how to read
32 with great patience
33 Step by step
34 the first piece of music
35 out of tune
36 the most beautiful music
37 felt a new hope
38 From then on
39 some great news
40 were going to have
41 hundreds of people
42 our music
43 sends us trash, send back music

교과서 확인학습 B p.142~143

1 From Trash to Music
2 Tears of joy are rolling down my cheeks.
3 I'm so happy and thrilled.
4 If I were a bird, I would fly.
5 I look around.
6 The other members in my orchestra are hugging one another.
7 Our concert has just finished and everyone is standing and giving us a big hand.
8 None of us ever expected that this day would come.
9 It has been a long journey.
10 My name is Andrea and I'm a violinist in the Recycled Orchestra.
11 Why is it called the Recycled Orchestra?
12 It's because our musical instruments are made of objects from a landfill.
13 That's why it's also known as the Landfill Harmonic Orchestra.
14 Most of us in the orchestra are from Cateura, a small town in Paraguay.
15 There is a huge landfill in our town.
16 Some people even say that Cateura itself is a giant landfill.
17 Many of us are poor.
18 There weren't many hopes and dreams in our town.
19 Everything began to change, however, when we met Favio Chávez.
20 Favio was an environmental educator and a musician.
21 He wanted to teach us music, but there was a big problem.
22 There were only a few musical instruments in the whole town.
23 We couldn't afford to buy new ones.
24 But Favio didn't give up.
25 He said that we could make musical instruments with objects from the landfill.
26 A talented man named Nicholas was able to put this idea into practice.
27 He made violins from oil drums.
28 He turned water pipes into flutes.
29 We had another problem.
30 No one knew how to play musical instruments.
31 We didn't even know how to read music.
32 Favio taught us with great patience.
33 Step by step, we began to make some sounds on our instruments.
34 I still remember the first piece of music that we played.
35 It was very short and mostly out of tune.
36 But it was the most beautiful music to us.
37 We felt a new hope in our hearts.
38 From then on, we gathered to practice every day.

39 One day, Favio told us some great news.
40 We were going to have a concert, a real concert!
41 And here we are now in front of hundreds of people.
42 They love our music.
43 The world sends us trash, but we send back music!

시험대비 실력평가

p.144~147

01 (A) thrilled (B) are (C) giving
02 If I were a bird, I would fly.
03 ②, ⑤ 04 ⑤ 05 ④
06 by → as 07 ③ 08 ones
09 we could make musical instruments with objects from the landfill
10 ④ 11 ③ 12 ② 13 ⑤
14 ④ 15 ② 16 landfill
17 ③, ⑤ 18 ③
19 온 마을에 악기가 단지 몇 개뿐이었고, 새 악기를 살 형편도 아니었던 것
20 buying → to buy 21 ①, ④, ⑤
22 in tune → out of tune 23 ② 24 ③

01 (A) 감정을 나타내는 동사는 수식받는 명사가 감정을 느끼게 되는 경우에 과거분사를 써야 하므로 thrilled가 적절하다. (B) 주어가 The other members이므로 수의 일치를 시켜 복수 동사 are로 쓰는 것이 적절하다. (C) standing과 병렬구문을 이루도록 giving으로 쓰는 것이 적절하다.

02 현재 사실에 반대되는 내용을 가정하고 있으므로, 가정법과거로 쓰는 것이 적절하다.

03 ⓑ와 ②, ⑤: 완료 용법, ①, ④: 계속 용법, ③: 경험 용법

04 그들 중 아무도 이 날이 올 거라고 예상하지 못했다. ④ applaud: 박수를 치다, 갈채를 보내다

05 앞에 나오는 내용과 상반되는 내용이 뒤에 이어지므로 however가 가장 적절하다. ① 대신에, ② 그러므로, ③ 즉[말하자면], ⑤ 게다가

06 be known as: ~로 알려져 있다, be known by: ~에 의해 알 수 있다

07 이 글은 'Andrea가 속한 오케스트라는 Recycled Orchestra라고 불리는데, 그 이유는 그들의 악기들이 파라과이의 작은 마을인 카테우라의 거대한 쓰레기 매립지에서 나온 물건들로 만들어졌기 때문'이라는 내용의 글이므로, 주제로는 ③번 '오케스트라가 Recycled Orchestra라고 불리는 이유'가 적절하다. ① description: (~이 어떠한지에 대한) 서술[기술/묘사/표현]

08 one/ones: 앞에 이미 언급했거나 상대방이 알고 있는 사람·사물을 가리킬 때 명사의 반복을 피하기 위해 사용, ⓐ의 ones는 앞 문장의 musical instruments를 가리킨다.

09 with objects from the landfill: 쓰레기 매립지의 물건들로

10 이 글은 'Favio 선생님이 Nicholas 아저씨의 도움으로 쓰레기 매립지의 물건들로 악기를 만드는' 내용의 글이므로, 제목으로는 ④번 '쓰레기를 악기로'가 적절하다.

11 마을에 무슨 악기가 있었는지는 알 수 없다. ① He was an environmental educator and a musician. ② He wanted to teach music. ④ With objects from the landfill. ⑤ A talented man named Nicholas.

12 ⓐ with patience = patiently: 인내심 있게, ⓑ on: ('수단'을 나타내어) ~으로[~에]

13 '우리에게 또 다른 문제가 있었다. 아무도 악기를 연주할 줄 몰랐다. 우리는 심지어 악보를 읽는 방법도 알지 못했다.'는 말로 미루어, 앞에 올 내용으로는 '악기를 구하는 어려움'이 적절하다.

14 'Cateura의 어린이들이 연주했던 첫 곡이 무엇이었는지'는 대답할 수 없다. ① No, there wasn't. ② No, there wasn't. ③ Favio did. ⑤ They thought it was the most beautiful music.

15 주어진 문장의 It에 주목한다. ②번 앞 문장에서 물어보고 있는 '오케스트라가 Recycled Orchestra라고 불리는 이유'를 가리키므로 ②번이 적절하다.

16 landfill: 쓰레기 매립지, 매우 많은 양의 쓰레기가 묻혀 있는 크고 깊은 구멍

17 ⓐ와 ③, ⑤: 재귀대명사의 강조 용법(재귀대명사가 주어, 목적어 등과 동격으로 쓰여 뜻을 강조하는 용법, 생략 가능), ①, ②, ④: 재귀 용법(재귀대명사가 타동사, 전치사 등의 목적어로 쓰이는 경우)

18 ⓐ put ~ into practice: ~을 실행에 옮기다, ⓑ turn A into B: A를 B로 바꾸다

19 (A) 다음에 이어지는 내용을 쓰는 것이 적절하다.

20 afford는 to부정사를 목적어로 취하는 동사이다.

21 step by step = gradually = by degrees = little by little: 점차로, 차근차근, 하나씩, ② 나란히, ③ 자주, 매번

22 '연주했던 첫 곡은 매우 짧고 대부분은 음이 맞지 않았다'고 해야 하므로, 'in tune'을 'out of tune'으로 고치는 것이 적절하다. in tune: 곡조[음]가 맞는, out of tune: 음이 맞지 않는

23 ⓒ와 ①, ③, ④: 부사적 용법, ②, ⑤: 명사적 용법

24 이 글은 '악기를 연주할 줄도 모르고 악보를 읽는 방법도 알지 못했던 단원들이 어려운 훈련 과정을 거쳐 마침내 공연을 하게 되는 과정'에 관한 글이므로, 주제로는 ③번 '공연을 하게 되기까지의 힘든 과정'이 적절하다.

서술형 시험대비 p.148~149

01 a big hand
02 As[Because, Since] I am not a bird, I don't fly.
03 (A) joy (B) none
04 That's why it's also known as the Landfill Harmonic Orchestra.
05 is → are
06 (A) the Recycled Orchestra (B) a landfill
07 named
08 we could make musical instruments with objects from the landfill
09 (A) oil drums (B) water pipes
10 (A) musical instruments (B) talented
11 we should[could]
12 We were going to have a concert, a real concert!
13 hundred → hundreds

01 give a big hand: 큰 박수를 보내다, clap: 박수를 치다, enthusiastically: 열광적으로
02 가정법과거는 현재 사실과 반대되는 가정을 나타낼 때 사용하는 것이므로, 직설법으로 고칠 때 현재시제로 고치는 것이 적절하다.
03 공연이 이제 막 끝났고 글쓴이는 '기뻐서' 울고 있다. 청중들이 박수를 보내고 있고 오케스트라의 단원들 중 '아무도' 이 날이 올 거라고 예상하지 '못했다.' weep for joy: 기뻐서 울다, applaud: 박수를 치다, 갈채를 보내다
04 That's why ~: 그것이 ~한 이유이다, be known as: ~로 알려지다
05 주어가 'Most of us'이므로 수의 일치를 시켜 복수 동사 are로 고치는 것이 적절하다.
06 그 오케스트라의 악기들이 쓰레기 '매립지'에서 나온 물건들로 만들어지기 때문에 사람들은 그 오케스트라를 'Recycled Orchestra' 또는 Landfill Harmonic Orchestra로 부른다.
07 'Nicholas라는 이름의' 남자라고 해야 하므로 과거분사 named로 쓰는 것이 적절하다. named Nicholas는 주어인 A talented man을 수식한다.
08 '우리가 쓰레기 매립지의 물건들로 악기를 만들 수 있다'는 것을 가리킨다.
09 그는 '기름통'으로 바이올린을, 그리고 '수도관'으로 플루트를 만들었다.
10 Favio 선생님은 쓰레기 매립지의 물건들로 '악기'를 만들 수 있다는 생각을 한 환경 교육가이자 음악가였고, Nicholas는 Favio 선생님의 생각을 실행에 옮길 수 있었던 '재능이 많은' 사람이었다.
11 의문사+to부정사 = 의문사+주어+should[can]+동사원형
12 '우리가 공연을, 진짜 공연을 하게 될 것이었다!'를 가리킨다.
13 hundreds of: 수백의, 수백 명의

영역별 핵심문제 p.151~155

01 ① 02 ③ 03 take part
04 made 05 ③ 06 excited
07 ⑤ 08 ⑤
09 the man who[that] was born without a right hand
10 ④ 11 ⑤ 12 ③
13 (C) – (B) – (A) – (D) 14 ③ 15 ⑤
16 ② 17 how to contact
18 were[was], would make
19 (1) we should read (2) I should do
(3) to contact (4) to leave (5) which, to take
20 played, could win
21 (1) when to take out
(2) which dress to wear
(3) whom to meet
22 ③ 23 ② 24 ②
25 There were only a few musical instruments in the whole town.
26 ⑤ 27 ② 28 ②, ④ 29 ③

01 talented: 재능 있는 / 그녀는 사진작가일 뿐만 아니라 재능 있는 음악가이기도 하다.
02 cheer for: 응원하다 / 그들은 그들이 좋아하는 팀과 선수들을 응원한다.
03 participate in: 참가하다, 참여하다 take part in: ~에 참가하다 / 그들은 그가 그 행사에 참가하기를 기대했다.
04 be made of: ~로 만들어지다 / 그것들은 고대 그리스 신전들처럼 돌로 만든 것이 아니다. be made into ~: ~로 만들어지다 / 그녀의 베스트셀러는 곧 TV 미니 시리즈로 만들어질 것이다. made from: ~로 만든 / 많은 생산품들이 수작업보다는 기계로 제작된다.
05 'I'm looking forward to의 to는 전치사로 뒤에 명사 또는 동명사(-ing)를 쓴다. ③을 제외한 모든 보기는 to 뒤에 동명사가 나왔다. ① What do you say to 동명사 ~?: ~에 대해 어떻게 생각해? / 오늘 밤 외식하는 거 어때? ② prefer A to B: B보다 A를 더 좋아하다 / 나는 등산보다 걷기를 더 좋아한다. ③ be used to 동사원형: ~하기 위해 사용되다 / 싱크대를 청소하기 위해 무엇을 써야 하니? ④ adjust to 동명사: ~에 적응하다 / 그녀는 혼자 사는 것에 적응하는 데 한참이 걸렸다. ⑤ when it comes to 동명사: ~에 관해서는, ~에 관한 한 / 치과에 가는 일이라면 난 정말 겁쟁이가 돼.
06 사람이 흥분하는 것으로 과거분사형의 형용사가 올바르다.
07 ⑤ 보라가 공연에서 기타를 연주해 본 적이 있는지는 알 수 없다.
08 지호가 Jim Abbott에 관한 영화를 토요일에 같이 보자고 제안하는 말에, 소녀가 'Sure.(물론이지.)'로 대답하면서 토요일에 보자고 말하는 것이 어울리므로 ⑤가 적절하다.

09 who는 주격 관계대명사로, 'who was born without a right hand'가 'the man'을 수식하고 있다. who 대신에 that을 사용할 수 있다. be born: 태어나다 without: ~ 없이

10 주어진 문장은 '어제 체육 수업 중에 손을 다쳤어.'로 노래하는 동안 기타를 쳐 줄 수 없는 이유이므로, 거절을 나타내는 'I'd love to, but I can't.' 다음에 들어가는 것이 적절하다.

11 take part in: ~에 참가하다

12 (B) 'have p.p.'는 과거의 특정 시점에서 시작된 일이 현재까지 계속되고 있음을 나타내는 현재완료 형태로, 여기서는 계속적 용법으로 사용되고 있다. for+숫자+시간 단위: ~동안 (C) while: ~하는 동안

13 (C) 오늘 오후에 무엇을 할 것인지 질문하고 (B) 축구를 할 거라 대답 하면서 같이 하자고 제안하자 (A) 거절하며, 조부모님 댁에 방문해야 한다고 대답한다. (D) 상대방은 그럼 다음번에 같이 하자고 말한다.

14 ③번의 if는 간접의문문에 쓰였지만 나머지는 모두 가정법의 조건절을 이끌고 있다.

15 the dress가 wear의 목적어로 나와 있으므로 what을 when 등으로 고치거나 the dress를 삭제해야 한다.

16 가정법과거는 'If+주어+were/동사의 과거형 ~, 주어+조동사의 과거형+동사원형 …'의 형태로 나타낸다.

17 how to contact: 어떻게 연락할지

18 가정법과거에는 조건절에 동사의 과거형이 나오고 주절에는 '조동사의 과거형(would/should/could/might)+동사원형'이 나온다. 'be'동사는 주어의 인칭 및 수와 무관하게 'were'를 쓰지만, 구어체에서는 주어가 'I' 또는 3인칭 단수인 경우 'was'를 쓰기도 한다.

19 (1)~(4) 의문사+to부정사 = 의문사+주어+should/can+동사원형 (5) 의문사 which가 의문형용사로 쓰여 to부정사와의 사이에 명사가 올 수 있다.

20 가정법과거는 'If+주어+were/동사의 과거형 ~, 주어+조동사의 과거형(would/should/could/might)+동사원형 …'의 형태이다.

21 (1), (3) 의문사+to부정사 = 의문사+주어+should/can+동사원형 (2) 의문사 which가 의문형용사로 쓰여 to부정사와의 사이에 명사가 올 수 있다.

22 ③번은 '오케스트라가 Recycled Orchestra로 불리는 이유'를 가리키고, 나머지는 다 'Recycled Orchestra'를 가리킨다.

23 huge: 거대한, 막대한, 엄청난, tiny: 작은, 조그마한

24 ②번 다음 문장의 He에 주목한다. 주어진 문장의 Favio를 받고 있으므로 ②번이 적절하다.

25 a few는 '약간의, 몇 개의'라는 뜻의 수량형용사로 셀 수 있는 명사 앞에 위치한다.

26 Nicholas는 기름통으로 '바이올린'을 만들었고 수도관으로 '플루트'를 만들었다.

27 바로 앞 문장에서 '그들은 우리의 음악을 사랑한다.'라고 했으므로, 세상은 우리에게 쓰레기를 보내지만, 우리는 '음악'을 돌려보낸다고 하는 것이 적절하다. ④ garbage: 쓰레기

28 (A)와 ②, ④: 명사적 용법, ①, ⑤: 부사적 용법, ③: 형용사적 용법

29 (B)와 ③: (부사) (쉬지 않고) 계속하여, ① (전치사) ~ 위에 (무엇의 표면에 닿거나 그 표면을 형성함을 나타냄), ② (전치사), (요일, 날짜, 때를 나타내어) ~에, ④ (전치사), ~하자마자 [~한 즉시], ⑤ (전치사), [소속] ~의 일원으로

단원별 예상문제

p.156~159

01 ① 02 ④ 03 ① 04 ②
05 ② 06 ⑤ 07 look forward to
08 ⓐ who/that ⓑ watched
09 I'm really looking forward to flying a drone in the park.
10 (B) → (D) → (A) → (C) 11 award
12 I'm really looking forward to watching it.
13 ③
14 (1) If she had a flying carpet, she could travel all over the world. / As she doesn't have a flying carpet, she can't travel all over the world.
(2) If it snowed a lot, I would ski in the mountains. / Since it doesn't snow a lot, I won't ski in the mountains.
(3) He taught us how to use the machine. / He taught us how we should use the machine.
15 ③, ④
16 Because their musical instruments are made of objects from a landfill.
17 ③ 18 ④ 19 environmental
20 musical instruments 21 ②
22 No one knew how to play musical instruments.
23 ①, ⑤

01 ①은 반의어 관계이지만 이외의 보기들은 동의어 관계이다. ① bored: 지루해하는, thrilled: 아주 신이 난 ② award: 상, prize: 상 ③ journey: 여행, trip: 여행, 소풍 ④ mostly: 대부분, 일반적으로, mainly: 주로, 대개는 ⑤ take care of: 돌보다, look after: 돌보다, 살피다

02 put ~ into practice: ~을 실행에 옮기다 / 그들이 제안한 것을 실행에 옮겨야 할 때였다.

03 give a big hand: 큰 박수를 보내다 / 그들에게 큰 박수를 보내 주시지 않겠습니까?

04 a few+셀 수 있는 명사: 약간의, 몇 개의 / 나는 그 가게에서 몇 가지를 샀다.

05 제목을 묻지는 않았다. (A) What are you going to do this weekend?(이번 주말에 뭐 할 거니?) (B) What is it about?(무슨 내용이니?) (C) Who is the main actor?(주연 배우가 누구니?) (D) Do you want to join me?(나와 함께 가고 싶니?)

06 'I'd love to, but I can't.'는 '그러고 싶지만, 할 수 없어.'라는 뜻으로 상대방의 제안을 거절할 때 사용할 수 있는 표현이다. 그러므로 제안하는 말인 'Do you want to join me?(나와 함께 가고 싶니?)'의 대답이 될 수 있으므로 ⑤가 적절하다.

07 look forward to (동)명사: ~를 기대하다, 고대하다 / 당신이 그것을 즐길 것이라고 생각해서 그것이 일어나기를 바라다

08 ⓐ 선행사 'a boy'를 주격 관계대명사절인 'who became a famous dancer'가 수식하고 있다. who 대신에 관계대명사 that을 사용할 수 있다. ⓑ last year(작년)라는 시간의 부사구 때문에 과거시제를 써야 한다. 또한 흐름상 뮤지컬을 연기하는 것이 아니라 보는 것이 적절하므로 watched가 적절하다.

09 look forward to (동)명사: ~를 기대하다, 고대하다

10 수학 숙제를 끝냈는지 질문하자 (B) 아직 못 끝냈다고 대답하며, 수학이 어렵다고 말한다. (D) 수학이 어렵다는 것에 동의하면서, 하지만 동시에 흥미롭다고 말한다. (A) 그러면 수학 숙제를 도와줄 수 있는지 묻자 (C) 거절을 하면서 남동생을 돌봐야 한다고 거절의 이유를 말해준다.

11 award: 상 / 어떤 것을 잘해서 누군가에게 주어지는 상이나 증명서

12 'I'm looking forward to ~.'는 앞으로 일어날 일에 대한 기대를 말할 때 사용하는 표현으로, '나는 ~하기를 기대한다.'의 의미이며 to 다음에는 명사나 동명사가 온다.

13 ① If I knew the truth, I would tell it to you. ② If there were no corn, there would be no frozen pizza. ④ Were it not for trade unions, wages would not be so high as they are. ⑤ But for his idleness, he would be a good man.

14 (1), (2) 가정법과거 문장은 현재시제의 직설법으로 바꿔 쓸 수 있다. (3) '의문사+to부정사'는 '의문사+주어+should+동사원형'으로 바꿔 쓸 수 있다.

15 ③ The message will tell you whom to contact. ④ Do you want to know how to make friends?

16 그들의 악기들이 쓰레기 매립지에서 나온 물건들로 만들어지기 때문이다.

17 ⓐ와 ③: 물건, 물체, ① 목적, 목표, ② 반대하다(동사), ④ 목적어, ⑤ [사고·감정·행동 등의] 대상, objects of consideration: 고려의 대상이 되는 것들

18 파라과이의 작은 마을인 카테우라에는 거대한 쓰레기 매립지가 있고 몇몇 사람들은 심지어 카테우라 자체가 거대한 쓰레기 매립지라고 말한다고 했을 뿐이므로, '카테우라가 거대한 쓰레기 매립지'라는 말은 옳지 않다.

19 environment의 형용사형이 되어야 한다.

20 '악기'를 가리킨다.

21 주어진 문장의 'we began to make some sounds'에 주목한다. ②번 앞 문장에서 Favio 선생님이 엄청난 인내심으로 우리를 가르쳐주신 결과 '우리가 악기로 어떤 소리를 만들어 내기 시작한' 것이므로 ②번이 적절하다.

22 how to+동사원형: ~하는 방법, 어떻게 ~할지

23 ⓑ와 ①, ⑤: 관계대명사, ②와 ④: 동격의 접속사(뒤에 완전한 문장이 이어짐.) ③ 그(앞에서 말한 사람이나 사물·말하는 이나 듣는 이가 이미 알고 있는 사람이나 사물을 가리킬 때 씀)(지시형용사)

서술형 실전문제

p.160~161

01 (f), I'd love to, but I can't. → Sure. 또는 OK.

02 (1) I'm really looking forward to riding a horse.
(2) I can't wait to ride a horse.

03 (1) I'd love to, but I can't.
(2) I'm sorry, but I can't.

04 (1) As I don't have a time machine, I won't go back in time and meet King Sejong.
(2) I don't have a better camera, so I can't take better photos.
(3) If she were not working, she could go to a movie with Jack.
(4) Were he in Seoul today, he would come to my house.
(5) Without people to be governed, there could be no government.

05 (1) They want to know how people decide how much they can eat.
(2) I don't know which one I should say first.
(3) The most important grammar rule to master is when to use "I" and when to use "me."

06 Why do they(people) call it the Recycled Orchestra?

07 itself

08 (A) because (B) objects (C) why

09 the first piece of music that we played

10 so that, colud[might], in order that, could[might]

01 'Can I join you?(나도 너와 함께 해도 될까?)'란 질문에, 'I'd love to, but I can't.(그러고 싶지만, 안 돼.)'로 대답하고, 토요일에 보자는 것을 어울리지 않는다. 그러므로 함께해도 된다는 긍정의 대답과 어울린다.

02 기대를 나타낼 때 사용하는 표현으로 'I'm looking forward to (동)명사 ~.(나는 ~하기를 기대한다.)', 'I can't wait to 동사원형 ~.(나는 ~하는 것이 기다려져.)' 등이 있다.

03 상대방의 제안에 거절하는 말에는 'I'd love to, but I can't.', 'I'm sorry, but I can't.', 'I'm afraid I can't.', 'Your suggestion sounds great, but ~.' 등이 있다.

04 (1)~(3) 가정법과거 문장은 현재시제의 직설법으로 바꿔 쓸 수 있다. (4) 가정법으로 고친 후, if를 생략하고 were를 문두에 쓰고 도치시킨다. (5) if there were no = if it were not for = were it not for = without = but for

05 '의문사+to부정사'는 '의문사+주어+should[can]+동사원형'으로 바꿔 쓸 수 있다.

06 they[people]를 능동태의 주어로 하여 고치는 것이 적절하다.

07 강조 용법(재귀대명사가 주어, 목적어 등과 동격으로 쓰여 뜻을 강조하는 용법, 생략 가능)의 재귀대명사를 쓰는 것이 적절하다.

08 (A) 오케스트라가 Recycled Orchestra라고 불리는 이유는 악기들이 쓰레기 매립지에서 나온 물건들로 만들어지기 '때문'이라고 해야 하므로 because가 적절하다. It's because ~: 그것은 ~ 때문이다. (B) 악기들이 쓰레기 매립지에서 나온 '물건들'로 만들어졌다고 해야 하므로 objects가 적절하다. object: 물건, 물체, (욕망, 연구, 관심 등의) 대상, subject: (논의 등의) 주제, (다뤄지고 있는) 문제, 학과, 과목, (C) '그것이 오케스트라가 Landfill Harmonic Orchestra로도 알려진 이유'라고 해야 하므로 why가 적절하다. That's why ~: 그것이 ~한 이유이다

09 '우리가 연주했던 첫 곡'을 가리킨다.

10 부사적 용법(목적)을 나타내는 to부정사는 so that ~ may(can) 또는 in order that ~ may(can)로 바꿔 쓸 수 있다.

창의사고력 서술형 문제 p.162

|모범답안|

01 I'm looking forward to / I'd love to, but I can't.

02 (1) If he had enough time, he would visit us.
(2) If it were not rainy, I would go swimming.
(3) If I had a car, I would not have to walk.
(4) Without the fog, flights would not be delayed.

03 (A) Admiral Yi Sun-sin
(B) you never gave up in difficult situations
(C) saved (D) with only 12 ships
(E) how to make geobukseon

단원별 모의고사 p.163~167

01 ⑤ 02 ①
03 (1) looking (2) turned (3) afford (4) take
04 (1) (o)ne another (2) (c)heer for (3) few (4) take part (5) able to (6) give, a big hand
05 (B) → (A) → (D) → (C) 06 ④ 07 ③
08 I can't wait to watch it. 09 (A) in (B) for
10 ④ 11 ② 12 ② 13 ③
14 (1) Please tell me where I should park my car.
(2) He hasn't decided when he should leave for America.
(3) I'm trying to decide what I should take with me.
15 ② 16 ④
17 (1) If she were[was] an adult, she would travel all around the world.
(2) If I were[was] a king, I would give people presents.
(3) How to start is the most important part of all.
(4) I don't know what to do if there were[was] a fire in the building.
(5) Could you tell me where to park?
18 ④ 19 ⑤ 20 ② 21 ①, ③, ④
22 (A) only a few (B) violins (C) flutes 23 ③
24 The world sends us trash, but we send back music!
25 ④

01 frightened: 두려워하는 scared: 무서워하는, 겁먹은

02 (A) That's why ~: 그것이 ~한 이유이다. / Simon은 너를 좋아해. - 그것이 그가 너와 있고 싶어하는 이유야. (B) how to 동사원형: ~하는 방법, 어떻게 ~할지 / 커피 추출기를 어떻게 사용하는지 아세요?

03 (1) look forward to (동)명사: ~를 기대하다, 고대하다 / 나는 그와 일하는 것을 기대하고 있다. (2) turn A into B: A를 B로 바꾸다 / 그 왕자는 마녀에 의해 개구리가 되었다. (3) can't afford to 동사원형: ~을 할 형편이 못되다 / 우리는 새 컴퓨터를 살 여유가 없다. 왜냐하면 너무 비싸기 때문이다. (4) take care of: ~를 돌보다 / 난 그녀에 대해 걱정하지 않아요. 그녀는 스스로를 돌볼 수 있어요.

04 (1) one another: 서로 (2) cheer for: 응원하다 (3) a few+셀 수 있는 명사: 약간의, 몇 개의 (4) take part in: ~에 참가하다 (5) be able to 동사원형: ~할 수 있다 (6) give a big hand: 큰 박수를 보내다

05 (B) 상대방이 행복해 보인다고 말하면서, 무슨 일 때문에 기분이

좋은지 질문하자 (A) Jackson의 콘서트를 볼 것이라고 대답한다. (D) 좋겠다고 말하자 (C) Jackson의 콘서트를 볼 것이 기대된다고 말한다.

06 주어진 문장은 제목을 물어보는 질문으로, 'Our Hero'로 대답할 수 있으므로 ④가 적절하다.

07 was won → won ⓐ named는 동사 name(이름 짓다)의 과거분사형으로 '이름이 ~인'의 의미를 가지며, 앞의 명사 'baseball player'를 수식하고 있다. ⓑ bear: 낳다 be born: 태어나다 ⓒ tried와 won은 접속사 and로 연결되어 있다. won은 win(이기다)의 과거형이다. ⓓ be made into ~: ~로 만들어지다 ⓔ be going to 동사원형: ~할 것이다

08 'I'm looking forward to (동)명사 ~.'는 '나는 ~하기를 기대한다.'라는 뜻으로, 기대를 나타낼 때 사용하는 표현이다. 'I'm looking forward to (동)명사 ~.' 대신 쓸 수 있는 표현으로, 'I can't wait to ~'가 있는데 'can't wait to' 다음에는 동사원형을 써야 한다.

09 (A) take part in: ~에 참가하다 (B) for+숫자+시간 단위: ~ 동안

10 빈칸 (C)에는 대회에서 노래하는 동안 기타를 쳐 줄 수 있는지 묻는 물음에 대한 대답으로, 어제 체육 수업 중에 손을 다쳤다는 말이 뒤에 나오므로 못 친다는 대답이 적절하다. 상대방의 제안을 거절할 때 사용할 수 있는 표현으로는 'I'd love to, but I can't.', 'I wish I could, but I have to ~.' 등이 있다.

11 ① Alex는 기타를 칠 수 있는가? (네) ② 몇 시에 수민이를 응원하러 Alex가 대회에 갈 것인가? ③ 얼마 동안 Alex가 기타를 배웠는가? (3년) ④ 수민이는 무슨 대회에 참여할 예정인가? (노래대회) ⑤ 왜 Alex는 대회에서 기타를 연주할 수 없는가? (어제 체육 수업에서 손을 다쳐서.)

12 (A) A가 'Sounds fun.'이라고 하고 있으므로 행진을 볼 것을 기대하는 표현이 어울린다. 'I'm looking forward to (동)명사 ~.'는 '나는 ~하기를 기대한다.'라는 뜻으로, 기대를 나타낼 때 사용하는 표현이다. (B) A가 '그때 페이스페인팅을 하러 간다.'고 하고 있으므로 못 간다고 말하는 것이 어울린다. 거절하는 'I'd love to, but I can't.(그러고 싶지만, 할 수 없어.)'가 적절하다.

13 ③ 내가 의사이기 때문에, 아픈 사람들을 도울 수 있다. ①, ②, ④, ⑤ 내가 의사라면, 아픈 사람들을 도울 수 있을 텐데. (내가 의사가 아니기 때문에, 아픈 사람들을 도울 수 없다.)

14 '의문사+to부정사'는 '의문사+주어+should[can]+동사원형'으로 바꿔 쓸 수 있다.

15 ②번의 if는 간접의문문으로 명사절을 이끄는 접속사이며, 나머지는 모두 가정법의 조건절을 이끄는 종속접속사이다.

16 If there were no ~ = If it were not for ~ = Were it not for ~ = Without ~ = But for ~

17 (1), (2) '만약 ~라면 …할 텐데'라는 뜻으로, 현재 사실을 반대로 가정하거나 실현 가능성이 없는 일에 대해서 가정할 때 사용하는 가정법과거로 'If+주어+were/동사의 과거형 ~, 주어+조동사의 과거형(would/should/could/might)+동사원형 …'의 형태로 쓴다. (3)~(5) '의문사+to부정사'는 'what/when/where/how/which/who(m)+to부정사'의 형태로 쓰이며, 문장 속에서 주어, 목적어, 보어 역할을 하는 명사구로 사용된다.

18 오케스트라가 Recycled Orchestra라고 불리는 이유가 악기들이 '쓰레기 매립지'에서 나온 물건들로 만들어지기 때문이라고 하는 것이 적절하다. ① 공장, ③ 작업장, ⑤ 악기점

19 ⓑ와 ⑤: 전치사, [역할·자격·기능·성질 따위를 나타내어] ~으로(서)(의), ① 접속사, [이유·원인] ~이므로, ~ 때문에, ② 전치사, 예를 들면, ~처럼[같이](= such as, like), ③ [보통 'as ~ as ...'로 형용사·부사 앞에서] …와 같은 정도로, 마찬가지로 (as ~ as ...에서, 앞의 as가 지시부사, 뒤의 as는 접속사), ④ 접속사, [비례] ~함에 따라, ~할수록

20 ⓐ objects from the landfill: 쓰레기 매립지의 물건들, ⓑ 재료를 이용하여 다른 물건으로 만드는 경우, 전치사 from을 사용한다.

21 (A)와 ②, ⑤: 명사적 용법, ①, ④: 부사적 용법, ③: 형용사적 용법

22 비록 온 마을에 악기가 '단지 몇 개뿐'이었고 새 악기를 살 형편도 아니었지만, Cateura의 어린이들은 Favio 선생님과 Nicholas 아저씨 덕분으로 '바이올린'과 '플루트'와 같은 악기들을 가질 수 있었다.

23 이 글은 '악기를 연주할 줄도 모르고 악보를 읽는 방법도 알지 못했던 단원들이 어려운 훈련 과정을 거쳐 마침내 공연을 하게 되는 과정'에 관한 글이므로, 어울리는 속담으로는 '고진감래'가 적절하다. ③번은 '제때의 한 땀(은 나중의 아홉 땀을 던다) (문제를 즉각 처리하면 훨씬 더 수월하게 해결할 수 있다는 뜻)', 나머지는 다 '고진감래'를 나타내는 속담이다. ④ 고생 끝에 낙이 온다.

24 sends trash to us도 sends us trash와 같은 뜻이지만, 10 단어로 영작하기 위해 4형식으로 쓰는 것이 적절하다. send back: 돌려보내다

25 그들이 연주했던 첫 곡은 매우 짧고 대부분은 음이 맞지 않았다. in tune: 곡조[음]가 맞는

교과서 파헤치기

단어 TEST Step 1 p.02

01 나중에, 후에	02 장소	03 투표하다
04 벽화	05 배경	06 굽다
07 보람 있는	08 근처, 이웃	09 (특정한) 장소, 자리
10 준비하다	11 양로원	12 선택하다, 선정하다
13 배달하다	14 현장, 장소	15 경험
16 친절한	17 책꽂이	18 털
19 짐을 꾸리다	20 지원하다	21 재활용 쓰레기통
22 배열하다	23 없애다, 제거하다	24 나누다
25 분명하게	26 문제되다, 중요하다	
27 깨끗한	28 예의 바르게	29 기부, 기증
30 운영자, 관리자	31 심다	32 응답하다
33 제안하다	34 자원봉사; 자원봉사하다	
35 치우다, 줍다	36 ~와 사이좋게 지내다	
37 ~을 자랑스러워하다		38 모이다
39 ~을 명심하다	40 휴식을 취하다	
41 꼭 ~하다	42 제시간에 도착하다	
43 ~에게 도움을 주다		

단어 TEST Step 2 p.03

01 background	02 manager	03 pack
04 paint	05 donation	06 matter
07 neat	08 site	09 rewarding
10 amusement park		11 experience
12 apply	13 clearly	14 recycling bin
15 arrange	16 vote	17 select
18 spot	19 wall painting	20 nursing home
21 politely	22 shelf	23 deliver
24 neighborhood	25 prepare	26 remove
27 divide	28 suggest	29 volunteer
30 village	31 reply	32 wing
33 share	34 board	35 pick up
36 be proud of ~	37 line up	38 give a bath
39 take a break	40 get together	41 be on time
42 get along with ~		43 give ~ a hand

단어 TEST Step 3 p.04

1 matter, 중요하다 2 location, 장소 3 plant, 심다
4 deliver, 배달하다 5 pack, 짐을 꾸리다
6 remove, 제거하다 7 drawing, 그림
8 volunteer, 자원봉사자 9 bake, 굽다
10 donation, 기부, 기증 11 divide, 나누다
12 arrange, 정리하다 13 background, 배경
14 select, 선택하다, 선정하다
15 amusement park, 놀이 공원 16 manager, 관리자

대화문 TEST Step 1 p.05~07

Listen and Speak 1 A

What, for / packing, donation, give me a / want, to / write, address on / problem

Listen and Speak 1 B

this mess / baking / Why, baking, many / They're for, nursing home / nice of / Can you give, hand / do you want me / put, gift boxes, each

Listen and Speak 1 C

1 doing / packing for, move, Can you help / What do you want, to do / put the clothes into

2 are, doing / packing for, move, Can you help me / want me to do / move, outside

3 What are you doing / packing for, move, Can you help me / What do you want me to do / take out

Listen and Speak 2 A

Enjoy / will, is on / Don't worry about / Make sure you feed, after / should

Listen and Speak 2 B

Make groups of, sit, to make, Keep in mind, make sure, before you start, Second, when, let's

Listen and Speak 2 C

1 to go / Make sure, lock / Anything / that's

2 time to / Make sure you clean / Anything else

3 It's time to go / Make sure, water the plants / will, else

Real Life Talk Watch a Video

What can I do / here for, volunteer work / must be / What do you want me to do / read, for the blind, recording room / Should, go / go into / anything to keep in / Make sure you, slowly and clearly / do my best

Real Life Talk Step 3

1 I'm here for / for coming / do you want me to do / give, a bath / Is there anything, keep in mind / Make sure, brush, fur

2 I'm here for the volunteer / Thanks for / What do you want me to do / for the blind / Is there anything to keep in mind / sure, slowly, clearly

대화문 TEST Step 2

p.08~10

Listen and Speak 1 A

B: What are all these boxes and books for?

G: I'm packing the books for the donation center. Can you give me a hand?

B: Sure. What do you want me to do?

G: Please write the address on the boxes.

B: No problem.

Listen and Speak 1 B

B: What is this mess?

G: I'm baking cookies.

B: Why are you baking so many cookies?

G: They're for the people at the nursing home.

B: That's very nice of you.

G: Can you give me a hand?

B: Sure. What do you want me to do?

G: Please put the cookies in the gift boxes. Three cookies in each box.

B: Okay.

Listen and Speak 1 C

1 A: What are you doing?

B: I'm packing for my move tomorrow. Can you help me?

A: Sure. What do you want me to do?

B: Please put the clothes into the box.

A: No problem.

2 A: What are you doing?

B: I'm packing for my move tomorrow. Can you help me?

A: Sure. What do you want me to do?

B: Please move the chairs outside.

A: No problem.

3 A: What are you doing?

B: I'm packing for my move tomorrow. Can you help me?

A: Sure. What do you want me to do?

B: Please take out the trach.

A: No problem.

Listen and Speak 2 A

B: Enjoy the concert, Mom.

W: I will. Thanks. Your dinner is on the table.

B: All right. Don't worry about me.

W: Make sure you feed the dog after you have dinner.

B: Okay. Mom, you should go now. Dad is waiting in the car.

Listen and Speak 2 B

B: Hello, class. Make groups of four people and sit around the tables. Today we're going to make bacon and egg sandwiches. Keep in mind two rules for our class. First, make sure you wash your hands before you start. Second, be careful when you use a knife. All right, let's start.

Listen and Speak 2 C

1 A: It's time to go home.

B: Yes. Make sure you lock the doors.

A: Okay, I will. Anything else?

B: No, that's it. See you tomorrow.

2 A: It's time to go home.

B: Yes. Make sure you clean the board.

A: Okay, I will. Anything else?

B: No, that's it. See you tomorrow.

3 A: It's time to go home.

B: Yes. Make sure you water the plants.

A: Okay, I will. Anything else?

B: No, that's it. See you tomorrow.

Real Life Talk Watch a Video

Woman: Good morning. What can I do for you?

Tony: Hi. I'm here for the volunteer work.

Woman: Oh, you must be Tony.

Tony: That's right. What do you want me to do today?

Woman: Please read this book for the blind in the recording room.

Tony: No problem. Should I go in now?

Woman: Yes. Please go into Room 7.

Tony: Okay. Is there anything to keep in mind?

Woman: Yes. Make sure you read slowly and clearly.

Tony: Okay. I'll do my best.

Real Life Talk Step 3

1 A: Hi, I'm Minsu. I'm here for the volunteer work.

B: Thanks for coming, Minsu.

A: What do you want me to do today?

B: Please give the dog a bath.

A: Okay. Is there anything to keep in mind?

B: Yes. Make sure you brush the fur first.

A: Okay, I will.

2 A: Hi, I'm Tony. I'm here for the volunteer.

B: Thanks for coming, Tony.

A: What do you want me to do today?

B: Please record a book for the blind.

A: Okay. Is there anything to keep in mind?

B: Yes. Make sure you read slowly and clearly.

A: Okay, I will.

본문 TEST Step 1 p.11~12

01 Paint, Better Tomorrow
02 My name is
03 This, front, wall
04 so, aren't they
05 take, front, paintings
06 old neighborhoods bright
07 Last, village with
08 light went on, head
09 thought, in, art
10 Why don't we, like
11 suggested, idea, meeting
12 found, teen volunteer, on
13 to, wall painting, neighborhood
14 applied for, later, selected
15 day, finally came
16 had us meet, site
17 in, poor condition
18 strange writings, drawings, parts
19 Other parts, on
20 removed, over, with, paint
21 let us paint
22 decided, something cute, near
23 divided into, began
24 was in, group with
25 chose, spot, paint, character
26 painted, did, background drawings
27 for about, hours
28 After, finished, together, shared
29 was very proud of
30 so, that, landed on
31 much harder than drawing
32 agreed, wasn't perfect
33 But, didn't matter
34 a little brighter, happier
35 proud of ourselves
36 didn't just paint, on
37 a better tomorrow, painted

본문 TEST Step 2 p.13~14

01 Better Tomorrow
02 My name is
03 This is me, front
04 aren't they
05 take pictures, wall paintings
06 old neighborhoods bright
07 Last month, with wall paintings
08 As, a light went on in my head
09 thought, I'm in
10 Why don't we, like
11 suggested this idea
12 found, on the Internet
13 to do a wall painting
14 applied for, later, was selected
15 finally came
16 had us meet, painting site
17 was in very poor condition
18 strange writings and drawings
19 Other parts
20 painted over, with white paint
21 let us paint
22 decided to, something cute
23 divided into
24 was in the group
25 chose my spot, movie character
26 painted, did, background drawings
27 for about
28 finished, got together, shared, experiences
29 was very proud of
30 so, that, landed on
31 Drawing, much harder than
32 wasn't perfect
33 matter
34 a little brighter and happier
35 were proud of ourselves
36 didn't just paint
37 a better tomorrow

본문 TEST Step 3 p.15~16

1 더 나은 내일을 그려라
2 안녕. 내 이름은 호민이야.
3 벽화 앞에 있는 사람이 나야.
4 날개가 예뻐, 그렇지 않니?
5 많은 사람들이 벽화 앞에서 사진 찍는 것을 좋아해.
6 벽화는 오래된 마을을 밝고 새롭게 만들어.
7 지난달에 나는 여수에 있는 벽화 마을을 방문했어.
8 내가 사진을 찍을 때 머릿속에 좋은 생각이 떠올랐어.
9 나는 생각했어. "나는 학교 미술 동아리에 있잖아.
10 우리가 이것처럼 벽화를 그리면 어떨까?"
11 나는 이 아이디어를 다음 동아리 모임에서 제안했고, 동아리 부원들은 그것을 아주 좋아했어.
12 우리는 인터넷에서 청소년 봉사 프로젝트를 찾았어.
13 그 프로젝트는 우리 마을에 벽화를 그리는 것이었어.
14 우리는 거기에 지원했고, 2주 후에 우리 동아리가 선택되었어!
15 마침내 프로젝트 날이 되었어.
16 프로젝트 책임자는 우리를 오전 9시에 그림 그리는 곳에서 만나게 했어.
17 벽은 상태가 별로 좋지 않았어.
18 몇 군데에는 이상한 낙서와 그림이 있었어.
19 다른 부분에는 오래된 포스터들이 붙어 있었어.
20 우리는 먼저 포스터들을 제거하고 낙서와 그림을 흰 페인트로 덧칠했어.
21 책임자는 우리가 원하는 어떤 것이든 그리게 했어.

22 우리는 그 벽이 초등학교 근처에 있어서 귀여운 뭔가를 그리기로 했어.
23 우리는 세 그룹으로 나뉘어 그리기 시작했어.
24 나는 민수와 지원이와 같은 그룹이었어.
25 나는 내 구역을 정해서 가장 좋아하는 영화 캐릭터를 그리기 시작했어.
26 민수는 몇 송이의 꽃을 그렸고 지원이는 배경 그림을 그렸어.
27 우리 동아리는 약 다섯 시간 동안 그림을 그렸어.
28 끝난 후에 우리는 모여서 그날의 경험을 함께 이야기했어.
29 민수는 자신이 그린 꽃 그림을 정말 자랑스러워했어.
30 그는 "내 꽃이 정말 진짜 같아서 벌이 꽃에 앉았어."라고 말했어.
31 나는 "벽에 그리는 것이 종이에 그리는 것보다 훨씬 힘들었어."라고 말했어.
32 우리 모두는 우리 벽화가 완벽하지는 않다는 것에 동의했어.
33 하지만 그것은 중요하지 않았어.
34 우리는 동네를 조금 더 밝고 행복하게 만들었어.
35 우리는 우리 자신이 자랑스러웠어.
36 우리는 그날 벽에 그림만 그린 게 아니었어.
37 우리가 그린 것은 바로 더 나은 내일이었어.

본문 TEST Step 4-Step 5 p.17~21

1 Paint a Better Tomorrow
2 Hi. My name is Homin.
3 This is me in front of the wall painting.
4 The wings are so pretty, aren't they?
5 Many people like to take pictures in front of wall paintings.
6 They make old neighborhoods bright and new.
7 Last month, I visited a village with wall paintings in Yeosu.
8 As I was taking a picture, a light went on in my head.
9 I thought, "I'm in the school art club.
10 Why don't we do wall paintings like these?"
11 I suggested this idea at the next club meeting, and the members loved it.
12 We found a teen volunteer project on the Internet.
13 The project was to do a wall painting in our neighborhood.
14 We applied for it, and two weeks later, our club was selected!
15 The day of the project finally came.
16 The project manager had us meet at the painting site at 9 a.m.
17 The wall was in very poor condition.
18 There were strange writings and drawings on some parts.
19 Other parts had old posters on them.
20 We removed the posters first and painted over the writings and drawings with white paint.
21 The manager let us paint anything we wanted.
22 We decided to paint something cute because the wall was near an elementary school.
23 We divided into three groups and began painting.
24 I was in the group with Minsu and Jiwon.
25 I chose my spot and started to paint my favorite movie character.
26 Minsu painted some flowers and Jiwon did some background drawings.
27 Our club painted for about five hours.
28 After we finished, we got together and shared the day's experiences.
29 Minsu was very proud of his flower painting.
30 He said, "My flower is so real that a bee landed on it."
31 I said, "Drawing on a wall was much harder than drawing on paper."
32 We all agreed that our wall painting wasn't perfect.
33 But it didn't matter.
34 We made our neighborhood a little brighter and happier.
35 We were proud of ourselves.
36 We didn't just paint pictures on a wall that day.
37 It was a better tomorrow that we painted.

구석구석지문 TEST Step 1 p.22

After You Read B

1. Paint, Better Tomorrow
2. DATE, April
3. MEETING TIME
4. like painting
5. make your neighborhood brighter
6. Right now, poor condition
7. need to remove, paint over, with white paint
8. anything you want
9. email

Word Power

1. got up, prepared for
2. said goodbye to
3. Try to get along with, have fun
4. replied, got on

Think and Write

1. Volunteer Work
2. volunteered, Library
3. read, to children
4. tried to, like, voice actor
5. volunteer, had, arrange, on the shelves
6. so, that, take a break every, minutes
7. After, finished, looked, neat
8. felt, proud
9. rewarding experience

구석구석지문 TEST Step 2 p.23

After You Read B

1. Project: Paint a Better Tomorrow
2. DATE: April 15
3. MEETING TIME: 9 a.m.
4. Do you like painting?
5. Do you want to make your neighborhood brighter?
6. Right now, the wall is in very poor condition.
7. You need to remove the old posters and paint over the strange writings with white paint.
8. You can paint anything you want!
9. email: volunteer@1365.go.kr

Word Power

1. Sally got up early and prepared for school.
2. She said goodbye to her mom.
3. Her mom said, "Try to get along with your friends and have fun."
4. Sally replied, "Okay, I will," and got on the school bus.

Think and Write

1. Volunteer Work Diary
2. I volunteered at Dream Library.
3. I read English books to children.
4. I tried to read like a voice actor.
5. The volunteer manager had me arrange the books on the shelves.
6. The books were so heavy that I had to take a break every 30 minutes.
7. After I finished, the shelves looked very neat.
8. I felt very proud.
9. It was a fun and rewarding experience.

단어 TEST Step 1 p.24

01 빛나는, 반짝거리는
02 흙
03 모험
04 머리, 지능
05 (구멍 등을) 파다
06 (심장이) 고동치다, 때리다
07 털다
08 폭넓은, 폭이 ~인
09 (사람을) 배치하다
10 편리한
11 잔혹한, 잔인한
12 뼈
13 (연극, 영화에서의) 연기
14 형사, 탐정
15 (일을) 거르다, 빼먹다
16 운전사가 없는
17 유용한, 도움이 되는
18 편리, 편의
19 훔치다
20 구덩이, 구멍
21 가벼운
22 결혼하다
23 요약, 개요
24 근육
25 잠들지 않은, 깨어 있는
26 키우다, 기르다
27 돌려주다, 반품하다
28 장면
29 품성, 인격
30 맨 아래, 바닥
31 불행히도
32 조심스럽게
33 갑자기
34 물건
35 내려놓다
36 ~로 가득 차다
37 ~을 의미하다
38 ~을 집다
39 결국 ~이 되다
40 ~의 바닥에서
41 찾아보다
42 ~의 것이다, ~ 소유이다
43 ~와 사랑에 빠지다

단어 TEST Step 2 p.25

01 steal
02 dig
03 adventure
04 muscle
05 character
06 dirt
07 brain
08 suddenly
09 brush
10 assign
11 hole
12 summary
13 carefully
14 bone
15 scene
16 wide
17 shiny
18 sleepy
19 convenience
20 actually
21 detective
22 skip
23 yell
24 light
25 awake
26 beat
27 unfortunately
28 raise
29 bottom
30 convenient
31 return
32 cruel
33 acting
34 popular
35 fall in love with
36 in fact
37 stand for ~
38 day off
39 put down
40 end up
41 stay awake
42 at the bottom of
43 look up

단어 TEST Step 3

p.26

1 awake, 잠들지 않은, 깨어 있는 2 wide, 폭이 ~인
3 bottom, 맨 아래, 바닥 4 shiny, 빛나는, 반짝거리는
5 hole, 구덩이, 구멍 6 skip, (일을) 거르다, 빼먹다
7 day off, 휴일, 쉬는 날 8 object, 물건
9 brush, 털다 10 dig, (구멍 등을) 파다 11 muscle, 근육
12 tube, 통, 관 13 acting, (연극, 영화에서의) 연기
14 assign, (사람을) 배치하다 15 steal, 훔치다
16 yell, 고함치다

대화문 TEST Step 1

p.27~29

Listen and Speak 1 A

Welcome to / Long, no, How, been / How, here from / by subway / How, feel about / clean

Listen and Speak 1 B

did, hear / What / can, during classes from / heard / How, feel / useful, look up words I don't know / can also find / helpful

Listen and Speak 1 C

1 Can I ask / try, best / How, feel, single / easy, unhealthy
2 ask, difficult / try / How do you feel / helpful but scary
3 Can I ask you / try my best / How do you feel about / helpful but cruel

Listen and Speak 2 A

Did you enjoy / a lot / What did you like most / acting was / with you on

Listen and Speak 2 B

Why, always drinking / help me stay awake / I'm with you on, too much caffeine / help me focus on / know that too much caffeine / should drink, less often / Maybe

Listen and Speak 2 C

1 How do you feel about reading / anytime / with you on that, not good for
2 How do you feel about skipping / more / I'm with you on that / may not work
3 How do you feel about eating / a lot of fat / I'm with you on that / I don't agree, can save

Real Life Talk Watch a Video

What / They're items I ordered / don't you / How do you feel about / at all / difficult to know what, actually looks like / with you on / difficult to return / right, convenient / convenience, everything

Real Life Talk Step 2

1 feel about shopping / a lot / Can you tell me / shop whenever / I'm with you
2 How do you feel about raising / tell me, reason / work to take care of / don't agree, cute, make us happy

Check up Dialogue Champion

How do you feel about using, in class / useful, search for information / with you on that

대화문 TEST Step 2

p.30~32

Listen and Speak 1 A

B: Hi, Amy. Welcome to Korea.
G: Long time no see, Minho. How have you been?
B: Great. How did you come here from the airport?
G: I came here by subway.
B: How do you feel about the subway in Korea?
G: I think it's very clean.

Listen and Speak 1 B

G: Brian, did did you hear the news?
B: What news?
G: We can use smartphones during classes from next week.
B: Yes, I heard that.
G: How do you feel about it?
B: I think it will be very useful. I can look up words I don't know.
G: Yeah. We can also find information on the Internet.
B: Right. It will be very helpful.

Listen and Speak 1 C

1 A: Can I ask you a difficult question?
B: Sure. I'll try my best.
A: How do you feel about the single food diet?
B: I think it's easy but unhealthy.
2 A: Can I ask you a difficult question?
B: Sure. I'll try my best.
A: How do you feel about the AI robot?
B: I think it's helpful but scary.
3 A: Can I ask you a difficult question?
B: Sure. I'll try my best.
A: How do you feel about animal testing?
B: I think it's helpful but cruel.

Listen and Speak 2 A

B: Did you enjoy the movie?
G: Yes, I liked it a lot.
B: What did you like most about it?
G: The acting was so great.
B: I'm with you on that.

Listen and Speak 2 B

B: Hey, Jessica. Why are you always drinking energy drinks?

G: Because they help me stay awake.

B: I'm with you on that, but they have too much caffeine.

G: Well, they help me focus on my studies.

B: Did you know that too much caffeine can hurt your bones?

G: Oh, I didn't know that.

B: I think you should drink energy drinks less often.

G: Maybe you're right. Thanks, Tom.

Listen and Speak 2 C

1 A: How do you feel about reading books on a smartphone?
B: I think it's good. We can read anytime.
A: I'm with you on that. / I don't agree. It's not good for our eyes.

2 A: How do you feel about skipping breakfast?
B: I think it's good. We can sleep more.
A: I'm with you on that. / I don't agree. Our brain may not work well.

3 A: How do you feel about eating fast food?
B: I think it's bad. Fast food has a lot of fat.
A: I'm with you on that. / I don't agree. We can save time.

Real Life Talk Watch a Video

Tony: What are all these boxes, Suji?

Suji: They're items I ordered online.

Tony: You like shopping on the Internet, don't you?

Suji: Yes, I do. How do you feel about online shopping, Tony?

Tony: I don't like it at all.

Suji: Why?

Tony: It's very difficult to know what an item actually looks like.

Suji: I'm with you on that.

Tony: It's also difficult to return an item if you don't like it.

Suji: You're right, but I think it's very convenient.

Tony: Well, convenience isn't everything.

Real Life Talk Step 2

1 A: How do you feel about shopping on the Internet?
B: I like it a lot.
A: Can you tell me the reason?
B: I can shop whenever I want.
A: I'm with you on that.

2 A: How do you feel about raising pets?
B: I don't like it.
A: Can you tell me the reason?
B: It's a lot of work to take care of them.
A: I don't agree. They're so cute and make us happy.

Check up Dialogue Champion

A: How do you feel about using smartphones in class?

B: I think smartphones are useful in class. We can search for information on them.

A: I'm with you on that.

본문 TEST Step 1 p.33~34

01 Dig harder 02 harder, the faster, yelled
03 harder since, muscle hurt
04 thirsty, hungry
05 to go home 06 for, would be, at
07 a terrible name
08 there was no lake
09 hot, full of sand
10 In fact, even 11 place for bad
12 what, like, doing
13 sent, stealing, pair of
14 didn't really steal
15 in, place at, wrong
16 walking home from school
17 Suddenly, pair, fell from
18 hit him on, head
19 with, tell, what happened
20 few, stopped, why, running
21 for, belonged to, famous
22 why, ended up at
23 was assigned to
24 There, six other boys
25 had cool names like
26 Each, had, dig, hole
27 to, about, deep, wide
28 digging to build character
29 more, dug, stronger, became
30 took less, finish, each
31 finishing, something shiny, dirt
32 heart beat faster
33 something interesting, given, off
34 picked up, brushed off
35 small gold tube
36 couldn't be, since, light
37 There, letters, bottom, tube
38 did, stand for 39 beat even faster

본문 TEST Step 2 p.35~36

01 Dig harder 02 The harder, the faster, yelled
03 any harder since, hurt
04 thirsty, hungry 05 go home
06 Unfortunately, for, would be
07 a terrible name
08 there, no lake 09 hot, full of sand
10 In fact, even 11 a place for bad boys
12 like, doing 13 was sent, for stealing
14 didn't really steal
15 in the wrong place, wrong time
16 walking home from school
17 a pair of, fell from
18 hit him on the head
19 with, what happened
20 A few minutes, stopped, why he was running
21 for, belonged to
22 That was why, ended up
23 was assigned to
24 six other boys 25 cool, like
26 one hole every day
27 about, deep, wide
28 to build character
29 The more, the stronger
30 It took, to finish, each day
31 something shiny in the dirt 32 beat faster
33 anyone who, be given the day off
34 picked up, brushed off
35 small gold tube
36 couldn't be, since
37 letters, at the bottom of
38 stand for 39 beat even faster

본문 TEST Step 3 p.37~38

1 "더 열심히 파, Stanley!
2 네가 열심히 파면 팔수록, 너는 더 빨리 끝낼 거야!" Sir 씨가 소리를 질렀다.
3 Stanley Yelnats는 모든 근육 하나하나가 아팠기 때문에 더 열심히 팔 수가 없었다.
4 그는 목이 마르고 배가 고팠다.
5 그는 집에 가고 싶었다.
6 불행히도, 앞으로 18개월 동안 Stanley의 집은 바로 여기 Green Lake 캠프가 될 것이었다.
7 Green Lake 캠프는 형편없는 이름이었다.
8 그곳은 초록색도 아니었고 호수도 없었다.
9 Green Lake 캠프는 뜨거웠고 온통 모래였다.
10 사실 그곳은 캠프조차 아니었다.
11 그곳은 나쁜 소년들을 위한 곳이었다.
12 그렇다면 Stanley 같이 착한 소년이 여기서 무엇을 하고 있었을까?
13 그는 운동화 한 켤레를 훔쳤다는 이유로 캠프에 보내졌다.
14 Stanley가 정말로 운동화 한 켤레를 훔친 것은 아니었다.
15 그는 그저 잘못된 시간에 잘못된 장소에 있었다.
16 어느 날, 그는 학교에서 집으로 걸어가고 있었다.
17 갑자기, 낡은 운동화 한 켤레가 하늘에서 떨어졌다.
18 그 운동화는 그의 머리에 맞았다.
19 그는 그의 아버지에게 무슨 일이 일어났는지 말하기 위해 운동화를 가지고 달리기 시작했다.
20 몇 분 후에, 경찰이 Stanley를 멈춰 세웠고 그가 왜 달리고 있었는지를 그에게 물었다.
21 Stanley에게는 불행히도, 그 운동화는 유명한 야구 선수인 Clyde Livingstone의 것이었다.
22 그것이 Stanley가 Green Lake 캠프에 오게 된 이유였다.
23 Stanley는 캠프에서 D 그룹에 배치되었다.
24 Stanley의 그룹에는 6명의 다른 소년들이 있었다.
25 그들은 모두 X-Ray, Zigzag, Zero와 같은 멋진 이름을 가지고 있었다.
26 각 소년은 매일 구덩이 하나를 파야 했다.
27 그것은 150cm 정도 깊이와 150cm 정도 너비여야 했다.
28 Sir 씨는 "너희들은 인격을 수양하기 위해 구덩이를 파고 있는 것이야."라고 말했다.
29 Stanley는 많이 파면 팔수록, 더 힘이 세졌다.
30 하루하루 구덩이를 끝내는 데 시간이 덜 걸렸다.
31 그가 온 지 두 번째 주, Stanley가 자기 구덩이를 끝내 가고 있었을 때, 그는 흙 속에서 빛나는 뭔가를 봤다.
32 Stanley의 심장은 더 빨리 뛰었다.
33 그는 흥미로운 뭔가를 발견한 사람은 그 날을 쉬게 된다고 들었다.
34 그는 조심스럽게 그 빛나는 물체를 집어 흙을 털어 냈다.
35 그것은 작은 금색 통이었다.
36 그러나 그것은 너무 가벼웠기 때문에 진짜 금일 리가 없었다.
37 그 통의 바닥에는 KB라는 두 글자가 있었다.
38 KB는 무엇을 의미할까?
39 Stanley의 심장은 훨씬 더 빨리 뛰었다.

본문 TEST Step 4-Step 5 p.39~43

1 "Dig harder, Stanley!
2 The harder you dig, the faster you'll finish!" yelled Mr. Sir.
3 Stanley Yelnats couldn't dig any harder since every single muscle hurt.
4 He was thirsty and hungry.
5 He wanted to go home.

6 Unfortunately, Stanley's home for the next 18 months would be right here, at Camp Green Lake.
7 Camp Green Lake was a terrible name.
8 It wasn't green and there was no lake.
9 Camp Green Lake was hot and full of sand.
10 In fact, it wasn't even a camp.
11 It was a place for bad boys.
12 Then what was a good boy like Stanley doing here?
13 He was sent to the camp for stealing a pair of sneakers.
14 Stanley didn't really steal a pair of sneakers.
15 He was just in the wrong place at the wrong time.
16 One day, he was walking home from school.
17 Suddenly, a pair of old sneakers fell from the sky.
18 The sneakers hit him on the head.
19 He started running with the sneakers to tell his father what happened.
20 A few minutes later, the police stopped Stanley and asked him why he was running.
21 Unfortunately for Stanley, the sneakers belonged to a famous baseball player, Clyde Livingstone.
22 That was why Stanley ended up at Camp Green Lake.
23 Stanley was assigned to Group D in the camp.
24 There were six other boys in Stanley's group.
25 They all had cool names like X-Ray, Zigzag and Zero.
26 Each boy had to dig one hole every day.
27 It had to be about 150cm deep and 150cm wide.
28 Mr. Sir said, "You are digging to build character."
29 The more Stanley dug, the stronger he became.
30 It took less time to finish his hole each day.
31 In his second week, as Stanley was finishing his hole, he saw something shiny in the dirt.
32 Stanley's heart beat faster.
33 He heard that anyone who found something interesting would be given the day off.
34 He carefully picked up the shiny object and brushed off the dirt.
35 It was a small gold tube.
36 But it couldn't be real gold since it was too light.
37 There were two letters, *KB*, at the bottom of the tube.
38 What did KB stand for?
39 Stanley's heart beat even faster.

구석구석지문 TEST Step 1 p.44

After You Read B

1. August 5th
2. Unfortunately, there is no lake
3. in, have cool names like
4. have to dig, about, deep, wide
5. anyone who, something interesting, get the day off
6. hope, can be

Word Power

1. bought a pair of shoes for
2. found a pair of glasses
3. packed three pairs of jeans

Think and Write

1. was a teacher in
2. was very popular
3. Many rich men, to marry her
4. fell in love with, poor man
5. tried to hurt
6. Later, found dead, became sad, left

구석구석지문 TEST Step 2 p.45

After You Read B

1. Monday, August 5th
2. Unfortunately, the camp isn't green and there is no lake.
3. I'm in Group D. My group members have cool names like X-Ray, Zigzag and Zero.
4. We have to dig one hole about 150cm deep and 150cm wide.
5. The good news is this: anyone who finds something interesting can get the day off.
6. I hope I can be the one.

Word Power

1. She bought a pair of shoes for 15 dollars.
2. I found a pair of glasses under the chair.
3. He packed three pairs of jeans in his bag.

Think and Write

1. Kate Barlow was a teacher in Green Lake.
2. She was very popular.
3. Many rich men in the town wanted to marry her.
4. But Kate fell in love with Sam, a poor man.
5. The rich men tried to hurt Sam.
6. Later, Sam was found dead. Kate became sad and left the town.

Lesson 5

단어 TEST Step 1 p.46

01 아무도 ~않다 02 바다 03 ~할 형편이 되다
04 재능 있는 05 지루해하는 06 구르다, 굴러가다
07 무서워하는, 겁먹은 08 걱정하는
09 신이 난, 흥분한 10 응원하다 11 연설
12 여행 13 쓰레기 매립지
14 대부분, 일반적으로 15 나타나다
16 놀란, 놀라는 17 황홀해하는, 아주 신이 난
18 전쟁, 전투 19 곡, 곡조, 선율 20 교육자
21 환경의 22 인내심 23 상.
24 악기 25 공연 26 존경하다
27 거대한 28 볼, 뺨 29 붙이다
30 제목 31 쓰레기 32 운동, 체육관
33 무인 항공기 34 오케스트라, 관현악단
35 응원하다 36 그때부터 37 ~를 돌보다
38 포기하다 39 ~에 참가하다 40 서로
41 큰 박수를 보내다 42 ~을 실행에 옮기다
43 음이 맞지 않는

단어 TEST Step 2 p.47

01 drone 02 educator 03 performance
04 respect 05 giant 06 landfill
07 mostly 08 afford 09 appear
10 none 11 cheek 12 award
13 battle 14 violinist 15 thrilled
16 worried 17 surprised 18 talented
19 bored 20 trash 21 patience
22 stick 23 roll 24 scared
25 environmental 26 cheer 27 excited
28 speech 29 still 30 tune
31 gym class 32 journey 33 parade
34 musical instrument 35 give up
36 be known as 37 take part in 38 cheer for
39 from then on 40 one another 41 be made of
42 take care of 43 put ~ into practice

단어 TEST Step 3 p.48

1 talented, 재능 있는 2 afford, ~할 형편이 되다
3 thrilled, 황홀해하는, 아주 신이 난
4 step by step, 점차로, 차근차근, 하나씩
5 cheek, 볼, 뺨 6 practice, 실행, 실천
7 scared, 무서워하는, 겁먹은 8 roll, 구르다, 굴러가다
9 landfill, 쓰레기 매립지 10 trash, 쓰레기
11 award, 상 12 look forward to, ~를 기대하다, 고대하다
13 patience, 인내심 14 tune, 곡, 곡조, 선율
15 orchestra, 오케스트라, 관현악단 16 bored, 지루해하는

대화문 TEST Step 1 p.49~51

Listen and Speak 1 A

Welcome to, looking forward to playing, excited to, See you on

Listen and Speak 1 B

what are, reading / reading, about, named / who was born without / even won / was made into, going to watch / I'm really looking forward to watching / join / on

Listen and Speak 1 C

1. What's, on / excited, I'm going to travel / sounds / really looking forward to
2. look happy / excited, learn to fly / I'm really looking, to flying
3. look happy, going on / so excited, I'm going / looking forward to watching, performance

Listen and Speak 2 A

finish, math homework / difficult / interesting, too / help me with / I'd love to, have to take care of

Listen and Speak 2 B

going to take part in / how to play, right / I've played, for / Can you play, while / but I can't, hurt, gym class / sorry to hear / cheer for

Listen and Speak 2 C

1. going to do / want to / but I can't, have to / next time
2. are you going to / going to, join me / I'd love to, to visit / next time

Real Life Talk Watch a Video

What are you going / going to watch / it about / about a boy who became / looking forward to watching / interesting, main actor / watched, last year / want to join / but I can't, volunteer / next

Real Life Talk Step 2

1. are, going to / I'm going to watch, looking forward to watching / fun / love to, but I can't, my face

painted

2. going to do next / at, I'm really looking forward, playing it / Sounds / to join / I'd love to, but, longest

대화문 TEST Step 2 p.52~54

Listen and Speak 1 A

B: Hey, Bora. Welcome to our rock band.

G: Thanks. I'm looking forward to playing in a concert with you.

B: We're excited to have a new guitar player.

G: Yeah. See you on Friday.

Listen and Speak 1 B

G: Jiho, what are you reading?

B: I'm reading a book about baseball player named Jim Abbott.

G: Oh, the man who was born without a right hand?

B: That's right. He tried really hard and even won the MVP award.

G: Yeah. His story was made into a movie. I'm going to watch it this Saturday.

B: Really? What's the title?

G: *Our Hero*. I'm really looking forward to watching it.

B: Can I join you?

G: Sure. See you on Saturday.

Listen and Speak 1 C

1. A: You look happy today. What's going on?
   B: I'm so excited. I'm going to travel to Jeju-do.
   A: That sounds great!
   B: Yes. I'm really looking forward to riding a horse.
2. A: You look happy today. What's going on?
   B: I'm so excited. I'm going to learn to fly a drone.
   A: That sounds great!
   B: Yes. I'm really looking forward to flying a drone in the park.
3. A: You look happy today. What's going on?
   B: I'm so excited. I'm going to see Jackson's concert.
   A: That sounds great!
   B: Yes. I'm really looking forward to watching Jackson's performance.

Listen and Speak 2 A

G: Minho, did you finish the math homework?

B: Not yet. Math is difficult.

G: Yes, but it's interesting, too.

B: Then can you help me with my math homework?

G: I'd love to, but I can't. I have to take care of my brother.

Listen and Speak 2 B

G: Alex, I'm going to take part in a singing contest next Monday.

B: That's great, Sumin!

G: You know how to play the guitar, right?

B: Yes, I've played the guitar for 3 years.

G: Great. Can you play the guitar while I sing in the contest?

B: I'd love to, but I can't. I hurt my hand in gym class yesterday.

G: Oh! I'm sorry to hear that.

B: Thanks. But I'll be there to cheer for you.

Listen and Speak 2 C

1. A: What are you going to do this afternoon?
   B: I'm going to ride my bike. Do you want to join me?
   A: I'd love to, but I can't. I have to do my homework.
   B: Okay, then next time.
2. A: What are you going to do this afternoon?
   B: I'm going to play soccer. Do you want to join me?
   A: I'd love to, but I can't. I have to visit my grandparents.
   B: Okay, then next time.

Real Life Talk Watch a Video

Linda: Hi, Tony! What are you going to do this weekend?

Tony: I'm going to watch the musical, *Billy Elliot*.

Linda: *Billy Elliot*? What is it about?

Tony: It's about a boy who became a famous dancer. I'm looking forward to watching it.

Linda: Sounds interesting. Who is the main actor?

Tony: Jason Kim. He's a great dancer.

Linda: He's my favorite actor. I watched his musical last year.

Tony: Oh, really? Do you want to join me?

Linda: I'd love to, but I can't. I have volunteer work this weekend.

Tony: Okay. Maybe next time!

Real Life Talk Step 2

1. A: What are you going to do first?
   B: I'm going to watch a parade at 10:30. I'm really looking forward to watching it.
   A: Sounds fun.
   B: Do you want to join me?
   A: Yes, I'd love to. / I'd love to, but I can't. I'm

going to get my face painted at that time.

2. A: What are you going to do next?

B: I'm going to play a water balloon game at 12:30. I'm really looking forward to playing it.

A: Sounds fun.

B: Do you want to join me?

A: Yes, I'd love to. / I'd love to, but I can't. I'm going to have the longest hot dog at that time.

본문 TEST Step 1 p.55~57

01 Trash to Music
02 Tears, joy, rolling down
03 so happy, thrilled
04 were, would fly
05 look around
06 other, hugging one another
07 has, finished, giving, hand
08 None, ever expected, would
09 has been, long journey
10 name, a violinist in
11 Why is it called
12 because, made of, from
13 why, also known as
14 Most, us, are from
15 There, huge landfill, town
16 even, itself, giant landfill
17 Many, us, poor
18 weren't many hopes, dreams
19 began, change, however, met
20 an environmental educator, musician
21 teach us music, problem
22 only, few, instruments, whole
23 couldn't afford to, ones
24 didn't give up
25 with objects from, landfill
26 named, put, into practice
27 made, from, drums
28 turned, into flutes
29 had another problem
30 No, how to play
31 even, how to read
32 with great patience
33 by step, sounds, instruments
34 remember, piece, music, played
35 short, mostly out, tune
36 the most beautiful music
37 felt, new hope, hearts
38 From then on, gathered
39 One, some great news
40 were going to have
41 front, hundreds of people
42 love our music
43 sends us trash, back

본문 TEST Step 2 p.58~60

01 Trash, Music
02 Tears of joy, rolling down
03 thrilled
04 were, would fly
05 look around
06 The other members, one another
07 has just finished, giving us a big hand
08 None, ever expected
09 It has been, journey
10 I'm a violinist
11 Why is it called
12 because, are made of, from, landfill
13 That's why, known as
14 Most of, are from
15 a huge landfill
16 itself, giant landfill
17 Many of us, poor
18 many hopes and dreams
19 began to change, however
20 an environmental educator, musician
21 teach us music
22 only a few, whole town
23 couldn't afford to
24 give up
25 with objects from the landfill
26 named, was able to put, into practice
27 made, from
28 turned, into
29 another problem
30 how to play
31 how to read
32 taught, with great patience
33 Step by step
34 the first piece of music, played
35 mostly out of tune
36 the most beautiful music
37 felt a new hope
38 From then on, gathered to practice
39 some great news
40 were going to have
41 front, hundreds of people
42 our music
43 sends us trash, send back music

본문 TEST Step 3 p.61~63

1 쓰레기를 음악으로
2 기쁨의 눈물이 내 볼에 흘러내리고 있다.
3 나는 정말 기쁘고 황홀하다.
4 내가 새라면, 날아오를 텐데.
5 나는 주변을 본다.
6 우리 오케스트라의 다른 단원들은 서로 껴안고 있다.
7 우리의 공연은 이제 막 끝났고 모든 사람들이 서서 우리에게 큰 박수를 보내고 있다.
8 우리 중 아무도 이 날이 올 거라고 예상하지 못했다.

9 긴 여정이었다.
10 내 이름은 Andrea이고 나는 Recycled Orchestra의 바이올리니스트이다.
11 오케스트라가 왜 Recycled Orchestra라고 불리냐고?
12 그것은 우리의 악기들이 쓰레기 매립지에서 나온 물건들로 만들어지기 때문이다.
13 그것이 오케스트라가 Landfill Harmonic Orchestra로도 알려진 이유이다.
14 오케스트라의 우리들 대부분은 파라과이의 작은 마을인 카테우라 출신이다.
15 우리 마을에는 거대한 쓰레기 매립지가 있다.
16 몇몇 사람들은 심지어 카테우라 자체가 거대한 쓰레기 매립지라고 말한다.
17 우리들 중 많은 이들이 가난하다.
18 우리 마을에는 꿈과 희망이 많지 않았다.
19 그러나 우리가 Favio Chávez 선생님을 만났을 때 모든 것이 바뀌기 시작했다.
20 Favio 선생님은 환경 교육가이자 음악가였다.
21 그는 우리에게 음악을 가르치고 싶어 했지만, 큰 문제가 있었다.
22 온 마을에 악기가 단지 몇 개뿐이었다.
23 우리는 새 악기를 살 형편도 아니었다.
24 그러나 Favio 선생님은 포기하지 않았다.
25 그는 우리가 쓰레기 매립지의 물건들로 악기를 만들 수 있다고 말했다.
26 재능이 많은 Nicholas 아저씨가 이 생각을 실행에 옮길 수 있었다.
27 그는 기름통으로 바이올린을 만들었다.
28 그는 수도관을 플루트로 바꾸었다.
29 우리에게 또 다른 문제가 있었다.
30 아무도 악기를 연주할 줄 몰랐다.
31 우리는 심지어 악보를 읽는 방법도 알지 못했다.
32 Favio 선생님은 엄청난 인내심으로 우리를 가르쳤다.
33 점차로, 우리는 악기로 어떤 소리를 만들어 내기 시작했다.
34 나는 아직도 우리가 연주했던 첫 곡을 기억한다.
35 그 곡은 매우 짧고 대부분은 음이 맞지 않았다.
36 그러나 그것은 우리에게 가장 아름다운 곡이었다.
37 우리는 마음속에 새로운 희망을 느꼈다.
38 그때부터, 우리는 매일 연습을 하기 위해 모였다.
39 어느 날, Favio 선생님은 우리에게 엄청난 소식을 말해 줬다.
40 우리는 공연을, 진짜 공연을 하게 될 것이었다!
41 그리고 여기 우리는 지금 수백 명의 사람들 앞에 있다.
42 그들은 우리의 음악을 사랑한다.
43 세상은 우리에게 쓰레기를 보내지만, 우리는 음악을 돌려보낸다!

본문 TEST Step 4-Step 5

p.64~69

1 From Trash to Music
2 Tears of joy are rolling down my cheeks.
3 I'm so happy and thrilled.
4 If I were a bird, I would fly.
5 I look around.
6 The other members in my orchestra are hugging one another.
7 Our concert has just finished and everyone is standing and giving us a big hand.
8 None of us ever expected that this day would come.
9 It has been a long journey.
10 My name is Andrea and I'm a violinist in the Recycled Orchestra.
11 Why is it called the Recycled Orchestra?
12 It's because our musical instruments are made of objects from a landfill.
13 That's why it's also known as the Landfill Harmonic Orchestra.
14 Most of us in the orchestra are from Cateura, a small town in Paraguay.
15 There is a huge landfill in our town.
16 Some people even say that Cateura itself is a giant landfill.
17 Many of us are poor.
18 There weren't many hopes and dreams in our town.
19 Everything began to change, however, when we met Favio Chávez.
20 Favio was an environmental educator and a musician.
21 He wanted to teach us music, but there was a big problem.
22 There were only a few musical instruments in the whole town.
23 We couldn't afford to buy new ones.
24 But Favio didn't give up.
25 He said that we could make musical instruments with objects from the landfill.
26 A talented man named Nicholas was able to put this idea into practice.
27 He made violins from oil drums.
28 He turned water pipes into flutes.
29 We had another problem.
30 No one knew how to play musical instruments.
31 We didn't even know how to read music.
32 Favio taught us with great patience.

33 Step by step, we began to make some sounds on our instruments.
34 I still remember the first piece of music that we played.
35 It was very short and mostly out of tune.
36 But it was the most beautiful music to us.
37 We felt a new hope in our hearts.
38 From then on, we gathered to practice every day.
39 One day, Favio told us some great news.
40 We were going to have a concert, a real concert!
41 And here we are now in front of hundreds of people.
42 They love our music.
43 The world sends us trash, but we send back music!

구석구석지문 TEST Step 1

p.70

After You Read B

1. feel
2. feel thrilled, just performed, first concert
3. Why, called
4. That's because, musical instruments are made of, from a landfill
5. amazing
6. None of, how to play musical instruments, with great patience
7. wonderful story

Think and Write

1. Dear Admiral
2. respect, because, gave up in difficult situations
3. saved, country
4. It, that, won, with only 12 ships
5. If, had, would go to meet
6. like to ask, how to make
7. my hero
8. Sincerely

Project Step 3

1. bottle shaker
2. To make, a bottle, buttons
3. Clean, put, in the bottle
4. Close, decorate it
5. can also put different things like, it
6. Different, different sounds
7. Listen to, group's bottle shaker

구석구석지문 TEST Step 2

p.71

After You Read B

1. Reporter: Congratulations! How do you feel now?
2. Andrea: I feel thrilled. We just performed our first concert.
3. Reporter: Why is the orchestra called the Recycled Orchestra?
4. Andrea: That's because our musical instruments are made of objects from a landfill.
5. Reporter: That's amazing.
6. Andrea: Yeah. None of us knew how to play musical instruments, but Favio taught us with great patience.
7. Reporter: That is a wonderful story.

Think and Write

1. Dear Admiral Yi Sun-sin,
2. I'm Sumin. I really respect you because you never gave up in difficult situations.
3. You saved the country and the people.
4. It was amazing that you won the battle with only 12 ships.
5. If I had a time machine, I would go to meet you!
6. I'd like to ask you how to make geobukseon.
7. You're my hero. Thank you.
8. Sincerely yours, Sumin

Project Step 3

1. This is a bottle shaker.
2. To make it, you need a bottle and buttons.
3. Clean the bottle and put the buttons in the bottle.
4. Close the bottle and decorate it.
5. You can also put different things like rice or sand in it.
6. Different items make different sounds.
7. Listen to my group's bottle shaker.

적중100

영어 기출 문제집

정답 및 해설

동아 | 이병민